FEARFUL SYMMETRY
A STUDY OF WILLIAM BLAKE

FEARFUL SYMMETRY

A STUDY OF

WILLIAM BLAKE

BY NORTHROP FRYE

PRINCETON UNIVERSITY
PRESS

TO

DR. PELHAM EDGAR

FEARFUL SYMMETRY was a hard book to write, not only because it was my first, and not only because of its subject. Every major poet demands from his critic a combination of direction and perspective, of intensive and extensive reading. The critic must know his poet's text to the point of possession, of having it all in his head at once, as well as knowing whatever aspect of the poet's "background" is relevant to his approach. At the same time he should be able to place his poet in a broad literary context. The doctoral thesis is useful for encouraging intensive reading, but of very little use for gaining literary perspective, which takes years to develop and cannot be hurried. The present book never went through the thesis stage, and my interest in Blake had from the beginning been of the extensive kind. Its fifth and last complete rewriting consisted largely of cutting out of it a mass of critical principles and observations, some of which found their way into my next long book, *Anatomy of Criticism*. This may explain why *Fearful Symmetry* takes the form, not of the fully documented commentary which is what I should prefer to write now, but of an extended critical essay in the Swinburne tradition. The subject of that essay is Blake in his literary context, which means, not Blake's "place in literature," but Blake as an illustration of the poetic process.

In the early stages I felt all the resistance against grappling with a specific symbolic language, which "has to be got up like so much Gothic," in Professor Douglas Bush's words, that so many other critics of Blake had felt. If Blake were unique, or even rare, in demanding this kind of preparation, I should perhaps not have finished the book. But there are so many symbolic constructs in literature, ranging from Dante's Ptolemaic universe to Yeats's spirit-dictated *Vision*, that one begins to suspect that such constructs have something to do with the way poetry is written. For readers brought up to ask only emotional reverberation or realistic detail from poetry, it comes as a disillusioning shock to learn that, as Valéry says, cosmology is a literary art. The statement of Los in *Jerusalem*: "I must Create a System, or be enslav'd by another Mans" has been quoted out of context by many critics, including myself on occasion. We should take it in its context, not identifying the "I" with Blake, but seeing it as defining a necessary activity of the poetic process. One should never think of Blake as operating or manipulating a "system" of thought, nor should we be misled by his architectural metaphors to think of his symbolic language as something solidified and crustacean. Part of the context of Los's remark is this:

> Striving with Systems to deliver Individuals from those Systems;
> That whenever any Spectre began to devour the Dead,
> He might feel the pain as if a man gnawd his own tender nerves.

Cosmology is a literary art, but there are two kinds of cosmology, the kind designed to understand the world as it is, and the kind designed to transform it into the form of human desire. Platonists and occultists deal with the former kind, which after Newton's time, according to Blake, became the accepted form of science. Cosmology of this type is speculative, which, as the etymology of that word shows, is ultimately intellectual narcism, staring into nature as the mirror of our ordinary selves. What the mirror shows us is what Blake calls "mathematic form," the automatic and mindless universe that has no beginning nor end, no up nor down. What such a universe suggests to us is resignation, acceptance of what is, approval of what is predictable, fear of whatever is unpredictable. Blake's cosmology, of which the symbol is Ezekiel's vision of the chariot of God with its "wheels within wheels," is a revolutionary vision of the universe transformed by the creative imagination into a human shape. This cosmology is not speculative but concerned, not reactionary but revolutionary, not a vision of things as they are ordered but of things as they could be ordered. Blake is often associated with speculative cosmologists, but the psychological contrast with them is more significant than any resemblances. Blake belongs with the poets, with the Milton whose Raphael advised Adam that while studying the stars was all very well, keeping his own freedom of will was even more important. Blake's poetry, like that of every poet who knows what he is doing, is mythical, for myth is the language of concern: it is cosmology in movement, a living form and not a mathematical one. "The Word is what gives movement to number," as Yeats says.

There is a broad consistency in Blake's mythology: there are some uncertain points, such as the role of Los in *Europe*, but on

the whole he meant the same things by Orc and Urizen and Enitharmon all through his poetic life. The combination of radical
and evangelical sympathies—so frequent in England, so rare elsewhere—remained with him to the end. He hailed with delight the
apocalyptic element in the American and French revolutions, the
glimpse of eternal freedom that they gave. But he also saw growing, in France and England alike, a "Deism" or self-righteous mob
rule, two mobs which most hated, not each other, but the sane
voice of prophecy telling them how much of what they were doing,
in war and peace alike, was futile and stupid and wrong. In his
earlier work Blake thought of the essential "Mental fight" of
human life as the revolt of desire and energy against repression,
though even then he was careful to say that reason was the form
of desire and energy, which are never amorphous except when
they are repressed. Later he tended more to see this conflict as one
of the genuine reason, or what he called intellect, against rationali-
zation. "The tygers of wrath are wiser than the horses of instruction," but Blake thought of his own poetry as instructive, and the
horses of instruction in their turn are wiser than the balky mules
of hysteria.

Blake wrote during the Napoleonic Wars, in one of

> the central Cities of the Nations
> Where Human Thought is crushd beneath the iron hand of
> Power.

I wrote *Fearful Symmetry* during the Second World War, and
hideous as that time was, it provided some parallels with Blake's
time which were useful for understanding Blake's attitude to the
world. Today, now that reactionary and radical forces alike are
once more in the grip of the nihilistic psychosis that Blake described so powerfully in *Jerusalem*, one of the most hopeful signs
is the immensely increased sense of the urgency and immediacy of
what Blake had to say.

NORTHROP FRYE

Toronto, Canada
March 1969

CONTENTS

ILLUSTRATIONS

(following page 50)

PART ONE

THE ARGUMENT

GON. How lush and lusty the grass looks!
    how green!
ANT. The ground indeed is tawny.
SEB. With an eye of green in 't.
ANT. He misses not much.
SEB. No; he doth but mistake the truth
        totally.—THE TEMPEST, ACT II, SCENE I.

1   *THE CASE AGAINST LOCKE*

THIS book offers an explanation of Blake's thought and a commentary on his poetry. No effort has been made to deal at all adequately with Blake's biography or with his work as painter and engraver: a study of his relation to English literature is primarily what has been attempted. The attempt is not unique, though the amount of critical writing on Blake's poetry is perhaps not as large as it is often vaguely stated to be. After deducting the obsolete, the eccentric and the merely trivial, what remains is surely no greater in volume than a poet of such importance is entitled to. It is large enough, however, to justify a statement of what is believed to be peculiar to this study.

Many students of literature or painting must have felt that Blake's relation to those arts is a somewhat quizzical one. Critics in both fields insist almost exclusively upon the angularity of his genius. Blake, they tell us, is a mystic enraptured with incommunicable visions, standing apart, a lonely and isolated figure, out of touch with his own age and without influence on the following one. He is an interruption in cultural history, a separable phenomenon. The historian of painting has to abandon all narrative continuity when the time comes to turn aside and devote a few words to Blake's unique output. The historian of poetry is not quite so badly off; but even so it is only by cutting out two-thirds of Blake's work that he will be able to wedge the rest of it in with that of the minor pre-Romantics.

For Blake is more than most poets a victim of anthologies. Countless collections of verse include a dozen or so of his lyrics, but if we wish to go further we are immediately threatened with a formidable bulk of complex symbolic poems known as "Prophecies," which make up the main body of his work. Consequently the mere familiarity of some of the lyrics is no guarantee that they will not be wrongly associated with their author. If they indicate that we must take Blake seriously as a conscious and deliberate artist, we shall have to study these prophecies, which is more than many specialists in Blake's period have done. The prophecies form what is in proportion to its merits the least read body of poetry in the language, and most of the more accessible editions of Blake omit them altogether, or print only those fragments which seem to the editor to have a vaguely purplish cast.

There is no *a priori* reason for this, apart from one or two hazy impressions which need only a passing mention. One is, that Blake wrote lyrics at the height of his creative power and that he later turned to prophecy as a sign that he had lost it. Yet his earliest book, *Poetical Sketches*, is evenly divided between lyrics and embryonic prophecies, and one of his last and most complicated prophecies contains his most famous lyric. Another is, that Blake is to be regarded as an ultrasubjective primitive whose work involuntarily reflects his immediate mood. The *Songs of Innocence* are then to be taken at their face value as the outpourings of a naïve and childlike spontaneity, and the *Songs of Experience* as the bitter disillusionment resulting from maturity—for when Blake engraved the latter he was no longer a child of thirty-two but a grown man of thirty-seven. It is logical inference from this that the prophecies can reflect only an ecstatic self-absorption on which it is unnecessary for a critic to intrude.

Now of course it is quite true that Blake was a neglected and isolated figure, obeying his own genius in defiance of an indifferent and occasionally hostile society; and he himself was well aware that he was "born with a different face."[1] But he did not want to be: he did not enjoy neglect, and he had what no real artist can be without, an intense desire to communicate. "Those who have been told," he pleaded, "that my Works are but an unscientific and irregular Eccentricity, a Madman's Scrawls, I demand of them to do me the justice to examine before they decide."[2] It is pathetic to read his letters and see how buoyant is his hope of being understood in his own time, and how wistful is the feeling that he must depend on posterity for appreciation. And it was not only recognition he wanted: he had a very strong sense of his personal responsibility both to God and to society to keep on producing the kind of imaginative art he believed in. He despised obscurity, hated all kinds of mystery, and derided the idea that poets do not fully comprehend what they are writing.[3] All his poetry was written as though it were about to have the immediate social impact of a new play. Besides, if we look at some of the other poets of the second half of the eighteenth century—Smart, Cowper, Chatterton, Macpherson, Fergusson, Collins, Burns—we shall find the percentage of mental breakdowns and social maladjustments among them abnormally high. It is clear that the spiritual loneliness of Blake was not so much characteristic of him as of his age.

Therefore, as no one will deny that Blake is entitled to the square deal he asked for, we propose to adopt more satisfactory hypotheses and see what comes out of them. These are, first, that all of Blake's poetry, from the shortest lyric to the longest prophecy, must be taken as a unit and, *mutatis mutandis,* judged by the same standards. This means that the longer and more difficult prophecies will have to bear the weight of the commentary. They are what a great poet chose to spend most of his time on, and they are what he hoped to be remembered for, as a poet, by posterity. He may have been mistaken in this, as poets often are about their own work, but if he was the error is too consistent and gigantic to be ignored. Second, that as all other poets are judged in relation to their own time, so should Blake be placed in his historical and cultural context as a poet who, though original, was not aboriginal, and was neither a freak nor a sport.

One of the most striking things about Blake is his genius for crystallization. He is perhaps the finest gnomic artist in English literature, and his fondness for aphorism and epigram runs steadily through his work from adolescence to old age. To produce the apparent artlessness of the lyrics he was ready to do the very considerable amount of rewriting and excision that his manuscripts show. The meticulous clarity of his engraving is as evident in the great sweep of *Paolo and Francesca*, in the Dante series, as in the microscopic marginal detail on the poems. It seems difficult to imagine, then, how Blake came to find an artistic satisfaction, or even relief, in writing such confused and chaotic monologues as the prophecies are generally considered to be. I quote from an intelligent and sensitive study of his painting:

By way of more than passing interest, it is worthy of note that in the garden of the house grew a grape-vine; but no grapes were enjoyed, for Blake held that it was wrong to prune the vine. Had Blake submitted that vine to pruning, he might have enjoyed its fruit; and had he submitted the luxuriant vine of his Prophetic Books to more diligent pruning, more people might have lived to enjoy their fruit also. It would be one of those strange chances with which Life is for ever teasing the children of men, that Blake should produce the larger number of his books from a house from the windows of which he could see a parable from which he was not willing to learn.[4]

Anyone who has glanced at the original versions of "The Tyger" or "The Fly" may perhaps wonder why the man who did the pruning of these poems should have been afraid of a grapevine. However, the story of the unpruned vine is merely one of the anecdotes that regularly go the rounds of artists' biographies, the source of this one being probably Vasari's Life of Piero di Cosimo; we are concerned here only with the theory of wanton luxuriance. Blake's poetry consists of one volume of youthful work published without his co-operation, a proof copy of another poem, a few manuscripts, and a series of poems the text of which was laboriously engraved backhanded on copper plates and accompanied by a design. And when these poems were once engraved Blake seldom altered anything more fundamental than the color-scheme:

> Re-engrav'd Time after Time,
> Ever in their youthful prime,
> My designs unchang'd remain.[5]

The inference is clear: the engraved poems were intended to form an exclusive and definitive canon. And in this canon there is much evidence, not only of pruning, but of wholesale transplanting and grafting. His longest poem, *The Four Zoas*, Blake left abandoned in a manuscript full of lively sketches and loaded with deletions and corrections. Much of its material was later used in *Milton* and *Jerusalem*, which he did engrave; but, proportionately, Blake may be said to have blotted more lines than any other important poet of English literature.

Further, Blake's poems are poems, and must be studied as such. Any attempt to explain them in terms of something that is not poetry is bound to fail. Many students of Blake have been less interested in what he wrote than in what he read, and have examined the prophecies chiefly as documents illustrating some nonpoetic tradition such as mysticism or occultism. This, though it also ignores Blake's vociferous assertions that he belongs to no tradition whatever except that of the creative artists, is again a perfectly logical inference from the overemphasis on his uniqueness already mentioned. If even the lyrics are so isolated in the history of literature, the prophecies can represent only a complete break with the literary tradition itself.

I am not speaking now of merely vulgar misunderstandings. No one who has read three lines of our straightforward and outspoken poet can imagine that he wished to be pursued by a band of superstitious dilettantes into the refuge of a specialized cult. Whatever Blake's prophecies may be, they can hardly be code messages. They may need interpretation, but not deciphering: there can be no "key" and no open-sesame formula and no patented system of translation. The amateur of cabalism who accepts obscure truisms for profound truths, and sentimental platitudes for esoteric mysteries, would do well to steer clear of Blake. No: I mean the tendency to describe Blake in terms of certain stereotypes which imply that he can be fully appreciated only by certain types of mind, and which tend to scare the ordinary reader away from him. The poet who addressed the four parts of his most complicated poem, *Jerusalem*, to the "Public," Jews, Deists and Christians— to anyone who cares to look at it—the poet who boasted of being understood by children,[6] would have resented this treatment strongly. It is true, however, that the poet who said "Exuberance is Beauty"[7] demands an energy of response. He is not writing for a tired pedant who feels merely badgered by difficulty: he is writing for enthusiasts of poetry who, like the readers of mystery stories, enjoy sitting up nights trying to find out what the mystery is.

The usual label attached to Blake's poetry is "mystical," which is a word he never uses. Yet "mysticism," when the word is not simply an elegant variant of "misty" or "mysterious," means a certain kind of religious technique difficult to reconcile with anyone's poetry. It is a form of spiritual communion with God which is by its nature incommunicable to anyone else, and which soars beyond faith into direct apprehension. But to the artist, *qua* artist, this apprehension is not an end in itself but a means to another end, the end of producing his poem. The mystical experience for him is poetic material, not poetic form, and must be subordinated to the demands of that form. From the point of view of any genuine mystic this would be somewhat inadequate, and one who was both mystic and poet, never finally deciding which was to be the adjective and which the noun, might be rather badly off. If he decided for poetry, he would perhaps do better to use someone else's mystical experiences, as Crashaw did St. Teresa's.

I do not say that these difficulties are insurmountable, or that there are no such things as mystical poets. But they are very rare birds, and most of the poets generally called mystics might better be called visionaries, which is not quite the same thing. This *is* a word that Blake uses, and uses constantly. A visionary creates, or dwells in, a higher spiritual world in which the objects of perception in this one have become transfigured and charged with a new intensity of symbolism. This is quite consistent with art, because it never relinquishes the visualization which no artist can do without. It is a perceptive rather than a contemplative attitude of mind; but most of the greatest mystics, St. John of the Cross and Plotinus for example, find the symbolism of visionary experience not only unnecessary but a positive hindrance to the highest mystical contemplation. This suggests that mysticism and art are in the long run mutually exclusive, but that the visionary and the artist are allied.

Such a distinction cannot be absolute, of course, and one type blends into the other. But Blake was so completely a visionary and an artist that I am inclined to think that most true mystics would reject his attitude as vulgar and insensitive. Porphyry speaks of his master Plotinus as having four times in his life, with great effort and relentless discipline, achieved a direct apprehension of God. Blake says:

> I am in God's presence night & day,
> And he never turns his face away.[8]

To Blake, the spiritual world was a continuous source of energy: he harnessed spiritual power as an engineer harnesses water power and used it to drive his inspiration: he was a spiritual utilitarian. He had the complete pragmatism of the artist, who, as artist, believes nothing but is looking only for what he can use. If Blake gets into the rapt circle of mystics it is only as Mercury got into the Pantheon, elbowing his way through with cheerful Cockney assurance, his pockets bulging with paper, then producing his everlasting pencil and notebook and proceeding to draw rapid sketches of what his more reverent colleagues are no longer attempting to see.

· 2 ·

ANY attempt to explain Blake's symbolism will involve explaining his conception of symbolism. To make this clear we need Blake's own definition of poetry:

Allegory addressed to the Intellectual powers, while it is altogether hidden from the Corporeal Understanding, is My Definition of the Most Sublime Poetry; it is also somewhat in the same manner defin'd by Plato.[9]

It has often been remarked that Blake's early lyrics recall the Elizabethans: it is not so generally realized that he reverts to them in his critical attitude as well, and especially in this doctrine that all major poetry is allegorical. The doctrine is out of fashion now, but whatever Blake may mean by the above definition, it is clear that there is a right and a wrong way of reading allegory. It is possible, then, that our modern prejudice against allegory, which extends to a contemptuous denial that Homer or Virgil or Shakespeare can be allegorical poets, may be based on the way of the "corporeal understanding."

What is the corporeal understanding? Literally, it is bodily knowledge: the data of sense perception and the ideas derived from them. From this point of view *poetry* is something to be explained, and the notion that any kind of commentary will ever explain any kind of poetry is of course vulgar. Even if there is a hidden meaning, a poem which contains no more than what an explanation of that meaning can translate should have been written in the form of the explanation in the first place. And if the literal sense of poetry is intelligible, the possibility that it may also be explained allegorically might better be left alone.

The corporeal understanding, then, cannot do more than elucidate the genuine obscurities, the things requiring special knowledge to understand, like the contemporary allusions in Dante. The more it busies itself with the real meaning of the poem the more involved it gets, and Blake, like other difficult poets, has been wrapped in a Laocoön tangle of encyclopedias, concordances, indexes, charts and diagrams. The "intellectual powers" go to work rather differently: they start with the hypothesis that the poem in front of them is an imaginative whole, and work out the implications of that hypothesis. "Every Poem must necessarily be a perfect Unity,"[10] said Blake: the identity of content and form is the axiom of all sound criticism. There is therefore nothing mysterious about the intellectual powers: on the contrary, the one thing they must include is a sense of proportion. If one wishes to make a necklace out of some beads and a string, one would be well advised to start with the string and apply the beads to it. In the opposite procedure of laying the beads down in a line and trying to stick the string through them, a comparatively simple task becomes one of incredible difficulty.

Blake's idea that the meaning and the form of a poem are the same thing comes very close to what Dante appears to have meant by "anagogy" or the fourth level of interpretation: the final impact of the work of art itself, which includes not only the superficial meaning but all the subordinate meanings which can be deduced from it.[11] It is therefore hoped that if the reader finds his ideas of Blake at all clarified by the present book, he will be led to the principle which underlies it. This is that, while there is a debased allegory against which there is a reasonable and well-founded prejudice, there is also a genuine allegory without which no art can be fully understood. It is of course confusing that the same word is used in both senses, and when Blake says in one place that his poetry is allegory addressed to the intellectual powers and in another that one of his paintings is "not Fable or Allegory, but Vision,"[12] he does little to clear up the confusion. The allegory that is addressed to the intellectual powers, however, is not a distortion of poetry any more than poetry is a distortion of prose. It is a literary language with its own idioms and its own syntactical arrangement of ideas. If a critic were to say that Homer's theme demands a rugged simplicity which is spoiled by the complicated inflections of the language he used, he would be displaying nothing except his ignorance of Greek. Similarly, if a critic is ignorant of the language of allegory, he will demonstrate nothing but that ignorance if, in dealing with any genuinely allegorical writer, Spenser for instance, or Langland, or Hawthorne, he complains of the intrusion of allegory into characterization, or descriptions of nature, or whatever else is more congenial to his prejudices. As ignorance of the methods and techniques of allegorical poetry is still almost universal, the explicitly allegorical writers have for the most part not received in modern times much criticism which is based directly on what they were trying to do. If Blake can be consistently interpreted in terms of his own theory of poetry, however, the interpretation of Blake is only the beginning of a complete revolution in one's reading of all poetry. It is, for instance, quite impossible to understand Blake without understanding how he read the Bible, and to do this properly one must read the Bible oneself with Blake's eyes. Then comes the question of how he read some of his other essential sources, Ovid's *Metamorphoses*, for instance, or the Prose Edda, and how he related their symbolism to his own. As one proceeds, one emerges from a haze of suggestive allusions into a new kind of poetic thought, and one begins to feel, as one does in learning any language, the support of an inner logical discipline. At this point hidden links in the symbolism become visible, and they lead in their turn to further associations, until the intellectual powers are able to read without translating.

If this book can explain Blake properly, it will suggest that Blake is a reliable teacher of a poetic language which most contemporary readers do not understand, or if they do, do not realize it. Blake did not invent that language, and he is not a special kind of poet; he is merely a poet who, as he says, makes a commonplace understanding of him impossible. But once he is understood and the language of allegory learned by means of him, a whole new dimension of pleasure in poetry will be opened up which will add increased depth and range, not only to the more explicitly allegorical writers, but to any poet who addresses the intellectual powers. Blake himself wrote a brilliant criticism of Chaucer, not an obviously allegorical poet, in which he provides an illustration of the method. In the depths of his labyrinthine *Jerusalem* he promises us "the end of a golden string,"[13] and that refers, as will be shown in due course, not to a technique of mystical illumination as is generally assumed, but to a lost art of reading poetry.

Of course an attempt to outline the Blakean approach to poetry is not the same thing as a study of Blake's sources or influence. One's impression of Blake is that he read little, could not read any language with comfort except his own and perhaps French,[14] and preferred marginally cursing authors he hated, like Reynolds and

Bacon, to discovering parallels in kindred spirits. Blake is the kind of writer who may show startling resemblances to someone he had not read, such as Traherne, and no resemblance at all to someone he had read attentively, such as Paine. Conversely, such a writer as Gérard de Nerval, who had presumably not read Blake, is much closer to him than Yeats, who edited him. In the study of Blake it is the analogue that is important, not the source; and even essential sources such as the Bible and Milton are of value only as sources of analogues. Blake is warning us of this when he says:

> I must Create a System or be enslav'd by another Man's.
> I will not Reason & Compare: my business is to Create.[15]

It is always dangerous to assume that any poet writes with one eye on his own time and the other confidentially winking at ours. Yet the impression that there is something peculiarly modern and relevant to the twentieth century about Blake is very strong. "Blake and Modern Thought" is the title of at least two studies of Blake; and his devotees are never tired of finding that contemporary ideas have been anticipated by him. We shall have to return to this subject, but there is one aspect of it which may be noticed here. A modern writer on Blake is not required to discuss his sanity, for which I am grateful: I could not do so without being haunted by one of his own epigrams: "The Man who pretends to be a modest enquirer into the truth of a self evident thing is a Knave."[16] But that Blake was often called mad in his lifetime is of course true. Wordsworth called him that, though Wordsworth had a suspicion that if the madman had bitten Scott or Southey he might have improved their undoubtedly sane poetry.[17] The point is, not that the word "mad" applied to Blake is false, but that it is untranslatable. When Samuel Johnson speaks in his diary of disorders of mind he experienced which were very near to madness, both what he meant by madness and what he implied by sanity have dropped out of our language. He thought of madness as a completely sterile, chaotic and socially useless deviation from normal behavior. Whatever art he approved of he considered sane and balanced, benefiting society and adjusted to society. In the nineteenth century a reaction against this attitude set in, and the opposition of artist and society reached a very high tension which suggested that genius itself is a morbid secretion of society, and art a disease that cures the world homeopathically.

Now one interesting thing about Blake is that he combines the attitude of Johnson with the nineteenth century position. He felt the whole force of the social opposition to his kind of art, but he never allowed its propaganda to influence him even negatively. He was called mad so often that towards the end of his life he even became interested in insanity, struggled through part of a once famous book on the subject and made drawings of lunatic heads.[18] But he never believed that there was much of creative value in morbidity, disease or insanity in themselves. The sources of art are enthusiasm and inspiration: if society mocks and derides these, it is society that is mad, not the artist, no matter what excesses the latter may commit:

I then asked Ezekiel why he eat dung, & lay so long on his right & left side? he answer'd, "the desire of raising other men into a perception of the infinite."[19]

What Blake demonstrates is the sanity of genius and the madness of the commonplace mind, and it is here that he has something very apposite to say to the twentieth century, with its interest in the arts of neurosis and the politics of paranoia.

· 3 ·

BLAKE distinguishes between opinions and principles, saying that everyone changes the former and that no one, not even a hypocrite, can change the latter.[20] But even in matters of opinion Blake shows little variation, though there would certainly have been much more had he received his fair share of sympathetic criticism. His principles he held with bulldog tenacity all his life. The lyrics of his adolescence, the prophecies of his middle period, the comments which blister the margins of books he read on a sickbed at seventy, are almost identical in outlook. He himself says that his notes on Reynolds, written at fifty, are "exactly Similar" to those on Locke and Bacon, written when he was "very Young."[21] Even phrases and lines of verse will reappear as much as forty years later. Obstinacy in maintaining what he believed to be true was itself one of his leading principles, and he notes with sardonic amusement its success with those who opposed him: "as if genius and assurance were the same thing!"[22] Consistency, then, foolish or otherwise, is one of Blake's chief preoccupations, just as "self-contradiction" is always one of his most contemptuous comments.

Therefore, if the engraved poems of Blake form a canon, as we have suggested, anything admitted to that canon, whatever its date, not only belongs in a unified scheme but is in accord with a permanent structure of ideas. Omission may be deliberate or accidental—we can seldom be sure which—but admission is a seal of approval extending to more than poetic merit. This does not mean that Blake's poetry is the vehicle of a "message," but that he is in a somewhat restricted sense of the term a "metaphysical" poet. The structure of ideas common to his poems, then, is what we must first examine.

His engraving process was perfected about 1788, and the first products of it were three series of aphorisms, two called *There Is No Natural Religion* and the third *All Religions Are One*. These aphorisms are evidently intended to be a summarized statement of the doctrines in the engraved canon, and as they are largely concerned with Blake's theory of knowledge, it will be following Blake's own order to start from there. Our supporting quotations will be drawn as far as possible from writings outside the more difficult prophecies, in order to avoid their technical vocabulary.

· 4 ·

THAT an eighteenth century English poet should be interested in contemporary theories of knowledge is hardly surprising. Blake had carefully read and annotated Locke's *Essay on the Human Understanding* in his youth, though his copy has not turned up. But as Locke, along with Bacon and Newton, is constantly in Blake's poetry a symbol of every kind of evil, superstition and tyranny, whatever influence he had on Blake was clearly a negative one. The chief attack on Locke in the eighteenth century came from the idealist Berkeley, and as idealism is a doctrine congenial to poets, we should expect Blake's attitude to have some points in common with Berkeley's, particularly on the subject of the mental nature of reality, expressed by Berkeley in the phrase *esse est percipi*: "to be is to be perceived":

Mental Things are alone Real; what is call'd Corporeal, Nobody Knows of its Dwelling Place: it is in Fallacy, & its Existence an Imposture. Where is the Existence Out of Mind or Thought? Where is it but in the Mind of a Fool?[23]

The unit of this mental existence Blake calls indifferently a "form" or an "image." If there is such a thing as a key to Blake's thought, it is the fact that these two words mean the same thing to him. He makes no consistent use of the term "idea." Forms or images, then, exist only in perception. Locke's philosophy distinguishes sensation from reflection: the former is concerned with perception, the latter with the classification of sensations and the development of them into abstract ideas. These latter afford inclusive principles or generalizations by which we may build up the vast unselected mass of sense data into some kind of comprehensible pattern. The eighteenth century's respect for generalization comes out in Samuel Johnson, who dwells frequently on the "grandeur of generality," saying that "great thoughts are always general," and that "nothing can please many, and please long, but just representations of general nature."[24] Blake, evidently, thinks differently:

What is General Nature? is there Such a Thing? what is General Knowledge? is there such a thing? Strictly Speaking All Knowledge is Particular.

To Generalize is to be an Idiot. To Particularize is the Alone Distinction of Merit. General Knowledges are those Knowledges that Idiots possess.[25]

Blake is discussing Reynolds' theories of painting, but as one of his main points against Reynolds is the Lockian basis of his aesthetics, it is quite safe to use these quotations here. The second remark, though of course itself a generalization, means that the image or form of perception is the content of knowledge. Reflection on sensation is concerned only with the mere memory of the sensation, and Blake always refers to Locke's reflection as "memory." Memory of an image must always be less than the perception of the image. Just as it is impossible to do a portrait from memory as well as from life, so it is impossible for an abstract idea to be anything more than a subtracted idea, a vague and hazy afterimage. In fact, it is far less real than an afterimage. Sensation is always in the plural: when we see a tree we see a multitude of particular facts about the tree, and the more intently we look the more there are to see. If we look at it very long and hard, and possess a phenomenal visual memory, we may, having gone away from the tree, remember nearly everything about it. That is far less satisfying to the mind than to keep on seeing the tree, but, though we no longer have a real tree, we have at least a memory of its reality. But the abstract idea of "tree" ranks far below this. We have now sunk to the mental level of the dull-witted Philistine who in the first place saw "just a tree," without noticing whether it was an oak or a poplar.

But even the idea "tree" retains some connection, however remote, with real trees. It is when we start inferring qualities from things and trying to give them an independent existence that the absurdities of abstract reasoning really become obvious. We do this as a kind of mental shorthand to cover up the deficiencies of our memories. Blake says, in a note on Berkeley's *Siris*:

Harmony and Proportion are Qualities & not Things. The Harmony and Proportion of a Horse are not the same with those of a Bull. Every Thing has its own Harmony & Proportion, Two Inferior Qualities in it. For its Reality is its Imaginative Form.[26]

This implies, for one thing, that "proportion" means nothing except in direct relation to real things which possess it; and for another, that the differences between the proportions of a bull and a horse are infinitely more significant than the mere fact that both of them have proportion. In short, things are real to the extent that they are sharply, clearly, particularly perceived by themselves and discriminated from one another. We have said that the idea "tree" represents a dull and vague perception of the forms of trees; but such a word as "proportion," taken by itself, represents a flight from reality that even a dense fog or a pitch-black night could be no more than a mere suggestion of. The first point in Blake to get clear, then, is the infinite superiority of the distinct perception of things to the attempt of the memory to classify them into general principles:

Deduct from a rose its redness, from a lilly its whiteness, from a diamond its hardness, from a spunge its softness, from an oak its heighth, from a daisy its lowness, & rectify everything in Nature as the Philosophers do, & then we shall return to Chaos, & God will be compell'd to be Eccentric if he Creates, O happy Philosopher.[27]

The acceptance of the *esse-est-percipi* principle unites the subject and the object. By introducing the idea of "reflection" we separate them again. The abstract philosophers say that things do not cease to exist when we stop looking at them, and therefore there must be some kind of nonmental reality behind our perception of them. Thus Locke attempts to distinguish the "secondary qualities" of perception from "primary qualities" which he assigns to a "substratum" of substance. A still cruder form of the same theory is atomism, the belief in a nonmental and unperceived unit of the object-world. "An atom," Blake said, is "a thing which does not exist"[28]—as of course it does not, in the sense in which he meant the word. Democritus had expounded this theory in Classical times: it had been developed by Epicurean philosophers, and Bacon, who "is only Epicurus over again," and whose "philosophy has ruined England," had been enthusiastic about Democritus.[29] Newton's corpuscular theory of light belongs to the same method of thought.[30] Atomism is another attempt to annihilate the perceived differences in forms by the assertion that they have all been constructed out of units of "matter." If we try to visualize a world of tiny particles all alike, we again summon up the image of a dense fog or a sandstorm which is the inevitable symbol of generalization. How could forms have been developed out of such a chaos? There is no "matter": there is a material world, but that is literally the "material" of experience, and has no reality apart from the forms in which it subsists, except as an abstract idea on the same plane as that of "proportion."

If to be is something else than to be perceived, our perceptions do not acquaint us with reality and we consequently cannot trust them. We are then forced back on altering the method of perception in the hope that something more real will turn up. Bacon, whose "first principle is Unbelief,"[31] started a program of conducting experiments for this purpose. Blake is quite ready to admit that "the true method of knowledge is experiment"[32]; but he insists that everything depends on the mental attitude of the experimenter. If you cannot accept what you see as real, the fact that you see it in a microscope or a test tube makes no difference. Anyone who, like Descartes, begins by doubting everything except his own doubts, will never end in certainties, as Bacon promises. Where is the certainty to come from? Blake is never tired of ridiculing Locke's

> Two Horn'd Reasoning, Cloven Fiction,
> In Doubt, which is Self contradiction.[33]

and he asks ironically what would happen if the object took the point of view of the subject:

> He who Doubts from what he sees
> Will ne'er Believe, do what you Please.
> If the Sun & Moon should doubt,
> They'd immediately Go out.[34]

This last remark has a double edge. The attempt to separate the object from the subject gets us no further than a mere hypothesis of the "substratum" or "atom" type. But, if the mountain will not go away from Mohammed, Mohammed can always go away from the mountain. Locke's "reflection" is designed to withdraw the subject from the object, to replace real things with the shadowy memories of them which are called "spectres" in Blake's symbolism. But all that can be produced from this must be spun out of the philosopher's own bowels like a spider's web, a fantastic and egocentric daydream. Hence, while the Epicurean atomist and the solipsist or navel-gazer are superficially opposed to one another, the attempt to separate the subject and the object is common to them both, and consequently they differ only in emphasis. We shall meet with extensions of this principle later on.

· 5 ·

BERKELEY draws a distinction, though his treatment of it is not as thorough as it might be, between the ideas we have of the existence of other things and the "notion" we have of our own existence. We know that we are a reality beyond others' perceptions of us, and that if *esse est percipi*, then *esse est percipere* as well.

Now insofar as a man is perceived by others (or, in fact, by himself), he is a form or image, and his reality consists in the perceived thing which we call a "body." "Body" in Blake means the whole man as an object of perception. We need another word to describe the man as a perceiver, and that word must also describe the whole man. "Soul" is possible, though it has theological overtones suggesting an invisible vapor locked up in the body and released at death. Blake will use this word only with a caution:

Man has no Body distinct from his Soul; for that call'd Body is a portion of Soul discern'd by the five Senses.[35]

At the time that he wrote the aphorisms referred to above he used
the rather cumbersome term "Poetic Genius," for reasons that will
presently appear: "the Poetic Genius is the true Man," he says, and
"the body or outward form of Man is derived from the Poetic
Genius."[36] The commonest word, however, is "mind," and Blake
frequently employs it. We use five senses in perception, but if we
used fifteen we should still have only a single mind. The eye does
not see: the eye is a lens for the mind to look through. Perception,
then, is not something we do with our senses; it is a mental act.
Yet it is equally true that the legs do not walk, but that the mind
walks the legs. There can be therefore no distinction between
mental and bodily acts: in fact it is confusing to speak of bodily
acts at all if by "body" we mean man as a perceived form. The only
objection to calling digestion or sexual intercourse mental activities is a hazy association between the mind and the brain, which
latter is only one organ of the mind, if mind means the acting man.
It is perhaps better to use some other word. If man perceived is a
form or image, man perceiving is a former or imaginer, so that
"imagination" is the regular term used by Blake to denote man as
an acting and perceiving being. That is, a man's imagination is his
life. "Mental" and "intellectual," however, are exact synonyms of
"imaginative" everywhere in Blake's work. "Fancy" also means
the imagination: "fantasy," on the other hand, relates to the memory and its "spectres."

To be perceived, therefore, means to be imagined, to be related
to an individual's pattern of experience, to become a part of his
character. There is no "general nature," therefore nothing is real
beyond the imaginative patterns men make of reality, and hence
there are exactly as many kinds of reality as there are men. "Every
man's wisdom is peculiar to his own individuality,"[37] and there is
no other kind of wisdom: reality is as much in the eye of the be-
holder as beauty is said to be. Scattered all through Blake's work
are epigrams indicating this relativity of existence to perception:

> Every Eye sees differently. As the Eye, Such the Object.
> Every thing possible to be believed is an image of truth.
> The Sun's Light when he unfolds it
> Depends on the Organ that beholds it.[38]

Blake does not deny the unity of the material world: a farmer and a painter, looking at the same landscape, will undoubtedly see the same landscape:

. . . All of us on earth are united in thought, for it is impossible to think without images of somewhat on earth.[39]

This fact has its importance in Blake's thought; but the reality of the landscape even so consists in its relation to the imaginative pattern of the farmer's mind, or of the painter's mind. To get at an "inherent" reality in the landscape by isolating the common factors, that is, by eliminating the agricultural qualities from the farmer's perception and the artistic ones from the painter's, is not possible, and would not be worth doing if it were. Add more people, and this least common denominator of perception steadily decreases. Add an idiot, and it vanishes.

The abstract reasoner attempts to give independent reality to the qualities of the things he sees, and in the same way he tries to abstract the quality of his perception. It is to him that we owe the association of mind and brain. The intellect to him is a special department concerned with reasoning, and other departments should not meddle with it. Emotion is another department, formerly ascribed to the heart, and still retaining a fossilized association with it. As for the sexual impulse, that is "bodily"; that is, it belongs to a third department called "body" by a euphemism. Thought being largely reflection, it is an "inward" activity: those who specialize in "outward" activity are not thinkers, but the practical people who do things. Scientists should be trained to see the sun as a fact; artists to see it emotionally as beautiful. That is, the artist's imagination is not concerned with seeing things, but with seeing an abstraction called the "beauty" in things; the scientist does not see anything either, but merely the "truth" in it. Thus we get Philistines saying that if we add any enthusiasm about beauty to our perception of things it will blur the clarity with which we see them; while the sentimental assert that the warm-blooded mammalian emotional perception which tenderly suckles its images is superior to the reptilian intellectual who lays cold abstract eggs. This last is a point of view with which Blake's is often confused.

All this pigeonholing of activity is nonsense to Blake. Thought *is* act, he says.[40] An inactive thinker is a dreamer; an unthinking doer is an animal. No one can begin to think straight unless he has a passionate desire to think and an intense joy in thinking. The sex act without the play of intellect and emotion is mere rutting; and virility is as important to the artist as it is to the father. The more a man puts all he has into everything he does the more alive he is. Consequently there is not only infinite variety of imaginations, but differences of degree as well. It is not only true that "every eye sees differently," but that "a fool sees not the same tree that a wise man sees," and that "the clearer the organ the more distinct the object."[41] Hence if existence is in perception the tree is *more* real to the wise man than it is to the fool. Similarly it is more real to the man who throws his entire imagination behind his perception than to the man who cautiously tries to prune away different characteristics from that imagination and isolate one. The more unified the perception, the more real the existence. Blake says:

"What," it will be Question'd, "When the Sun rises, do you not see a round disk of fire somewhat like a Guinea?" O no, no, I see an Innumerable company of the Heavenly host crying, "Holy, Holy, Holy is the Lord God Almighty."[42]

The Hallelujah-Chorus perception of the sun makes it a far more real sun than the guinea-sun, because more imagination has gone into perceiving it. Why, then, should intelligent men reject its reality? Because they hope that in the guinea-sun they will find their least common denominator and arrive at a common agreement which will point the way to a reality about the sun independent of their perception of it. The guinea-sun is a sensation assimilated to a general, impersonal, abstract idea. Blake can see it if he wants to, but when he sees the angels, he is not seeing more "in" the sun but more of it. He does not see it "emotionally": there is a greater emotional intensity in his perception, but it is not an emotional perception: such a thing is impossible, and to the extent that it is possible it would produce only a confused and maudlin blur—which is exactly what the guinea-sun of "common sense" is. He sees all that he can see of all that he wants to see; the perceivers of the guinea-sun see all that they want to see of all that they can see.

In Blake the criterion or standard of reality is the genius; in

Locke it is the mediocrity. If Locke can get a majority vote on the sun, a consensus of normal minds based on the lower limit of normality, he can eliminate the idiot who goes below this and the visionary who rises above it as equally irrelevant. This leaves him with a communal perception of the sun in which the individual units are identical, all reassuring one another that they see the same thing; that their minds are uniform and their eyes interchangeable. The individual mind thus becomes an indivisible but invariable unit: that is, it is the subjective equivalent of the "atom." Blake calls the sum of experiences common to normal minds the "ratio," and whenever the word "reason" appears in an unfavorable context in Blake, it always means "ratiocination," or reflection on the ratio.

There are two forms of such ratiocination. There is deductive reasoning, or drawing conclusions from a certain number of facts which we already possess, a process in which every new fact upsets the pattern of what has already been established: "Reason, or the ratio of all we have already known, is not the same that it shall be when we know more."[43] Then there is inductive reasoning, which is equally circular because it traces the circumference of the universe as it appears to a mediocre and lazy mind:

The bounded is loathed by its possessor. The same dull round, even of a universe, would soon become a mill with complicated wheels.[44]

We distinguish between voluntary and involuntary activities, between conscious and unconscious planes of the mind, and it is from this that Blake's idea of degrees of imagination is derived. "My legs feel like a walk" is recognized to be a half-humorous figure of speech; but "my heart beats" is accepted as literal. It is not altogether so: the imagination beats the heart; but still the automatic nature of the heartbeat is not in question. Blake's objection to Locke is that he extends the involuntary action into the higher regions of the imagination and tries to make perceptive activity subconscious. Locke does not think of sight as the mind directing itself through the eye to the object. He thinks of it as an involuntary and haphazard image imprinted on the mind through the eye by the object. In this process the mind remains passive and receives impressions automatically. We see the guinea-sun automatically: seeing the Hallelujah-Chorus sun demands a voluntary and conscious imaginative effort; or rather, it demands an exuberantly active mind which will not be a quiescent blank slate. The imaginative mind, therefore, is the one which has realized its own freedom and understood that perception is self-development. The unimaginative is paralyzed by its own doubt, its desire to cut parts of the mind off from perception and parts of perception out of the mind, and by the dread of going beyond the least common denominator of the "normal." This opposition of the freedom of the acting mind and the inertia of the response to an external impression will also meet us again.

· 6 ·

Such freedom is extravagant only if there is no inner unity to the character of the perceiver. Perceptions form part of a logically unfolding organic unit, and just as an acorn will develop only into an oak, and not just any oak but the particular oak implicit in it, so the human being starts at birth to perceive in a characteristic and consistent way, relating his perception to his unique imaginative pattern. This is what Blake means when he explodes against the denial of innate ideas with which Locke's book opens:

Reynolds Thinks that Man Learns all that he knows. I say on the Contrary that Man Brings All that he has or can have Into the World with him. Man is Born Like a Garden ready Planted & Sown. This World is too poor to produce one Seed.

Innate Ideas are in Every Man, Born with him; they are truly Himself. The Man who says that we have No Innate Ideas must be a Fool & Knave, Having No Con-Science or Innate Science.[45]

It perhaps should be pointed out that Locke is denying what from Blake's point of view would be innate generalizations, and Blake does not believe in them any more than Locke does. Blake is protesting against the implication that man is material to be formed by an external world and not the former or imaginer of the material world. We are not passively stimulated into maturity: we grow into it, and our environment does not alter our nature, though it may condition it. Blake is thus insisting on the importance of the distinction between wisdom and knowledge. Wisdom is the central form which gives meaning and position to all the facts which are acquired by knowledge, the digestion and assimilation of whatever in the material world the man comes in contact with.

Sense experience in itself is a chaos, and must be employed either actively by the imagination or passively by the memory. The former is a deliberate and the latter a haphazard method of creating a mental form out of sense experience. The wise man will choose what he wants to do with his perceptions just as he will choose the books he wants to read, and his perceptions will thus be charged with an intelligible and coherent meaning. Meaning for him, that is, pointing to his own mind and not to, for instance, nature. It thus becomes obvious that the product of the imaginative life is most clearly seen in the work of art, which is a unified mental vision of experience.

For the work of art is produced by the entire imagination. The dull mind is always thinking in terms of general antitheses, and it is instructive to see how foolish these antitheses look when they are applied to art. We cannot say that painting a picture is either an intellectual or an emotional act: it is obviously both at once. We cannot say that it is either a reflective or an active process: it is obviously both at once. We cannot say that it is "mental" or "bodily": no distinction between brainwork and handwork is relevant to it. We cannot say that the picture is a product of internal choice or external compulsion, for what the painter wants to do is what he has to do. Art is based on sense experience, yet it is an imaginative ordering of sense experience: it therefore belongs neither to the "inside" nor the "outside" of the Lockian universe, but to both at once.

The artist is bound to find the formless and unselected linear series of sense data very different from what he wishes to form, and the difficulties inherent in this never disappear for him. The composition of music is an imaginative ordering of the sense experience of sound, yet so different from random sense experience of sounds that the latter for most composers is a nuisance to their composing and must be shut out of their ears. The painter is even worse off, for though Beethoven's deafness did not destroy the hearing of his imagination, the painter cannot shut his eyes. For Blake the acquiring of the power to visualize independently of sense experience was a painful and laborious effort, to be achieved only by relentless discipline. But at the same time the senses are the basis of all art. No painter ever painted an abstract idea; he paints only what he can visualize, and art owes its vividness and directness of impact, as compared with reasoning, to the fact that the concrete is more real than the general.

It is, then, through art that we understand why perception is superior to abstraction, why perception is meaningless without an imaginative ordering of it, why the validity of such ordering depends on the normality of the perceiving mind, why that normality must be associated with genius rather than mediocrity, and why genius must be associated with the creative power of the artist. This last, which is what Blake means by "vision," is the goal of all freedom, energy and wisdom.

But surely it is absurd to connect this with the *esse-est-percipi* doctrine. To be is to be perceived; therefore the object is real in proportion as the perceiver is a genius; therefore a tree is more real to a painter than to anyone else. This sounds dubious enough, and more so when we raise the question: what is the reality of a painted tree? If it is painted from life, it is an imitation of life, and must therefore be less real; if it is visualized independently of sense experience, does it not come out of the memory just as abstract ideas do? And if the whole work of art in which it occurs is an imaginative ordering of experience, then similarly the work of art is an imitation or a memory of experience. According to Plato the bed of sense experience, itself an imitation of the form or idea of the bed, is imitated by the painter. And while it is not surprising that Blake should be fond of pointing out that the Muses Plato worshiped were daughters of memory rather than imagination, there is still Plato's argument to meet.

Now it is true that we derive from sense experience the power to visualize, just as Beethoven derived from his hearing the power to "visualize" sounds after he had lost it. It may even be true that we do not visualize independently of sense without the help of memory. But what we see appearing before us on canvas is not a reproduction of memory or sense experience but a new and independent creation. The "visionary" is the man who has passed through sight into vision, never the man who has avoided seeing, who has not trained himself to see clearly, or who generalizes among his stock of visual memories. If there is a reality beyond our perception we must increase the power and coherence of our perception, for we shall never reach reality in any other way. If the reality turns out to be infinite, perception must be infinite too. To visualize, therefore, is to realize. The artist is *par excellence* the man who struggles to develop his perception into creation, his sight into vision; and art is a technique of realizing, through an ordering of sense experience by the mind, a higher reality than linear unselected experience or a second-hand evocation of it can give.

It is no use saying to Blake that the company of angels he sees surrounding the sun are not "there." Not where? Not in a gaseous blast furnace across ninety million miles of nothing, perhaps; but the guinea-sun is not "there" either. To prove that he sees them Blake will not point to the sky but to, say, the fourteenth plate of the Job series illustrating the text: "When the morning stars sang together, and all the sons of God shouted for joy." *That* is where the angels appear, in a world formed and created by Blake's imagination and entered into by everyone who looks at the picture. It appears, then, that there are not only two worlds, but three: the world of vision, the world of sight and the world of memory: the world we create, the world we live in and the world we run away to. The world of memory is an unreal world of reflection and abstract ideas; the world of sight is a potentially real world of subjects and objects; the world of vision is a world of creators and creatures. In the world of memory we see nothing; in the world of sight we see what we have to see; in the world of vision we see what we want to see. These are not three different worlds, as in the religions which speak of a heaven and hell in addition to ordinary life; they are the egocentric, the ordinary and the visionary ways of looking at the same world.

The fact that in the world of vision or art we see what we want to see implies that it is a world of fulfilled desire and unbounded freedom. The rejection of art from Plato's *Republic* is an essential part of a vision of the human soul which puts desire in bondage to reason, a vision of a universe turning on a spindle of necessity, and an assumption that a form is an idea rather than an image. Works of art are more concentrated and unified than sense experience, and that proves that there is nothing chaotic about the unlimited use of the imagination. Hence an antithesis of energy and order, desire and reason, is as fallacious as all the other antitheses with which timid mediocrity attempts to split the world. Imagination is energy incorporated in form:

Energy is the only life, and is from the Body; and Reason is the bound or outward circumference of Energy.[46]

Blake's poem *Visions of the Daughters of Albion* ends in an apotheosis of desire; *Jerusalem* in one of intellect. Those who have succeeded in mentally separating the inside from the outside, the top from the bottom, the convex from the concave, will call these poems hopelessly inconsistent with each other. But a thinker who has no desire to think cannot think, and thus all thought, like all sexual intercourse, is a fulfillment of desire. And one who desires but cannot imagine what it is he wants is not getting very far with his desire, which, if it were real, would attempt to achieve an intelligible form.

Nearly all of us have felt, at least in childhood, that if we imagine that a thing is so, it therefore either is so or can be made to become so. All of us have to learn that this almost never happens, or happens only in very limited ways; but the visionary, like the child, continues to believe that it always ought to happen. We are so possessed with the idea of the duty of acceptance that we are inclined to forget our mental birthright, and prudent and sensible people encourage us in this. That is why Blake is so full of aphorisms like "If the fool would persist in his folly he would become wise."[47] Such wisdom is based on the fact that imagination creates reality, and as desire is a part of imagination, the world we desire is more real than the world we passively accept.

· 7 ·

Now of course the arts are only a few of many social phenomena which are summed up in such words as "culture" or "civilization." These words in fact give a much clearer idea of what Blake means by "art." The religious, philosophical and scientific presentations of reality are branches of art, and should be judged by their relationship to the principles and methods of the creative imagination of the artist. If they are consistent with the latter, they fulfill a necessary function in culture: if they are not, they are pernicious mental diseases.

We have said that the artist uses ideas, but *qua* artist is not otherwise concerned with their truth. This exactly corresponds to the doctrine that reality is in the individual mental pattern. As compared with religion, for instance, art keeps the pragmatic individual synthesis, whereas religion as generally understood is both dogmatic and communal. The religious synthesis, therefore, in trying to fulfill the needs of a group, freezes the symbols both of its theology and ritual into invariable generalities. Religion is thus a social form of art, and as such both its origin in art and the fact that its principles of interpretation are those of art should be kept in mind:

The Religions of all Nations are derived from each Nation's different reception of the Poetic Genius, which is every where call'd the Spirit of Prophecy.[48]

"All Religions are One" means that the material world provides a universal language of images and that each man's imagination speaks that language with his own accent. Religions are grammars of this language. Seeing is believing, and belief is vision: the *substance* of things hoped for, the *evidence* of things not seen.

A metaphysical system, again, is a system; that is, an art-form, to be judged in terms of its inner coherence. "Every thing possible to be believ'd is an image of truth," which means a form of truth, and if Plato's or Locke's philosophy makes sense in itself, it is as truly a form or image of reality as a picture, and an image of the same kind. To try to verify a philosophical or religious system in relation to an objective nonmental "truth" is to dissolve an imaginative form back into the chaos of the material world, and this kind of verification will destroy whatever truth it has. Even in science there is no use looking beyond the human mind for reassurance. As a matter of fact in stressing the concrete and the primacy of sense experience Blake is much closer to the inductive scientist than to the "reasoner," and his unfavorable comments on science always relate to certain metaphysical assumptions underlying the science of his day laid down by Bacon and Locke. As long as science means knowledge organized by a commonplace mind it will be part of the penalty man pays for being stupid; the value of science depends on the mental attitude toward it, and the mental attitude of Bacon and Locke is wrong. As for history, that, even when it has overcome the difficulty of having to deal with documents which are invariably a pack of lies, is a linear record of facts like our daily sense experience, and has like it to be ordered by the imagination. "Reasons and opinions concerning acts are not history," says Blake: "Acts themselves alone are history"[49]—history is imaginative material to be synthesized into form, not memory to be reflected upon.

Blake is not simply rationalizing his own job to the limit: his defense of the supremacy of art is a well-established one in literary criticism, and he has no wish to curtail the variety of culture. He does not say that science is wrong; he says that a commonplace mind can make a wrong use of it. He does not say that philosophy is quibbling; he says it would be if philosophers had no imagination. And still less has his teaching to do with that of most of those who tell us that we should make our lives a work of art and live beautifully. The cultivators of "stained-glass attitudes" do not usually mean by beauty the explosion of energy that produces the visions of the dung-eating madman Ezekiel.

· 8 ·

WHATEVER may be thought of Blake's doctrine of the imagination, one thing should at least be abundantly clear by now. Any portrayal of Blake as a mystical snail who retreated from the hard world of reality into the refuge of his own mind, and evolved his obscurely beautiful visions there in contemplative loneliness, can hardly be very close to Blake. That identifies his "imagination" with his interpretation of Locke's "reflection," which is unnecessarily ironic. It is true that we often confuse the imaginary with the imaginative in ordinary speech, and often mean, when we say that something is "all imagination," that it does not exist; but such modes of speech and thought, however intelligible in themselves, cannot be used in interpreting Blake.

Though Blake is an interesting eighteenth century phenomenon even in philosophy, Locke's reputation can perhaps be left to take care of itself. To meet the difficulties in his theory of imagination we must in any case proceed to his religious ideas, and leave the epistemology of Locke and Berkeley for the more rarefied atmosphere of Swedenborg.

Samuel Johnson attempted to refute Berkeley by kicking a stone: in doing so he merely transferred his perception of the stone to another sense, but his feeling that the stone existed independently of his foot would possibly have survived even a mention of that fact. Berkeley's argument was that there is a reality about things apart from our perception of them, and, as all reality is mental, this reality must be an idea in the mind of God. Now God and man are different things to Berkeley, and this sudden switch from one to the other leaves a gap in the middle of his thought. Blake, by postulating a world of imagination higher than that of sense, indicates a way of closing the gap which is completed by identifying God with human imagination:

Man is All Imagination. God is Man & exists in us & we in him.

The Eternal Body of Man is The Imagination, that is, God himself. ... It manifests itself in his Works of Art (In Eternity All is Vision).[1]

Man in his creative acts and perceptions is God, and God is Man. God is the eternal Self, and the worship of God is self-development. This disentangles the idea raised in the preceding chapter of the two worlds of perception. This world is one of perceiver and perceived, of subject and objects; the world of imagination is one of creators and creatures. In his creative activity the artist expresses the creative activity of God; and as all men are contained in Man or God, so all creators are contained in the Creator.

This doctrine of God further explains how a visionary can be said to be normal rather than abnormal, even though his appearance may be rare. The sane man is normal not because he is just like everyone else but because he is superior to the lunatic; the healthy man is normal because he is superior to the cripple. That is, they are most truly themselves. The visionary is supreme normality because most of his contemporaries are privative just as cripples and lunatics are. Whatever he is from their point of view, he is more of a man than they, and it is his successes that make him truly "human," not his failures or weaknesses, as they are apt to say. Hence the visionary expresses something latent in all men; and just as it is only in themselves that the latter find God, so it is only in the visionary that they can see him found. As imagination *is* life, no one is born without any imagination except the stillborn, but those who cut their imagination down as far as they can, deny, as far as they can, their own manhood and their divinity which is that manhood. They will therefore turn their backs on the genius who greatly acts and greatly perceives; but they retain the power to enter into kinship with him:

The worship of God is: Honouring his gifts in other men, each according to his genius, and loving the greatest men best: those who envy or calumniate great men hate God; for there is no other God.[2]

The identity of God and man is qualified by the presence in man of the tendency to deny God by self-restriction. Thus, though God is the perfection of man, man is not wholly God: otherwise there would be no point in bringing in the idea of God at all. On the other hand, the infinite variety of men is no argument against the unity of God. Such ideas as "mankind" and "humanity" are only generalized; but the fact that an acorn produces only an oak indicates the fact of species or class as clearly as it indicates the fallacy of a generalized tree. Blake's word "form" always includes this unity of species: he says, for instance:

> The Oak is cut down by the Ax, the Lamb falls by the Knife,
> But their Forms Eternal Exist For-ever.[3]

Similarly, God is not only the genius but the genus of man, the "Essence" from which proceed the individuals or "Identities" mentioned in Blake's note on Swedenborg:

Essence is not Identity, but from Essence proceeds Identity & from one Essence may proceed many Identities. . . .

If the Essence was the same as the Identity, there could be but one Identity, which is false. Heaven would upon this plan be but a Clock. . . .[4]

(Blake is attacking what seems to him a tendency to pantheism in Swedenborg.) Just as the perceived object derives its reality from being not only perceived but related to a unified imagination, so the perceiver must derive his from being related to the universal perception of God. If God is the only Creator, he is the only Perceiver as well. In every creative act or perception, then, the act or perception is universal and the perceived object particular.

And we have already met the converse of this principle, that when the perception is egocentric the perceived object is general. There are thus two modes of existence. The ego plays with shadows like the men in Plato's cave; to perceive the particular and imagine the real is to perceive and imagine as part of a Divine Body. A hand or eye is individual because it is an organ of a body: separated from the body it loses all individuality beyond what is dead and useless. That is why the imagination is constructive and communicable and why the "memory" is circular and sterile. The universal perception of the particular is the "divine image" of the *Songs of Innocence*; the egocentric perception of the general is the "human abstract" of the *Songs of Experience*. This is the basis of Blake's theory of good and evil which we shall meet in the next chapter.

There are two corollaries of this. One is that we perceive *as* God: we do not perceive God. "No man hath seen God at any time," because true perception is creation, and God cannot be created. We may see the divine aspect of great men, but when we do the divine in us recognizes itself. The other is, that, as we cannot perceive anything higher than a man, nothing higher than Man can exist. The artist proves this by the fact that he can paint God only as a man, though if he is reproducing senile and epicene ideas of God he will paint an enfeebled old man out of compliment to them. But there is no form of life superior to our own; and the acceptance of Jesus as the fullness of both God and Man entails the rejection of all attributes of divinity which are not human:

Man can have no idea of any thing greater than Man, as a cup cannot contain more than its capaciousness. But God is a man, not because he is so perceiv'd by man, but because he is the creator of man.[5]

Naturally those brought up on abstract ideas will begin by denying both of these postulates, so let us see what success they have with their theology.

· 2 ·

WE have quoted Blake as saying that the idea of "proportion" means nothing except in relation to a concrete thing which possesses it. The proportions of a real thing are part of its "living form." We can only detach the idea of proportion from reality through what he calls "mathematic form"; generalized symmetry without reference to perceived objects. Now this idea of "mathematic form" has always had a peculiar importance for abstract reasoners, who try to comprehend God's creative power through the abstract idea of creation, or "design."

Hence there is a recurrent desire to believe that some simpler pattern, expressible perhaps in some mathematical formula, underlies the complications of our universe. I say complications, for this line of thought takes the world as complicated rather than complex. Pythagoras began with the patterns of simple arithmetic and the cardinal numbers; the *Timaeus* attempted to work out the geometrical shapes considered most fitting (this word will meet us again) from which to deduce all phenomena; and with the elaboration of the Ptolemaic universe the tendency spread in all directions. Many of its manifestations, particularly those that still survive, are occult, or at least highly speculative. But actually the whole tendency to symmetrical pattern-making in thought is very inadequately described as occultism, which is only a specialized department of it. Pattern-making extends over philosophy from Pythagoras to the Renaissance as a kind of intermediate stage between magic and science.

These latter two are psychologically very similar, we are told; both attempt to manipulate the laws of nature for man's purposes. And if this tendency to explain the world as a complication of simple mathematical formulae is, as we suggest, intermediate between magic and science and psychologically allied to both, we should expect Blake's attitude to it to be much the same as his attitude to science. Briefly, it may be said that the whole Pythagorean tradition in thought, from the *Timaeus* to our own day, has nothing to do with Blake and appears in him only in the form of parody. He simply did not believe in "the mystical Mathematicks of the City of Heaven." "The Gods of Greece & Egypt were Mathematical Diagrams—See Plato's Works,"[6] he says. It sounds flippant, but it was the most serious criticism he had to offer.

It is worth insisting on this, because occultists are frequently attracted to Blake, and the above statement may well surprise anyone who has noticed the role that recurring cardinal numbers and even diagrams play in the later prophecies. But real things have mathematical principles inherent in them, and a work of art, which is a synthesis of real things, has mathematical principles inherent in its unity. Blake distinguishes between the art of "mathematic form," like Greek architecture, which displays a tendency to generalized symmetry, and the art of "living form," like Gothic architecture, which has kept that symmetry properly subordinated.[7] But the Gothic arch and spire would soon collapse without mathematical principles. The Apocalypse in the Bible is an imaginative and visionary work of art, but it is not the less so for making a symbolic use of the number seven. The recurrence of this number is part of its unity as a poem, not an attempt to indicate a sevenfold aspect of things in general. Similarly in Blake all recurrent numbers and diagrams must be explained in terms of their context and their relation to the poems, not as indicating in Blake any affinity with mathematical mysticism.

· 3 ·

THE poetic basis of symmetrical thought is now fairly clear to us since the Copernican universe replaced the Ptolemaic one. But the later system has developed new methods of conceiving an impersonal and abstract God which are equally antithetical to Blake, and these, being more contemporary, bear the main brunt of his attack, and form the basis for his treatment of Newton. The vast size of the Copernican universe has encouraged many timid souls to feel that the creation of it must be ascribed to an impersonal Power, whose nature can be understood only through our ideas of mechanical force. Hence the true followers of such a God are "men of destiny"; men of force or cunning rather than intelligence or imagination, and those unfortunate enough to possess the latter would do well to avoid him, or rather it. It is true that the more striking manifestations of this religion are later than Blake: when to the ice-cold and ether-breathing deity of the Copernican system there was added the immense stretch of geological time, in which nothing particularly cheerful seems to have occurred, gods like the "immanent Will" of Hardy's *Dynasts* were developed of a ferocity unknown to Blake's age. Blake, however, in his depiction of the chilling terror of his character Urizen, the god of empty space and blind will, shows a remarkably prophetic insight into these dinosaur-haunted theologies.

He himself regards the "immanent Will" account of God as superstitious. Not, of course, because he has any more faith in the benevolent avuncular God who explains away all suffering and injustice at the Last Judgment and proves himself to have had the best intentions all along. Nor does he agree with those who accept it negatively and feel that its "right worship is defiance."[8] He disagrees with it on the same ground that he disagrees with Locke's account of abstract ideas. Locke extends involuntary and automatic reflexes to include the passive reception of sense impressions, which to Blake should be the products of an active consciousness. Similarly, the worshiper of "immanent Will" is extending the subconscious activity of the heartbeat from sense experience to the whole universe. And he does it by exactly the same process of trying to find a least common denominator for his general principles. A man, a dog and a tree are all alive; therefore life must be inherently and really some kind of "life force" common to them which can only be identified with the lowest possible limit of life—protoplasm, perhaps. But as the boundary between living things and moving things is difficult to trace, the "immanent Will" is bound to sink below "life force" to take in all other forms of motion in a more inclusive generalization still.

It is much better, as in the previous case, to go to work the other way. A man, a dog and a tree are all alive; but the man is the most alive; and it is in man that we should look for the image, or form, of universal life. There can be no "life force" apart from things possessing it: universal life is the totality of living things, and God has intelligence, judgment, purpose and desire because we are alive and possess these things.

The Darwinian universe merely adds the tyranny of time and will to the tyranny of space and reason with which Blake was already acquainted, and suggests a generalized energy abstracted from form supplementing the generalized form abstracted from energy which we find in Locke's conception of substance. "No Omnipotence can act against order," Blake says.[9] If Blake had lived a century later he would undoubtedly have taken sides at once with Butler and Shaw and claimed that alterations in an organism are produced by the development of the organism's "imagination"; and the doctrine of environmental stimulus in time would have fitted into the same plane in his thought as Locke's doctrine of involuntary sense perception in space.

As a matter of fact Blake does use the persistence of life as an argument that the hold of life on the world is not precarious. Lightning may kill a man, but it cannot beget him: life can come only from life, and must go straight back to the creation at least, which implies the primacy of creative over destructive energy. Worshipers of the "immanent Will" see its most striking effects in the latter, and in the irony and tragedy it suggests, but this must be subordinate to the power of incubation. We have already noticed that Blake's words "form" and "image" mean a species persisting through time: "The Oak dies as well as the Lettuce, but Its Eternal Image & Individuality never dies, but renews by its seed."[10] Further, when Blake says: "Each thing is its own cause and its own effect,"[11] he means that life is not itself caused by anything external to it, and that there is no causality which is not part of an organic process. Accidents happen, but when they do they are not part of a larger superhuman scheme; they are part of the breakdown of human schemes, and their "meaning" depends on what the human mind does with them.

Blake was familiar enough with the earlier manifestations of life-force worship in eighteenth century primitivism. That postulated a "nature" as the body of life from which man has sprung, and that too attempted to cut parts away from the human imagination by asserting that the latter was diseased and adulterated insofar as it had developed away from nature. Blake had no use for the noble savage or for the cult of the natural man; he disliked Rousseau enough to give an attack on him a prominent place in *Jerusalem*. Civilization is in more than one sense supernatural: it is something which man's superiority over nature has evolved, and the central symbol of the imagination in all Blake's work is the city. "Where man is not, nature is barren,"[12] he says. Of all animals, man is the most hopelessly maladjusted to nature: that is why he outdistances the animals, the supreme triumph of the imagination which has developed and conquered rather than survived and "fitted."

· 4 ·

THUS we find ourselves unable to conceive of anything superhuman in the direction of either design or power. The same thing happens when we try to conceive a "perfect" God. Perfection, when it means anything, means the full development of all one's imagination. This is what Jesus meant when he said "Be ye therefore perfect." But many timid abstract thinkers feel that this is irreverent, and that perfection lies in the completeness with which a quality is abstracted from a real thing. God is thus thought to be "pure" goodness. Such a God could never have created Falstaff, to whom he would be vastly inferior. If this idea of "pure" perfection is pressed a little further it dissolves in negatives, as all abstract ideas do. God is infinite, inscrutable, incomprehensible—all negative words, and a negative communion with some undefined ineffability is its highest development. What Blake thinks of this he has put into one of his most brilliant epigrams:

> God Appears & God is Light
> To those poor Souls who dwell in Night,
> But does a Human Form Display
> To those who Dwell in Realms of day.[13]

It is an old quibble that God cannot move because to move is to alter and to alter would be to lessen his perfection. As long as this means abstract perfection, the argument is unanswerable: a negatively perfect God is not a Creator.

In the first chapter of Genesis we read of a God, or Gods, called Elohim, who can be reconciled with a philosophical First Cause. So completely is he a God of unconscious and automatic order that he created the sun, moon and stars chiefly to provide a calendar for Jewish ritual, and rested on the Sabbath to institute a ceremonial law. In the next chapter we come across a folklore God named Jehovah, a fussy, scolding, bad-tempered but kindly deity who orders his disobedient children out of his garden after making clothes for them, who drowns the world in a fit of anger and repeoples it in a fit of remorse. Such a God has much to learn, but he comes far closer to what Jesus meant by a Father than the other, and gets a correspondingly higher place in Blake's symbolism.[14]

Even when we try to think of the superhuman in terms of intelligence and imagination we run into difficulties. To be is to be perceived, and we perceive nothing higher than man. The one certain inference from this is that we cannot conceive an essentially superhuman imagination, and when we try to imagine above human nature we always imagine below it. It has been said that grasshoppers are like gods in that they are without blood or feeling. Such gods are therefore as much inferior to man as grasshoppers are, or would be if they could exist. We can imagine men who can do things we cannot; who can fly, who perspire instead of excreting food, who converse by intuition instead of words. But these are differences in attributes, not in substance: the latter we cannot imagine. In Blake there are no characters who represent anything qualitatively superior to man in the way that a man is superior to a fish. There is no "chain of being" in Blake and no trace of any of the creatures invented by those who believe in a chain of being: no gods, no eons, no emanations (in the Gnostic sense: Blake's use of this term is different), no world-soul, no angelic intelligences bound on the spindle of necessity. If they had any intelligence they would get off it, as man got off the spindle of nature.

This is important as throwing some light on Blake's idea of inspiration. It is true that Blake often makes remarks implying an external spiritual agency. He speaks, for instance, of his poems as "dictated," and of himself as their "secretary."[15] But usually the term "angel" or "spirit" in Blake, when not used in an ironic sense, means the imagination functioning as inspiration, and the fact that inspiration often takes on a purpose of its own which appears to be independent of the will is familiar to every creative artist. Blake says, for instance: "Every man's leading propensity ought to be call'd his leading Virtue & his good Angel."[16] It is the same with the "dictation" of his poetry:

When this Verse was first dictated to me, I consider'd a Monotonous Cadence . . . to be a necessary and indispensible part of Verse. But I soon found . . .

If the inspiration were anything external to Blake he would have had no choice in the matter. "Spirits are organized men," he says, and he would agree with Paul that "the spirits of the prophets are subject to the prophets."[17]

The spirit which is the organized man may also be, however, the imagination which has got itself disentangled from its present world through the process we call death. The imagination cannot exist except as a bodily form, but the body is only what others on the same plane of existence see of the soul or mind. Hence when the imagination changes its world it can change its bodily form as completely as the lepidoptera which have suggested most of the images of immortality. Christianity has always insisted on the resurrection of the body, though the two facts that the risen body is spiritual and that it is a body are hard to keep both in mind at once. All belief in ghosts or shades or in any form of spirit conceived as less than bodily is superstitious: there is no *animula vagula blandula* in Blake.

· 5 ·

THERE is no divinity in sky, nature or thought superior to our selves. Hence there is in Blake no acceptance of the *données* of existence as such, no Leibnitzian idea of the perfection of *established* order. Nor is there any idea of finding in nature external hints or suggestions of God; all such intuitions are implanted by the mind on nature. Nature is there for us to transform; it is neither a separate creation of God nor an objective counterpart of ourselves. Blake criticized Wordsworth sharply for ascribing to nature what he should have ascribed to his own mind and for believing in the correspondence of human and natural orders:

> How exquisitely the individual Mind
> (And the progressive powers perhaps no less
> Of the whole species) to the external World
> Is fitted:—and how exquisitely, too—
> Theme this but little heard of among men—
> The external World is fitted to the Mind.

"You shall not bring me down to believe such fitting & fitted," is Blake's comment on this passage.[18]

We arrive at the emotions of acceptance and obedience only at the price of stifling part of our imaginations. In terms of man's desires, we see nothing outside man worthy of respect. Nature is miserably cruel, wasteful, purposeless, chaotic and half dead. It has no intelligence, no kindness, no love and no innocence. Man under natural law is more pitiful than Diogenes' plucked cock. In a state of nature man must surrender intelligence for ferocity and cunning, kindness and pity for a relentless fight to survive, love for the reproductive instinct, innocence for obedience to humiliating laws.

When we look up from the earth to the whizzing balls of ice and fire in the sky we see there merely an extension of nature. It is instinctive with the ignorant to worship the sun as the giver of life, and superstition of this sort is described by Blake as ignorant honesty, beloved of God and man.[19] The advance of knowledge in revealing the deadness and remoteness of the sun should not destroy this instinct for worship, but it should eliminate the sun as a possible object of it. Unthinkable distances and endless resources for killing anyone who might conceivably approach them is all the response the heavens afford to the exploring imagination. They therefore cannot be connected with any feeling of love, reverence, loyalty or anything else we associate with a personal God. And an impersonal God can be worshiped only by the servile, the self-hypnotized, the hypocritical, or at most the resigned.

However, it is all very well to abuse nature, but the divinity in us which Blake postulates is hardly more reassuring. We are capable of depths of cruelty and folly that sink below anything in nature. Yet is not the source of evil the natural weakness of man's body, the form his mind takes in the physical world? Our sight is feeble compared to the lynx; our movements stumbling and foolish compared to a bird; our strength and beauty grotesque compared to the tiger. Once we begin to think in terms of wish and desire, we find ourselves beating prison bars. Our desire to see goes far beyond any telescope. We are ashamed of our bodies, and though the shame itself is shameful, particularly when we realize that they are the forms of our souls, it is there, and it is hard to love a Creator who could, for instance, make our "places of joy & love excrementitious."[20] We are fearfully and wonderfully made, but in terms of what our imaginations suggest we could be, we are a hideous botch. The man who does not use his imagination is the natural man, and the natural man, according to all versions of Christianity except Deism, can do nothing good; yet what does the imagination do except reveal to us our own impotence?

The realization that the world we desire and create with our imaginations is both better and more real than the world we see leads us to regard the latter world as "fallen." It is a cheap print or reproduction of what was once the vision of the unbounded creative power of God, and all great visions in art lead up to visions of the unfallen world, called Paradise in the Bible and the Golden Age in the Classics. "The Nature of my Work is Visionary or Imaginative," said Blake; "it is an Endeavour to Restore what the Ancients call'd the Golden Age."[21] In Christian terms, this means that the end of art is the recovery of Paradise. The Bible tells us that in Paradise man was integrated with God: nature to him was not ocean and wilderness but his own property, symbolized by a garden or park which is what the word "Paradise" means; animals were neither ferocious nor terrified, and life had no pain or death.

In Blake there are certain modifications of the orthodox account of the Fall. One is that as all reality is mental, the fall of man's mind involved a corresponding fall of the physical world. Another is, that as God is Man, Blake follows some of the Gnostics and Boehme in believing that the fall of man involved a fall in part of the divine nature. Not all, for then there would be no imagination left to this one; but part, because it is impossible to derive a bad world from a good God, without a great deal of unconvincing special pleading and an implicit denial of the central fact of Christianity, the identity of God and Man. The conclusion for Blake, and the key to much of his symbolism, is that the fall of man and the creation of the physical world were the same event.

All works of civilization, all the improvements and modifications of the state of nature that man has made, prove that man's creative power is literally supernatural. It is precisely because man is superior to nature that he is so miserable in a state of nature. Now in a state of nature, in which we use as little imagination as possible, our minds exist in the form only of our dirty, fragile, confined bodies, and from that point of view man is a speck of life precariously perched on a larger speck in a corner of a huge, mysterious, indifferent, lifeless cosmos. When the subject exists in a cramped distortion the object will necessarily exist in a monstrous distortion. The visionary insists that everything in the physical world which we call real is a matter of perspective and associations:

> How do you know but ev'ry Bird that cuts the airy way,
> Is an immense world of delight, clos'd by your senses five?[22]

There is nothing particularly lovable about a wolf or a fox, but there may be about a dog. Man has caught and trained the dog; he has developed the dog's intelligence and has projected his own imagination on him. He loves the dog more than the wolf because there is more of man in the dog. We get out of nature what we put into it, and the training of a dog is an imaginative victory over nature. So an artist catches and trains the objects of his

vision; he can put human imagination into them, make them intelligible and responsive. In a picture every detail is significant and
relevant to the whole design. That is an image of the world the
visionary wants to live in; a world so fully possessed by the human
imagination that its very rocks and clouds are more alive and more
responsive than the dogs in this world are. Up to a point we can
talk to a dog and make him talk back; we cannot make a tree talk
back, but in a higher world we could create the tree as completely
as we create sons and daughters in this world. The Classical dryad
represents a partial attempt to transform an object of perception
into a creature:

. . . the forms of all things are derived from their Genius, which by the
Ancients was call'd an Angel & Spirit & Demon.[23]

The *Metamorphoses* of Ovid record the converse process, of hu-
manized creatures dwindling into objects of perception, which implies that they are images of the fall of man. As our imaginations
expand the world takes on a growing humanity, for to see things
as created by God and in God is the same as seeing things as created by Man and in Man:

> . . . Each grain of Sand,
> Every Stone of the Land,
> Each rock & each hill,
> Each fountain & rill,
> Each herb & each tree,
> Mountain, hill, earth & sea,
> Cloud, Meteor & Star,
> Are Men seen Afar.[24]

The fallen world is the world of the *Songs of Experience*: the
unfallen world is the world of the *Songs of Innocence*. Naturally
those who live most easily in the latter are apt to be, from the
point of view of those absorbed wholly in the former, somewhat
naïve and childlike. In fact most of them are actually children.
Children live in a protected world which has something, in epitome, of the intelligibility of the state of innocence, and they have
an imaginative recklessness which derives from that. The child
who cries to have the moon as a plaything, who slaps a table for
hurting him when he bumps his head, who can transform the most
unpromising toy into a congenial companion, has something which

the adult can never wholly abandon without collapsing into mediocrity.

The paradisal Eden of the Bible is described in terms of a pastoral placidity which may suggest to an unsympathetic reader that Adam fell because he outgrew it: the suggestion is much stronger in *Paradise Lost*. Yet this association of innocence with naïveté is by no means adequate. An unfallen world completely vitalized by the imagination suggests human beings of gigantic strength and power inhabiting it, such as we find hinted at in the various Titanic myths. The vision of such beings would be able to penetrate all the mysteries of the world, searching into mountains or stars with equal ease, as in this description of the bound Titan Orc:

> His eyes, the lights of his large soul, contract or else expand;
> Contracted they behold the secrets of the infinite mountains,
> The veins of gold & silver & the hidden things of Vala,
> Whatever grows from its pure bud or breathes a fragrant soul;
> Expanded they behold the terrors of the Sun & Moon,
> The Elemental Planets & the Orbs of eccentric fire.[25]

Even in those moments when most "we feel that we are greater than we know," this feeling is not so much one of individuality as of integration into a higher unit or body of life. This body, of course, is ultimately God, the totality of all imagination. But even men who cannot reach the idea of God believe in the reality of larger human bodies, such as nations, cities or races, and even speak of them as fathers or mothers. It takes a genuine faith to see a nation or race as a larger human being, or form of human existence, and a good deal of such faith is undoubtedly idolatry. Still, there is a partial idea of God in it, and in a Utopia or millennium it would become direct knowledge or vision, such as Milton suggests when he says that "a Commonwealth ought to be but as one huge Christian personage, one mighty growth, and stature of an honest man."[26] Hence these gigantic forms which inhabit the unfallen world are, on nearer view, human aggregates of the kind which inspire loyalty even in this world:

. . . these various States I have seen in my Imagination; when distant they appear as One Man, but as you approach they appear multitudes of Nations.[27]

This exactly fits what we have just said, that the fall of man involved a fall in part but not all of the divine nature. The particu-

lar "Giant form" or "Eternal" to which we belong has fallen, the
aggregate of spirits we call mankind or humanity and Blake calls
Albion (Adam in Blake has his regular place as the symbol of the
physical body or the natural man). When Albion or mankind fell,
the unity of man fell too, and although our imagination tells us
we belong to some larger organism even if we cannot see it as God,
in the meantime we are locked up in separated opaque scattered
bodies. If the whole of mankind were once more integrated in a
single spiritual body the universe as we see it would burst.

Theology distinguishes between "natural" and "revealed" religion, the former being the vision of God which man develops
with his fallen reason and the latter the vision communicated to
him by inspired prophets. To Blake "There Is No Natural Religion." The only reason that people believe in it is that they are
unwilling to believe in the identity of God and Man. If there is evil
in nature, it must be our fault and not God's; therefore God created the world good, the extent to which man's fall altered that
goodness being a disputed point. But if we stop trying to rescue
the credit of an abstract and pure goodness, we can easily see that
all religion is revealed. The Greek word for revelation is "apocalypse," and the climax of Christian teaching is in the "Revelation"
or Apocalypse at the end of the Bible which tells us that there is an
end to time as well as a beginning and a middle, a resurrection as
well as a birth and a death; and that in this final revelation of the
unfallen world all mystery will vanish: John's symbol is the burning of the Great Whore who is called Mystery. Such a revelation
involves the destruction of the present world, when the sun will
be turned into darkness and the moon into blood and the stars will
fall from heaven like ripe figs. It moves on to a new heaven and
earth (*i.e.*, an earth renewed or revealed in the form of heaven),
in which the chaos of nature becomes our own garden, as in Paradise, a world no longer continuously perceived but continually
created:

> In futurity
> I prophetic see
> That the earth from sleep
> (Grave the sentence deep)
> Shall arise and seek
> For her maker meek;

And the desart wild
Become a garden mild.[28]

Now when something is revealed to us we see it, and the response to this revelation is not faith in the unseen or hope in divine promises but vision, seeing face to face after we have been seeing through a glass darkly. Vision is the end of religion, and the destruction of the physical universe is the clearing of our own eyesight. Art, because it affords a systematic training in this kind of vision, is the medium through which religion is revealed. The Bible is the vehicle of revealed religion because it is a unified vision of human life and therefore, as Blake says, "the Great Code of Art."[29] And if all art is visionary, it must be apocalyptic and revelatory too: the artist does not wait to die before he lives in the spiritual world into which John was caught up. To quote Wordsworth again in a passage which explains why Blake admired as well as criticized him:

. . . The unfettered clouds and region of the Heavens,
Tumult and peace, the darkness and the light—
Were all like workings of one mind, the features
Of the same face, blossoms upon one tree;
Characters of the great Apocalypse,
The types and symbols of Eternity.[30]

According to Wordsworth the perceived forms of the eternal world are those which are constantly perceived in this one, and it is not in the grandiose or exceptional experience that "the types and symbols of Eternity" are to be found. Blake is merely extending this principle when he says in "Auguries of Innocence":

To see a World in a Grain of Sand
And a Heaven in a Wild Flower,
Hold Infinity in the palm of your hand
And Eternity in an hour.[31]

Such perception, as the title of the poem makes clear, is an "augury" of the paradisal unfallen state. The last two lines bring us to the next step in the argument.

Those who, like Locke, attempt to separate existence from perception are also separating time from space, as we exist in time and perceive in space. Those who, like the artists, accept the mental nature of reality, know that we perceive a thing at a definite moment, and that there is thus a quality of time inherent in all perception; and, on the other hand, that existence is in a body, which has a spatial extension. We are back again to Blake's doctrine that "Reason is the bound or outward circumference of Energy," that energy and form, existence and perception, are the same thing. Consequently every act of the imagination, every such union of existence and perception, is a time-space complex, not time plus space, but time *times* space, so to speak, in which time and space as we know them disappear, as hydrogen and oxygen disappear when they become water.

This is what the words "eternal" and "infinite" mean in Blake. Eternity is not endless time, nor infinity endless space: they are the entirely different mental categories through which we perceive the unfallen world. A spiritual world which is visualized as a world of unchanging order, symbolized by the invariable interrelations of mathematics, is not an eternal world but a spatial one, from which time has simply been eliminated. And, to complete the antithesis, a spiritual world visualized as one of unchanging duration is a world of abstract time, from which the "bounding outline" or spatial limits of existence have been eliminated. The Lockian can conceive of eternity and infinity only in either or both of these ways: that is why he uses two words, one suggesting time and the other space, for the same thing. But his two categories have nothing to do with real infinity and eternity; nor, in fact, has he two of them: all he has in each case is the indefinite, which is the opposite of the infinite or eternal, and one of the most sinister words in Blake's symbolism.

Clock time is a mental nightmare like all other abstract ideas. An impalpable present vanishing between an irrevocable past and an unknown future, it is the source of all our ideas of fate and causality. It suggests an inexorable march of inevitably succeeding events in which everything is a necessary consequence of causes stretching back to an unknown God as a First Cause and stretching on into a future which would be completely predictable if it were not too complicated. Its only possible symbol not only for Blake but even for those who believe in it is the chain, which is also a symbol of slavery. At best time is "the mercy of Eternity"[32]; its swiftness makes more tolerable the conditions of our fallen state.

To the imaginative eye there is a more definite shape to time. In most religious allegories, including Blake's, this is indicated by the boundaries ascribed to it, a beginning at the creation or fall and an end at the apocalypse. This is a convenient way of expressing the fact that the fallen world is temporal and the unfallen eternal, but it is not essential, and is even misleading when carried too far. "In the beginning God created the heaven and earth": if we try to visualize what happened *before* that, we get an impression of extraordinary bleakness. This is because we cannot think of eternity except by extending time indefinitely, when we think of it as a continuation of this world:

Many suppose that before the Creation All was Solitude & Chaos. This is the most pernicious Idea that can enter the Mind. . . . Eternity Exists, and All things in Eternity, Independent of Creation which was an act of Mercy.[33]

Orthodox ideas of the joys of heaven and the torments of hell also deal with the indefinite rather than the eternal.

The religious idea of "salvation" depends on transcending this view of time. The man survives the death of the natural part of him as the total form of his imaginative acts, as the human creation out of nature which he has made. When Blake says, "Eternity is in love with the productions of time,"[34] he means in part that every imaginative victory won on this earth, whether by the artist, the prophet, the martyr, or by those who achieve triumphs of self-sacrifice, kindliness and endurance, is a permanent reality, while the triumphs of the unimaginative are lost. Existence and perception being the same thing, man exists eternally by virtue of, and to the extent of, his perception of eternity. Any doctrine of personal immortality which conceives of it either as the survival of the individual or of the disappearance of the individual into some objective form of generalized being, such as matter or force or the collective memory of posterity, is again thinking of the eternal as the indefinite.

The same principles apply to space. The universe stretches out to indefiniteness in all directions, and to the fallen eye it is without any kind of limit or outline. All that this suggests to the imagination is the latter's own insignificance and helplessness. Yet somehow we manage to shrug it off and go on with our own concerns. By doing so we indicate that as far as our lives go there is something about time and space that is not real, and something about us that is. However man may have tumbled into this world of indefinite space, he does not belong to it at all. Real space for him is the eternal here; where we are is always the center of the universe, and the circumference of our affairs is the circumference of the universe, just as real time is the "eternal Now"[35] of our personal experience. The ordinary man assumes, as a working hypothesis, that all the universe outside his range is not worth bothering one's head about unduly. The visionary sees, as the final revelation of the Word which God speaks to his mind, that the whole "outside" universe is a shadow of an eclipsed Man.

· 6 ·

ACCORDING to Locke ideas come from space into the mind; according to Blake space is a state of mind. But, as fallen man sees around him only the ruins of a fallen world which his own fall produced, space is a low state of mind. In higher states, where the world we live in is not objective but created, space is no longer an indefinite extent but the form of what we create. This portion of Blake's argument comes, *mutatis mutandis*, from Swedenborg.[36] Let us now return to that crucial passage about the two suns discussed in the last chapter and give it again in its proper context:

Error is Created. Truth is Eternal. Error, or Creation, will be Burned up, & then, & not till Then, Truth or Eternity will appear. It is Burnt up the Moment Men cease to behold it. I assert for My Self that I do not behold the outward Creation & that to me it is hindrance & not Action; it is as the dirt upon my feet, No part of Me. "What," it will be Question'd, "When the Sun rises, do you not see a round disk of fire somewhat like a Guinea?" O no, no, I see an Innumerable company of the Heavenly host crying, "Holy, Holy, Holy is the Lord God Almighty." I Question not my Corporeal or Vegetative Eye any more than I would Question a Window concerning a Sight. I look thro' it & not with it.

We have said that there are at least three levels of imagination. The lowest is that of the isolated individual reflecting on his memories of perception and evolving generalizations and abstract ideas. This world is single, for the distinction of subject and object is lost and we have only a brooding subject left. Blake calls this world Ulro; it is his hell, and his symbols for it are symbols of sterility, chiefly rocks and sand. Above it is the ordinary world we live in, a double world of subject and object, of organism and environment, which Blake calls Generation. No living thing is completely adjusted to this world except the plants, hence Blake usually speaks of it as vegetable. Above it is the imaginative world, and Blake divides this into an upper and a lower part, so that the three worlds expand into four.

Imagination very often begins with a vision of wonderful and unearthly beauty. The writings of many visionaries are full of a childlike delight in a paradisal world which is the same world that other people see, but seen differently. Traherne's *Centuries of Meditations* is a typical book of this kind: the feeling that with the purging of vision one is enabled to possess the entire universe is particularly strong there. Sexual love dwells in the same paradisal state, and from such a love we may proceed up a ladder of love to an imaginative awakening, as in the traditional philosophy of love derived from the *Symposium*.

Love and wonder, then, are stages in an imaginative expansion: they establish a permanent unity of subject and object, and they lift us from a world of subject and object to a world of lover and beloved. Yet they afford us only a lower Paradise after all. Wonder would doubtless have been defined by Blake differently from Johnson's "effect of novelty upon ignorance,"[37] but perhaps he would only have substituted "innocence" for the last word. Ultimately, our attitude to what we see is one of mental conquest springing from active energy. Love and wonder are relaxations from this state: they do not produce the visions of art but an imaginative receptivity. The "Renaissance of Wonder" to Blake could be nothing more than a preliminary imaginative revolt from the fallen world. The imaginative intensity which finds delight and beauty in considering the lilies may remain suffusing us with a vague and unlocalized joy, and with this we may well be content. But the impulse to make some kind of creation out of it is still there, and poetry and painting are the result of the perseverance of vision into conquest. The highest possible state, therefore, is not the union of lover and beloved, but of creator and creature, of energy and form. This latter is the state for which Blake reserves the name Eden. The lower Paradise he calls Beulah, a term derived from Isaiah which means "married," and is used to describe the relation of a land to its people.[38] Eden in Blake's symbolism is a fiery city of the spiritual sun; Beulah is the garden of Genesis in which the gods walk in the cool of the day.

As Ulro is a single and Generation a double world, so Beulah is triple, the world of lover, beloved and mutual creation; the father, the mother and the child. In Eden these three are contained in the unified imagination symbolized in the Bible by the four "Zoas" or living creatures around the throne or chariot of God, described by Ezekiel and John.[39] This world therefore is fourfold, expanding to infinity like the four points of the compass which in this world point to the indefinite. To recapitulate:

> Now I a fourfold vision see,
> And a fourfold vision is given to me;
> 'Tis fourfold in my supreme delight
> And threefold in soft Beulah's night
> And twofold Always. May God us keep
> From Single vision & Newton's sleep![40]

(The twofold vision here, however, is not that of Generation, but the ability to see an unfallen world as well as a fallen one.)

· 7 ·

WE began this chapter by showing that for Blake there can be no question of finding God through either the understanding or the will. That is because the distinction between them, which it is necessary to make first in order to get rid of one of them later, is a distinction based on the "Two Horn'd Reasoning, Cloven Fiction" of the Lockian universe. Those for whom subject and object, existence and perception, activity and thought, are all parts of a gigantic antithesis, will naturally conceive of man as split between an egocentric will and a reason which establishes contact with the nonego. Believers in the cloven fiction tend to come to rest finally in either a will-philosophy or a reason-philosophy, trying in each case to minimize the importance of the one they reject, because they are seeking to unify their ideas by reducing the problem from the double world of Generation to the single world of Ulro. One group assumes that will and energy exist by themselves *in vacuo*, and the other makes similar assumptions about necessity and established order.

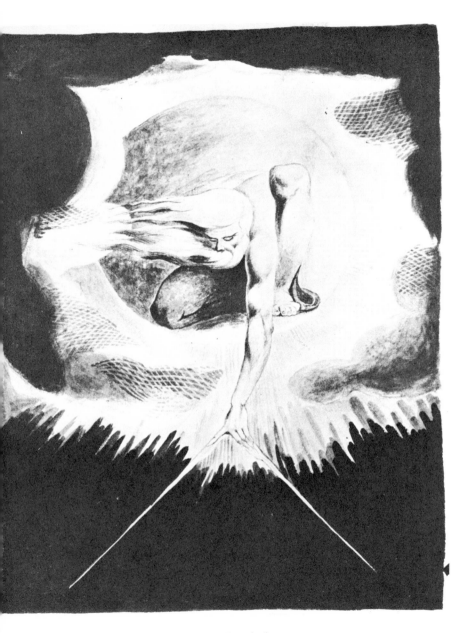

1. *Europe,* Frontispiece

2. Two Songs of Experience

In the flames stood & view'd the armies drawn out in the sky
Washington Franklin Paine & Warren Allen Gates & Lee:
And heard the voice of Albions Angel give the thunderous command:
His plagues obedient to his voice flew forth out of their clouds
Falling upon America, as a storm to cut them off
As a blight cuts the tender corn when it begins to appear.
Dark is the heaven above, & cold & hard the earth beneath;
And as a plague wind fill'd with insects cuts off man & beast;
And as a sea o'erwhelms a land in the day of an earthquake;

Fury, rage, madness! in a wind swept through America
And the red flames of Orc that folded roaring fierce around
The angry shores, and the fierce rushing of th' inhabitants together:
The citizens of New-York close their books & lock their chests;
The mariners of Boston drop their anchors and unlade;
The scribe of Pensylvania casts his pen upon the earth;
The builder of Virginia throws his hammer down in fear.

Then had America been lost, o'erwhelm'd by the Atlantic,
And Earth had lost another portion of the infinite,
But all rush together in the night in wrath and raging fire
The red fires rag'd! the plagues recoil'd! then rolld they back
                                                    with fury

3. *America*, Plate 14

Albion rose from where he labourd at the Mill with Slaves
Giving himself for the Nations he danced the dance of Eternal Death

4. *Glad Day*

Every ornament of perfection. and every labour of love,
In all the Garden of Eden, & in all the golden mountains
Was become an envied horror. and a remembrance of jealousy:
And every Act a Crime, and Albion the punisher & judge

And Albion spoke from his secret seat and said

All these ornaments are crimes, they are made by the labours
Of loves: of unnatural consanguinities and friendships
Horrid to think of. when enquired deeply into: and all
These hills & valleys are accursed witnesses of Sin
I therefore condense them into solid rocks, stedfast!
A foundation and certainty and demonstrative truth:
That Man be separate from Man, & here I plant my seat.

Cold snows drifted around him: ice coverd his loins around
He sat by Tyburns brook, and underneath his heel, shot up!
A deadly Tree, he namd it Moral Virtue, and the Law
Of God who dwells in Chaos hidden from the human sight.

The Tree spread over him its cold shadows. (Albion groand)
They bent down, they felt the earth and again enrooting
Shot into many a Tree! an endless labyrinth of woe!

From willing sacrifice of Self, to sacrifice of (miscall'd) Enemies
For Atonement: Albion began to erect twelve Altars,
Of rough unhewn rocks, before the Potters Furnace,
He namd them Justice, and Truth. And Albions Sons
Must have become the first Victims, being the first transgressors
But they fled to the mountains to seek ransom: building A Strong
Fortification against the Divine Humanity and Mercy,
In Shame & Jealousy to annihilate Jerusalem.

5. *Jerusalem*, Plate 28

6. *Vision of the Book of Job,* Plate 20

We saw in the last chapter that for Blake the subjective navel-gazer and the objective atomist make the identical blunder of chopping the world in two, and differ only about which piece of it they are to seize. Those who seek understanding and power form a similar, or rather part of the same, false contrast. One group pursues God into an indefinite omnipotence, the other into an indefinite omniscience, and both lose sight of his humanity and personality. We may put the same point in another way. The will and the reason may be good or bad: if they are to be good, they must meet the standards or conditions of goodness. The will has to meet the standards ordinarily called justice and morality; the reason has to meet the standard of truth. Now these forms of the "good" as we should expect, have in common the impersonal and general quality of law. That two and two make four is equally true for everyone; that a murderer shall be hanged applies to all members of the state which adopts such a law. Here again, the "subject" with which we start seems to get lost in both directions, and to disappear into the uniformity of guinea-sun perceivers.

Hence the "good" is traditionally threefold in division, and includes a middle term of "beauty" which, unlike the other two, seems to have a personal and human reference, and, though it undoubtedly posssesses laws, they are laws of a much more flexible kind, which are able to allow for the differences that actually do exist among human beings. Now it is clear that Blake's dislike of antithetical modes of thought will not be appeased by adding a middle term, even one regarded as a *tertium quid*. "Beauty" to Blake is not a third form of the good, but good itself, the union in which the reality of the other two consists; it is pursued not by feeling or emotion or any part of the personality, but by the imagination which is "the Real Man."[41] The product of "beauty" is art; art is civilization; and it is only civilization that can give any value or any meaning to those impersonalizing tendencies of the mind which build up the imaginative forms of science and morality. Thus Blake's identification of religion with art is utterly different from the Romantic identification of the religious and æsthetic experiences. There is no place in his thought for æsthetics, or general theories of abstract beauty.

· 8 ·

If the highest state of man is fourfold in Blake's symbolism, we should expect him to reject the doctrine of a threefold God. Here Blake follows his master Swedenborg, who attacked the orthodox Trinity as tritheistic. In *Paradise Lost*, Blake complains, "the Father is Destiny, the Son a Ratio of the five senses, and the Holy Ghost Vacuum."[42] In theology something is usually done with the conceptions of power and wisdom, but the middle term, as in the ethical diagram, is apt to prove embarrassing and be tacitly dropped. Yet the conception of God as a Holy Spirit, the giver and incubator of life, the indwelling person of God, the eternal Self, is, once again, the unity in which the reality of the other two consists. It was the Holy Spirit that spoke by the prophets, which means that it continues to speak by the artists who have prophetic imaginations. The "inspiration" which artists have is therefore the breath or spirit of God which dwells in the artist and is the artist. Such inspiration is the only proof we have of the existence of a spiritual power greater than ourselves. Art, then, is "the gift of God, the Holy Ghost."[43]

What did the Holy Spirit that spoke by the prophets speak about? It prophesied the Messiah; that is, it saw God as man and understood that "God becomes as we are, that we may be as he is."[44] In Milton this Messiah is a ratio of the five senses because he created the fallen world with its guinea-sun. Such a creative principle is a Nous, a reason or mathematical order, the automatism by which nature maintains enough permanence to keep from dissolving into nonexistence. This Nous is to be visualized as a Father rather than a Son, a hoary "Ancient of Days" such as stretches out his compasses (notice the mathematical symbol) in the frontispiece to *Europe*.[45] Jesus is not a Nous but a Logos, a compelling Word who continually recreates an unconscious floundering universe into something with beauty and intelligence. The Son and the Holy Spirit are therefore the same thing. And this Son or Spirit is also the universal Man who is the unified form of our scattered imaginations, and which we visualize as a Father. The three persons of the Trinity are to be connected by ors rather than ands, and the real God is fourfold, power, love and wisdom contained within the unity of civilized human imagination. This

God is a God-Man, the Jesus in whose eternal and infinite risen body we find our own being after we have outgrown the imaginative infancy which the orthodox conception of the Fatherhood of God implies for us. The final revelation of Christianity is, therefore, not that Jesus is God, but that "God is Jesus."[46]

The life of man is polarized between the Creator and the Creation, more abundant life in the larger human mind and body of God and acceptance of the minimum life of nature and reason. Any real religion contains much to encourage the imagination, but it is likely also to try to give some divine sanction to the fallen world. Hence when its followers come to the place where they should make the supreme effort to become part of a universal human and divine creator (this place in Blake is the upper limit of Beulah), they find nature and reason blocking the way in a divine disguise. Here they must choose between the Word and the World, and if their choice is wrong they will be like Goethe's Faust, who, unable to grasp the meaning of *"das Wort,"* translates it as *"die That,"* the thing made as opposed to its Maker, and falls into the power of a devil.

A certain amount of natural religion exists in all Christian Churches, but it is only in Blake's own time that the cult of reason and nature has been precipitated from Christianity and made into a dogmatic system with all loopholes for the imagination sealed off. This system is Deism, a term Blake associates, not only with both Voltaire and Rousseau, but with the whole culture of the Age of Reason and the return to nature. For Deism, God is a hypothesis necessary to account for the beginning of the chain of causality; otherwise human life should be confined to nature and reason. That is, its Father is destiny, its Logos the ratio of the five senses, and its Spirit of love and beauty a vacuum—the faults of Milton's thinking unified into a single systematic falsehood. Locke was responsible for Deism, whether he was a Deist himself or not; for his cloven fiction is the source of its separation of the divine and the human. This cleavage in religion produces an antithesis of idolaters: one the egocentric contemplative who broods over his soul, the other the antinomian who pursues a life of selfish expediency. Now while one may find handsome crops of both kinds of tares in all religions, it is only in Deism, which plants no wheat, that they cease to become hypocrites.

We shall never understand why Blake so hated Deism unless we understand not only what it was to him, but what he saw that it would soon become. That is, we must accept in Blake a certain amount of prophecy in the literal sense of anticipating the probable future, and must see in his conception of Deism a mental attitude which is still with us, the monstrous hydra which is the perverted vision of human society as an atomic aggregate of egos instead of as a larger human body. The closer man comes to the state of nature, the more he clings to the "reason" which enables him to deal with nature on its own terms. The natural society, whether we see it in primitive tribes or in exhausted civilizations, is a complicated mechanism of prescribed acts which always have a rational explanation, but make no sense whatever in terms of passion, energy, insight or wisdom. The natural man is not the solitary majestic lion that he would like to be: he is a buzzing and spineless insect, a flying head cut off at the neck, like the cherubs in Reynolds, equipped with a venomous sting and a stupefied sense of duty. So at least he appears in Blake, both as the Deist of Blake's time and as the "Druid" which Blake predicted he would soon become.

An apocalyptic mind, however, is apt to feel that his own time is the darkest hour before the dawn, and to Blake the appearance of this consolidated system of error suggested that it might well be followed by some prophet who, by refuting it, might be the herald of a genuine apocalypse. Swedenborg had said that the Last Judgment took place in the spiritual world in 1757. This did not impress Blake unduly, but neither did he forget altogether that he had been born in that year.[47]

We now come to Blake's ethical and political ideas, which, like his religion, are founded on his theory of knowledge. It is impossible for a human being to live completely in the world of sense. Somehow or other the floating linear series of impressions must be ordered and united by the mind. One must adopt either the way of imagination or the way of memory; no compromise or neutrality is possible. He who is not for the imagination is against it. Religion insists that however mixed good and bad may be in this world, there are eternally only heaven and hell, with a great gulf between. For the apocalypse or vision of eternity is at the same time a Last Judgment, an absolute separation of sheep from goats, of the men who have used their varying amounts of talents from the men who have hidden theirs. In eternity all the confused and eclectic and weakly tolerant are obviously on the wrong side. Hence the duty of the imaginative man is to force the issue and compel decisions.

To the extent that a man has imagination he is alive, and therefore the development of the imagination is an increase of life. It follows that restricting the imagination by turning from instead of passing through perception is a reduction of life. It must then tend in the direction of death, so that all imaginative restraint is ultimately, not that it always proceeds to ultimates, a death-impulse. Hence evil is negative: all evil consists either in self-restraint or restraint of others. There can be no such thing, strictly speaking, as an evil act; all acts are good, and evil comes when activity is perverted into the frustration of activity, in oneself or others. But Blake himself is clearer than any paraphrase:

But as I understand Vice it is a Negative. . . . Accident is the omission of act in self & the hindering of act in another; This is Vice, but all Act is Virtue. To hinder another is not an act; it is the contrary; it is a restraint on action both in ourselves & in the person hinder'd, for he who hinders another omits his own duty at the same time. Murder is Hindering Another. Theft is Hindering Another. Backbiting, Undermining, Circumventing, & whatever is Negative is Vice.[1]

To the theologian all vice resolves itself into pride or self-will, and in a way this is also true of Blake, but perhaps such words as the medieval *"accidia,"* the Elizabethan "melancholy" or Baudelaire's *"ennui"* are closer to Blake's conception of negative evil. Blake's own word for it is "jealousy." By turning away from the world to be perceived we develop an imaginative idleness which spreads a sickness and lassitude over the whole soul, and all vices spring from this. It does not matter whether the sickness is expressed inwardly or outwardly. Murder is obviously an expression of the same death-impulse that suicide is, and all evil acts are more or less murderous. "Sooner murder an infant in its cradle than nurse unacted desires,"[2] says Blake: self-denial for no imaginative reason is suicide *in petto*; slander is murdering a reputation which is as vital to a man as his throat. This death-impulse, this perverted wish to cut down and restrict the scope of life, is the touchstone not only of all the obvious vices, but of many acts often not classified as such, like teasing, instilling fear or discouragement, or exacting unthinking obedience. It is quite inadequate to call self-interest a motive of evil conduct, though the death-impulse may be disguised in that form. Self-interest implies a good deal of control: in all extreme vices there is a mania in which one is hagridden by a "ruling passion." Self-interest may explain the profiteer, but not the miser:

Those who say that men are led by interest are knaves. A knavish character will often say, "of what interest is it to me to do so and so?" I answer, "of none at all, but the contrary, as you well know. It is of malice and envy that you have done this; hence I am aware of you, because I know that you act, not from interest, but from malice, even to your destruction."[3]

The development of the imagination is a continuous process of synthesis. The perverted imagination with nothing real to work on is forced to turn analytic and dissective, and all dissected things are uniformly hideous. We can see this most clearly in cadavers, but only because we can see it at all there: the idea of a "proportion" with the proportions of all things mixed up in it is equally monstrous, and the idea of a rose with its "secondary qualities" of color and scent removed equally unlovable. Blake always thinks of cruelty as something very close to mischievous curiosity. The prototype of Nero is the bored schoolboy pulling wings off a butterfly. Fear, another fruitful source of evil, is not so much the horror of the unknown as a fascinated attraction to it. The mind of the reflecting reasoner feels a kinship with mystery which paralyzes him into remaining in it; and he does not want it removed. Columbus and Marco Polo were not popular when they returned home, and the prophets, the explorers of the spiritual world, are notoriously unwelcome in their own countries.

We may develop this conception of cruelty and fear a little further. We saw in the first chapter that the "memory," by separating the subject and object, may quite consistently turn a man into either a navel-gazer or an atomist, but that from the point of view of the imagination it does not matter which. In the second chapter we saw that the same tendency in religion may make a man either an inert contemplative or an antinomian. In ordinary life exactly the same distinction holds. A man may specialize in self-restraint or in restraint of others. The former produces the vices which spring from fear; the latter those which spring from cruelty. But the thwarting of imagination is the basis of both: all the cruel are frightened, and all the fearful are cruel.

The relation between these two groups does not extend beyond the social and political, for whatever gods they may have do not exist, and they appear in life as tyrants and victims of tyrants. They are numerous enough, and the imaginative rare enough, to present a uniform picture of a group of tyrants exploiting a larger group of victims all through history. The image of parasite and host is the best one for them, as it brings out Blake's point that both groups are essentially passive. The parasite is passive because it clings to the host; the host, because it endures the parasite. Tyranny is seldom (in the long run, never) imposed on people from without; it is a projection of their own pusillanimity. Tyranny and mob rule are the same thing. The tyrant in Blake is always an isolated, inscrutable brooder—the inscrutability of the king's mind, incidentally, is a favorite theme of Bacon's—and because he is that he is truly representative of his victims. For in the state of "memory" or reflection we withdraw into ourselves and are locked up there with our own keys in a dark spiritual solitude in which we are unable to conceive activity except in terms of hindrance and restraint.

This seems to contradict what we have said about imagination as self-development. But self-development leads us into a higher state of integration with a larger imaginative unit which is ultimately God. Hence the paradox that one gains his life by losing it, which Jesus taught. The selfish or egocentric are incapable of *developing* themselves; that comes from expansion outward, not withdrawal inward. Hence there are two selves in man absolutely opposed to one another, the better self which grows and lives and the worse self which rots and withers, the good and the evil angel:

Man is a twofold being, one part capable of evil & the other capable of good; that which is capable of good is not also capable of evil, but that which is capable of evil is also capable of good.[4]

Blake accepts the doctrine of original sin with the modification that man is not "simple & yet capable of evil," which we shall consider in a moment. We are born into a fallen world and are therefore born with a "natural" tendency to make the most rather than the best of it, to accept it as final reality. But if man were really natural he would be a simple being like an animal in whom selfishness and self-development are the same thing. Most apologies for tyranny are based on analogies from nature, based in their turn on the assumption either that man is essentially natural or that nature is divinely ordered. But the polities of the wolf pack and the beehive are not good enough for us. Both the tyrant and his victim are in a state of nature, and both are in that state of animal self-absorption which Blake calls the Selfhood. This word, a very important one in his thought, will be used henceforth to replace "memory" and "reflection."

Man has within him the principle of life and the principle of death: one is the imagination, the other the natural man. In the natural world the natural principle will win out eventually and the man will die. As an individual ego reflecting on his sensations of an outer space-world while existing in time, the natural man is a dying man; and like most chronic invalids the ego is fretful, irascible, cruel, bothered by trifles, jealous and inordinately vain. Its only freedom is in domineering over or hindering others; its only happiness is in solitary possession; and in everything it does it seeks, like Cleopatra, for a painless form of suicide.

The only possible cure for the original sin of this Selfhood of the natural man is vision, the revelation that this world is fallen and therefore not ultimate. There is no such thing in the long run as necessary evil. "Mercy, Pity, Peace and Love" appear to be only palliatives against the antecedent evils of cruelty, war and jealousy, which may suggest that they could not exist without evil, as a doctor cannot exist without disease. But that is nonsense: destroy the evil, and the four virtues will be seen to be the attributes of unfallen Man. We have already mentioned the significance in this connection of the contrasting lyrics "The Human Abstract" and "The Divine Image." The destruction of the appearance of this world must precede the vision of the same world purified, and, subject and object being inseparable, the Selfhood must be annihilated before the true self can appear.

Now all the kindly and honest people who act as though they believed evil to be neither necessary nor desirable are on the right side. But an honest man is not quite the noblest work of God until the faith by which the just live develops into full imaginative vision. The fully imaginative man is therefore a visionary whose imaginative activity is prophecy and whose perception produces art. These two are the same thing, perception being an act.

Those whose minds are befuddled with the two contradictory notions of mystery and necessity, derived from reflecting on space and time respectively, will naturally think of a prophet as someone with a mysterious knack of foretelling an inevitable future. This is exactly what the prophet cannot be. The "seer" has insight, not second sight: he is not a charlatan but the contrary of one, an honest man with a sharper perception and a clearer perspective than other honest men possess. The imagination in seeing a bird sees through it an "immense world of delight"; the imagination in looking at society not only sees its hypocrisies but sees through them, and sees an infinitely better world. The prophet can see an infinite and eternal reality, but nobody can see an indefinite future, except conditionally:

Prophets, in the modern sense of the word, have never existed. Jonah was no prophet in the modern sense, for his prophecy of Nineveh failed. Every honest man is a Prophet; he utters his opinion both of private & public matters. Thus: If you go on So, the result is So. He never says, such a thing shall happen let you do what you will. A Prophet is a Seer, not an Arbitrary Dictator.[5]

It is the superior clarity and accuracy of the prophet's vision that makes him an artist, and that makes the great artist prophetic.

· 2 ·

Tyranny is the co-operation of parasite and host; no tyrant maintains himself by force, but by trading on his victims' fears. So although "A tyrant is the worst disease, and the cause of all others,"[6] the tyrant can at any rate be seen, and the imagination can handle anything that can be seen. It is the sense of the indefinite unseen, acquired by turning away from perception, which is capable of restraining imagination, and, as "everybody hates a king,"[7] he would soon be destroyed if there were no sense of a mysterious power lurking behind him: if, in short, there were no divinity to hedge the king. Tyranny requires a priesthood and a god first, and these make it permanent. Religion has been called the opiate of the people; but religion in its conventionally accepted and socially established form is far more dangerous than any opiate, the effects of which are transitory. As long as we ascribe the real source of tyranny to temporal power we may overthrow that power only to find in the very act of shouting *écrasez l'infâme* that *l'infâme* has quietly attached itself to the new government and we have to begin all over again. As Paul said, in the passage Blake took as a motto for *The Four Zoas*:

For we wrestle not against flesh and blood, but against principalities, against powers, against the rulers of the darkness of this world, against spiritual wickedness in high places.[8]

There is only one false religion as there is only one true one; and it has two infallible marks. First, it postulates some kind of God who is unknown and mysterious because he is not inside us but somewhere else: where, only God knows. Second, it preaches submission, acceptance and unquestioning obedience. The sting is in the tail. Religion of this kind being invented only to buttress the *status quo*, it is always "State Religion, which is the source of all Cruelty."[9] This is seen in its clearest form in the worship of a deified Caesar, but subtler tyrants have preferred various kinds of loyal disguise. Blake says for instance of Bacon's *Essays*:

Everybody knows that this is epicurism and libertinism, and yet everybody says that it is Christian philosophy. How is this possible? Everybody must be a liar and deceiver? No! "Everybody" does not do this; but the hirelings of Kings and Courts, who made themselves "everybody," and knowingly propagate falsehood.[10]

Besides, the anti-imaginative structure must be made as complete as possible, for the imagination is always finding holes in it; in fact, it is always finding it transparent. As that same Bacon remarked, truth comes more easily from error than from confusion. It is the business of imagination to force all falsehood into a denial of truth, to show error as error, to clarify it by reducing the neutral ground. False or state religion has thus altered its forms in the course of centuries, not because it is capable in itself of any development, but because it has had to meet the increasing comprehensiveness of the imagination which has followed the work of the prophets and Jesus. We have already seen how Blake regarded Deism as a consolidation of error which indicated an imminent final rejection of it.

In the unfallen world objects of perception are alive and intelligent; and a faint echo of the animation of that world survives in the animism of primitive religion. The nymphs, satyrs and fauns of Classical mythology are older and more authentic than the Olympian hierarchy. With the separation of existence and perception, however, the natural object became attached to the latter and its spirit or Genius to the former, so that gradually a belief in invisible deities grew up. The eleventh plate of *The Marriage of Heaven and Hell*, the paragraph beginning "The ancient Poets animated all sensible objects with Gods or Geniuses," traces this process with a clarity that might impress even a modern student of the subject. In the later poems Blake contrasts the "fairies" of the more original belief with the "heathen gods" who succeeded them.[11] These gods were invariably selfish and cruel, as a God whose interests do not run counter to those of man cannot be invoked in support of a tyranny. Ovid shows them particularly interested in stifling and suppressing the artists who attempted to rival them (*i.e.*, create better gods), as in the stories of Marsyas and Arachne.

It is in the God of official Christianity, however, invented as a homeopathic cure for the teachings of Jesus, that state religion has produced its masterpiece. This God is good and we are evil; yet, though he created us, he is somehow or other not responsible for our being evil, though he would consider it blasphemous either to assert that he is or to deny his omnipotence. All calamities and miseries are his will, and to that will we must be absolutely resigned even in thought and desire. The powers that be are ordained of him, and all might is divine right. The visions of artists and prophets are of little importance to him: he did not ordain those, but an invariable ritual and a set of immovable dogmas, which are more in keeping with his ideas of order. Both of these are deep mysteries, to be entrusted to a specially initiated class of servants. He keeps a grim watch over everything men do, and will finally put most of them in hell to scream eternally in torment, eternally meaning, of course, endlessly in time. A few, however, who have done as they have been told, that is, have done nothing creative, will be granted an immortality of the "pie in the sky when you die" variety.

It is easy to call this popular misunderstanding, but perhaps harder to deny that orthodox religion is founded on a compromise with it. If God moves in a mysterious way, a mysterious God *may* be capable of anything. And as all mysteries are nightmares, this one increases in horror the longer we continue to think of what he *may* do to us. But as only the worst of men would torture other men in hell endlessly, given the power, those who believe God does this worship the devil, or the worst elements in man. And this devil takes his duties as Prince of this world very seriously. In practice he is far worse than his most devoted admirer would dare admit. In practice all established Churches are irrevocably committed to the defense of their establishment, and any time of crisis shows clearly that, as far as the orthodox are concerned:

God is only an Allegory of Kings & nothing Else. . . . God is The Ghost of the Priest & King, who Exist, whereas God exists not except from their Effluvia.[12]

In early days this God had a hankering for human blood, for he would naturally regard suicide or murder as the most reverent homage that could be paid to him. The Old Testament shows him grudgingly retiring under pressure of the prophets and being forced to content himself with murdered animals, but the feeling that human sacrifice is the ultimate gesture of respect still persists, and periodically causes holy wars and crusades. This creature Blake calls, outside the prophecies, "Old Nobodaddy," and here he is, contemplating the French Revolution:

> The King awoke on his couch of gold,
> As soon as he heard these tidings told: . . .

Then he swore a great & solemn Oath:
"To kill the people I am loth,
But If they rebel, they must go to hell:
They shall have a Priest & a passing bell."

Then old Nobodaddy aloft
Farted & belch'd & cough'd,
And said, "I love hanging & drawing & quartering
Every bit as well as war & slaughtering.
Damn praying & singing,
Unless they will bring in
The blood of ten thousand by fighting or swinging."[13]

Although this God is personal, there is a recurrent tendency
to think of him as impersonal. He constantly relapses into Fate
or Necessity as soon as his pretensions are examined at all seriously.
Being a mere shadow of the tyrant's demand that we submit
passively to him whatever we think or want to do, and not having
any more intelligible program of obedience (even the ten commandments only tell us what we must *not* do), Nobodaddy turns
out to be much like our old friend the immanent Will. Perfect
obedience to him would be unconscious and automatic, like the
circling of the stars. The believers in him tell us that the whole
universe obeys God in this way except us, and that we do not
because we are evil and have fallen. Well, so we have; but the
fatal mistake in orthodox thought comes at the next step. All good
comes from God, and as, the orthodox say, God is not man, man
must be "simple & yet capable of evil." Such a man must, therefore,
look "beyond" the human world for salvation, and there is nothing
beyond the human world except the spatial beyond which is
nature, and which suggests all these ideas of uncritical docility.
Hence routine and passive life comes to be thought good; all that
is independent, free and energetic comes to be associated with
evil.

This exaltation of the routine and the passive is congenial to
all forms of fatalism, among which Blake puts predestination,
because they assert that we are not to do what we can in this world
but what we must. The same idea is enforced in society by law.
Law at its best is impartial; it assumes equality among all men,
and so exactly corresponds to the equality of dullness which asserts
that only the guinea-sun can "really" be seen. In other words,

it puts normality at the lower limit just as Lockian philosophy does. Every real thing contains within it its unique law of growth and coherence, and hence "One Law for the Lion & Ox is Oppression,"[14] just as one idea of proportion to cover them both is nonsense. A generalizing law permits of no exceptions, but everything that lives is an exception to it. Penal laws are based on the assumption that the "general" interest must be preserved, and preserved by compulsion. Therefore they "court Transgression."[15]

The worship of mediocrity goes much further than this. Greek ethics, for instance, is based on a hesitation and diffidence which is designed not to alter social conditions. Blake wrote such aphorisms as "The road of excess leads to the palace of wisdom"[16] with one eye on the Greek "Nothing in excess." Prudence is defined by Blake as "a rich, ugly old maid courted by Incapacity," and in the prophecies he speaks of the four Classical virtues as the four pillars of Satan's throne.[17] But official Christianity is no better; it too tells us that humility and modesty are great virtues, and that in exalting oneself above a certain level there is grave danger, for anything that might attract the attention of the Setebos-God it worships is sure to exasperate him. This corresponds to the experimental scientist's teaching that we should reserve judgment and not commit ourselves to anything until we are sure of being well within the guinea-sun conception of reality. Hence Blake says not only:

> If the Sun & Moon should doubt,
> They'd immediately Go out.

but also:

> Humility is only doubt,
> And does the Sun & Moon blot out.[18]

All moral virtue of this kind ends in lugubrious and portentous dullness.

If such a morality were based on nothing more than expediency, it would be bad enough, but at least it would relate only to particular actions. This uncomplicated denial of imagination might, however, expose its reactionary basis a little too clearly. It is safer to fall back on the original point that all good is from God and all evil from man, that the former is symbolized by routine obedience and the latter by independence. When this idea is pressed a little, it becomes obvious that all activity is really evil and hence the passive and inert is the good. We are back again at the idea of negative perfection. A negatively perfect God, we said, a God who is pure goodness, can do nothing. A negatively perfect man is in the same dilemma.

"Everything that lives is holy,"[19] and as long as we equate good and evil with life and death, the words mean something. But adjusting one's life to a normal level of the kind recommended by moral virtue is no more "good" than any other form of fashionable self-mutilation, such as foot-binding or waist-pinching. The morally good man tries to obey an external God instead of bringing out the God in himself. The external God being only the shadow of Caesar, the good man finds himself obeying the latter instead. Caesar being only the shadow of popular timidity, the good man finds himself in the end doing what everyone else does. Morality as such is slave morality. That is what the Bible means when it says that while man was in Eden he possessed the tree of life, but when he turned to the tree of the knowledge of good and evil he found that he had the tree of death:

By this it will be seen that I do not consider either the Just or the Wicked to be in a Supreme State, but to be every one of them States of the Sleep which the Soul may fall into in its deadly dreams of Good & Evil when it leaves Paradise following the Serpent. . . . The Combats of Good & Evil is Eating of the Tree of Knowledge. The Combats of Truth & Error is Eating of the Tree of Life.[20]

The conception of the saving power of God held by orthodox Christians would be correct if it were not worked out in terms of an antithesis of divine and human wills rather than a unity of divine and human imagination. "If man," Blake asks, "is consider'd as only evil & god only good, how then is regeneration effected which turns the evil to good?"[21] The power of becoming our own best selves must be within us: there can be no oracles to approach and no incantations to memorize. Satan in the Bible is called *diabolos* or accuser because he is forever reminding man of his own insufficiency and causing him to despair of deliverance, and his henchmen spread throughout society the state of mind called by Blake the "accusation of sin," the final triumph of the death-impulse, the complete torpor and paralysis of the mind.

For Satan is not himself a sinner but a self-righteous prig. As Blake explains:

We do not find any where that Satan is Accused of Sin; he is only accused of Unbelief & thereby drawing Man into Sin that he may accuse him.[22]

As long as God is conceived as a bloodthirsty bully this priggishness takes the form of persecution and heresy-hunting as a service acceptable to him. But we saw that under examination Old Nobodaddy soon vanishes into a mere perpetual-motion machine of causation. And as Deism is an isolation of what is abstract and generalized in Christianity, Satan in Blake's day has become a Deist, and has turned to subtler forms of persecution, to ridicule and shoulder-shrugging and pointing out contemptuously how little evidence there is for any kind of reality except that of natural law.

Yet Deism professed to be in part a revolutionary force. The American and French revolutions were largely Deist-inspired, and both appeared to Blake to be genuinely imaginative upheavals. He wrote poems warmly sympathizing with both, hoping that they were the beginning of a world-wide revolt that would begin his apocalypse. He met and liked Tom Paine, and respected his honesty as a thinker. Yet Paine could write in his *Age of Reason*:

I had some turn, and I believe some talent for poetry; but this I rather repressed than encouraged, as leading too much into the field of imagination.

The attitude to life implied by such a remark can have no permanent revolutionary vigor, for underlying it is the weary materialism which asserts that the deader a thing is the more trustworthy it is; that a rock is a solid reality and that the vital spirit of a living man is a rarefied and diaphanous ghost. It is no accident that Paine should say in the same book that God can be revealed only in mechanics, and that a mill is a microcosm of the universe. A revolution based on such ideas is not an awakening of the spirit of man: if it kills a tyrant, it can only replace him with another, as the French Revolution swung from Bourbon to Bonaparte. And if it abolishes tyrants altogether, it can only do so by establishing a tyranny of custom so powerful that the tyrant will not be necessary, as in the ant-republic. An inadequate mental attitude to liberty can think of it only as a leveling-out. Democracy of this sort is a placid ovine herd of self-satisfied mediocrities. Blake watched this tendency growing as he became more disillusioned with the French and American revolutions, and at the end of his life he was still protesting:

> But since the French Revolution Englishmen are all intermeasurable by one another: certainly a happy state of agreement, in which I for one do not agree.[23]

The difference between the Deist and the Blakean ideas of a free and democratic society corresponds again to the difference between the guinea-sun and the angelic sun. In Deism there is not only the belief that the physical world is the only real one, but also a feeling of satisfaction at remaining within it, a certain enthusiasm about accepting the conditions it imposes. Now it seems reasonable enough to take the world as we find it, trying to be as contented in it as possible, and make others so, without straining after more elusive pleasures, perhaps less substantial ones. But if it were possible to do this the human race would have settled into Utopian serenity centuries ago. It remains true that the physical world is not good enough for the imagination to accept, and if we do accept it we are left with our Selfhoods, our verminous crawling egos that spend all their time either wronging others or brooding on wrongs done to them. The end of all natural religion, however well-meaning and good-natured, is a corrupt and decadent society rolling downhill to stampeding mass hysteria and maniacal warfare. This is the historical succession to Deism which Blake in *Jerusalem* symbolizes as "Druidism," for reasons to be explained in due course.

If there is greater imaginative power in the revolutionary impulse, it is not so much because of what it accomplishes as because of what it is in itself. Revolution is always an attempt to smash the structure of tyranny and create a better world, even when revolutionaries do not understand what creation implies or what a better world is. The apocalypse will necessarily begin with a slaughter of tyrants, and Christ came, Blake says, to deliver those bound under the knave, not to deliver the knave.[24] Later on we shall trace in greater detail the waning of Blake's interest in the revolutionary movements of his time: all we need to say just now is that for Blake the central problem of social and political liberty is the release of imagination. Hence the initial stage in attaining this, for Blake as for Milton before him and for Carlyle and others after him, is to establish the role of the great man in society. The goal of prophecy is the Messiah, the divine man. This involves the question of the nature of the great man: we shall see later why to Blake the great man can be only the visionary prophetic artist, never the Carlylean hero or the Nietzschean Superman. Society is best off when it is sufficiently aware of its own defects to let the prophet scold it, and the "honest man" say what he likes.

· 3 ·

THEREFORE the real war in society is the "Mental Fight" between the visionaries and the champions of tyranny. The latter are not the tyrants themselves but visionary renegades: poets like Virgil who write for Caesar; philosophers who "teach doubt & Experiment"[25]; generalizing painters like Titian and Rubens; theological apologists of Nobodaddy. As they are guardians of society and moral virtue, Blake calls them "Angels"; for those who, like himself, call the whole structure of society in question there is no word but "Devils." Angels, though wrong, are essential to imagination, for the reason given above, that the basis of tyranny is not error but confusion. Those who really believe in tyranny and work out a coherent defense of it clarify confusion into error and thereby demonstrate its opposite to be true. The uses to society of the Devil and the Angel, Blake says, are about equal, because "to be an Error & to be Cast out is a part of God's design."[26] Hence there must be in society a continuous fight between radical and conservative imagination. "Without Contraries is no progression,"[27] but this is the only kind of contrariety that can progress. Blake, in dealing with artists he considers Angels, lays about him with the destructive fury of a Friar John, without stopping to think whether he is being unfair to them or not. They can take care of themselves. Blake is engaged in "intellectual War"[28]; he thinks of his state of Eden as an eternal Valhalla of conflicts waged with bows of burning gold and arrows of desire.

But attacking Angels is only part of the prophet's work; another part is concerned with the conquering of neutrals. These are not strong enough to fight, because they are victims of revenge-morality. For those who live under the curse of the law see in every vigorous act the uncompleted half of a movement toward inertia, to be followed and neutralized at once by its opposite. Hence revenge or attack comes to be a typical response to activity. And as retribution tends to the neutralizing of activity, retribution is not only bad in itself but a waste of time. Wars, penal codes and persecutions never become positive acts; and while they will always exist as long as the world is fallen, they are never more than the endless working-out of a decimal proved millenniums ago to be recurring.

The first step in escaping from this is the complete renunciation of all the forms of punishment which are so dear to the Selfhood. "Forgiveness of sins" is a cardinal principle with Blake, the antidote for the "accusation of sins" which poisons the imagination. Forgiveness of this sort implies three things. First, a previous condemnation. "Severity of judgment is a great virtue,"[29] said Blake: all sins (manifestations of hindrance or restraint) should be violently resented and denounced by the visionary. Weak and lazy people who are not actually being frightened at the moment tend to lose all interest in such matters under the guise of a good-humored tolerance, and in these moods of comparative courage they feel that the importance of sin is greatly exaggerated. It is very different when they do become frightened, for then they at once begin to point to others and scream to have them destroyed. But it is now the visionary's turn to be tolerant. As all vengeance is evil and as "the voice of honest indignation is the voice of God,"[30] resentment and retribution are irreconcilable. Punishing a man strengthens society; strengthening society is strengthening mediocrity. The second step in forgiveness is the separation of the man from his sin, and the third the release of the imaginative power which makes this possible. The prophet, who wants to be delivered from evil, denounces the condition the man is in; society, which wants only to be delivered from the inconveniences attached to evil, denounces the man only. The prophetic vision is focused on a Messiah or incarnation of God; the mediocre or guinea-sun vision is focused on a scapegoat:

In Hell all is Self Righteousness; there is no such thing there as Forgiveness of Sin; he who does Forgive Sin is Crucified as an Abettor of Criminals, & he who performs Works of Mercy in Any shape whatever is punish'd &, if possible, destroy'd, not thro' envy or Hatred or Malice, but thro' Self Righteousness that thinks it does God service, which God is Satan.[31]

The visionary is characterized by the two emotions of wrath and pity, called by Blake Rintrah and Palamabron. The former is peculiar to him. The Angel cannot feel the honest indignation which is the voice of God: he may simulate it to the point of deceiving himself, but there will always be a concealed selfish reason for expressing it. On the other hand, he is not always merciless; he may think of punishment as necessary and regret the necessity. Necessity is the tyrant's plea, not love of punishment. (The point here is not that punishment is never necessary, but that if it is necessary it is therefore not free, and indicates the failure of society to achieve freedom.) Blake says in the prophecies that Satan has the science of pity but not the science of wrath.[32] The prophet may flail his enemies with a haughty and arrogant contempt; this is the *saeva indignatio* of Rintrah which begins *The Marriage of Heaven and Hell*. But behind this is not only the prophet's infinite tenderness for the weak and foolish, but his own sense of exceptional responsibility and of the exceptional infamy of deserting his work:

But if we fear to do the dictates of our Angels, & tremble at the Tasks set before us; if we refuse to do Spiritual Acts because of Natural Fears or Natural Desires! Who can describe the dismal torments of such a state!—I too well remember the Threats I heard!—"If you, who are organized by Divine Providence for spiritual communion, Refuse, & bury your Talent in the Earth, even tho' you should want Natural Bread, Sorrow & Desperation pursues you thro' life, & after death shame & confusion of face to eternity. . . .[33]

A man who writes like this does not write difficult poetry to relieve his private feelings or mock a sympathetic reader, though perhaps we are beyond this stage by now. But while Blake lays a heavy emphasis on the didactic nature and social impact of art, he has nothing of that distrust of the ability of art to carry its own message which has spoiled many conscientious prophets. The visionary is disinterested because his vision is clear and accurate, and if his presentation of that vision is perfect in form he has done all he can. He cannot construct an inferior kind of art or prophecy for weaker people. On the other hand he may practice self-denial without restricting his imaginative development: if he thinks poverty a social evil he is not inconsistent if he remains poor in order to say so.

The fight between Devils and Angels is a fight between the two opposed principles of self-development and Selfhood, and because each springs from the self the latter may speak the language of the former and imitate its processes. This struggle is carried on in all four imaginative states, Eden, Beulah, Generation and Ulro.

· 4 ·

IN Eden the two fundamental processes of the imagination, Blake says, are war and hunting; that is, struggle and search, perverted here into different kinds of murder. In the unfallen world the creative joy of the artist expands into that of the Creator God twisting the sinews of the tiger's heart; that of the exploring scientist into the vision of the Titan Orc piercing into "the Elemental Planets & the orbs of eccentric fire."

It is difficult for the man without a genuine apocalyptic, we have said, to understand that such virtues as mercy, pity, peace and love are not mere palliatives of antecedent evils and do not exist by virtue of them. We know good by evil in this world: when we try to think of "Good by itself and Evil not at all," in spite of ourselves we think of the protected child's world. The Bible, Milton, even the Bunyan whose idea of mental warfare was so courageous, tend to describe Heaven in terms of protection, relaxation and peace. Blake suggests that an eternal joy is a positive thing, an achievement in a world of gratified desire. But when we try to visualize this world, does not Paradise become a mere kindergarten in which we may run and play as we like, with knives and boiling water carefully put out of our reach? Without *risk* would not the highest kind of pleasure be apt to pall? If twisting a tiger's heart in the next world is as dangerous as twisting his tail in this one, the Creator may well smile if he wins out; but surely a world in which the lion is said to lie down with the lamb is a world of stuffed lions.

Hence, it may be argued, the great men in this world are not only the great creators but the great destroyers or conquerors as well; the heroes whom Blake would consider not great men but great nuisances, or great epidemics. For danger leads to domination, in thought as in etymology. Lordship among other creators, then, would be nobler than the merely secure lordship over creatures, and the Napoleons of this world symbolize the fact. Thus Nietzsche's realization that man is something to be surpassed led him to celebrate struggle, or will to power, rather than conquest, conquest in this world being often an anticlimax.

But to Blake all energy is creative, all creation of one Creator, and all energy exists only in form, or fulfillment. God can no more strive with God than Satan can cast out Satan, much less destroy or subdue God. A "master race" would be more locked up in gloomy spiritual solitude than ever: the "will to power" never escapes from time, and therefore never loses the sense of the eternal and infinite as ironic, because forever elusive. When we see that all men are part of the larger body of a single Man we can also see that only the pleasure of creation is real, and that creation is the only outcome of conflict which satisfies the imagination. The pleasure of mastery is morbid, and the pleasure of danger a gambler's delirium. Perhaps the use of this word "pleasure" confuses the issue: Blake does not often use it, and it is in fact rather a passive and receptive word. The poet who said that "Active Evil is better than Passive Good"[34] might well have said that active pain is better than passive pleasure, in which case he would have come much closer to Nietzsche, or even to the sadists he is sometimes confused with. Blake does not talk about pleasure and pain, but about joy and sorrow, which are words that do mean something; and eternity to him is simply that plane of existence on which joy, or the fulfillment of desire, becomes possible. The absence of joy in Nietzsche's philosophy would put him on the side of the Angels for Blake.

· 5 ·

THE natural man who attempts the state of Beulah or love is in a state of "jealousy." The abstract reasoner cannot see a tree without dragging its shadow off to the cave of his own mind, and a post-Blakean myth of great imaginative accuracy shows that the attitude of the natural or "cave" man to his wife is not greatly different. The Selfhood cannot love in the sense of establishing a kinship with the beloved: it can regard the latter only as a possession, something to contemplate in solitude. These irreconcilable attitudes to love are represented in "The Clod and the Pebble" in the *Songs of Experience*. Mastery over woman produces the same morbidity and imaginative idleness as mastery over man, and Blake uses the word "jealousy" to cover the Selfhood's attitude to both.

Abstract ideas are called spectres by Blake, and Spectre with a capital letter is the Selfhood. The corresponding term is "Emanation," which means the total form of all the things a man loves and creates. In the fallen states the Emanation is conceived as outside, and hence it becomes the source of a continuously tantalizing and elusive torment. In imaginative states it is united with and emanates from the man, hence its name. The imagination, therefore, achieves a single spiritual union, which is why monogamous marriage, the fallen approximation of it, has got itself so firmly established in society. Of course the legal and ecclesiastical idea of marriage as a trap baited with the sex act and snapped at consummation Blake, like Milton, thought obscene. His warnings, however, are not directed against marriage but against the "soft Family-Love"[35] which is one of the most formidable bulwarks of social conservatism. The notion that a child is a possession of its parents is very hard to eradicate, especially in loving parents; and this kind of parental love is denounced by Blake as a vicious appetite. The most elaborate form of it is the Platonic educational love which has for its goal the retention of the boy in the larger family unit of the city-state.[36]

Sexual love, however, is the door through which most of us enter the imaginative world, and for many it affords the sole glimpse into that world. It is thus especially pathetic when a chance to love is thwarted or missed, and especially important for the Selfhood to place a strong guard over this door to send enquirers in the wrong direction. This door, the guard says, does not lead to fuller humanity; it goes the opposite way to nature. This is the "animal" or lower part of you that you are now exploring, and is a form of excretion which the loftiest spirituality cuts out of life entirely.

The guard is lying, of course. Mating and copulating may be "animal," but imaginative love is part of our divine birthright. The whole notion of shame which the guard inspires is typical of Selfhood "jealousy," and it breeds several different diseases, all closely related. Blake did not need to survive to this century to learn that prudery and prurience are much the same thing, or that there can be a good deal of autoerotic frustration in virginity. He makes both points with great explicitness all through his work, as in this plaintive lament of a dead spinster:

> An old maid early—e'er I knew
> Ought but the love that on me grew;
> And now I'm cover'd o'er & o'er
> And wish that I had been a whore.[37]

Sexual abstinence is more melodramatic than autoeroticism: Nobodaddy is a jealous God, and the killing of love is as dear to him as the killing of life, which, of course, it includes. Here again the myth of a higher "soul" and a lower "body" rears its foolish head. The latter, we are told, is "tainted" and "corrupt"; the former becomes "pure" when separated from the body and purged of fleshly desires. As the body *is* the soul seen from the perspective of this world, it is easy to see how murderous this denial of those simple desires which are imaginative needs must be. Blake has put this into his terrible lyric on the sunflower in the *Songs of Experience*, the flower which wistfully follows the sun across the sky all day, a perfect symbol of the "vegetable" life rooted in this world and longing to be free. But all the *Songs of Expe-. rience* are deeply acid-bitten, and even the "pale Virgin shrouded in snow" is not so tragic a figure of useless imaginative waste as the harlot.[38] Society is never so self-righteous as when accusing the harlot of sin and doing nothing to free her from it, yet she is an inevitable result of its own blaspheming of love, and the plagues which blight the marriage hearse are no more an accidental result of that blasphemy than violent death is an accidental result of war.

The elaborate erotic apparatus of more respectable females, coyness, shyness, modesty, jealousy, teasing, luring the man on and then holding him off, concealing and revealing the body at once, and so on, are not to be dismissed as either silly or amusing: they are, like marriage, symbols of a profound imaginative reality. The material world is in a way feminine to the perceiver; it is the body which receives the seed of his imagination, and the works of the imagination which are the artist's children are drawn from that body. We think of Nature as feminine, and so she is. But as the artist develops he becomes more and more interested in the art and more and more impatient of the help he receives from nature. In the world of Eden there is only energy incorporating itself in form, creator and creature, which means that somewhere (on the upper limit of Beulah, as it happens) this permanent objective body which nourishes and incubates the imaginative form drops out. Nature, in simpler language, is Mother Nature, and in the perfectly imaginative state there is no mother. The fall of man began with the appearance of an independent object-world, and continued into this state of Generation, where we begin life in helpless dependence on Mother Nature for all our ideas. This independent nourishing force in nature Blake calls the female will.

The worship of a female principle, therefore, specifically a maternal principle, is not imaginative, and is only possible to natural religion. In Eden there is no Mother-God. In many religions God is certainly worshiped as a trinity of father, mother and child, as in Beulah, but in the more highly developed ones God is always the Supreme Male, the Creator for whom the distinction between the beloved female and created child has disappeared. The reappearance of the Madonna in Christianity is thus a corruption of that religion, and is in direct contradiction to Jesus' own teachings. Mother-worship is womb-worship, a desire to prolong the helplessness of the perceiver and his dependence on the body of nature which surrounds him.

Women are of course the only possible images of the female will in this world, though it does not follow that they are to be identified with it. All female-worship is disguised nature-worship, and all Petrarchan and chivalric codes directed to the adoration of a mistress are imaginatively pernicious for that reason. The female antics mentioned above which have degenerated from these codes reproduce, in the fallen world, the elusive and treacherous beauty of a separate nature; and the separation of nature from man, which drives him from reflection to melancholy, and from melancholy to suicidal madness, has usually been symbolized in art by the love, or rather jealousy, of a viciously willful woman. In Blake's symbolism the two great symbols of the female will are the Madonna and Child, the infant imagination wrapped in the arms of a mother, and the Court of Love code with its curious reversal of sexual roles in which a coy mistress is the "lord."

· 6 ·

THE more mundane struggles of the visionary in the world of Generation are largely concerned with money. Money to Blake is the cement or cohesive principle of fallen society, and as society consists of tyrants exploiting victims, money can exist only in the two forms of riches and poverty; too much for a few and not enough for the rest. *La propriété, c'est le vol* may be a good epigram, but it is no better than Blake's definition of money as "the life's blood of Poor Families,"[39] or his remark that "God made Man happy & Rich, but the Subtil made the innocent, Poor."[40] A money economy is a continuous partial murder of the victim, as poverty keeps many imaginative needs out of reach. Money for those who have it, on the other hand, can belong only to the Selfhood, as it assumes the possibility of enjoyment through possession, which we have seen to be impossible; and hence of being passively or externally stimulated into imagination. An equal distribution of money, even if practicable, would therefore not affect its status as the root of all evil. Corresponding to the consensus of mediocrities assumed by law and Lockian philosophy, money assumes a dead level of "necessities" (notice the word) as its basis. Art on this theory is high up among the nonessentials; pleasure, in society, tends to collapse very quickly into luxury and affectation.

Peace is this money economy functioning; war is the same economy breaking down, and proceeding from partial to total murder of the victim. Blake speaks of "Heroism a Miser,"[41] meaning that wars are fought to get money and that brave deeds in battle therefore go to enrich profiteers. Or, to put it in words of one syllable:

> The Prince's Robes & Beggar's Rags
> Are Toadstools on the Miser's Bags.[42]

Into this money economy the visionary must fit himself somehow, and he usually finds that integrity and prosperity point in very different directions. Society on the whole does not want him, and occasionally tells him that he ought to be poor and thereby suffer enough to make himself a great genius. "Poverty is the Fool's Rod,"[43] said Blake; nor did he care for the other view, which he died too soon to feel the real force of, that a visionary must present a socially acceptable morality first and his visions afterwards. Not that Blake is any great exponent of *la vie de Bohème*, but, as he says, an artist cannot be dissipated unless he has something to dissipate.[44]

· 7 ·

COMING down to Ulro we reach the problem skirted around in the first chapter of the difference between the imaginative and the imaginary, between the vision and the hallucination. This contrast is a perfectly valid one, but usually it is wrongly stated on an assumption of separate subjects and objects. Either the thing seen is thought to be "outside" the mind and real, or "inside," in which case it is "just imagination," and unreal. But this distinction does not work, and the question may be argued for centuries whether ghosts, for instance, are objectively real or subjectively unreal without being settled.

Now whether we "really" see something or just "imagine" we see it, the thing visualized is in both cases equally a datum of experience. But two mental attitudes to perception are possible. The way of what we have called the normal genius is imaginative, divine, universal, and therefore communicable; what cannot be communicated is not imagined but derived from reflection. Further, the unfallen world is infinite and eternal, and what exists in that world persists in this one. This persistent reality is the basis of all vision. Superficially, the vision of Quixote, who saw a windmill as a hundred-armed giant, is very similar to the vision of Blake:

> For double the vision my Eyes do see,
> And a double vision is always with me.
> With my inward Eye 'tis an Old Man grey;
> With my outward, a Thistle across my way.[45]

But in seeing the giant Quixote lost his imaginative control of the windmill.

When the diseased or lunatic mind has what it calls visions, the latter have certain characteristics which do not appear in

those of the visionary. In the first place, they are consistent only
with a series of associations peculiar to the individual, and only
in terms of that have they any communicable value. They can
therefore seldom produce the imaginative response in us that
Blake's vision of the sun as a company of angels does, when he
illustrates it in the Job series. In the second place, they are haphazard, and appear and vanish in defiance of the imaginative will.
In the third place, they are evil and monstrous, corresponding
to the Selfhood's fears of what may exist outside perception, and
to the generalizations in which various real things are mixed
together.

The response of the Selfhood to vision, therefore, is the same
as its response to sight. In responding to sight it withdraws and
reflects; in responding to vision it runs away and hides under the
bedclothes. In responding to sight it is passively affected by an
external stimulus; in responding to vision it is haunted and pursued by some external power conceived as both irresistible and
evil. The imagination, on the other hand, makes the ghost perceived by it the slave of a sketchbook. Spirits of all kinds appeared
to Blake, but only as unpaid models; they were forced to stand
around and pose, open their mouths to display their teeth better,
and were not allowed to depart before he had finished with them
on any such thin excuse as the necessity of getting away at cock-
crow.

We may notice that in all four areas of imaginative conflict the
Selfhood sets up a parody of the imagination. The physical fight
of the hero parodies the mental fight of the artist; the jealous
wife and teasing mistress parody the emanation; money and morality parody the community of minds; the ghost or nightmare
parodies the vision. This pattern of superficial resemblance combined with profound contrast, the illustration of the doctrine
that truth clarifies error into the negation of itself, reaches its
culmination in the parody of Christ by Antichrist. Our next task
is to describe Blake's conception of Jesus, in which our main
source must be *The Everlasting Gospel.*

· 8 ·

THE Holy Spirit spoke by the prophets, all visionaries speak with
the voice of God, but in Jesus God and Man became one. For Jesus

was a perfect man, not in the negative sense of a man without sin—had he been perfect in that way he could never have existed at all, even as a myth—but as a man who "was all virtue, and acted from impulse, not from rules."[46] Everything he did was an imaginative act bringing more abundant life, and his whole gospel reduces itself to forgiveness of sins, in the sense above discussed.

His impact on society was that of a revolutionary and iconoclast, as that of all prophets must be. He found the Jews worshiping their own version of Nobodaddy, a sulky and jealous thundergod who exacted the most punctilious obedience to a ceremonial law and moral code. He tore this code to pieces and broke all ten commandments, in theory at least. He had no use for the Pharisees' Sabbath or for the paralysis of activity thought to be most acceptable to their frozen God on that day. All the devotion to ritual fopperies of the kind that lazy minds think of as possessing some kind of mysterious magical virtue got the same treatment. Jesus met the guardians of law and conventional piety with jeers and insults and merciless exposures of their hypocrisy and ignorance. He started disputing with doctors very early, and reduced both the smugly pious Pharisees and the smugly skeptical Sadducees to an infuriated silence. He himself was a vagrant and did not work at his trade, giving the bag to Judas to carry, but he never ceased to denounce the ambitious and self-made as fools and swindlers. So far from honoring his father and mother—the only positive command in the Decalogue—he found that complete imagination involves a break with a family. He ran away from home at twelve, told his followers that they must hate their parents, and said to his own mother, "Woman, what have I to do with thee?"[47] When he was brought a harlot to be accused, condemned and murdered in the approved way, he showed that the self-righteousness which made killing her a pleasure was something far worse than her sin. Finally Jesus became so obnoxious to society that society could stand him no longer, and, as he refused all compromise or even defense, he really compelled the custodians of virtue and vested interests to murder him. From their point of view they were quite right, and their charge of blaspheming their God amply justified.

At the same time the common people heard him gladly; publicans and sinners welcomed him; lepers, pariahs and beggars called to him; children swarmed after him. He was more interested in sinners than the righteous; Pharisees did not recognize him as a prophet, but the adulterous woman of Samaria did. When he talked of God he did not point to the sky but told his hearers that the Kingdom of Heaven was within them. Nor did he tell them how to live a Christian life in society. He asked the impossible, demanded perfection, and threw out wildly unpractical suggestions. He said that God was a Father and that we should live the imaginatively unfettered lives of children, growing as spontaneously as the lilies without planning or foresight. The God of his parables is an imaginative God who makes no sense whatever as a Supreme Bookkeeper, rewarding the obedient and punishing the disobedient. Those who labor all day for him get the same reward as those who come in at the last moment. His kingdom is like a pearl of great price which it will bankrupt us to possess. If we want wise and temperate advice on living we shall find it in Caesar sooner than in Christ; there is more of it in Marcus Aurelius than there is in the Gospels.[48] Sensible people will tell us that it is foolish to throw everything to the winds, to give all one's goods to the poor and live entirely without caution or prudence. But they will not tell us the one thing we need most to know: that we are all born into a world of liquid chaos as a man falls into the sea, and that we must either sink or swim to land because we are not fish.

For all Jesus' teaching centers on the imminent destruction of this world and the eternal permanence of heaven and hell, these latter being not places but states of mind. Jesus however did not discuss this in terms of good and evil, but in terms of life and death, the fruitful and the barren. The law of God that we must obey is the law of our own spiritual growth. Those who embezzle God's talents are praised; those who are afraid to touch them are reviled.

There is much haughtiness and arrogance in Jesus, much speaking with authority and much blasting invective. This is the indignation of the prophet. Yet we have seen that resentment excludes retribution, and Jesus forgave all sins continuously until his last gasp on the cross. For the same reason he renounced all the attributes of the conquering Messiah, refused to fight tyranny with tyranny, and withdrew completely from the vendettas of society.

It is therefore nonsense to believe that Jesus forgave sins only because he was biding his time for a more hideous revenge later on. Hell is the Selfhood "jealousy" defined by Blake as "the being shut up in the possession of corporeal desires which shortly weary the man,"[49] and this is the only hell that Jesus spoke of.

The higher state of heaven is achieved by those who have developed the God within them instead of the devil. Those who have fed the hungry and clothed the naked are here, because they have realized the divine dignity of man. These are the just who, as Paul said, live by faith, and the just, being potentially visionaries, attain that vision after death. Faith, which may be "blind," attains its consummation in vision, and Jesus promised that some of his followers would not taste death before they had that vision. In other words, it is not necessary to die to get it. Faith, Jesus said, can remove mountains. But mountains in the world of experience are entirely motionless; what kind of faith can remove them? Well, a landscape painter can easily leave one out of his picture if it upsets his imaginative balance. And that kind of vision, which sees with perfect accuracy just what it wants to see, pierces the gates of heaven into the unfallen world.

Jesus was not only a teacher but a healer, and the true healer does not "cure"; he helps the sick man to cure himself. Jesus tore off all the veils of timidity and caution and prudence and moderation and confronted his hearers with the ultimate contrast of full imagination or Selfhood, himself or Caiaphas. He could bring God out of a fisherman or a tax-collector, and he could frighten a weakling until all his hysterias and bugaboos ran shrieking out of him. Therefore he continuously worked what are called miracles. Now just as prophecy is vulgarly considered to be fortune-telling, so miracles are vulgarly considered to be mysterious tricks which cannot be explained except on the assumption that the worker of them is all that he says he is. Miracles of this kind belong to the more popular and ignorant levels of religion: they are a crude form of scientific experiment. The miracles of Jesus depended on the belief of the recipient. A real miracle is an imaginative effort which meets with an imaginative response. Jesus could give sight to the blind and activity to the paralyzed only when they did not want to be blind or paralyzed; he stimulated and encouraged them to shatter their own physical prisons. Miracles reveal what the imagination can do. The opposite of revelation is mystery, and a miracle which remains mysterious is a fraud, especially if it is an authentic miracle:

Jesus could not do miracles where unbelief hindered, hence we must conclude that the man who holds miracles to be ceased puts it out of his own power to ever witness one. The manner of a miracle being performed is in modern times considered as an arbitrary command of the agent upon the patient, but this is an impossibility, not a miracle, neither did Jesus ever do such a miracle. . . .[50]

Jesus' teaching avoids generalizations of the sort that translate into platitudes in all languages. Examples, images, parables, and the aphorisms which are concretions rather than abstractions of wisdom, were what he preferred. These are the units of art, and are addressed only to those who are willing to understand them; no art works automatically on the unresponsive any more than a miracle does. Coleridge's "willing suspension of disbelief" is a negative statement of the desire to see which all art implies. Such a desire is simple and childlike rather than complex; but to the generalizer there is nothing so esoteric as a straightforward story which compels him to focus his vision on something concrete. He prefers plain statements of general truth: those, he feels, are addressed to all men equally, like the guinea-sun. He is more at home with "Blessed are the meek, for they shall inherit the earth": that expresses the general truth that one may become rich and respected by not offending anybody:

> The Vision of Christ that thou dost see
> Is my Vision's Greatest Enemy: . . .
> Thine is the friend of All Mankind,
> Mine speaks in parables to the Blind.[51]

There is no Christian visible Church, Christian theology, Christian morality, Christian society or Christian ceremony. Religion, says Blake, is "Civilized Life such as it is in the Christian Church,"[52] and the Christian Church in this sense is nothing but "Active Life"[53] or the free use of the imagination. Nobody can be "converted" to Christianity in the sense of exchanging one faith for another:

. . . By their Works ye shall know them; the Knave who is Converted to Deism & the Knave who is Converted to Christianity is still a Knave, but he himself will not know it, tho' Every body else does.[54]

Imagination is life, and Jesus, by "taking away the remembrance of sin," released it, bringing more abundant life. He not only judges the quick and the dead; he judges them according to whether they are quick or dead. He did not curse Pilate; he cursed the barren fig-tree. The imagination always follows Jesus, and cannot do otherwise. There is no natural religion; all religion is revelation; revelation is apocalypse; apocalypse is vision. The only "church" Jesus founded was a communion of visionaries, and Baptism and the Lord's Supper symbolize, Blake says, "Throwing off Error & Knaves from our company continually & Recieving Truth or Wise Men into our Company continually."[55] The essence of the socially acceptable and moral Antichrist, then, is "the outward Ceremony,"[56] its recurrent ritual imitating the Nobodaddy who chases his tail forever in the sky.

Heaven is not a place guarded by immigration officials interested only in passports and certificates, nor is it the higher class to which we are promoted by passing an examination showing what we have learned in this world. Heaven *is* this world as it appears to the awakened imagination, and those who try to approach it by way of restraint, caution, good behavior, fear, self-satisfaction, assent to uncomprehended doctrines, or voluntary drabness, will find themselves traveling toward hell, as Ignorance did in Bunyan, hell being similarly this world as it appears to the repressed imagination:

Men are admitted into Heaven not because they have curbed & govern'd their Passions or have No Passions, but because they have Cultivated their Understandings. The Treasures of Heaven are not Negations of Passion, but Realities of Intellect, from which all the Passions Emanate Uncurbed in their Eternal Glory. The Fool shall not enter into Heaven let him be ever so Holy. Holiness is not The Price of Enterance into Heaven. Those who are cast out are All Those who, having no Passions of their own because No Intellect, Have spent their lives in Curbing & Governing other People's by the Various arts of Poverty & Cruelty of all kinds. . . .[57]

Notice the pejorative use of the term "holiness" in the above passage, which is regular in Blake except in direct connection with the state of innocence. The conception of the holy first stirs in the primitive mind in connection with symbols of an unknown fear; it develops in darkened temples where the "holy place" is guarded and veiled, and matures in a feeling of awful reverence which expresses itself in sacrifice. The term is also associated more loosely with hoary age and the last extremity of moral virtue; but in all its meanings it connotes a mental paralysis founded on mystery, like the "holy dread" of *Kubla Khan*. In the passage quoted above Blake goes on to say, in a blinding flash of contempt, "The Modern Church Crucifies Christ with the Head Downwards." It is clear that when Blake defines his art as allegory addressed to the intellectual powers, by intellectual powers he must have meant, strained as the interpretation may seem to some, intellectual powers. To his theory of art we must now turn.

A LITERALIST OF THE
IMAGINATION

BLAKE's conception of art is not only central in his thinking but distinctive of him as a thinker, and though he reminds us frequently of Berkeley or Swedenborg, he was what neither Berkeley nor Swedenborg was, a practising artist. The other two stressed, certainly, the role of the imagination in their philosophy and theology; but they themselves were dealing with the latter two subjects and fully intended to preserve their independence. Blake, however, had no interest in doing this at all, and, aided by his practical knowledge of how the creative imagination works, pushed boldly on where they stopped short. Further, those whose ideas run along lines similar to Blake's often have great difficulty in coming to terms with sense experience, and Blake's training as a painter was an important, no doubt the decisive, factor in enabling him to do so. For here as everywhere else in Blake's thought we go back to his theory of knowledge.

The common statement that all knowledge comes from sense experience is neither true nor false; it is simply muddled. The senses are organs of the mind, therefore all knowledge comes from mental experience. Mental experience is a union of a perceiving subject and a perceived object; it is something in which the barrier between "inside" and "outside" dissolves. But the power to unite comes from the subject. The work of art is the product of this creative perception, hence it is not an escape from reality but a systematic training in comprehending it. It is difficult to see things that move quickly and are far away: in the world of time and space, therefore, all things are more or less blurred. Art sees its images as permanent living forms outside time and space. This is the only way in which we can stabilize the world of experience and still retain all its reality:

All that we See is Vision, from Generated Organs gone as soon as come, Permanent in The Imagination, Consider'd as Nothing by the Natural Man.[1]

To Plato, whose Muses were daughters of Memory, knowledge was recollection and art imitation: to Blake, both knowledge and art are recreation.

Rational syntheses such as philosophy, theology and science do not create new images or forms. They establish new relationships among the images we already have. They make a partial synthesis by part of the mind of partial images; therefore they are bound to be partial in their appeal and must be entirely subject to imagination in spite of themselves. Reason is a vehicle which the healthy mind drives under its own control, not a Juggernaut. We never argue or become convinced without motives which lie beyond the persuasive force of reason, nor should we. The explanatory disciplines are general and explicit, taking in their whole audience at once as a single unit. But there is no general truth of equal importance and interest to everyone. Applause, it has been said, is the echo of a platitude, but the applause itself indicates that the response comes from the entire personality and is therefore an organic part of it. We have here an agreement of minds on the guinea-sun level. The difference between the platitude and the aphorism, hinted at earlier, is that the platitude involves no disturbance of a commonplace standard of values. A platitude may be true, even universally true; but it would not occur to us to call it profoundly true. We do not call a statement profound unless we are pleased with its wit.

Art proves the inadequacy of abstract and rational ideas by the rule that examples and illustrations are more powerful than doctrines or precepts. And we say that examples and illustrations are "vivid," which means alive. They are addressed to the body which is the form of the soul; they represent a communication from the whole mind and they demand total response. Art is based on sense experience, and what we see or hear is taken in directly by the imagination:

Knowledge is not by deduction, but Immediate by Perception or Sense at once. Christ adresses himself to the Man, not to his Reason.[2]

Christ brought no new doctrines: he brought new stories. He did not save souls; he saved bodies, healing the blind and deaf that they might hear his parables and see his imagery. He stands outside the history of general thought; he stands in the center of individual wisdom.

Wisdom is the application of the imaginative vision taught us by art. We conquer knowledge by forced marches, learning more

id more as we continually press on. Wisdom is the unhurried
expanding organic health of the powerful and well-knit imagina-
on, and it depends on a combination of practice and relaxation.
: is difficult for the man who has knowledge without wisdom to
elax his mind into receptivity in front of a picture or poem. To
im it contains a communicable residue of general statements
alled the meaning, and to clutch this and carry it off is his sole
esire. In art we learn as the child learns, through the concrete
lustration of stories and pictures, and without that childlike
esire to listen to stories and see pictures art could not exist. We
cquire greater control over abstract ideas as we grow older: if
hat is part of the expanding child's vision, well and good: if it
eplaces that vision, maturity is only degeneration. The wise man
as a pattern or image of reality in his mind into which every-
hing he knows fits, and into which everything he does not know
ould fit, and therefore his approach to knowledge is something
hat the dung-beetles of unorganized learning cannot even grasp.
More! More! is the cry of a mistaken soul," said Blake: "less
han All cannot satisfy Man."[3]

Art is suggestive rather than explicit: it makes no attempt to
persuade into a general agreement or provide mediocre levels of
explanation. And the whole value of all cultural disciplines is in
his objective statement of vision. To get any value out of a philosopher, we must finish his book and make our response to it as an
art-form, as the imaginative projection of a creative mind. There
s a sneer at Aristotle's *Analytics* in *The Marriage of Heaven and
Hell*, presumably because of its title: all wisdom comes in unified
yntheses of experience, and nothing else is vision. The philosopher's choice of form has everything to do with his rank as a
philosopher. Most readers of Plato assume that his dialogue form
was adopted at random to expound a system of general ideas in
a series of graded lessons. But the supremely suggestive and ferti-
izing quality of Plato's philosophy lies in the fact that he was the
only philosopher who was artist enough to master a visionary
orm, and hence *par excellence* the philosopher who suggests an
nfinity of responses instead of compelling a single one.

Religions ordinarily claim to have this total appeal to the
imagination and to demand the total response denied to the
reason and the will, both of which they say they include. But

wherein does anything that is genuine in religion differ fro
art? The most obvious difference between them is that art is pu
revelation and religion full of mystery. And the chief reason wh
people insist on substituting religion for art, and on maintainir
a mystery in religion, is that only in abstractions can they fir
absolutes, and only in absolutes can they find an unchangir
invariable support for their imaginations. No work of art clair
to be more than one of an infinity of mental syntheses. It includ
no solid body of impersonal spiritual truth; it suspends judgmer
on the inherent truth of all creeds and regards all explanato
and dogmatic systems as art-forms. Art is not in any religior
sense substantial. Not only do the plastic arts decay and vanis
but literature and music, which have better powers of surviva
are still exhaustible, not a permanent support such as religic
affords. All art, even the greatest, is flawed, and our total respon
to it is bound to include a certain critical detachment.

That is as it should be. Passive dependence upon an objectiv
and permanent support leads not to the Fatherhood of God, bu
to the Motherhood of nature. It is the relaxed and childlike co
fidence of Beulah, a liquid imagination which needs a solid co
tainer and longs to hear what Blake calls "comfortable notes
It represents the imagination of the child, or the "gentle souls
like St. Teresa who get a job guarding a gate in *Jerusalem*,[4] or th
sick souls who accuse themselves of sin and feel that fear is a
essential part of the imagination, or the miserable souls oppresse
by tyranny and calamity. All of these have vision, though of
somewhat myopic kind; they all see images of the truth. But th
do not see as clearly and accurately as the exuberant soul glowir
with health and energy. Under the stress of the loss of a child c
the horror of war an imagination, however powerful, is apt t
drop at on e from Eden to Beulah, to find refuge in the everlastin
arms of a transcendent Father or Mother. Religions which hav
no intention of arising from Beulah stress the value of sufferin
and humility in order to keep the imagination there: the sta
of Eden to them is proud and demonic, a state in which or
forgets God. But one forgets God in that state only in the sen:
in which one forgets one's health by being healthy: one is merel
released from the tyranny of "memory."

Religion, then, is raw imaginative material clarified by ar

orm" and "image" being the same word in Blake, art is the form
religion because it is the image of religion. Blake has a certain
nderness for the mellower forms of superstition: belief in fairies
id nymphs he thinks of as potential rather than degraded imag-
ation.[5] Similarly, he would regard idolatry as a good thing if
were not that between the maker and the owner of the idol
imes a third spirit in the idol itself. The nonhuman quality of
is spirit perverts both art and religion. Now art which is con-
ived as illustrating a religion to which it is subordinated also
fers to a third spiritual power. If the artist is great enough this
es not matter. But iconic art, that is, works of art whose author-
ip and merits matter less than their power to stimulate wor-
ipers to reflect and meditate, is barbaric. The value of a con-
entional religious symbol for religion depends entirely on how
od it is as art. Our response to the tremendous Madonnas of
imabue may be healthy and fully imaginative, not because we
elieve in the Madonna whether we do or not, but because we
an see the picture, and enter into the vision. But the notion that
Madonna by a bad artist can be of any religious value to anyone,
owever ignorant of art, because it is a Madonna, is unhealthy
nd cramping to the imagination. The appreciation of the painter's
echnical skill in painting a religious picture is not only more
ivilized; it is further from idolatry than the abstracted response
rawn away to the general idea which the picture represents.
lence:

A Poet, a Painter, a Musician, an Architect: the Man Or Woman
vho is not one of these is not a Christian.
You must leave Fathers & Mothers & Houses & Lands if they stand
n the way of Art.
Prayer is the Study of Art.
Praise is the Practise of Art.
Fasting &c., all relate to Art.
The outward Ceremony is Antichrist.[6]

· 2 ·

THE totality of imaginative power, of which the matrix is art, is
what we ordinarily call culture or civilization. Everything worth
doing and done well is an art, whether love, conversation, religion,
education, sport, cookery or commerce. Because the world is

fallen we think of art as ornament succeeding necessities; but a
life moves upward to achieve ornament, for ornament is fre
and necessities are necessary:

The Bible says That Cultivated Life Existed First. Uncultivated Li
comes afterwards from Satan's Hirelings. Necessaries, Accomodatio
& Ornaments are the whole of Life. Satan took away Ornament Firs
Next he took away Accomodations, & Then he became Lord & Mast
of Necessaries.[7]

And this culture is what maintains all order and security i
society. Reason and order being "the bound or outward circum
ference of Energy," the imagination is always constructive, an
all interference or anarchy is of the Selfhood. The essentials o
the free state were defined in America as life, liberty and th
pursuit of happiness. But one cannot pursue happiness: one mu
pursue something else that will give happiness; and the onl
happiness that exists is derived from the free creative life. A
state is free, then, in proportion to the amount of free life i
permits, just as it is a slave-state in proportion to the amoun
of death or imaginative restraint for which it is organized. Jus
as reason is the circumference of energy, so necessity is the ci
cumference of freedom: *noblesse oblige*. Penal codes and repre
sive laws cannot produce order: they are conceived as a despera
defense against chaos: order is not a matter of morality but o
morale. Compulsion and obedience follow the anarchic will o
tyranny: our imaginations, being one in God, achieve, when u
restricted, a spontaneous co-operation. That is part of what Blak
means when he says that empire follows art and not art empire

This conception of culture as the source of order in societ
and as more complete in its appeal than religion, may remind u
to some extent of *Culture and Anarchy*; enough, at any rate, t
make us wonder why so strongly "Hebraic" a thinker and despise
of the Classics as Blake should hold such views. Blake believe
like Arnold, that culture preserves society: he did not believe, a
Arnold apparently did, that society preserves culture. Society t
Blake is an eternally unwilling recipient of culture: every geniu
must fight society no matter what his age. Arnold's view of bot
culture and society is conservative, traditional and evolutionary
Blake's is radical, apocalyptic and revolutionary. Arnold think

the prophet not so much as a visionary as a preacher of moral
ruples, and in his thought the boundary line between Hebrews
id Philistines becomes even more vague and fluctuating than it
as in history.

Inspiration is the artist's empirical proof of the divinity of his
iagination; and all inspiration is divine in origin, whether used,
rverted, hidden or frittered away in reverie. All imaginative
id creative acts, being eternal, go to build up a permanent
ructure, which Blake calls Golgonooza, above time, and, when
is structure is finished, nature, its scaffolding, will be knocked
vay and man will live in it. Golgonooza will then be the city
God, the New Jerusalem which is the total form of all human
lture and civilization. Nothing that the heroes, martyrs, proph-
s and poets of the past have done for it has been wasted; no
onymous and unrecognized contribution to it has been over-
ɔked. In it is conserved all the good man has done, and in it is
mpleted all that he hoped and intended to do. And the artist
io uses the same energy and genius that Homer and Isaiah had
ll find that he not only lives in the same palace of art as Homer
d Isaiah, but lives in it at the same time.[9]

· 3 ·

E now proceed to Blake's theory of painting, leaving his theory
poetry for the next chapter. The essential principle of this is
iple enough. Art is the incorporation of the greatest possible
aginative effort in the clearest and most accurate form. Per-
ɔtion is the union of subject and object, and creation is the
npletion of this union. Unity and clarity are therefore the
ie thing, and unity is the product of integrated power. The
ld imagination produces great art; the timid one small art.
t the healthy eye does not see more broadly and vaguely than
weak eye; it sees more clearly. The genius proves himself one
his accuracy; the mediocrity proves himself one by his vague-
ss.

Lockian views of art will necessarily be founded on the idea
an accidental contact of an independent subject with an inde-
ndent object; consequently a general antithesis between sub-
tive and objective art will run all through them. Reynolds'
ws of art are founded, Blake says, on Burke's *Treatise on the*

Sublime and Beautiful, which Blake calls an application of Locke theory of knowledge to aesthetics. Blake's comment on Burke presents fewer difficulties in interpretation than some of his writing

> I read Burke's Treatise when very young. . . . I felt the Same Contemp & Abhorrence then that I do now.[10]

According to Burke, there are two elements in art, the conceptio and the execution. The former is what the artist generates within himself: it is in other words a form of reflection. The latter repr sents the result of the application of this reflection to the oute world. Hiatus between conception and execution, then, is th first fact of criticism. The more powerful the reflection, the mo complete the withdrawal, and the greater the likelihood that th application will be vague and rough; and vice versa. So all a is split down the middle into the "sublime," great conceptior inclined to be imperfect in execution, and the "beautiful," tr umphs of execution implying a patient and therefore not a su premely vigorous genius. (This account, of course, is intende to give Blake's view of Burke, not an impartial summary of th *Treatise*.)

Here again is precisely the same dichotomy which we have m so often already, between subjective and objective separations subject and object. The antitheses between the navel-gazer an atomist in thought, the hermit and antinomian in religion, th victim and tyrant in society, correspond in art to that of the su lime and the beautiful. It is all too consistent with Lockia reasoning to make works of art, which are concrete things, fit general classification of qualities, and to make genius subservier to aspects and trends. Duality of this kind is a cautious an dubious derogation of art; it establishes a dogmatic axiom tha there is no such thing as positive perfection, no absolutely gre genius, no possibility of real inspiration or fully integrated visior Because Michelangelo and Raphael had great minds, Reynolc must say that they neglected the smaller beauties of art[11]; becaus Milton had a great mind, Johnson must say that his genius coul not carve cherry-stones and therefore produced bad sonnets.

Blake cannot understand why we should require artists t specialize either in lofty beginnings or in high finish. We do n reflect first and write or paint afterwards: art is the activity c

riting or painting. We do not experience an internal tornado
nd then see what we can salvage from the wreck: the conception
kes on its own form and shape only in the execution. We cannot
onceive more than we produce: we may dream of great master-
ieces and then find that what we do afterwards is inferior to the
ream, but a dream of doing something great is not seeing a
icture in the mind's eye and realizing it in paint. What the
ainter really visualizes is what he can succeed in making appear
n the canvas. If he complains that he originally "imagined"
omething much finer, why is his attitude now one of remembering
nd not still one of imagining? Conception and execution, then,
re absolutely the same thing, and a fissure between them can only
e produced by the entering wedge of social chaos:

> have heard many People say, "Give me the Ideas. It is no matter
> vhat Words you put them into," & others say, "Give me the Design,
> t is no matter for the Execution." These People know Enough of
> Artifice, but Nothing Of Art. Ideas cannot be Given but in their
> ninutely Appropriate Words, nor Can a Design be made without its
> ninutely Appropriate Execution. . . . Execution is only the result of
> nvention.[12]

There can be no such thing, therefore, as a genius whose work is
ketchily done because he is in too great a hurry to get down his
onception before he forgets it. "Mechanical Excellence is the
Only Vehicle of Genius"[13]; the inexorable power of vision will
not be satisfied with anything short of absolute clarity. The
gusty and stormy artist is not bold but timid. He hides his work in
uggestive clouds for fear that the clear glare of intense vision will
reveal its deficiencies too unsparingly. Blake makes no spasmodic
gestures; he is not an incarnation of a thundergod; he wants no
emotional storm upsetting the balanced imaginations of those
vho see his pictures:

> intreat, then, that the Spectator will attend to the Hands & Feet,
> o the Lineaments of the Countenances; they are all descriptive of
> Character, & not a line is drawn without intention, & that most
> discriminate & particular. As Poetry admits not a Letter that is Insignif-
> cant, so Painting admits not a Grain of Sand or a Blade of Grass
> Insignificant—much less an Insignificant Blur or Mark.[14]

All vagueness and obscurity in art, all uncompleted and roughly
sketched statements, come from "leaving something to the imagina-

tion," and artists who think of imagination as a residue of visio
are not to be trusted.

The other side of Burke's antithesis deals with art that has th
meticulous attention to detail without the driving power of geniu.
In such a case the detail will lack significance, or relevance to th
central unity of the design. The expertness of a Ter Borch i
painting the sheen of satin or the starch of a ruff is also bor
of timidity. Here we are expected to scatter the charge of ou
response and look at the picture as an aggregate of variou
triumphs of expertness. To concentrate upon the picture as
unified vision will reveal that Ter Borch is, again, not creatin
but recording, though the stimulus here is present and outsid
instead of past and inside.

The silliest idea that can enter the artist's head is that natur
has been prefabricated by a fully conscious and intelligent mind
and that art should imitate instead of recreating nature. An artis
who holds such a view saws off the branch he is sitting on, for ar
could not exist without taking it for granted that nature is th
material world and not the formed world. Unimaginative realisn
evokes only the smug pleasure of recognition. The painter become
popular because he assures everyone else that he sees no mor
than they see. He paints the guinea-sun; he is satisfied with a fallel
world. But art which is only nature at secondhand is quite rightl
regarded by society as a dispensable luxury. One cannot pain
flowers better than they paint themselves, and if one has nothing
else to say about flowers one can produce only a smudged and
oily reminder of them. Here the iconic heresy comes back int
art, applied to nature instead of religious vision. Yet Reynold
is full of cautious and doubtful fears about the ability of th
painter to accomplish anything without forcing his mind to
vacuous stupor of contemplative inertia. He says, for instance

The mind is but a barren soil; a soil which is soon exhausted and wil
produce no crop.

Blake faced with such a remark is rather in the position of th
profane man who cannot "do the subject justice"; but he doe
his best, taking refuge in the heaven-defying blasphemy of th
Pharisee's prayer:

The mind that could have produced this Sentence must have been a Pitiful, a Pitiable Imbecillity. I always thought that the Human Mind was the most Prolific of All Things & Inexhaustible. I certainly do Thank God that I am not like Reynolds.[15]

Closely akin to this distrust of the unifying subject and dependence on some "outside" crutch or prop for it is the use of a generalized technical formula. In poetry, for instance, we find Dryden and Pope adopting a ready-made heroic couplet and using it as a Procrustean bed to stretch all their ideas upon. In all genuine art the finished product is the exact shape of the conception, and it is impossible that a long poem in couplets can avoid being formless for more than a few lines at a time. The artist cannot achieve complete control of his medium without complete freedom to do so. The only "free verse" worth reading is verse that is free to reproduce with perfect accuracy every detail of the content in the form. To the objection that Pope has as much right to work his poem out in couplets as Blake has to work his picture out in a rectangle, Blake would perhaps have said that the rectangle is one of the boundaries of the medium, like language in poetry, whereas the couplet is a barrier thrown across the medium.

Blake regards what he considers the unimaginative recurrence of the couplet as a step in the direction of the freezing of art into "outward Ceremony." In nature, along with the frozen love of the mating etiquette of animals and the frozen economy of the insect state, we have frozen art-forms like the peacock's tail and the nightingale's song, beautiful of course, but capable only of repetition and not of recreation. The repetitive and imitative instincts go together, leading art downward into a hell of narrowing circles.

It is much better to travel in the opposite direction. We are all born in dependence upon an outer world, and only gradually learn to unite it to our minds. Hence repetition and imitation are the beginning of art; they are what we call practice. There can be nothing effortless for the powerful imagination bursting its way out of a fallen world. Nothing sluggish or inert has any place in art, and that is why art is difficult:

Without Unceasing Practise nothing can be done. Practise is Art. If you leave off you are Lost.[16]

This practice consists of "making many Finish'd Copies both of Nature & Art & of whatever comes in his way from Earliest Childhood"[17]; that is, of copying pictures and drawing from models. All young artists must go through a discipline so incessant and grueling that only genuine talent can supply the energy to drive through it and the ambition to emerge from it a master and not a plodder. Plodding, or mechanically repeated imitation, of course gets nowhere; but it will usually be found that the plodder's inability to turn a fully balanced imagination on his practice will make it even mechanically imperfect. "Servile Copying is the Great Merit of Copying,"[18] said Blake: the plodder is apt to generalize, not seeing either a picture or a model with the precise accuracy of genius.

All genuine lovers of art must agree that there can be no substitute for inborn genius and inspiration: in art there is no "moral virtue" of the kind that considers it unfair to discriminate against a man because he cannot help his lack of talent. But there is a difference between the amateurish and the professional conception of an inspired genius. To the professional the inspired genius is primarily a skilled laborer, and the greatest artists those in whom inspiration and craftsmanship coincide. Hence a society which produces great art is likely to be one that understands that the artist is a worker with a social function and the producer of goods for which there is a steady social demand. A society in which artists are socially isolated or have to live off the charity of patronage will do all the damage it can to all the genius that appears in it:

Liberality! we want not Liberality. We want a Fair Price & Proportionate Value & a General Demand for Art.[19]

· 4 ·

THE essential characteristic of mastery in art is the outline. The perceived form is particular and distinct and the abstraction general and vague because the former is real and the latter is not. The better our eyes the more clearly we see, and to see clearly is to discriminate clearly. And, Blake asks, "how do we distinguish the oak from the beech, the horse from the ox, but by the bounding outline?"[20] The outline defines the "living form," the thing we see in a coherent and integral unity. Negatively, it marks off a real thing from other real things, and prevents its disappearance into a generalized background. This is obvious enough in two dimensions; but even perception in depth is a matter of outlines, volumes and masses being only inferences from them. To draw a line is the primary step in incorporating energy in form. If a line were an infinite series of points, Zeno's paradox would be quite right; all things would be congealed in Being and movement would be impossible. But line *is* movement from one point to another: "A line is a line in its minutest subdivisions, straight or crooked. It is itself, not intermeasurable by anything else."[21] Striking out a line is a denial of all inertia and paralysis, all doubt and hesitation and reflection: it expresses the triumph of imaginative energy over a fallen world. Drawing a line asserts the reality of the particular thing against the liquid generalizations which expand indefinitely over the surface of thought. A line, therefore, is both movement and purpose: whatever the medium of the art, the line exists neither in time nor space, but in their eternal and infinite union:

The great and golden rule of art, as well as of life, is this: That the more distinct, sharp and wiry the bounding line, the more perfect the work of art, and the less keen and sharp, the greater is the evidence of weak imitation, plagiarism, and bungling. . . . The want of this determinate and bounding form evidences the want of idea in the artist's mind, and the pretence of the plagiary in all its branches. . . . What is it that builds a house and plants a garden, but the definite and determinate? . . . Leave out this line, and you leave out life itself; all is chaos again, and the line of the almighty must be drawn out upon it before man or beast can exist.[22]

This principle is not confined to painting. The first imaginative effort in music is also the striking-out of the melodic line, whether singly or in a pattern of counterpoint. Harmony is an inference from counterpoint, and music seen as a pattern of harmonies will vanish at once into cacophonous geometry:

Demonstration, Similitude & Harmony are Objects of Reasoning. Invention, Identity & Melody are Objects of Intuition.[23]

This seems to be Blake's only use of "intuition" as a synonym of imagination.

The power over the outline completes the victory of creation over perception. In music the systematic imitation of aural models, the songs of birds and the rippling of brooks, belongs to the more frivolous levels of the art. In Blake's opinion painting ought to have precisely the same imaginative integrity, the same freedom from external stimulus, that music has, and this is all he means when he says: "I assert for My Self that I do not behold the outward Creation." If a painter does not develop the ability to see with his mind's eye and evolve that vision into a picture, he has to depend on perception for all his subjects. And perception can suggest only minor subjects: the greatest themes, the visions of the Sistine ceiling or the Loggia, can no more be modeled from nature than a sonata can be.

All the arts are on the same level in imagination, but they differ in the readiness with which they lend themselves to imaginative treatment. The painter, unlike the composer, can only maintain the power to visualize independently of perception with a great deal of effort. When successful he finds, like all inspired artists, that his vision is often apparently involuntary. The great Ancient of Days, the frontispiece to *Europe*, hovered over a staircase for a long time before Blake painted it. But one great difficulty in the painter's way is that the tradition of painting since the Renaissance (an event which Blake, like Ruskin, regarded as an artistic disaster) has collapsed into passive dependence upon models. Hence the imaginative painter has a whole tradition to fight:

The spirit of Titian was particularly active in raising doubts concerning the possibility of executing without a model, and when once he had raised the doubt, it became easy for him to snatch away the vision time after time, for, when the Artist took his pencil to execute his ideas, his power of imagination weakened so much and darkened, that memory of nature, and of Pictures of the various schools possessed his mind. . . .[24]

Even the stupidest realist, of course, is forced to admit the necessity of "selection," which is only a dull and negative way of saying that all form in art comes from the mind. But what "selection" usually means is that the artist is afraid to proceed without a Lockian guarantee of reality: he waits until he finds something in nature which affords an external and unconscious resemblance to a work of art, and the work of art he makes from it preserves the memory of its resemblance to nature.

Blake however has his own version of the sublime and beautiful antithesis. The visionary, we remember, has two sciences, the science of wrath and the science of pity: the former the explosion of energy, the latter its fruit and incorporation. The two words "prophet" and "artist" point to a contrast between the Dionysiac and the Apollonian, the singer of the dithyramb and the singer of the paean, running all through art. This contrast Blake calls Rintrah and Palamabron, both of whom are different aspects of himself: one may compare Schumann's Florestan and Eusebius. But this is the positive way of expressing what Burke expresses negatively. Art is produced in an imaginative state which absorbs the whole individual, and certain qualities and characteristics of such work, relative to it as abstractions always should be to real things, will appear. But an artist who starts out to create a quality of art will get nowhere. This is the worst kind of imaginative timidity: an artist who is good for anything at all must go all out for his art, and let its qualities and characteristics look after themselves. Reynolds says:

A statue in which you endeavour to unite stately dignity, youthful elegance, and stern valour, must surely possess none of these to any eminent degree.

"Why not?" snapped Blake, and his whole hatred of Reynolds is in the question.[25]

All such qualities are what Blake calls physiognomic: they are inferred from the fact that no genius is like any other genius. The artist does not seek unity; he seeks to unite various things, and the divine imagination of God is similarly a unity of varieties. "Exuberance is Beauty," says Blake: no one ever has enough imagination unless he has too much, just as a volcano is never active until it spills over. But there is no spill in imagination: exuberance is not extravagance, Blake says, for extravagance also springs from distrust in the constructive power of the mind:

Variety does not necessarily suppose deformity, for a rose & a lilly are various & both beautiful. Beauty is exuberant, but not of ugliness, but of beauty, and if ugliness is adjoin'd to beauty it is not the exuberance of beauty; so, if Rafael is hard & dry, it is not his genius but an accident acquired, for how can Substance and Accident be predicated of the same Essence? I cannot conceive. But substance gives tincture to the accident, and makes it physiognomic.[26]

The painter must copy incessantly both nature and art, but he has no right to call copies creations. When he does we have not copying but imitation, which when another work of art is the model is plagiarism. Not all plagiarism, however, is dishonest in intention: it often springs from the Burke-Reynolds theory of the existence of qualities. Thus a student is told, not to copy Raphael, but to imitate Raphael's style, as though that were something detachable from Raphael. Or he is told to imitate the good qualities of painters and avoid their bad ones, or to add the coloring of Titian, the lighting of Correggio, the vigor of Rubens, the softness of Raphael, all together and make himself a supreme painter. If the eclectic were nothing more than a kind of offal-eating jackal of painting, he would still be bad enough, but he is worse: he is the man who tries to assimilate art to science, wisdom to knowledge, the individual view of an eternal world for an anonymous improvement in time. Science and improvement are all right in their way, but their way is not that of art, except within the advance of the individual from apprentice to master. Art never improves, even when social conditions do. There are no "Dark Ages" and no light ones[27]: genius is not made hereditary even by teaching, and all talk of "tradition," in the sense of a progressive improvement from one age to another, is only pedantic jargon. There is a place for this conception in Blake, as we shall see, but it is a different one from that which is usually assigned it by evolutionary views of art:

If Art was Progressive We should have had Mich. Angelos & Rafaels to Succeed & to Improve upon each other. But it is not so. Genius dies with its Possessor & comes not again till Another is Born with it.

Milton, Shakspeare, Michael Angelo, Rafael, the finest specimens of Ancient Sculpture and Painting and Architecture, Gothic, Grecian, Hindoo and Egyptian, are the extent of the human mind. The human mind cannot go beyond the gift of God, the Holy Ghost. To suppose that Art can go beyond the finest specimens of Art that are now in the world, is not knowing what Art is; it is being blind to the gifts of the spirit.[28]

· 5 ·

BAD painting will always go with a bad theory of knowledge, and will always be based on withdrawal, reflection, the oversimplified or shorthand equivalents for perception, which abstract ideas afford. Logically, complete generalization can have no perceptive form at all: it can only produce a picture of the plague of darkness even more thoroughgoing than Turner's, or renounce painting altogether in favor of the bare canvas, like the man in Mr. Huxley's *Crome Yellow*. The next best form of abstraction is camouflage, the art of concealing things against a general background.

There are two factors in camouflage: the concealment of outline and the unifying of color. The latter includes making light and shade independent of form. Camouflage is of course designed to baffle the eye, and works of pure camouflage are only puzzles. Another form of puzzle is provided by the painter who uses darkness as a positive basis and light as a sporadic scattering of it. The Dutch pictures with a candle in the center and the rest of the picture shading off to blackness at the edges are typical of this, and even Rembrandt and Vermeer do the same thing in subtler ways. They paint light, and they stress the difficulty and effort of seeing by means of it. Blake would not mind this "cold light & hot shade"[29] as an occasional paradox or *tour de force*. "A point of light is a Witticism,"[30] he says: the remark opens up an interesting association between Baroque painting and the metaphysical wit of Baroque poetry. But, taken seriously, it appeals to people for whom recollection in the dark is more reasonable than seeing in the light; for whom concealment, separation and mystery are fundamental data. As a systematic method of painting, it is a systematic assault upon vision. A hideous and gloomy brown sauce, a perfect image of a generalization, is spilled over the canvas, and through it, if we can find the right dark corner, we may dimly descry some spectral and ghostly evocation of the commonplace:

> Call that the Public Voice which is their Error,
> Like as a Monkey peeping in a Mirror
> Admires all his colours brown & warm
> And never once percieves his ugly form.[31]

It is not likely that Blake would have found much kinder words for those painters who, like Claude or Turner, are interested in light rather than darkness, as long as their outlines also blur into color-abstractions.

The unifying of color into a general "harmony" is the completion of this. Color is to painting what harmony is to music: an inference from the outline. And just as thinking of music as "harmonious" destroys its contrapuntal virility at once, so we can

look at a camouflaged blend of colors only with a baffled stare.
Perception in depth, the first effort of imaginative energy, becomes
impossible, and just as harmonious music is sensuous, so a painter
who is a great "colorist" demands, or rather coaxes, a nostalgic
and languid response:

Such Harmony of Colouring is destructive of Art. One species of
General Hue over all is the Cursed Thing call'd Harmony; it is like
the Smile of a Fool.[32]

All art is vigorous and controlled line-drawing: painting is
drawing on canvas; engraving is drawing on copper; music is
drawing on sound: whatever the medium, the imaginative impulse to conquer it is the same. All bad art fumbles, hesitates and
breaks up the line: all bad art has the disease of what Blake
calls "blotting and blurring." Broken volumes and masses imply
that the painter thinks of his subject as matter rather than
material; flecks and dots of color imply a mental affinity with
atomism or a Newtonian corpuscular theory of light. All attempts
to paint "atmosphere," or a generalized pictorial ether instead of
forms, are futile. No one ever paints spontaneously or easily in
this way, though it is part of the regular technique to pretend to
do so: thus the pictures of Salvator Rosa, whom Blake called "the
Quack Doctor of Painting," are "high Labour'd pretensions to
Expeditious Workmanship."[33] The output of Rubens is explained
by the fact that he employed "Journeymen": that is, "Rubens"
means a factory rather than an individual artist.

The response of the mind to an external stimulus develops an
art of accidental discovery. To stumble upon something especially
appropriate for painting may well be a pleasant minor occurrence
in art. The result is a kind of lucky or witty epigram: we have
already noticed that Blake speaks of the "point of light" school of
Dutch Baroque as epigrammatic. In our day photography, apart
from portraits, has a gnomic appeal of this kind, and Blake would
have considered a medium more mechanical than painting better
suited to it. Taking such accidents to be primary instead of
occasional gives us, in painting, the heresy of the picturesque,
which is only one of the many forms of ready-made subject. The
picturesque, whether found in the quack doctor Rosa or not, is
a type of art which takes wonder, or the contemplating of the

quizzical, to be an end as well as a beginning of imagination, and hence implies that the found object or random vision is of oracular significance.

Romantic or atmospheric painting we have already described as sacrificing detail for generalized unity. The realist painter has as different method of fogging the outlines which we have not yet touched on, but which is a necessary consequence of sacrificing unity for irrelevant detail. Every object in a picture has its primary and secondary outlines: a tree has its trunk and its leaves; a man has his body and his clothes; a room has its proportions and its furnishings. And while everything in a picture must be equally clear, every form has a pictorial center of rhythm from which all the rest flows. In drawing a clothed human figure this is obvious: "The Drapery is formed alone by the Shape of the Naked,"[34] said Blake. Eloquence and significance in drapery cannot exist except in relation to a body. This is why all the human figures in Blake's paintings are either naked or clad in the filmiest of nightdresses. Realism reverses this process and achieves a world of clothes, furniture and food, *Sartor Resartus* upside down, with clothes symbolizing reality and living things the evanescent. It takes particular pleasure in painting stuffed and starched garments which conceal the outlines of the body, in the inanimate complications of overdecorated rooms, in kitchens filled with dead game, pots, kettles and rubbish.

Blake frequently ridicules the triviality of mind which he considers such an attitude to painting shows, though he usually remains on the safe ground of defending free-flowing rhythm against fussy lifelessness:

> A Pair of Stays to mend the Shape
> Of crooked, Humpy Woman
> Put on, O Venus! now thou art
> Quite a Venetian Roman.[35]

But he has a deeper objection which would apply to better painting than this. Still life, or, in the more Blakean French phrase, *nature morte*, has proved an especially attractive subject to painters because it illustrates some of the most essential problems of the art. Besides, if the visionary is to see the world in a grain of sand, the intensity with which Cézanne saw apples or Van Gogh an old pair of boots is visionary in the best Blakean sense. But to Blake art exists in both time and space at once, and anything that concentrates on the spatial aspects of painting turns an accident of that medium into its essence. Hence it takes us back to the fatal doctrine that the solid and motionless is real and substantial whereas living things are motivated by something more ghostly and elusive. "Apples don't move," as Cézanne is said to have barked at a restless sitter. The line of thought here is moving away from vision into "mathematic form."

To Blake it is the life in things, the holy man in the cloud and the greybeard in the thistle, that the painter should evoke. Hence there are two kinds of symmetry, the living symmetry of the organism and the dead symmetry of the diagram. Art should be an organic unit of living symmetries, and to the vivid or lively imagination trees become nymphs and the sun an Apollo. The purely mathematical symbol of Egyptian pyramid is the product of a fantastically inert tyranny: its builder, in Blake's drawing, has a face combining stupidity and ferocity in a hideously self-satisfied leer. Even in Classical art, notably architecture, symmetry seems to exist for its own sake. The Gothic cathedral, on the other hand, is a huge reservoir of life: the springing spires and the grinning monsters bursting out of waterspouts, corbels, misericordias and archways quiver with the exuberance which is beauty to Blake. Apparently medieval artists were not sophisticated enough to think that the dead is more solid and permanent than the alive.

Similarly, the grotesque springing from exuberance is healthy art: the grotesque springing from "jealousy" is morbid. There is no ugliness to Blake except that which is produced by the "incapability of intellect"[36]; but still a study of life which suggests its imprisonment in death, which evokes Hamlet's incubus of corruption and disease, may well become injurious to art. Caricature of the type we find in Rowlandson is a by-product of the systematic distortion of the imagination, the putting of a corset on the mind instead of on Venus, which attempts to focus the imagination on some hidden reality behind the thing seen.[37] Blake also would probably have said that the astigmatic vision which runs through painting from El Greco to cubism is an experimental distorting of the mind as well, and that naïve fantastic painting out of the subconscious such as we have in Redon (the Douanier Rousseau is much closer to Blake and has been compared with him) also eliminates too much of the imagination.

· 6 ·

EVERYTHING Blake most hated in thought and life was deepened and intensified after his death, and painting is no exception. Impressionism in particular, with its breaking down of outline into color, its interest in scientific theories of light, and its laborious photographic detail, is a more complete denial of Blake's doctrines than anything he ever saw. It would be interesting to have his comments on Seurat. At the same time we should realize that much of Blake's intolerance was the partiality of loneliness. What to him was the unvarying dullness and monotony of the art of his time did not seem to him altogether an accidental result of blundering: it seemed to him to have some connection with the fact that his half-century of competent work was passed in poverty and neglect. Every year of his life proved to him conclusively that the art of Reynolds and Gainsborough was an essential part of the whole structure of Lockian philosophy, Deist religion, social injustice and warfare. In other words, his independence as an artist involved him, as the public had already been involved, in the vast network of commercial conspiracy by which dealers, critics and factory-painters got their pictures sold. As he says:

Commerce Cannot endure Individual Merit; its insatiable Maw must be fed by What all can do Equally well; at least it is so in England, as I have found to my Cost these Forty Years.[38]

But the antagonism between Blake and much of the modern spirit is deeper than this. Blake felt that art is infinitely great and must be equally so in all aspects; therefore he fought every tendency to throw a whole genius behind any one of these aspects. Piecemeal experimental exploration of art, such as science makes of nature, seemed to him to depend on a skillful use of formulas rather than on genuine vision. An ism in art is evidence in itself that the imagination of each believer in it is imperfect. Art should be as good as possible, and avoid distorting theories. In short, Blake felt that all theories of art were wrong *ipso facto* because art is more comprehensive than any theory about it; and he expressed this in a theory of his own which caused him to reject nine-tenths of post-Raphaelite painting. The rejections may be set aside: his defense of the dignity and importance of the art and of the responsibility of the possessor of vision is of lasting value. It is one thing to say that there is no natural religion, and another thing to say that there is no natural art, and to defend it by a lifetime of skilled and confident workmanship.

Even within Blake's own work, however, it is not so much the artists he attacks as those he defends that perplex the reader. However unfair or even silly he may be about Titian or Rembrandt, one can at any rate see what his point is; but can we really accept Giulio Romano, or the Carraccis, or even Poussin, as examples of what he wanted?[39] For Blake knew even Michelangelo and Raphael largely by prints; and it is impossible not to feel that had he ever really seen Raphael's work he would have entered at least as many caveats against him as he did against Milton or Swedenborg. His attitude brings him much closer to medieval art than to the Renaissance: he speaks highly of the Florentines, but even they have a good deal of "mathematic form" and reliance on nature in them, and it is clear that we cannot align Blake with the "pre-Raphaelites" who so stressed the latter quality. Perhaps it is only in the Sienese Trecento, where eloquent outline was the language of an imaginative vision of unequalled integrity and power, that the real spiritual ancestors of Blake are to be found.

Blake quotes with much resentment the remark of Gainsborough that the worst painters always choose the grandest subjects[40]: it is the sort of remark that encourages one to forget that the best painters choose them too. The question then arises of what the subject-matter for the painter who is independent of natural models should be, and this is a question which we can only answer by shifting the ground of discussion to poetry. And in dealing with this we find ourselves confronted at once with the word "symbolism," just as in dealing with his thought we found ourselves confronted with "mystic." Blake, we said, does not call himself a mystic but a visionary, and we are now in a position to see that it is much safer not to call him a mystic at all. He does not use the word "symbolism" either: we do not propose to draw the very radical conclusion that his poetry is not symbolic, but we do say that most of the meanings attached to the word are irrelevant to Blake.

WHEN we perceive, or rather reflect on, the general, we perceive as an ego: when we perceive as a mental form, or rather create, we perceive as part of a universal Creator or Perceiver, who is ultimately Jesus. Jesus is the Logos or Word of God, the totality of creative power, the universal visionary in whose mind we perceive the particular. But the phrase "Word of God" is obviously appropriate also to all works of art which reveal the same perspective, these latter being recreations of the divine vision which is Jesus. The archetypal Word of God, so to speak, sees this world of time and space as a single creature in eternity and infinity, fallen and redeemed. This is the vision of God (subjective genitive: the vision which God in us has). In this world the Word of God is the aggregate of works of inspired art, the Scripture written by the Holy Spirit which spoke by the prophets. Properly interpreted, all works of art are phases of that archetypal vision. The vision of the Last Judgment, said Blake, "is seen by the Imaginative Eye of Every one according to the situation he holds."[1] And the greater the work of art, the more completely it reveals the gigantic myth which is the vision of this world as God sees it, the outlines of that vision being creation, fall, redemption and apocalypse.

The Bible is the world's greatest work of art and therefore has primary claim to the title of God's Word. It takes in, in one immense sweep, the entire world of experience from the creation to the final vision of the City of God, embracing heroic saga, prophetic vision, legend, symbolism, the Gospel of Jesus, poetry and oratory on the way. It bridges the gap between a lost Golden Age and the time that the Word became flesh and dwelt among us, and it alone gives us the vision of the life of Jesus in this world. For some reason or other the Jews managed to preserve an imaginative tradition which the Greeks and others lost sight of, and possessed only in disguised and allegorical forms. The Classical poets, says Blake:

Assert that Jupiter usurped the Throne of his Father, Saturn, & brought on an Iron Age & Begat on Mnemosyne, or Memory, The Greek Muses, which are not Inspiration as the Bible is. Reality was Forgot,

& the Vanities of Time & Space only Remember'd & call'd Reality. Such is the Mighty difference between Allegoric Fable & Spiritual Mystery. Let it here be Noted that the Greek Fables originated in Spiritual Mystery & Real Visions, which are lost & clouded in Fable & Allegory, while the Hebrew Bible & the Greek Gospel are Genuine, Preserv'd by the Saviour's Mercy. The Nature of my Work is Visionary or Imaginative; it is an Endeavour to Restore what the Ancients call'd the Golden Age.[2]

We shall come to this distinction between allegory and vision in a moment. There are two obvious inferences from the passage: first, that Blake's poetry is all related to a central myth; and secondly, that the primary basis of this myth is the Bible, so that if we know how Blake read the Bible "in its infernal or diabolical sense"[3] we shall have little difficulty with his symbolism. The central principle of this diabolic interpretation is that the Bible is one poem, completely consistent in imagery and symbolism. Blake cared nothing about questions of authorship or historical accuracy: no one expects poetry, legend and saga to be reliable history or to come down to us ascribed to the right authors:

I cannot concieve the Divinity of the books in the Bible to consist either in who they were written by, or at what time, or in the historical evidence which may be all false in the eyes of one man & true in the eyes of another, but in the Sentiments & Examples, which, whether true or Parabolic, are Equally useful. . . .[4]

Nor did he care, in spite of the somewhat un-Blakean sound of "Sentiments & Examples," that Jehovah often urges a ferocious cruelty extremely repugnant to a civilized mind: if one gives up the attempt to extract a unified moral code out of the Bible this becomes a profoundly true vision of a false god. So Blake was ready to give a tolerant and sympathetic reading either to Swedenborg's *True Christian Religion* or to Paine's *Age of Reason*. His own ideas of the Bible were unaffected by Paine's iconoclasm, but he considered that the latter might be useful in breaking up a good deal of stupid orthodoxy: in doing that Paine was working for Christianity, and against only the socially accepted perversion of it, or Antichrist.

The Bible is therefore the archetype of Western culture, and the Bible, with its derivatives, provides the basis for most of our major art: for Dante, Milton, Michelangelo, Raphael, Bach, the great cathedrals, and so on. The most complete form of art is a cyclic vision, which, like the Bible, sees the world between the two poles of fall and redemption. In Western art this is most clearly represented in the miracle-play sequences and encyclopedic symbolism of the Gothic cathedrals, which often cover the entire imaginative field from creation to the Last Judgment, and always fit integrally into some important aspect of it.

However, while "The Old & New Testaments are the Great Code of Art,"[5] to regard them as forming a peculiar and exclusive Word of God is a sectarian error, the same one that the Jews made and that proved such a disaster to them. All myths and rituals hint darkly and allegorically at the same visions that we find in the Bible, which is why they have such a strong resemblance to Christian myths and rituals, a resemblance explained by early Church Fathers as diabolic parodies or Bibles of Hell, as Blake calls his own prophecies. There are many great visions outside the range of the Bible, such as the Icelandic Eddas and the *Bhagavadgita*, almost equally faithful to the central form of the Word of God, and the Bible no less than Classical legends comes from older and more authentic sources. For when Blake speaks of "the Stolen and Perverted Writings of Homer & Ovid," "set up by artifice against the Sublime of the Bible,"[6] he is not only implying the old Philonic doctrine that Plato and Ovid got their creation myths from Moses: he is also hinting at older Scriptures still from which the Bible itself has been derived:

The antiquities of every Nation under Heaven, is no less sacred than that of the Jews. . . . How other antiquities came to be neglected and disbelieved, while those of the Jews are collected and arranged, is an enquiry worthy both of the Antiquarian and the Divine.[7]

This feeling that the Bible does not exhaust the Word of God accounts for the phenomenon of what we may call contrapuntal symbolism, that is, the use of un-Christian mythology, usually Classical, to supplement and round out a Christian poem.

The cyclic vision in poetry is the true epic, whether based on the Bible, as in Dante and Milton, or outside its direct influence. The Classical epic represented by Homer and Virgil, which makes a rule of beginning in the middle, Blake thought comparatively formless[8]: much closer to his ideas are the more easy-going epics like Ovid's *Metamorphoses*, which starts at the creation and works down; or, in fact, even the philosophical epics which also deal with cosmological themes, like *De Rerum Natura*. So are the Gnostic systems, which are intolerably dull and puzzling considered as abstract theologies, but might have more interest if read as epic poems. The *Légendes des Siècles* indicate that the drawing-up of huge cyclic schemes did not perish with Blake, though perhaps only in *Back to Methusaleh* has English literature a contemporary example of a complete cyclic form.

The meaning of history, like the meaning of art, is to be found in its relation to the same great archetype of human existence. The inner form of history is not the same thing as the progress of time: a linear chronicle is a wild fairy tale in which the fate of an empire hangs on the shape of a beauty's nose, or the murder of a noble moron touches off a world war. And no poet concerned with human beings ever bothers to draw an individual as such: he is concerned with selecting the significant aspects of him. Significant in relation to what? In relation to the unity of his conception. But what makes that conception worth conceiving in the first place? Its relation, Blake would say, to the primary Word of God. We say that there is something universal in Quixote, Falstaff, Hamlet, Milton's Satan. But "something universal" is rather vague: just what is universal about them? As soon as we attempt to answer this, we begin in spite of ourselves to elaborate our own versions of the archetypal myth. The true epic is a cyclic vision of life, and the true drama, including narrative and heroic poetry, is an episode of that cyclic vision, just as Greek tragedies were slices from the Homeric banquet. Great art, therefore, is more conventional than most people realize, and if Chaucer and Shakespeare are read in their "infernal or diabolic sense" we shall find in them the same imaginative conceptions that we find in the cyclic visions. As Blake points out, the witches in *Macbeth* are the same three goddesses of destiny we meet in the Norns and Fates.[9] Of Chaucer Blake says:

Chaucer's characters live age after age. Every age is a Canterbury Pilgrimage; we all pass on, each sustaining one or other of these characters; nor can a child be born, who is not one of these characters of Chaucer. . . . Thus the reader will observe, that Chaucer makes every one of his characters perfect in his kind; every one is an Antique Statue; the image of a class, and not of an imperfect individual.[10]

· 2 ·

IN the artist the difference between the time-bound ego and the imaginative state in which great things are done is even more sharply marked than it is in the ordinary man. The artist may be conceited, irritable, foolish or dishonest, but it makes no difference what he is: all that matters is his imagination. We speak of So-and-So "the Man," meaning So-and-So when he is not being a poet; but it is only when So-and-So is using the imagination which is the "Real Man" and writing poetry that he is a man: the rest of the time he is on the ordinary Generation plane. That is why some of the greatest poets, Homer and Shakespeare for instance, hardly seem to have had a personal existence at all. They are inspired; that is, incarnations of the ability to write. As Blake goes on he becomes more and more impressed by the contrast between a man's imagination, his real life as expressed in the total form of his creative acts, and his ordinary existence; and he devotes a good deal of the first part of *Jerusalem* to working out the conflict between them.

Hence it is a blunder to limit the meaning of art to what the artist may be presumed to have intended. The artist's "intentions" are often on levels of consciousness quite unknown to himself. Some of these levels are subconscious and some superconscious: the latter may need the passing of centuries to clarify. The poet's "Spectre" may be dull, wrong-headed or erratic: the plain meaning of his imagination the poet may perfectly well repudiate as a "man." He is often a bad critic of his own work and is capable of saying inadequate and misleading things about it. Wordsworth will introduce his poems with comments like this:

Now the music of harmonious metrical language, the sense of difficulty overcome, and the blind association of pleasure which has been previously received from works of rhyme or metre of the same or similar construction, and indistinct perception perpetually renewed of language closely resembling that of real life, and yet, in the circumstance of metre, differing from it so widely—all these imperceptibly make up a complex feeling of delight, which is of the most important use in tempering the painful feeling always found intermingled with powerful descriptions of the deeper passions.

"I do not know who wrote these Prefaces," said Blake: "they are very mischievous & direct contrary to Wordsworth's own Practise."[11] One would never guess, from all this twaddle about "blind association," "indistinct perception," lukewarm tempering of passion, and meter as a difficult way of distorting prose, that its author could be capable of the clear-cut visions of the Lucy poems. Wordsworth's "Spectre" has obviously no right to open its mouth on the subject of Wordsworth's poetry, of which it knows nothing whatever.

The poet's meaning, then, is often quite different from what he may think he thought he meant, and in any case it is cumulative. Few great poets would be able to understand the reason for their fame in the following century. The inference is that all genuine poetry is something quite separate from the person who wrote it. A poem is like a child, an independently living being not fully born until the navel-string has been cut.

The lyric is no exception to this rule of objectivity. The poet can express himself in a lyric only by dramatizing the mental state or mood he is in, and the imaginative truth of the lyric refers to his state and not to himself. One may pass through state after state with bewildering rapidity: one may experience ten or twelve states of love or passion in as many seconds. But to create one must balance and harmonize one's states, and what one creates takes its unity of tone and mood from that stabilization. The lyric, then, is normally a snapshot or single vision of an imaginative state by a poet who is in but not necessarily of it, and Blake's engraved lyrics are grouped around the primary division of states into those of innocence and those of experience.

Of course a poet may give many useful suggestions about his own work, but we read the poem, not the poet, except by a figure of speech. Hence the primary activity of all communication with the poet is to establish the unity of his poem in our minds. We have quoted Blake as saying that every poem is necessarily a perfect unity. This unity has two aspects: a unity of words and a unity of images.

· 3 ·

BLAKE says very little about diction in poetry, and our account of his ideas on this point will have to take the form of a conjectural reconstruction; but the poet who said, and apparently meant, that "Poetry admits not a Letter that is Insignificant" must have had strong feelings about it.

Those who accept the Baconian and Lockian principle that words are the spectral ghosts of real things existing outside the mind will be hampered by several misconceptions which will forever prevent them from understanding what poetry is and why it exists. It is characteristic of people with vague minds and wandering attentions to speak of literature as "just a lot of words," meaning that words are inadequate and misleading substitutes for real things which the weakness and opacity of our minds compel us to adopt. But the assumption is false. If a tree fell in an uninhabited forest, would there be any sound? If sound means only waves set up in the air, yes; if it means waves set up in the air and striking a mind through its ear, no. But the latter meaning of sound is the only one that has any sense as well as sound. On the same principle, an object that has received a name is more real by virtue of it than an object without one. A thing's name is its numen, its imaginative reality in the eternal world of the human mind. That is another reason why Jesus is called the Word of God. Reality is intelligibility, and a poet who has put things into words has lifted "things" from the barren chaos of nature into the created order of thought. The Preacher says wearily that of making many books there is no end: the Apostle John, in the full exuberance of the spirit released in him by Jesus, proclaims that the world is not nearly big enough to hold all that might be written about the Word.[12]

Now as all creative power is human and not natural, it follows that words are of the pattern of the human mind and not that of nature—though of course nature has no pattern either apart from the mind. Therefore the meaning of a word does not depend on its relation to an outside world. The Baconian mind strives to make every word reproduce one definite "thing" or one reflected "idea," to the exclusion of all others: it is perpetually demanding definition in the sense of establishing a general law for each word that will meet every case. This cannot be done. A word's meaning depends partly on its context and partly on its relation to the mind of its hearer: all general meanings are only approximate. To the poet the word is a storm-center of meanings, sounds and associations, radiating out indefinitely like the ripples of a pool. It is precisely because of this indefiniteness that he writes poems. The poem is a unity of words in which these radiations have

ecome the links of imaginative cohesion. In a poem the sounds
nd rhythms of words are revealed more clearly than in ordinary
peech, and similarly their meanings have an intensity in poetry
hat a dictionary can give no hint of.

This respect for the imaginative integrity of poetry is the reason
or Blake's distrust of set patterns of meter and rhyme. Only
yrics, and not many of them, can be in a strict stanzaic form:
onger works must have much greater fluency if the sound, sense
nd subject are to make a complete correspondence at all times.
3lake says of his *Jerusalem*:

When this Verse was first dictated to me, I consider'd a Monotonous
Cadence, like that used by Milton & Shakespeare & all writers of
English Blank Verse, derived from the modern bondage of Rhyming,
o be a necessary and indispensible part of Verse. But I soon found
hat in the mouth of a true Orator such monotony was not only awk-
ward, but as much a bondage as rhyme itself. I therefore have pro-
luced a variety in every line, both of cadences & number of syllables.
Every word and every letter is studied and put into its fit place; the
errific numbers are reserved for the terrific parts, the mild & gentle
or the mild & gentle parts, and the prosaic for inferior parts; all are
necessary to each other.[13]

It is interesting that Blake cheerfully admits what to Poe was a
fatal objection to the long poem, that it occasionally must lapse
into the prosaic.

· 4 ·

THE question of the unity of imagery in poetry brings us to the
question of the right and wrong kinds of allegory referred to in
the opening chapter. A poem's "meaning" is its existence: as a
modern poet has said, poetry should not mean but be. Our understanding of it must be, like all understanding, "not by deduction,
but Immediate by Perception or Sense at once." In order to attain
this unified vision, a good deal of explanation may be necessary.
Poets are likely to be, as Gabriel Harvey says, curious universal
scholars, dealing with complex material in a very erudite way.
But when this explanation ceases to be a means to the end of
unifying the poem in our minds, and comes to be thought of as
the real form of the poem, everything goes wrong, and all the
poem's infinite variety is staled at once.

Hence what is usually called allegory, that is, art the meaning

of which points away from itself toward something else which i
not art, is a profane abomination. It would be far better if th
morals of Aesop's Fables, the signposts pointing from art t
ethics, were snipped off, because all the morality worth having i
already in the story, heightened by the fact that we are not boun
down to a single conclusion. The artist must have confidence tha
the work of art will carry its own "message" without putting in a
additional one for the Spectres. The allegory which is merely
set of moral doctrines or historical facts, ornamented to mak
them easier for simple minds, is not at all the kind of thing tha
the great allegorical writers were trying to produce. If it were
Dickens' remark that the chief function of allegory seems to b
to make one's head ache would require no qualification. In thi
sense of the word, Bunyan is not allegorical but Samuel Smiles is
Dante is not but medieval homilies at their dullest are. Here i
Blake's own statement on this point:

Fable or Allegory are a totally distinct & inferior kind of Poetry. Visior
or Imagination is a Representation of what Eternally Exists, Really &
Unchangeably. Fable or Allegory is Form'd by the daughters of Mem
ory. . . . Fable is allegory, but what Critics call The Fable, is Vision
itself. The Hebrew Bible & the Gospel of Jesus are not Allegory, bu
Eternal Vision or Imagination of All that Exists. Note here that Fable
or Allegory is seldom without some Vision. Pilgrim's Progress is full
of it, the Greek Poets the same; but Allegory & Vision ought to be
known as Two Distinct Things. . . .[14]

"Allegory" in the above sense is closely related to the kind of
symbolism which is founded on the simile. To say that a hero
is *like* a lion is a reference to something else on the same imaginative plane. Subject and object, as in Lockian philosophy, are
considered to be only accidentally related. Even an epic simile
enriches the symbolism only at the price of digressing from the
narrative. The artist, contemplating the hero, searches in his
memory for something that reminds him of the hero's courage,
and drags out a lion. But here we no longer have two real things:
we have a correspondence of abstractions. The hero's courage, not
the hero himself, is what the lion symbolizes. And a lion which
symbolizes an abstract quality is not a real but a heraldic lion.
Some lions are cowardly; some are old and sick; some are cubs;
some are female. And it is no use to say that a mature courageous

male healthy lion is an "ideal" one: we should need an old and sick lion for an old and sick hero. Whenever we take our eye off the image we slip into abstractions, into regarding qualities, moral or intellectual, as more real than living things. So Blake opposes to "Similitude" the "Identity," the latter being the metaphor which unites the theme and the illustration of it. Let us quote again a passage we have given before and put it beside a new one:

Harmony and Proportion are Qualities & not Things. The Harmony & Proportion of a Horse are not the same with those of a Bull. Every Thing has its own Harmony & Proportion, Two Inferior Qualities in it. For its Reality is its imaginative Form.

Aristotle says Characters are either Good or Bad; now Goodness or Badness has nothing to do with Character: an Apple tree, a Pear tree, a Horse, a Lion are Characters, but a Good Apple tree or a Bad is an Apple tree still; a Horse is not more a Lion for being a Bad Horse: that is its Character: its Goodness or Badness is another consideration.[15]

All symbolism that deals with qualities has too many bad qualities of its own to be of any use to art. Hence we must not expect to find in Blake any kind of personification, or attempt to give life to an abstraction. When we read in *The Four Zoas* that Los attempts to embrace Enitharmon but that she is jealous and goes over to the embraces of Urizen, it is neither very helpful nor very interesting to translate that as: "Time or Prophecy attempts to overcome Space but Space falls under the domination of Reason." The continuous translation of poetic images into a series of moral and philosophical concepts is what usually passes for the explanation of an allegory. Now a reconstruction of a poem in abstract nouns is not necessarily a false interpretation of part of its meaning. But it is a translation, which means that it assumes the reader's ignorance of the original language.

· 5 ·

ONCE again we see that art is neither inferior nor equal to morality and truth, but the synthesis of civilized life in which alone their general laws have any real meaning. Art is neither good nor bad, but a clairvoyant vision of the nature of both, and any attempt to align it with morality, otherwise called bowdlerizing, is intolerably vulgar. "Is not every Vice possible to Man," asked Blake, "described in the Bible openly?"[16] Art is neither true nor false, but a clairvoyant vision of the nature of both, and any attempt to estimate its merits by the accuracy with which it reproduces the data of history or science is foolish. A subtler problem, once again, is presented by religion, which claims to be the synthesis of morality and truth we have said that art is, and hence to be superior to it.

Let us go back to the eleventh plate of *The Marriage of Heaven and Hell,* already mentioned:

The ancient Poets animated all sensible objects with Gods or Geniuses, calling them by the names and adorning them with the properties of woods, rivers, mountains, lakes, cities, nations, and whatever their enlarged & numerous senses could percieve. . . .

Till a system was formed, which some took advantage of, & enslav'd the vulgar by attempting to realize or abstract the mental deities from their objects: thus began Priesthood;

Choosing forms of worship from poetic tales.

And at length they pronounc'd that the Gods had order'd such things.

Thus men forgot that All deities reside in the human breast.

Now just as the poet is brought up to speak and write one particular language, so he is brought up in the traditions of one particular religion. And his function as a poet is to concentrate on the myths of that religion, and to recreate the original imaginative life of those myths by transforming them into unique works of art. The essential truth of a religion can be presented only in its essential form, which is that of imaginative vision. "Every thing possible to be believ'd is an image of truth"; in which case everything possible to be believed by the ordinary man is actually to be seen by the visionary. The human imagination knows that man fell: the Biblical story of Adam and Eve is a vision of that fact which has frozen into a myth. Milton's reason told him that that story was "true"; his imagination told him that it was an image of truth, and stimulated him to recreate it in that form.

The artist *qua* artist neither doubts nor believes his religion: he sees what it means, and he knows how to illustrate it. His religion performs two great services for him. It provides him with a generally understood body of symbols, and it puts into his hands the visionary masterpieces on which it is founded: the Bible particularly, in the case of Christian poets. Many of these latter have petrified into sacred Scriptures supposed now to impart exclusive formulas of salvation rather than vision. It is the business of a poet, however, to see them as poems, and base his own poetry on them as such.

To do this he must bring out more sharply and accurately what the human mind was trying to do when it first created the beings we now call gods. Jupiter is a sky-god: he is a product of the imaginative tendency to see the sky as an old man, as Blake sees the thistle, and not as an abstraction called Heaven. Originally he was conceived as a tyrannical old bully because he represented the imaginative feeling of a hostile mystery in the sky-world. Venus became a beautiful harlot because the imagination sees "nature" as a woman and finds her lovely but treacherous. As the original "organized men," or "Giant forms,"[17] dwindle into gods, the clarity of their relationship to the archetypal myth becomes blurred, and irrelevant stories and attributes cluster around them. They become increasingly vague and general until, in their final stages, they are mere personifications; and by the time that Phoebus and Philomela have become highbrow synonyms for the sun and the nightingale, they have disappeared.

It is only in works of art that these hazy divinities can be provided with a distinctive context and given a particular meaning. "Venus" means nothing: an Aphrodite by Phidias, the Venus of Shakespeare's *Venus and Adonis*, the Venus of Lucretius' *De Rerum Natura*, do mean something, though very different things. Once again we come back to the point that religion is raw imaginative material clarified by art.

This is why we meet so many new names in Blake and find ourselves reading about Vala and Urizen instead of Venus and Zeus. It may be thought that the more familiar names would make the Prophecies easier, but actually it would make them more difficult. To Venus and Zeus we bring memories and associations rather than a concentrated response, and are thus continually impelled to search outside the poem being read for its meaning. And as no two poets can possibly mean the same thing by "Venus," we should have to go through a long process of discarding misleading associations which the use of a new name prevents at once. Those who think that a greater writer would be less exacting are under an illusion. Some poets, including Homer, Chaucer and Shakespeare, present a smooth readable surface for the lazy reader to slide over: others, including Dante, Spenser and Blake, make it impossible for any reader to overlook the fact that they contain deeper meanings. The wails of protest which the latter group arouses show only that the real profundity of the former group has not been touched. Blake has tried to show us, in his essay on Chaucer, how inadequate it is to bring preconceived notions of medieval monks and friars and merry widows to the *General Prologue*. It follows, of course, that the familiar names we do find in Blake, such as Reuben, Satan and Merlin, do not depend for their meaning on one's memory of Genesis, Milton or Malory.

The difference between Christianity and other religions is not the difference between truth and falsehood, for the gods of the Christian pantheon are, to the imaginative eye, the same white-whiskered tyrant, the same tortured dying god, the same remote and ineffable Queen of Heaven, that we find in all religions. Even the Bible must be shaken upside-down before it will yield all its secrets. The priests have censored and clipped and mangled: they give us a celibate Jesus born of a virgin without the slightest "stain" of sexual contact, which is blasphemous nonsense; and they tried to turn the fact that Christ came "to abolish the Jewish Imposture"[18] into an excuse for starting a new Christian imposture. The Bible is in a very special category compared with other works of art, but it too yields precedence to the imagination. (There is of course no place in Blake's thought for a "conflict" of the Bible with science: to read Genesis for biology is far sillier than to read *Macbeth* for Scottish history.) The central form of Christianity is its vision of the humanity of God and the divinity of risen Man, and this, in varying ways, is what all great Christian artists have attempted to recreate. Insofar as they regard the divinity worshiped by Christians as other than human, they produce cloudy and inaccurate visions. Milton's Satan comes off more clearly than his God because he has attempted to equate the latter with abstract goodness and perfection. There is nothing for such a God to do except recite the creed and rationalize the miserable agony of fallen man into a defense of his own virtue. Satan is human and real, a mixture of good and evil, imagination and Selfhood, and therefore has a place in a work of art.

Poetry cannot be made, either of morality and personifications, or of mythology and gods, as long as the artist considers himself to be an illustrator or a transcriber. Spenser (whom Blake does not mention but whom he had certainly read) had a tendency to personification and Milton to theology, and it is instructive to see in their work how their interest in them is always in inverse proportion to the quality of the writing. Shakespeare and Chaucer follow a sounder poetic policy. They avert their eyes from both gods and abstract nouns, and concentrate on living men and real things, on the particular rather than the general. Malbecco in Spenser "Forgot he was a man, and *Gealosie* is hight,"[19] but the characters of Shakespeare never dwindle into abstractions.

In the minds of Chaucer and Shakespeare was the universal Word of God, the archetypal vision of "All that Exists,"[20] which they had by virtue of their own genius, however much their reading may have contributed to it. They may not have been fully conscious that they possessed that vision, but that is why Othello and the Wife of Bath are not individuals but "Giant forms," exactly as Hercules and Juno originally were. They are, as we say, of universal significance, and that means precisely of the significance of the universe, the whole of life seen in the primary outlines of the human and divine mind—for Shakespeare and Chaucer, rightly understood, reveal these primary outlines just as the Bible does. If allegory means this universal significance in the artist's creation of particular things, then all art worth looking at or listening to, including music, is allegorical.

The ultimate significance of a work of art is simply a dimension added to its literal meaning, which can no more be separated from it than the depth of a pool of water can be separated from its surface. Dante says that the profoundest understanding of poetry, which he calls anagogy, "even in the literal sense, by the very things it signifies, signifies again some portion of the supernal things of eternal glory."[21] All moral, historical, political, biographical and other "interpretations" should lead us directly from the superficial to the complete apprehension of the same thing, the single image of reality which the work of art is. Dante's own *Commedia* is not affected by the fact that the geology of its hell, the geography of its purgatory, the astronomy of its paradise, are all impossible, and the theology of the whole poem rejected in part or *in toto* by many readers. Any fool knows that, but what he may not know is that the permanent form of the poem, which survives all the vacillations inseparable from "belief," is allegory addressed to the intellectual powers. The same is true of all other works of art whatever.

· 6 ·

THIS universal perception of the particular applies to natural objects as well as human forms. Ordinarily, our perception of the world is haphazard; it is often unrelated to our simultaneous mental processes, and hence when we use a real thing to "symbolize" a state of mind it seems to us only a fancied or arbitrary resemblance. At most, a natural object may symbolize a mental event because it "corresponds" to something in the mind. Here we still have Lockian dualism and its simile. But when we speak of the desire of the Selfhood or ego to restrict activity in others, it is rather inadequate to say that a prison is a "symbol" of the Selfhood. Prisons exist because Selfhoods do: they are the real things the Selfhood produces, and symbols of it only in that sense. To say that in Blake the sea is a symbol of chaos is incorrect if it assumes that "chaos" has any existence except in a number of real things which includes the sea. The sea is the image of chaos. "Image" and "form" being the same word in Blake, the sea is the form of chaos. As even chaos is only an abstract idea unless it is a perceived form, the sea is the reality of chaos.

And when we realize that everything exists in the form it does because man is fallen God, it becomes evident that all things are the realities of fall and regeneration. Art could not possess its infinite variety if archetypal visions could be represented only by a group of special symbols. In his poem called "Auguries of Innocence" Blake says:

> He who the Ox to wrath has mov'd
> Shall never be by Woman lov'd.

This is obviously not true of the state of experience: the title of the poem shows that Blake is talking about a Paradise or Beulah into which men who abuse oxen cannot enter. This "augury of innocence" is of the same order of thought as Jesus': "Blessed are the meek, for they shall inherit the earth." This is simple enough, but another couplet from the same poem is more complicated:

> The Bat that flits at close of Eve
> Has left the Brain that won't Believe.

The bat is black and prefers darkness to light. For this reason a superstitious man would see it as something ominous, and a Lockian poet would see it as a symbol of doubt. But to Blake it is neither of these things. Blake means precisely what he says. In human society everything from the Sistine ceiling to thumbscrews owes its form to man's mind and character in one of its various aspects. Similarly the character of everything in nature expresses an aspect of the human mind. We say that a snowflake has a symmetrical design, not because the snowflake has consciously produced it, but because we can see the design. We see that the snowflake has achieved something of which we alone can see the form, and the form of the snowflake is therefore a human form. It is the function of art to illuminate the human form of nature, to present the ferocity of the weasel, the docility of the sheep, the drooping delicacy of the willow, the grim barrenness of the precipice, so that we can see the character of the weasel, the sheep, the willow and the precipice. This vision of character, or total form, is something of course much more inclusive than the words given, which express only aspects of that character, can suggest.

"The man was like a lion" is a Lockian simile, an attempt to express a human character in natural terms. "The man was a lion" is a much more dramatic and effective figure, and more suggestive of their real relationship; but still it is essentially a simile with the word "like" omitted. But if we say "the lion is like a man" we are getting somewhere, and beginning to achieve the concentrated focus of the artist's vision on the lion which reveals his form to the human eye. As we proceed in our vision, everything positive and real about the lion becomes an aspect of our perception of him, and we can take the next step and say that the lion is entirely a human form, a human creature. All art interprets nature in human terms in this way, so vividly that we hardly dare admit what art tells us about the relation between tears and tempests, joy and sunshine, love and the moon, death and winter, resurrection and spring. The real bat, therefore, is that aspect of the human imagination which prefers darkness to light; and this bat is the exact opposite of the bat which is a symbol of doubt. The famous "Ghost of the Flea" similarly shows the human form of that insect.

The painted lion is not alive; the natural lion has not been emancipated into a human order. The painter's task is not a hopelessly quixotic attempt to capture his model's life, but to show its relationship to a universal human order, a Paradise in which lions owe their generation as well as their form to human minds. The most concentrated vision of the lion sees this archetypal human creature in the ferocious wildcat of nature, as Blake's poem on the tiger does. In some cases, including the flea, and perhaps the bat, this archetypal form was a product of the Fall, and would either disappear from Paradise or take on unrecognizable attributes, as in fact the Bible tells us is true of serpents.

Those who do not love living things do not love God or Man, as the Ancient Mariner found to his cost. But because some Greek poet loved the nightingale, he created from her the human figure of Philomela, and by doing so passed from love into vision, from a sensitive reaction to nature into the intelligent form of civilized human life, or Paradise. The story of Philomela is not a fantasy suggested by the nightingale, but a vision of the fall of the original human nightingale into its present natural shape. Blake says:

Think of a white cloud as being holy, you cannot love it; but think of a holy man within the cloud, love springs up in your thoughts, for to think of holiness distinct from man is impossible to the affections.[22]

But if the poet can see the world in a grain of sand, it is because he already has that archetypal vision of "All that Exists," of which everything he sees is a form or image. All Blake's poetry is related to his particular view of this vision, that "Central Form composed of all other Forms"[23] which he concedes to Reynolds. Within the huge framework of this central form, certain states of the human mind that created it inevitably appear and take on human lineaments, just as a pantheon crystallizes from a religious vision. Blake's characters are the "Giant forms" that religions worship as gods and artists visualize as "organized men."

Our next task is to outline Blake's central myth. Its boundaries, once more, are creation, fall, redemption and apocalypse, and it embraces the four imaginative levels of existence, Eden, Beulah, Generation and Ulro. It revolves around the four antitheses that we have been tracing in the first four chapters, of imagination and memory in thought, innocence and experience in religion, liberty and tyranny in society, outline and imitation in art. These four antitheses are all aspects of one, the antithesis of life and death, and Blake assumes that we have this unity in our heads.

· 7 ·

WE have dealt with Blake's point that in a perfectly imaginative state all individuals are integral units of a race, species or class, related to it as tissues and cells are to a body. This larger unit is not an abstraction or aggregate, but a larger human body or human being: the instructive ambiguity of these phrases has been noted. Hence whether we see the larger unit as one man or as a multitude of individuals is a matter of perspective. We have referred to Milton's vision of the English nation as one huge Christian personage. The most inclusive vision possible, then, is to see the universe as One Man, who to a Christian is Jesus. On nearer view Jesus is seen as a "Council of God"[24] or group of "Eternals" or Patriarchs, seen by ancient prophets as dwelling in a Golden Age of peace and happiness. On still nearer view these patriarchs, the memory of whom survives in the Bible under the accounts of Abraham, Isaac and Jacob, resolve themselves into vast numbers of individual men.

One of these Eternals, named Albion, has fallen. Albion includes, presumably, all the humanity that we know in the world of time and space, though visualized as a single Titan or giant. The history of the world from its creation, which was part of his fall, to the Last Judgment is his sleep. The yet unfallen part of God made seven attempts to awaken him, and in the seventh Jesus himself descended into the world of Generation and began his final redemption.

This myth of a primeval giant whose fall was the creation of the present universe is not in the Bible itself, but has been preserved by the Cabbala in its conception of Adam Kadmon, the universal man who contained within his limbs all heaven and earth, to whom Blake refers.[25] A somewhat more accessible form of the same myth is in the Prose Edda, a cyclic work systematizing the fragmentary apocalyptic poems of the Elder Edda, which to Blake contained traditions as antique and authentic as those of the Old Testament itself.[26] In the sleep of the giant Ymir, the Edda tells us, the earth was made of his flesh, the mountains of his bones, the heavens from his skull, the sea from his blood, the clouds from his brains—this last has a particularly Blakean touch.

The Greeks have also kept a dim memory of a Golden Age before the Fall in their legend of a lost island of Atlantis and of a giant who contained the world in the figure of Atlas, the Titan who bears the world on his back, a perfect image of the fallen Albion with nature outside him and pressing upon him, and of the etymology of that curious word "understanding." Atlantis, according to Plato's *Critias*, was settled by the god Poseidon (possibly Blake's "Ariston"), whose eldest son was Atlas: this corresponds to the English tradition, preserved in Spenser, that Albion, the eponymous ancestor of England, was the son of Neptune:

The giant Albion, was Patriarch of the Atlantic; he is the Atlas of the Greeks, one of those the Greeks called Titans.[27]

The fall of Albion included a deluge in which the center of Atlantis was overwhelmed and only the fragments of the British Isles were left. The settlement of America by the English and revolt of America against the dead hand of English tyranny is therefore the dawn of a new age in which Atlantis begins to appear above the waves. In the meantime England still exists in the spiritual world as Atlantis, and Blake's engraved poems are on its mountains.[28]

There are several accounts of the Fall in Blake which we shall summarize later, but the invariable characteristic of them is Albion's relapse from active creative energy to passivity. This passivity takes the form of wonder or awe at the world he has created, which in eternity he sees as a woman. The Fall thus begins in Beulah, the divine garden identified with Eden in Genesis. Once he takes the fatal step of thinking the object-world independent of him, Albion sinks into a sleep symbolizing the passivity of his mind, and his creation separates and becomes the "female will" or Mother Nature, the remote and inaccessible universe of tantalizing mystery we now see. Love, or the transformation of the objective into the beloved, and art, or the transformation of the objective into the created, are the two activities pursued on this earth to repair the damage of the Fall, and they raise our state to Beulah and Eden respectively.

On earth the cult of worshiping the independent object or

female will takes two chief forms. One is the superstitious reverence for a Mother God, the primitive fear of the sibyl or prophetess whom the Teutons called Vala. This is a symbolic form of nature-worship, and Blake gives the name Vala to nature in his symbolism. The other form is the worship not so much of vegetative nature as of the Queen of Heaven, the remote, mysterious beauty of the starry heavens. This produces on earth the blind devotion to a mistress who is expected to elude and tantalize the lover, the basis of the Troubadour code. The Queen of Heaven's name in Blake is Enitharmon.[29]

The fall of Albion, the company of nations living in the Golden Age, was followed at once by the appearance of the "female will." The story of Adam and Eve in the Bible, which represents a fairly late stage in the Fall, shows sin and death entering the world through a woman: the fact that Adam fell through adoration of Eve is however more clearly brought out in *Paradise Lost*. Of older provenance is the reference in Genesis to the sons of God intermarrying with the daughters of men, more fully elaborated in the Book of Enoch.[30] The story of Samson and Delilah is also, as Milton divined, another ancient myth dealing with a giant who fell through yielding to the female will; and so is the story of the murder of Sisera by Jael. The stories of Pandora and of the shutting-up of the prophet Merlin in a box by a woman are connected with the same theme, though referred to by Blake very obliquely, if at all. More important than any of these in Blake's symbolism are those five curious "daughters of Zelopehad" who wander in and out of the Hexateuch looking for a separate female inheritance.[31] One of them is named Tirzah, also the name of an Israelite capital of the Ten Tribes, and therefore a symbol of opposition to Jerusalem, the City of God. This Tirzah is associated with a beautiful woman in the Song of Songs. The five daughters represent the five senses and imply the passive dependence on sense experience which is symbolized in our being born from a mother. This is the meaning of the little poem "To Tirzah" which ends the *Songs of Experience*.

The word "emanation" in Blake means the object-world; creature in Eden, female in Beulah, object or nature in Generation, abstraction in Ulro. "Spectre" means the subjective counterpart to this in the two fallen states. Now the spiritual world is to Blake always something civilized, a city or a palace (in the highest imaginative state there would be no difference between a city and a palace, but a house of many mansions) surrounded by the garden or cultivated nature of the Biblical Paradise. Men lose the "opaque" qualities of their minds in higher imaginative states: therefore the spiritual world is a completely integrated body of imaginative men. The Christian Church is the nearest symbol of this on earth; but all visible churches are really part of a political body. This political body is symbolized in the Bible by Jerusalem, which in the Apocalypse becomes the New Jerusalem, the spiritualized church of the imaginative, the liberty of the sons of God united in brotherhood. Jerusalem is therefore the emanation of the awakened Albion. The Jesus who redeemed Albion suffered in the old Jerusalem, and when Albion awakes he will be with Jesus in the new one. The union of Albion and Jerusalem suggests a parallelism between English and Hebrew history which runs all through Blake's symbolism, and which underlies the famous hymn beginning "And did those feet in ancient time." This is natural, for the Last Judgment is seen by a poet "according to the situation he holds" and Blake's situation was that of an English Christian.

The seven attempts made by God to awaken Albion divide history into seven great periods, each with a dominating religion. These Blake identifies with the "Seven Eyes of God" mentioned in Zechariah, and he gives these "Eyes" the names of Lucifer, Moloch, the Elohim, Shaddai, Pachad, Jehovah and Jesus.[32] The "eighth eye" he occasionally speaks of is the apocalypse or awakening of Albion himself.

The Fall was not a single event, but required many generations, and covered the first three "Eyes" of God, described by Hesiod and Ovid as the silver, bronze and iron ages which followed the golden one. The silver age or Lucifer period was a time in which the universe was tearing apart in chaotic disorder, and gigantic energies, sprung from the body of Albion, were fighting for imaginative control of it. Myths of the war of Titans on Zeus in the Classics, and of the Jötuns on Odin in the Eddas, preserve accounts of a war of giants and gods. The giants are rightfully defeated, according to most of our Scriptures, because even the fallen order of nature which the gods established is preferable to chaos. But the feeling that Odin and Zeus are really usurpers can still be traced. Gradually, as the universe took its present form, the weakening human imagination was slowly pushed down and contracted into its present helpless state. Yet gigantic energies still remain in men, imprisoned, but struggling to be free. The revolt of Prometheus nearly destroyed Olympus; and in the Eddas it is prophesied that some day the chained Loki will burst free and begin the destruction of the world.[33] This imprisoned Titanic power in man, which spasmodically causes revolutions, Blake calls Orc. Orc is regarded as an evil being by conventional morality, but in Blake the coming of Jesus is one of his reappearances.

The victory of the sky-god over the Titans means that the universe slowly became more orderly and predictable, and that men, weaker than the Titans but still gigantic, turned to internecine war as history enters the "Moloch" brazen period. The new thundergod of moral law and tyrannical power, whom Blake calls Urizen, was a projection of the death-impulse, and these giants, at the nadir of the Fall, worshiped him in a cult of death consisting largely of human sacrifices. Since then, the belief that somehow it is right to kill men has been the underlying cause of all wars.

This is the period of Druidism, when giants erected huge sacrificial temples like Stonehenge and indulged in hideously murderous orgies. The burning of great numbers of victims in wicker cages went on for centuries and is referred to by Caesar and other Classical writers: Blake, for some reason, speaks of the "Wicker Man of Scandinavia," where such practices, according to his authority, were unknown.[34] Early explorers found the same custom in Mexico, indicating the world-wide spread of the Druid culture.[35] The main characteristics of Druidism, to be treated in more detail later, were megaliths or temples for human sacrifice, sun worship, serpent worship and tree worship—in Britain, of the oak.

During the Druid period the world took its present form, which means, as to be is to be perceived, that men's bodies were gradually shrinking down to the point at which they now perceive it. When the present body of man was achieved, the universe necessarily appeared to that body in its present shape. Its present shape is a stabilizing of the object-world, made permanent on a basis of "mathematic form" or mechanical order. Therefore the creation of the present body of man must have been part of this stabilization. Such a creation must have been an "act of Mercy" and the work of the yet unfallen God, for men by themselves in their fallen state have sunk below the instinct of self-preservation.

This process is described in the Biblical story of Adam and Eve, the Ask and Embla of the Eddas. Adam in Blake is the physical man, the soul in the form of the bodies we now see. He is called the "Limit of Contraction": that is, he has fallen as far as man can fall without losing his imagination altogether and the ability to recreate himself along with it. Along with his creation went the completion of the present universe, which Blake calls the "Mundane Shell," and, probably, the settling of animals and plants into their present natural order of spawning and preying, the aggregate of which Blake calls the "Polypus," a huge wriggling mass of life. This all took place in the third "Eye" of the Elohim. This word is plural in form, and Blake follows tradition in regarding the Elohim as a trinity. But on the principles of Blake's symbolism the trinity would become a collective singular at a little distance, and is so portrayed in the great picture of "The Elohim Creating Adam."[36] From Adam's time until the Last Judgment, a period for which Blake adopts the conventional figure of six thousand years, the remaining four eras or Eyes of God are divided into twenty-eight phases or "Churches," corresponding to the twenty-eight cities of Albion mentioned by Geoffrey of Monmouth.[37] The world of time and space is a "sublunary" world of cyclic change, and is associated with the twenty-eight-day lunar cycle.

The first twenty of these Churches cover the remainder of the Druid period and the fourth and fifth eyes of God, Shaddai and Pachad. They are known to us only from the genealogical lists of the Bible. Seth, Enoch, Methusaleh, Noah, Shem and the other patriarchs down to Abraham, who are said to have lived for centuries, are not individual men but civilizations or historical cycles which grew up in Africa and Asia.

We know the African culture only from its final decadence in Egypt, with its hieratic ritual, oppressive priestly code, tyrannical monarchy and the "mathematic form" of its pyramids. Apparently the Exodus in the Bible is a reminiscence of the founding of new Druid kingdoms in Asia at the beginning of the Shaddai period. The Noachic deluge, which may be partly a reminiscence of the overwhelming of Atlantis, is also connected with the same event, and symbolically it completes the establishing of the "Limit of Contraction" in Adam. When man falls, nature falls too; and when man is locked into an enfeebled body, born in helpless dependence on a precreated object, and a prey to selfishness, fear and all other symptoms of weakness, nature becomes a prey to sudden accidents and senseless cataclysms. When Blake speaks of the earthquake at Lisbon, which so exercised the theologians of design, as "the Natural result of Sin,"[38] he means that earthquakes are a natural result of living in a fallen world:

The Bible says that God formed Nature perfect, but that Man perverted the order of Nature, since which time the Elements are fill'd with the Prince of Evil, who has the power of the air.[39]

However that may be, the great "Druid" civilizations of Asia, particularly Mesopotamia, produced magnificent works of art and literature in their prime: again, history records only their late degenerate period. Of the literature, only the Old Testament survives. We can get some idea of what their art was like from the Greeks, however, for the Greek Muses were daughters of Memory, which means that Classical culture is a parasitic growth on the earlier Asiatic ones, and Classical mythology contains many echoes, usually misunderstood by its compilers, of earlier and more authentic visions:

No man can believe that either Homer's Mythology, or Ovid's, were the production of Greece or of Latium; neither will any one believe, that the Greek statues, as they are called, were the invention of Greek Artists; perhaps the Torso is the only original work remaining; all the rest are evidently copies, though fine ones, from greater works of the Asiatic Patriarchs.[40]

At any rate, one should give Blake credit for realizing that the marble mediocrities dug up in that age of Winckelmann were copies of something. The Trojan war symbolizes the taking-over of Asiatic culture by the Greeks. The beings of the earlier myths, which appeared on the walls of Solomon's Temple and were called Cherubim, were recognized as imaginative creations: the gods of the Greeks, derived from them, were conceived as independent of man:

Visions of these eternal principles or characters of human life appear to poets, in all ages; the Grecian gods were the ancient Cherubim of

Phoenicia; but the Greeks, and since them the Moderns, have neglected to subdue the gods of Priam. These gods are visions of the eternal attributes, or divine names, which, when erected into gods, become destructive to humanity. They ought to be the servants, and not the masters of man, or of society. They ought to be made to sacrifice to Man, and not man compelled to sacrifice to them; for when separated from man or humanity, who is Jesus the Saviour, the vine of eternity, they are thieves and rebels, they are destroyers.[41]

Troy in Blake therefore stands for the abstraction of the "fairies of Albion" into "Gods of the heathen." Hence the conquest of England by the Trojan Brutus symbolizes the final collapse of the great Druidic civilizations of antiquity, paralleling the Platonic account of the defeat of Atlantis by Athens. Geoffrey of Monmouth's history, the source of the Brutus story, is to Blake a repository of ancient prophetic poems which, like much of the Old Testament, has survived only in the form of a chronicle of kings and queens:

> Names anciently remember'd, but now contemn'd as fictions
> Although in every bosom they controll our Vegetative powers.[42]

The Trojan war is also, because based on the love of a whore, the source of all the chivalric female-will worship of the Middle Ages. After it, imaginative animism almost drops out of culture and a belief in abstract gods reigns supreme over most of the earth, the former surviving among the Druids only as esoteric traditions preserved by the caste of bards.

Before this had happened, however, the Jehovah cycle of history had begun with the founding of a new Hebrew culture, presented in the Bible as the escape of a patriarch (really a "Church") called Abraham, from Chaldea. The essential feature of this was the giving-up of human sacrifice in favor of animal sacrifice, symbolized in the story of the substitution of a ram for Isaac as a victim:

Adam was a Druid, and Noah; also Abraham was called to succeed the Druidical age, which began to turn allegoric and mental signification into corporeal command, whereby human sacrifice would have depopulated the earth.[43]

So far, so good; but truth precipitates error, and in every culture great imaginative work is done in the face of a consolidating tyranny. The growth of the Classical civilization was only part of this negative response to Abraham: the rest came in the establishment of a moral law and a ceremonial worship of a thunderous tyrant by Moses, the twenty-second "Church," completed by the integration of this into a political tyranny by David and Solomon, who represent the twenty-third.

According to Swedenborg, the Hexateuch is a compilation of earlier and later documents. The first eleven chapters of Genesis, down to Abraham, are ancient and belong to an original *Ur-Bibel*; but most of the Exodus account is drawn from earlier books, now lost. These consisted of a history and a prophecy, referred to in Numbers xxi, 14 and 27; also the "Book of Jasher."[44] The Exodus account as we have it is therefore somewhat confused, and an ancient prophetic poem has been rewritten from a priestly point of view. The Passover incident represents, like the Isaac story, the decline of human sacrifice, and the Exodus itself seems to go back to the emergence of an Asiatic civilization which probably took place nearer the time of Adam. But the real basis of the Exodus story was a poem in which Egypt symbolized Ulro and the Promised Land Eden. In that poem the imaginative energy which achieved the entry into Eden, the pillar of fire, was called Joshua, which means Jesus. (Blake usually calls it Orc, who is also Jesus, but in one poem Fuzon: he rejects the identification of Jesus and Joshua suggested in Milton's line, "And Joshua, whom the Gentiles Jesus call."[45]) The pillar of cloud, the power of tyranny which kept the Hebrews wandering in a wilderness trying to follow their elusive Sinaitic ghost (Urizen) was Egypt itself, which Moses represented. What is now given us as a ferocious butchery of Canaanite tribes was in the original the annihilation of the bogies of the Selfhood. The Biblical account makes little sense as history: at best it is historical reminiscence seen poetically, like the Trojan war in the *Iliad*. Hence when the prophets and psalmists speak of the deliverance of their people from Egypt, they are concerned only with the "anagogic" meaning of that event, which is, according to Dante, "the exit of the holy soul from the slavery of this corruption to the liberty of eternal glory."[46] This interpretation of the Exodus is fundamental to Blake's symbolism: the work which throws most light on Blake here is the Wisdom of Solomon, in which the plague of darkness, for instance, is treated as a symbol of the brooding terrors of the opaque Selfhood in language very close to Blake:

For while they thought that they were unseen in their secret sins, they were sundered one from another by a dark curtain of forgetfulness, stricken with terrible awe, and sore troubled by spectral forms.[47]

With the coming of Jesus or the seventh Eye the finale of history begins. The first consolidation of tyranny established to meet this new threat was the "Church Paul,"[48] absorbing Jesus into the old Pharisaic legalism. Next comes his further absorption into the Classical tyranny, represented by the Church Constantine, then the establishment of the female-will culture of the Middle Ages, the chivalric code and Madonna-worship associated with Charlemagne and Arthur. Finally comes the twenty-seventh Church in Luther and the Renaissance, the tyrannical precipitate of which is Deism. These twenty-seven "Heavens," as they are called, roll round us in a circle forever, and Deism is spiritually as far from Eden as Babylon or Egypt or Rome ever were.[49]

Only with the twenty-eighth, the last phase associated with Milton, does the apocalypse get under way (Swedenborg, we remember, said it began in Blake's birth year). Milton himself represents an imaginative penetration of the spiritual world unequalled in Christian poetry, and Blake, especially in his poem on Milton, attempts to clarify his vision still further. The apocalypse proper begins with the French and American revolutions, when the revolutionary iconoclasm of Orc, which was made manifest in Jesus, returns to the world to complete the seventh cycle. Then, as St. John says:

In the days of the voice of the seventh angel, when he shall begin to sound, the mystery of God should be finished, as he hath declared to his servants the prophets.[50]

Opposed to this is the development of empiric thought denying the reality of all states above Generation, which only needs a little pushing until it becomes a materialist tyranny so complete that humanity will finally be able to see all its ramifications as part of a single unified falsehood, an epiphany of Satan.

· 8 ·

But what is Satan? In the human mind he is the death-impulse or Selfhood which reduces men to becoming either death-dealing tyrants or torpid and inert victims of them. He is the "accuser" or principle of unbelief which makes tyrants revengeful and victims terrified, this mutual interaction of revenge and terror being the basis of fallen society. In this world Satan is therefore the objective counterpart of the death-impulse, the dead body or inert matter for which the most direct symbols are rock and sand. Yet matter is superior to chaos, and chaos to nonentity. The fact that physical death does not sink below matter must represent part of the same stabilizing of existence which is represented by the "Mundane Shell" and the body of Adam. Adam is the "Limit of Contraction," and Satan is the "Limit of Opacity"; Adam and Satan, therefore, are the bounds put to the Fall in life and death respectively. Hell, the abode of Satan, is Ulro, the world of abstractions which in aggregate are matter, nature, reason and memory. In Generation subject and object are in a relation which appears in Beulah more clearly as that of male and female, or lover and beloved. Hence Satan is described by Blake as a "Hermaphrodite," a sterile fusion of subject and object into an indivisible abstract or spectral world.

The Biblical account of the Fall, in the story of Adam and Eve, presents us with the two "Druidic" symbols of the tree and the serpent. Serpent-worship is, like human sacrifice, part of the psychology of the Fall. The serpent with its tail in its mouth is a perfect emblem of the Selfhood: an earth-bound, cold-blooded and often venomous form of life imprisoned in its own cycle of death and rebirth. As for the tree, there were two trees in Paradise, the tree of eternal life and the tree of the knowledge of good and evil. The former represents the unity of man with God: the account in Genesis seems to imply, though we shall look at it again, an abstract or superhuman God who is said to be jealous of man and expels him from Eden to prevent him from reaching for that tree. The restoration of the tree of life to man is therefore one of the features of the apocalypse. The water of life, symbolized in the Bible by the four rivers of Eden, which actually are the four senses of unfallen man, is also to be given freely to man after the last day.[51]

The other tree symbolizes several different aspects of the Selfhood. It is a tree of morality, conveying the knowledge that one lives a good life in a bad world by using the minimum of imagination. It is a symbol of nature, of the separate objective body of Generation which Blake always associates with the vegetable world. In the ninth book of *Paradise Lost,* after Eve has eaten of the apple, she bows to the tree and does it homage.[52] There, in the worship of an external spirit, is the beginning and end of all idolatry. But above all, this upas-tree of death which lost man Paradise symbolizes mystery, the elusiveness of the object. This aspect of it, though presented as a different tree, is beautifully brought out in Milton's banyan, which continually enroots itself in the earth, spreading a dense vegetable thicket wider and wider as it grows. When Adam and Eve shrink into the banyan grove to conceal and cover their fallen bodies, they are symbolically still in front of the tree of mystery. The growth of this tree is described in "The Human Abstract," which ends:

> The Gods of the earth and sea
> Sought thro' Nature to find this Tree;
> But their search was all in vain:
> There grows one in the Human Brain.

In this larger symbolic form the tree appears in Northern mythology as the world-ash Yggdrasil.

It was the serpent that tempted Adam to fall (it is not called the devil until much later), and the serpent then fell himself. But as Adam in Blake is the present human body which was established after a gigantic period, the serpent must among other things symbolize the fallen body of man. The "serpent body" forced to the ground to eat dust and clay is the constricted body of the natural man. The serpent's ability to shed its skin, on the other hand, makes it an emblem of death and rebirth, the persistence of the "living form" as a species in time. (There is no explicit association in Genesis between the bodies of Adam and Eve and that of the serpent, but there is a suggestive hint of one in *Paradise Lost* which may have attracted Blake's notice:

> As when he wash'd his servants' feet, so now
> As Father of his Family he clad
> Thir nakedness with Skins of Beasts, or slain,
> Or as the Snake with youthful Coat repaid.[53])

Orc, or human imagination trying to burst out of the body, is often described as a serpent bound on the tree of mystery, dependent upon it, yet struggling to get free. The erection of the brazen serpent in the wilderness therefore represents in disguised form the more clearly symbolic story of the earlier poem. The energy of Orc which broke away from Egypt was perverted into the Sinaitic moral code, and this is symbolized by the nailing of Orc in the form of a serpent to a tree. This was a prototype of the crucifixion of Jesus, and the crucifixion, the image of divine visionary power bound to a natural world symbolized by a tree of mystery, is the central symbol of the fallen world. Parallel to the image of the crucified Christ is the figure of Prometheus chained to a rock, imagination bound to Ulro. Both Titans were victims of Zeus-Jehovah or Urizen, and both are allotropic forms of Orc. Jesus redeems Adam in Generation; the Promethean fire will burn the "opaque" world to ashes in the final consummation. Some idea of this serpent-symbolism seems to underlie the Gnostic cult of the Ophites, who worshiped the serpent as Jesus and considered Jehovah an evil being.

Now if the fall of the serpent symbolizes the fall of Adam, or rather the fall of humanity to the Adamic form, the serpent before its fall must represent the Druid culture which preceded Adam. That culture in its dying stages was a period of ferocious war accompanied by prodigies of human sacrifice. It was the tyrannical side of the Selfhood run rampant. There were no quiescent victims, for human beings were still too strong: there were only the sacrificed captives. The unfallen serpent, then, would not be a scaly and shiny reptile, nor even the curious Miltonic animal that slides around on its rear, but a creature of terrible strength and beauty like the tiger, its scales glittering precious stones, its head crested with gold, the image of tyrannical pride, like Milton's Satan when his form had not yet lost all her original brightness.

It is this serpent, man's Selfhood or desire to assert rather than create, that stands between man and Paradise: the cherub with the flaming sword who guards the tree of life therefore is that demonic "serpent." The account in Genesis does not suggest this, but Ezekiel, in denouncing the King of Tyre, makes the identification, and relates the king's tyranny to it:

Thou hast been in Eden the garden of God; every precious stone was thy covering, the sardius, topaz, and the diamond, the beryl, the onyx, and the jasper, the sapphire, the emerald, and the carbuncle, and gold: the workmanship of thy tabrets and of thy pipes was prepared in thee in the day that thou wast created.

Thou art the anointed cherub that covereth; and I have set thee so: thou wast upon the holy mountain of God; thou hast walked up and down in the midst of the stones of fire.

Thou was perfect in thy ways from the day that thou wast created, till iniquity was found in thee.

By the multitude of thy merchandise they have filled the midst of thee with violence, and thou hast sinned: therefore I will cast thee as profane out of the mountain of God: and I will destroy thee, O covering cherub, from the midst of the stones of fire.[54]

The Greeks have preserved the memory of this Covering Cherub in their myth of the Hesperides, the Paradisal islands of the west under the domain of Atlas, where a mysterious tree with golden fruit is guarded by a dragon.

The fallen serpent is a worm "seventy inches long," lasting for "sixty winters"[55]; the demonic serpent or Covering Cherub is a dragon. The former is the helplessness of the victim; the latter the ferocity of the tyrant. But the dragon, in the Bible and elsewhere, is a symbol of something far worse than Satan the "Limit of Opacity": he is a symbol of the chaos which underlies it, waiting to burst in and overwhelm the entire cosmos. For the dragon in all mythologies is simply a conventional form of the monstrous, the unreal, the fire-breathing terror which the hero makes tangible only by killing. All monsters in heroic literature are, like Grendel, sprung of the race of Cain or the death-impulse, but much more hideous than this is the horror of something mysterious and undefined, the power of darkness. The creation of the fallen world is an "act of Mercy" because the stability and permanence of the dead inorganic world forms a barrier between our weak struggling lives and the total annihilation of all being in chaos.

The symbol of chaos in the Bible is water, specifically the sea, though sometimes conceived as "waters under the earth"; the wavering, uncertain, indefinite form which Blake hates so in art as the antithesis of what the imagination outlines. God created the world, Genesis begins, out of water or chaos. The Mesopotamian myth from which this was derived personifies this chaos as a sea-serpent or water-monster and God as a young hero who creates the cosmos by slaying the dragon. This is not in Genesis, but references to a divine struggle with chaos, which finally resulted in the waters being subdued and gathered into definite places, are scattered all through the Bible, especially in the Psalms. A deluge in the Bible therefore signifies a defeat of the imagination; and the fall of Albion began with a deluge which drowned Atlantis and produced the ocean that bears its name. The drying-up of water, on the other hand, as in the passage across the Red Sea, implies an imaginative advance. According to Job the power of God is nowhere more strikingly manifest than in keeping the sea within bounds, and in the apocalypse there shall be no more sea.[56]

This dragon of chaos is usually called Leviathan in the Bible, and Leviathan, the Covering Cherub in the fallen world, represents not only the tyranny of nature but the social tyranny among men which is part of it. The title of Hobbes' defense of tyranny is symbolically quite accurate, for the King of Egypt is called Leviathan by Ezekiel, just as the King of Tyre is called the Covering Cherub. Job, pondering the problem of injustice, finally realizes that the cruelty of man to man, the cruelty of nature to man, and the cruelty which fate inflicts, and God seems to inflict, on man, are all part of an indivisible pattern of tyranny, the tyranny of the state of nature. The poem ends in a vision of this in the form of two huge and untamable monsters, Leviathan, the "King over all the children of pride,"[57] being the more important. Had Job gone on, they would have merged into the dragon guarding Paradise. Had he gone still further, he would have reached his apocalypse or revelation of Paradise: that is, he would have pushed the dragon out of the way and walked boldly in.

In some places Leviathan is called Rahab, and Rahab is also the name of the harlot who received the spies of Joshua, and whose life was spared in the conquest of the Promised Land.[58] It is difficult to see what these two Rahabs can have to do with one another until we come to the Apocalypse and find there a Great Whore sitting on the back of a red dragon referred to as "that old serpent which is called the Devil, and Satan, which deceiveth the whole world."[59] This beast, a water-monster, is evidently the Covering Cherub seen from inside Paradise, and two smaller monsters, corresponding to the Leviathan and Behemoth of Job, are offspring of his. The Great Whore's rich clothes and precious stones recall the gilded serpent; she represents all human tyranny, for her name is Babylon and she sits on the seven hills of Rome;

she is all forms of state religion, for she is drunk with the blood of the saints; she is chaos, for she sits on many waters; and her whoredom represents the possessive love of the jealous Selfhood. She is, in short, the ultimate fallen form of nature or the "female will," Enitharmon and Vala combined in the time-world. Apocalypse means revelation, and the Great Whore is the chief thing revelation comes to remove, which is Mystery, a word used by Paul to refer to another consolidation of evil in the somewhat different form of the Antichrist.[60] The Great Whore of the Bible is the Medusa who turns men to stone, the *femme fatale* of the romantic poets whose kiss is death, whose love is annihilation, whose continual posing of the unanswerable riddle of life in this world is reflected in the mysterious female smiles of the Sphinx and Mona Lisa; and whose capacity for self-absorption has haunted art from ancient Crete to modern fashion magazines. The visionary sees nature as a veil (the sound-association with "Vala" should be noted) between himself and reality: the tearing of the veil of the mystery-temple by Jesus is therefore the first act in the apocalypse. As the vision consolidates, nature takes the human form of a beautiful harlot. The Whore and her beast, then, are the obstacles blocking up the view of the unfallen world; and when the Whore is stripped and burned all the evils of the Selfhood go from the Abyss, the chaos underlying matter, into the permanent second death of nonexistence.

In the Eddas Leviathan is the world-encircling serpent Midgard whom Thor once nearly landed on a fishing trip and once nearly lifted off the ground in the form of a cat. Behemoth is the great wolf Fenri, bound in this world by a chain called "Devouring" (a word often associated by Blake with the Selfhood), formed of nonexistent things like stones' roots and fishes' breath: this passage reads very like a Blakean satire on abstract ideas.[61] In the apocalypse described by the Sibyl in the Völuspa both wolf and serpent break loose: the former's jaws stretch to the top of heaven; the latter's poison is vomited over the earth.

There are in Blake, as in Swedenborg, two suns, one alive and unfallen, the source of life and light, and one dead, a "phantasy of evil Man."[62] The latter is the zodiacal sun, symbolizing the fallen conception of eternity as indefinite or endless recurrence. The image for this is the circle; and the serpent in a circular form with its tail in its mouth is therefore a perfect symbol of the zodiac, being so employed by the Druids. The precious stones with which the Covering Cherub or unfallen serpent is traditionally adorned then became zodiacal signs. In the priestly cult of Judaism the twelve stones on Aaron's breastplate, according to Josephus, represented the zodiac[63]; and the twelve sons of Jacob are connected with a zodiacal myth. This zodiacal pattern, which is frequent in Blake, always has the sinister significance of the unending cyclic repetition of time. Albion, for instance, has twelve sons associated with the "starry wheels," and their relation to the twelve sons of Jacob, who represent humanity, symbolizes the interdependence of the universe we see and the bodies which compel us to see it in that form. A similar myth may underlie the passage in Malory about the tomb of twelve kings with twelve images, each holding a candle, with Arthur above, like the Covering Cherub again, holding a drawn sword. Merlin the prophet said that when the candles went out the quest of the Sangreal (the medieval symbol of the apocalypse) would be achieved.[64] The general meaning of such a passage as the following should now be a little clearer:

In thoughts perturb'd they rose from the bright ruins, silent following
The fiery King, who sought his ancient temple, serpent-form'd,
That stretches out its shady length along the Island white. . . .
There stand the venerable porches that high-towering rear
Their oak-surrounded pillars, form'd of massy stones, uncut
With tool, stones precious, such eternal in the heavens,
Of colours twelve, few known on earth, give light in the opake,
Plac'd in the order of the stars. . . .
Then was the serpent temple form'd, image of infinite
Shut up in finite revolutions, and man became an Angel,
Heaven a mighty circle turning, God a tyrant crown'd.[65]

All over the world serpent and dragon myths descended from the Druids are found. St. George and the Dragon, Apollo and the Python, Beowulf and Grendel, Perseus and the Medusa who forces man down from Generation into the stony world of Ulro, are all images of the victory of the creative imagination over chaos. The Laocoön group originally portrayed, according to Blake, Jehovah and the two limits of the fallen world, Satan and Adam; the strangling serpents again represent the Fall.[66] Traditions of a Covering Cherub and a Red Dragon survived also in the North.

Gray's *Triumphs of Owen* tells us in a note that the latter was the device of the Cadwallader family, and this is repeated in the name of Arthur's father Uther Pendragon. The Arthurian legend contains many reminiscences of the more ancient one of Albion, of whom Arthur himself is a distorted reminiscence:

The stories of Arthur are the acts of Albion, applied to a Prince of the fifth century, who conquered Europe, and held the Empire of the world in the dark age, which the Romans never again recovered.[67]

This means that Blake accepts, not Geoffrey's literal account of the conquest of the Roman Empire by Arthur, but the symbolic meaning of that account; that in the Dark Ages Northern and Teutonic races, with their prophetess-worship which later developed into the Court of Love, overthrew the Roman Empire and established the Madonna-cult of the Roman Church. In Arthurian mythology, therefore, we should expect to find both Albion and Leviathan symbolism applied to Arthur in a rather confusing way. There is much to connect Arthur with Satan: we have mentioned the story in Malory which makes him the Covering Cherub, and in Malory also Arthur has a dream of a gilded serpent who turns out to be himself.[68] On the other hand, the legend that Joseph of Arimathea brought the Holy Grail to Glastonbury, while it symbolizes in part the establishment of the Roman Church in Britain, also contains echoes of the Atlantic Golden Age in which the feet of Jesus walked on English mountains. The relation of Arthur to Albion, in short, is very similar to that of Joshua to Jesus in the Bible, and Blake is anxious to keep the genuine vision disentangled from the historical distortion of it.

But if both the Arthurian legend and the myths of Adam in Genesis are later forms of a far older tale connected with Albion and Atlantis, it follows that Milton's long hesitation between Arthurian and Biblical themes, on the assumption that they were mutually exclusive, was unnecessary. Spenser got this point much clearer in *The Faerie Queene*, the first book of which deals with the slaying of a dragon by a knight of Arthur's court. If we look closely at Spenser's allegory, we can see that he is using the same symbols from the Bible that Blake is using, and in much the same way. St. George sets out to rescue the kingdom of Una from a monster. This kingdom was originally the Garden of Eden, Una's father being addressed as "king of Eden,"[69] and the present earth. That is, Una's parents represent a Golden Age in which the earth appeared as Paradise. The "infernall feend"[70] which expelled them is therefore the Covering Cherub, and St. George's real quest is the recovery of Paradise and the achievement of the apocalypse. His chief enemies throughout are Duessa, Blake's Rahab, who is identified with the Great Whore, an old man, Archimago, more or less Blake's Urizen, and Orgoglio, the giant of pride, or rather of "jealousy." The battle between St. George and "that old Dragon"[71] is fought in the Garden of Eden, St. George deriving his strength both from the tree of life and the water of life. Spenser, then, treats Arthurian and Biblical mythology with equal freedom as equally relative to an archetypal myth. Compared with him, Milton was badly hampered by an erroneous notion that the Biblical myth was "true" and the Arthurian one "false."

· 9 ·

As far as the poetic effect of Blake's mythology goes, it cannot of course be denied that when a character is presented as an individual or a god and his relationship to an archetype is left to take care of itself, an advantage in vividness is often gained. Blake was, it is obvious, so conscious of the shape of his central myth that his characters become almost diagrammatic. The heroism of Orc or the ululation of Ololon do not impress us as human realities, like Achilles or Cassandra, but as intellectual ideographs. It all depends on whether the reader has a taste for this kind of metaphysical poetry or not, on whether he is willing to read so uncompromising an address to the intellectual powers. It is not necessary to assume that qualities of poetry which are certainly not in Blake are qualities which Blake tried and failed to produce. One looks in a poet for what is there, and what there is in Blake is a dialectic, an anatomy of poetry, a rigorously unified vision of the essential forms of the creative mind, piercing through its features to its articulate bones. The figure is perhaps not one that he would have approved: his own is:

> I give you the end of a golden string,
>   Only wind it into a ball,

It will lead you in at Heaven's gate
Built in Jerusalem's wall.[72]

And if we have any doubts about the value of Blake's method, we have only to compare the poetic value of his reading of the Bible with that of the corporeal understanding. To the imaginative eye, the Bible begins in a world of chaos without form and void, continues through primitive legend and history to the prophets, proceeds from their far-off visions of a Redeemer and a New Jerusalem to Jesus, and from Jesus to the final blinding flash of revelation, the vision of the completed City of God and the disappearance of nature. To the corporeal understanding, the Bible begins in historical reminiscence and barbarous cosmology which, if often repulsive, is at any rate intelligible, proceeds to some irascible sermons on morality, the social insight of which is concealed in a good deal of fustian about a Messiah and a Last Day, goes on to the life and tragic death of a saintly teacher whose refined ethics were distorted into a grotesque myth by unintelligent disciples, and finally ends in the most impenetrably turgid allegory ever devised in language—if one can call its illiterate mixture of Greek words and Hebrew syntax a language. To the corporeal understanding, in short, the Bible's final "Revelation" is an utter mystery: that is, it bears the same name as the Great Whore whose destruction it foretells. A precisely similar paradox lurks in the mysterious symbolism of Blake.

PART TWO

THE DEVELOPMENT OF
THE SYMBOLISM

I call him Ork, because I know no beast,
Nor fish, from whence comparison to take.
                              ORLANDO FURIOSO,
                           tr. Harington, x, 87.

IT is clear that Blake was not a man with some unusual religious and moral ideas who felt that they would sound more oracular if put into the form, if one can call it that, of vaguely metrical rhapsodies. He was a poet whose poems were quite consistent with a theory of poetry. Our next task is to relate Blake's theory of poetry to the tradition of poetry, and to try to see him in the perspective of English literature. This attempt will take the writer away from Blake, where he is fairly sure of his ground, into many fields where his scholarship is casual, and will compel him to make bare assertions for which the full evidence would require another book. But the attempt must be made to complete the destruction of the myth that Blake is a literary freak. Blake is often thought of as a kind of intellectual Robinson Crusoe who was, as Greene said of Shakespeare, master of arts in neither university, and therefore built his palace of art out of odds and dead ends of European culture, adding a few lunatic fringes for decoration. But even a self-made thinker is not necessarily an untraditional one. It is true that in the study of Blake certain mysterious figures, Agrippa, Paracelsus, Boehme, Swedenborg, begin to loom up on the horizon, a cloudy phalanx whom many lovers of painting and poetry may not care to engage. Yet Blake insists so much on the supremacy of painting and poetry that we may not find them so important after all. He says of Swedenborg:

Any man of mechanical talents may, from the writings of Paracelsus or Jacob Behmen, produce ten thousand volumes of equal value with Swedenborg's, and from those of Dante or Shakespear an infinite number.[1]

Blake did not however consider even Shakespeare infallible, nor Dante when he got around to reading him, so we should not be surprised if his attitude to Paracelsus and Boehme shows the same independence of judgment he shows toward the others. "I will not Reason & Compare," he says; and even in dealing with other writers he was not a man to be always on his best academic behavior.

· 2 ·

ONE of the conspicuous features of Blake's thought which we have already met is a dislike of Classical culture and a preference for Hebrew prophecy almost equal to that of Jesus in *Paradise Regained*. Along with this goes a considerable respect for the medieval expressed in the formula "Grecian is Mathematic Form: Gothic is Living Form."[2] As an engraver Blake had been apprenticed in his youth to a man called Basire, the sort of man who would be called a member of the "old school" no matter what time he lived in. He had set Blake to making studies in Westminster Abbey, and Blake had emerged from this training a full-fledged member of the eighteenth century Gothic school; and his pro-Hebraic and anti-Classical bias is equally typical of his period, though not necessarily related to medievalism.

Classical culture to Blake was focused not on the individual but on the state, and on the social and political duties of the citizen. This meant that it was primarily a military culture, with all that that implies, including "State Religion, which is the source of all Cruelty." It was based on a proximate and expedient morality, of the kind that finds prophetic vision unreal. The only man resembling a prophet they had was Socrates, and even Socrates never questioned war or the structure of his society. Classical moralists carried the false heroics of the Homeric code into ordinary life and founded an ethic based on dignity and prudence, neither of which is an essentially imaginative quality; and Classical philosophy was as abstract as Classical art was derivative.

We have spoken of the curious relation between Blake's idea of culture and Matthew Arnold's. Both ascribed the vulgarity and Philistinism of the typical Englishman of their respective times, his acceptance of money as a necessity and of art as a luxury, to an overdose of moral virtue. Like Arnold, Blake advocated a relaxation of prudery, an increase of a culture founded on the "best self," and a return to sweetness and light. But according to Blake the prudery came from the crabbed Orphism of Plato, the negative virtue of Aristotle, the filial piety of Aeneas, the droning platitudes of Cicero and Seneca, the Selfhood-communings of Marcus Aurelius. "If Morality was Christianity," sneered Blake, "Socrates was the Saviour."[3] For sweetness and light we must turn to the

Bible, where God is a loving Father and his children burst into health and beauty like the lilies, where mountains jump for joy and trees clap their hands.

Of course not all of the Bible is like this. To Blake the "priest" is the central symbol of tyranny, as he is the spokesman of the belief in mystery which produces it. And there are plenty of priests in the Bible: they are there for a warning and serve as a foil for the prophets. The full meaning of Jesus' "forgiveness of sins" cannot be understood without Caiaphas and the Pharisees. Hence the prophets had to attack the priests as well as paint pictures of the state of innocence, and the Bible records their furious condemnation of war and injustice, of the rich grinding the faces of the poor and of trying to tickle God's nose with the smell of burning animals. They kept hammering at the tactless unanswerable questions no person of good taste and social instincts ever asks, because they continually saw all that men do in relation to fall, redemption (which they called the Exodus from Egypt) and apocalypse. They retained a social detachment that few if any Classical writers ever achieved, and were able to release an imaginative energy which the city-state choked off in Socrates.

It is because of its innate Hebraism that the Middle Ages, with all its faults, provided on the whole a better milieu for the visionary than Classical culture, although the great achievements of Gothic art were no more the direct product of the society they sprang from than those of any other art. True, Blake handsomely admits of Chaucer "that he was very devout, and paid respect to true enthusiastic superstition."[4] But there is one curious passage in which Blake speaks of Gothic architecture as the work of a persecuted minority, seeming to imply an association of Gothic architects, and perhaps of Grail romancers, with a kind of heretical freemasonry such as was later postulated by Rossetti. The medieval successor to the prophet was the monk, particularly the Franciscan. Like the prophet, the "grey monk" stands for the imaginative opposition to the priest, the Brother of Man against the Father impersonating Urizen, the preserver of culture against the repeater of ritual. It is the "monk of Charlemaine" (there is no anachronism in calling him "grey," as Charlemagne in Blake means the whole medieval period down to Luther) who, with the stigmata of the murdered Prince of Peace, comforts the victims of cruelty and war.[5] Chaucer's monk is energetic and vigorous, and as far as he can refuses to live the self-denying unimaginative life of the despiser of the world. But when he is asked for a tale he shows himself a deep student of poetry, gives a striking definition of tragedy and an encyclopedic list of tragic themes. Hence Blake insists that:

Though a man of luxury, pride and pleasure, he is a master of art and learning, though affecting to despise it. Those who can think that the proud Huntsman and Noble Housekeeper, Chaucer's Monk, is intended for a buffoon or a burlesque character, know little of Chaucer.[6]

· 3 ·

THERE is little point in unraveling all the strands of Blake's thought back to their primeval origins: we shall be better advised to start wherever they are first woven together in a form which seems to anticipate Blake. We must now leave Blake, though still speaking as far as possible from his point of view, and go back to the great cosmopolitan humanist culture which arose in Europe between the Renaissance and the Reformation. The writers and scholars who form this culture, Erasmus, Rabelais, Cornelius Agrippa, Paracelsus, Reuchlin, the More of *Utopia*, Ficino, and Pico della Mirandola being the most conspicuous names, seem to have emerged into a kind of visionary Christianity to which the present meanings of neither "Protestant" nor "Catholic" wholly apply. This is by no means a homogeneous group, but a later perspective brings out resemblances which are more profound than the differences. These writers wanted to preserve the central vision of Christianity, and yet most of them envisaged a greater reform of the Church than either Reformation or Counter-Reformation achieved. They had in common a dislike of the scholastic philosophy in which religion had got itself entangled, and most of them upheld, for religion as well as for literature, imaginative interpretation against argument, the visions of Plato against the logic of Aristotle, the Word of God against the reason of man.

If we examine the argument of Agrippa's *Vanity of the Arts and Sciences* we can see this more clearly. Agrippa's main thesis is that all scientific knowledge, which is symbolized by the serpent in Paradise, confuses the mind and is liable to abuse, "so that there is nothing more deadly, than to be as it were rationally mad."[7] His attacks, though good-humored enough, are extremely comprehensive, and cover every phase of human activity, ending as a climax with scholastic theology. True theology, he says, consists in prophecy and interpretation. Interpretation he bases more or less on the scheme of the four levels of allegory which comes down from Dante; prophecy he equates with vision. He ends with a panegyric on the Word of God, which is the tree of life and not the tree of knowledge. The argument of his book, then, is that the sole source of authority in religion is the Word of God, yet the authority for interpreting the Word of God must be the imagination. There is no question of "plain sense" for him: he explicitly says that Biblical prophecy is so often wrong on the literal level that it must be understood symbolically.[8]

This doctrine of the Word of God explains the interest of so many of the humanists, not only in Biblical scholarship and translation, but in occult sciences. Cabbalism, for instance, was a source of new imaginative interpretations of the Bible. Other branches of occultism, including alchemy, also provided complex and synthetic conceptions which could be employed to understand the central form of Christianity as a vision rather than as a doctrine or ritual, preserving a *tertium quid* which, without detracting from the reality of the religion, would also avoid both the iconic and the iconoclastic pitfalls. Thomas Vaughan, a disciple of Agrippa, says:

> The main motives which have occasioned the present rents and divisions of the Church are the ceremonies and types used in it. . . . But our reformers, mistaking these things for superstitions, turned them all out of doors. But verily it was ill done; for if the shadow of St. Peter healed shall not these shadows of Christ do much more? The papist, on the contrary, knowing not the signification of these types, did place a certain inherent holiness in them and so fell into a very dangerous idolatry. . . . The magicians they also instituted certain signs as the key to their Art, and these were the same with the former. . . . The magicians had a maxim among themselves "that no word is efficacious in magic unless it be first animated with the Word of God." Hence in their books there was frequent mention made of *Verbum and Sermo.* . . .[9]

This ambitious conception of a visionary and theosophical *via media* fell to pieces soon after the Reformation began. Something of it was retained however in that unhappy group of visionaries known as the Anabaptists. It was to this sect that the apocalyptic vision came most vividly. They were political anarchists because they regarded all social systems and established churches without exception as tyrannies. They looked for the millennium because they denied natural religion to the point of insisting that the whole physical world was a doomed illusion. They acknowledged no authority but that of the Scriptures and their own "inner light," a conception very close to Blake's theory of imagination. The Anabaptist leaven, working in Germany, produced Boehme, and through Boehme and its Quaker descendants it came into England.

The link between the Anabaptist "inner light" and Blake's vision brings us back to the interest in occultism. For one of the most important ideas that the humanists picked out of occultism was its theory of the creative imagination, most clearly set forth in the occult development of the "microcosm" conception. According to Paracelsus, for instance, man is an epitome of the universe, and the imagination is the power by which he relates that corresponding universe to himself. The difference between Paracelsus and Blake on this point is that Blake's interest in vision is that of an artist and Paracelsus' that of a doctor. Paracelsus is a physician whose theory of healing boils down to a powerful use of the imagination on the part of both healer and patient, and he believes that Jesus worked his miracles by imaginative power in the same way. Hence Paracelsus represents occultism in the aspect we have previously mentioned, as a halfway house between magic and science, partly Baconian experiment and partly imaginative conceptions which, because they assume a latent correspondence between human and natural orders, tend to become superstitions. Worse, Paracelsus seems to accept a kind of mezzanine level of reality between the spiritual and the physical, a level on which his dubious apparatus of gnomes and sylphs and the rest is chiefly to be found.

Another mixture of poetry and science, and one in many respects closer to Blake than Paracelsus is, is that curious development of apocalyptic philosophy which uses the language of alchemy, and in which the alchemic process has somewhat the same position that art has in Blake. To the alchemic visionary, gold, the material of the New Jerusalem, was the quintessence of the mineral world, that is, the dead or opaque part of the creation, the "Hermaphroditic Satanic world of rocky destiny."[10] A process of transforming metals to gold would be a redemption of this world:

it would symbolize, or even cause, by some form of sympathetic magic which the writer does not pretend to understand, the resurrection and apocalypse of man. The ultimate object of alchemy, from this point of view, was exactly what Blake said the object of his art was, "to Restore what the Ancients call'd the Golden Age."

Boehme is the first conspicuous example of the affinity between occult and left-wing inner-light Protestant traditions, deriving as he did from the alchemic philosophers on the one hand and the Anabaptists on the other. Boehme's works are, like Blake's, visionary poems in which the Biblical accounts of creation, fall, redemption and apocalypse are formed into an imaginative unity by the aid of complex ideas like *"Lust"* and *"Sude,"* which in a measure correspond to the characters of Blake's Prophecies. And, though his works seem to the outsider to present a more unattractive style and more impenetrable difficulties even than Blake's, they were translated and eagerly read in Renaissance England because that kind of visionary poetry was not despised then as it was despised in Blake's time.

It is particularly in his conception of the Creation and Fall that Boehme influenced Blake. This in Boehme occupies three stages, which Boehme calls "principles." The first "principle" is God conceived as wrath or fire, who torments himself inwardly until he splits open and becomes the second principle, God as love or light, leaving behind his empty shell of pain, which, because it is now God-forsaken, is abstract and dead. This pure pain is Satan or Lucifer, now cast off from God, who is also the inorganic matter of the created universe, the created universe being the third principle. The fall of Adam, therefore, was on the one hand a yielding to death and slavery to nature, and on the other a yielding to a tightly enclosed pain which is also the wrath of God. This last is very like Blake's Selfhood. Redemption thus involves not only the escape of the visionary power from the Selfhood, but a complete rejection of natural religion and the whole fallen order of nature.

The same occult-Anabaptist connection can also be demonstrated negatively in ridicule, notably in Jonson's great play *The Alchemist*. Jonson's Sir Epicure Mammon is a comic Faustus, even a comic Mephistopheles, watching a man he believes to be a saint struggling upward to achieve a regeneration of the physical world:

> I see no end of his labours. He will make
> Nature asham'd of her long sleep; when art,
> Who's but a step-dame, shall do more than she,
> In her best love to mankind, ever could.
> If his dream last, he'll turn the age to gold.[11]

The two Anabaptists Jonson introduces look like ordinary stage Puritans, but they are Anabaptists, and therefore not Puritans. They are there to round out the larger symbolism of the play as a realistic satire on the impact of apocalyptic vision upon hypocrites and scoundrels; and the scene in which a prostitute shouts out a long apocalyptic interpretation of the Bible, prophesying the immediate arrival of the Messianic kingdom, Daniel's fifth monarchy, is in octave counterpoint to the same theme.

Ralph, the Independent squire of Hudibras, has had a thorough occult education as well:

> A deep occult Philosopher,
> As learn'd as the *Wild Irish* are,
> Or Sir *Agrippa*, for profound
> And solid Lying much renown'd;
> He *Anthroposophus*, and *Floud*,
> And *Jacob Behmen* understood. . . .[12]

Butler is careful not to ascribe any such sympathies to Hudibras himself, who is a Presbyterian and derives from the scholastic tradition. The same association of inner light and the occult runs all through the introductory matter in *A Tale of a Tub*. But in that association a third strain of thought is included which is Platonic, or rather Neoplatonic, in origin.

The lower half of the mystical system of Plotinus is very similar to Blake's. In Plotinus the man is a single mental unit, yet also a unit of a single world-spirit; and the recognition of this universal spirit in material things is the source of beauty. In the Italian development of Platonic thought which began with Ficino, this idea is combined with the *Symposium* and with Court of Love conventions in such a way as to produce a mythology rather like Blake's theory of states. There are two great principles in life, Eros, which is energy and heat, and Venus, which is form and light. These two principles are subject and object in this world, male and female in a higher state, creator and creature in a still higher one. (We explain this mythology, it is obvious, in Blakean terms to show its relation to Blake, but even so the original is not seriously distorted.) Sexual love is the starting-point of imaginative development. At this stage we have only an adaptation of the Petrarchan "female will" philosophy, but as the lover goes up the imaginative ladder to the highest stage the female will drops out and what we have finally is a religious technique based on ecstatic imaginative vision. This vision is the climax of the Courtier's education in Castiglione, and enters English literature, if in a somewhat chastened form, with Spenser's Hymns to Love and Beauty. But in Spenser the ladder disappears and is replaced by a spiritual transformation which reverses the perspective from temporal to eternal; and Blake, who says that the states of existence are discrete and not continuous, also has no ladder.

To understand Blake's thought historically, we must keep in mind an affinity between three Renaissance traditions, the imaginative approach to God through love and beauty in Italian Platonism, the doctrine of inner inspiration in the left-wing Protestants, and the theory of creative imagination in occultism. In these traditions, again, we should distinguish certain elements which, though often found in the vicinity of Blake's type of thinking, were either ignored or condemned by him. The Renaissance development of the *Symposium* is Blakean: the Pythagorean tendencies derived from the *Timaeus* and the Cabbala are not. The occult idea that man can create a larger humanity from nature is Blakean: magic, sympathetic healing and evocation of spirits are not. The belief that the Bible is understood only by an initiated imagination is Blakean: the secret traditions of Rosicrucians and the rest do not lead us to Blake whatever they may be.

· 4 ·

AGRIPPA admits that the Spirit of God may seize on heathens as well as Christians, and that there may be prophecy outside the Christian faith. He mentions, among others, Cassandra, Teiresias, the Druids and the Sibyls.[13] Elizabethan critics, with their French and Italian preceptors, generally held that Classical mythology went back to legends of a much greater antiquity, represented by such names as Zoroaster and Orpheus, and that they in their turn were blurred but still genuine reminiscences of visions preserved accurately in the Bible. The result of this was the poetic technique we have called contrapuntal symbolism, in which pagan images are substituted for Christian ones in order to avoid irreverence, or used along with them for greater freedom and variety.

The resemblance in form between so many pagan and Christian legends cuts both ways: it makes the Bible more poetic and the Classics more prophetic. To the Renaissance poet, Hebrew psalms and prophecies are poetry as well as sound doctrine, hence they not only justify poetry and are models of style for it, but are to be read with the imagination as well as with the reason. On the other hand, heathens also believed their poets or prophets to be divinely inspired, and accepted them as their primary religious teachers. In both Hebrew and Classical cultures poets were the first lawgivers both in religion and in society. This is closely related to Blake's point that myths were originally poetic and not theological. Hence the Classical poems are not superficial; they are profound and concentrated visions of eternal truth, and must be interpreted as such.

Most of the Elizabethan methods of interpretation, deriving as they did partly from the Plutarchan attempt to varnish the gods into images of moral virtue and partly from the medieval homiletic tradition, were allegorical in the wrong sense, concerned with extracting moral platitudes and general ideas. But in Reynolds' *Mythomystes*, apart from much Cabbalistic pedantry of the sort that derives Bacchus from Noah by way of *Boachus, there is a keen sense of myth as the "essential form" of poetry:

. . . who can make that Rape of Proserpine,—whom her mother *Ceres* (that under the Species of Corne might include as well the whole Genus of the Vegetable nature) sought so long for in the earth,—to meane other then the putrefaction and suceeding generation of the Seedes we commit to Pluto, or the earth. . . .[14]

Reynolds is generally thought to be an antiquarian curiosity, but this explanation of the Proserpine myth is at least as "modern," if that is the opposite of the obsolete, as anything we can find in Dryden. Subsidiary allegorical traditions, like Bacon's attempt to explain Classical myths as Baconian and the alchemists' to explain them as alchemic, helped to encourage contemporary readers to read all poetry in the same way that one must read Blake's Prophecies.

But if in the Bible poetry, prophecy and divine inspiration are the same thing, and if in Classical poetry they are almost the same thing, is it not a possible inference that any poetry, even one's own, may be prophetic and divinely inspired? Elizabethan critics hover wistfully on the outskirts of this final arcanum, repeating to one another the Ovidian line:

Est deus in nobis; agitante calescimus illo.[15]

This "deus" of course is not really God: but "poet" means, etymologically, a maker or creator, God is a Creator, and therefore the creative artist at least imitates the creative activity of God. In "Puttenham," the opening sentences give us Coleridge's whole theory of a secondary imagination, the poet's approach to God through imagination involving a rejection of the philosopher's tendency to play with symmetrical and logical patterns:

A poet is as much to say as a maker. And our English name well conformes with the Greeke word, for of ποιεῖν, to make, they call a maker *Poeta*. Such as (by way of resemblance and reuerently) we may say of God; who without any trauell to his diuine imagination made all the world of nought, nor also by any paterne or mould, as the Platonicks with their Idees do phantastically suppose.[16]

The obvious conclusion is not denied by the parenthetic genuflection.

All these movements of thought we have been tracing converge on Blake's identification of the artist's genius with the Holy Spirit. The Holy Spirit spoke by the prophets and wrote the Scriptures; it is the indwelling Holy Spirit that enables us to respond to the Scriptures; the Holy Spirit comes nearest to being that aspect of God which the Neoplatonists approach through love and beauty; and in any case it is the giver of the life by which we approach it. Hence many religious poets show a tendency to make the Holy Spirit a sort of unofficial Christian muse, quite apart from its more strictly dogmatic functions, and Milton's appeal to the incubating Spirit in *Paradise Lost* is in the same tradition.

Christian interest in occult and Neoplatonic theories of imagination was not, as our examples have made obvious by now, confined to the Anabaptist tradition: it found its way into much more orthodox circles. For this interest had in the first place, we have said, arisen among humanists who were trying to see the Christian vision as a vision instead of as a logical system. The same approach seemed to many Anglicans the best way of reconciling the claims of catholicity and reform, and these were that thin but significant line of liberal visionaries who supplied so much of what was best in Anglican culture through the sixteenth and seventeenth centuries. The line of this tradition, in poetry, runs through Spenser, Henry Vaughan and Traherne to Christopher Smart in Blake's own time. Flanking it are the speculative works related to occult and imaginative modes of thought, notably those of Thomas Vaughan, Henry More and Sir Thomas Browne, which continue into the next century with Berkeley's *Siris*, which Blake read late and with little profit, and Law's translation of Boehme, with explanatory diagrams compared by Blake to the works of Michelangelo.[17]

Spenser, for instance, provides in *The Faerie Queene* a number of Christian ideas so intricately interwoven with romantic and Classical imagery that the sharp dogmatic distinction between the truth of Christianity and the falsehood of heathenism is very difficult to find. Then again, when Spenser identifies the apocalyptic Great Whore and the Pauline Antichrist with the Roman Church, he is not indulging in irresponsible abuse, but trying to see the part of Christianity he is rejecting in the perspective of the archetypal vision provided by the Bible. At the same time his Redcross Knight goes through a process of monastic discipline, penance and purgation. The implication of this is more or less Thomas Vaughan's point quoted above. The ritual is a vision of truth which has become false only because it has sunk to the level of physical acts within the order of nature. Reforming the Church, therefore, includes the emancipation of rite and ceremony into an imaginative vision in which their symbolic reality is purified of its natural element. This part of our task would be much easier if Blake had left us an extended comment on Spenser paralleling his essay on Chaucer.

The full consideration of Blake's debt to Milton will have to be postponed until we come to the poem by Blake which bears Milton's name. Though obviously far on the left of Calvinism Milton never adopted anything like an Anabaptist point of view, and whatever interest he may have had in occult philosophy does not seem to the present writer to have permeated very deeply into his thinking. But no one identifies poetry with prophecy or expresses the responsibility of the creative artist to God for his genius more clearly than Milton. Milton's "liberty" is practically the same thing as Blake's imagination, and whenever Milton talks about reason he means it in the sense of the "bound or outward circumference of Energy" which liberty supplies. Liberty for Milton is the total release of the whole man, and his main effort in defining it is to break down the partitions in which the timid and cautious attempt to keep its various aspects separate. That is, the "Christian liberty" of the theologians is not a different thing from political liberty; and the "liberty to know and utter" inevitably expands into the liberty to love.

It is in *Areopagitica* that Milton is nearest to Blake, and *Areopagitica* supplies for the student of Blake not only a guide to most of Blake's leading ideas but an illustration of many of his symbols. It was undoubtedly a major influence in forming Blake's doctrine that the Christian Church cannot exist outside the arts because the secondary Word of God which unites us to the primary Word or Person of Christ is a book and not a ceremony. Milton also shows that the impulse to destroy art by censorship makes general morality a criterion which the creative imagination must meet. But moral virtue of this kind is founded on the fallen state of man; it is the forbidden knowledge of good and evil, the tree of death which lost man Paradise, and therefore it can never give man back a vision of Paradise. The more one pursues moral virtue, the more obviously one becomes engaged in a pursuit of death. "The laziness of a licensing church" detests everything that has any exuberance; and its ultimate aim is the legalized "blank virtue" of the Pharisee, which Jesus saw for what it was, the "excremental whiteness" of the outside of a tomb.

For general truth does not exist. Truth exists only in the total form which the mind makes of reality, hence no doctrine which a man assents to because he is told to do so can be true for him. The City of God is built not out of continuous but out of contiguous stones, and social order is a unity of varieties, like the work of art, not the dead and frozen unity of unintelligent assent which all tyranny attempts to reach, "a staunch and solid piece of framework, as any January could freeze together."

The greatness of *Areopagitica* is that it speaks for liberty, not tolerance: it is not the plea of a nervous intellectual who hopes that a brutal majority will at least leave him alone, but a demand for the release of creative power and a vision of an imaginative culture in which the genius is not an intellectual so much as a prophet and seer. The release of creative genius is the only social problem that matters, for such a release is not the granting of extra privileges to a small class, but the unbinding of a Titan in man who will soon begin to tear down the sun and moon and enter Paradise. The creative impulse in man is God in man; the work of art, or the good book, is an image of God, and to kill it is to put out the perceiving eye of God. God has nothing to do with routine morality and invariable truth: he is a joyous God for whom too much is enough and exuberance beauty, a God who gave every Israelite in the desert three times as much manna as he could possibly eat. No one can really speak for liberty without passing through revolution to apocalypse:

He who thinks we are to pitch our tent here, and have attained the utmost prospect of reformation, that the mortal glass wherein we contemplate, can show us, till we come to beatific vision, that man by this very opinion declares, that he is yet far short of Truth.

For England is "rousing herself like a strong man after sleep," and, though God usually reveals his will to England first, the regeneration of England will inevitably spread to all humanity, and humanity will then appear as an awakening Man whose home is Jerusalem, the City of God. The Reformation purified Christianity: to purify Christianity is to release human liberty: to release liberty is to kindle a flame that can never be extinguished until it is merged in the final consummation of all things. And this liberty, properly understood, is the spirit of prophecy:

For now the time seems come, wherein Moses the great Prophet may sit in heaven rejoicing to see that memorable and glorious wish of his fulfilled, when not only our seventy Elders, but all the Lord's people are become Prophets.

The passage in the Bible that this refers to was taken by Blake as a motto for his own poem on Milton.[18]

The beatific vision of which Milton speaks is, from Blake's point of view, to be found in him in its complete integrity only here. In the epics there is still much that is generalized and doctrinal, as there is, in the opposite camp, in the liberal conformism of Vaughan and Traherne. For in Milton's day the Renaissance was cooling into its winter, and the thick "triple ice" of abstract thought, which Blake called Deism and Milton Catholicism, was forming over the living waters of truth once more. But it is already evident that Blake's affinities with that Renaissance go much deeper than a few Shakespearean echoes in his early songs. Had he been born at any time between, say, 1530 and 1630, he would have found a large public able to speak his language, his premises would have been accepted on their own merits, and he could have offered to the world, in Spenser's phrase, "a continued Allegory, or darke conceit,"[19] without being told that poets should not invent a private symbolism.

· 5 ·

THIS drama is called, *The Modern Prophets*, and is a most unanswerable satire against the late spirit of enthusiasm. . . . My friend designs to go on with another work against winter, which he intends to call, *The Modern Poets*, a people no less mistaken in their opinions of being inspired than the other.[20]

Thus *The Tatler* announces the arrival of the Augustan millennium, of an age of reason and common sense, a cultural growth which Blake abhorred in its root and all its branches. He hated its poets Dryden and Pope; he hated its enlightened philosophers Locke and Voltaire; he hated its elegantly skeptical historians Hume and Gibbon; he hated its fashionable portrait painters Reynolds and Gainsborough; and he involved its most famous critic in a highly undignified dispute with Scipio Africanus.[21] This part of Blake's thought is a completely negative one, and expounding it calls for the isolation of the anti-Blakean aspects of the Age of Reason; in short, for caricature. We shall hurry through this as quickly as possible, remembering however that the poet who said that Dryden and Pope "did not understand Verse" but pronounced the Falconer of *The Shipwreck* "an admirable poet"[22] is not airing a private grievance. To understand Blake on this point we must be able to see, beneath all his irascible intolerance, the dazed bewilderment of a belated child of an earlier and greater age, wondering what on earth he was doing, or what he was doing on earth, in the first period of English civilization that would have called him mad.

The Augustan conception of "nature" begins with a physical

world outside the mind which suggests not only all the artist's images but his ideas and forms. Hence the relation of the individual man to nature is uncomplicated by the presence within man of a divine power visualizing eternity. Pope's "Know then thyself, presume not God to scan" assumes an antithesis between God and man which leaves the latter, for the purposes of poetry, alone with the physical world. Hence Milton's eagle "kindling her undazzled eyes at the full mid-day beam" is too quixotic a bird for the poet; his model is rather the sensible hen who keeps her feet on the ground and finds in domestic life a concreteness that the heavens do not afford. It follows that the repression of creative power is one of the fundamental principles of art. As all that man really wants to see tears the physical world to pieces, from the Augustan point of view the full power of genius can never find expression: most of it will invariably go to waste in attempting higher flights, and therefore the technique of perfect expression is largely a technique of achieving a tactful and communicable mediocrity. Now while Blake would certainly not quarrel with ideals of clarity and correctness, he would deny that a clarity which means only that the minimum of imaginative response is to be appealed to has anything to be said for it. A common sense which denies the superiority of uncommon sense is systematic superficiality. Pope's address to Walsh at the end of an *Essay on Criticism* which is also an essay on creation has something far more than modesty in it, considering all the earlier talk about the checking and restraining of Pegasus:

> The Muse, whose early voice you taught to sing,
> Prescrib'd her heights, and prun'd her tender wing,
> (Her guide now lost) no more attempts to rise,
> But in low numbers short excursions tries.

One thinks of Blake's drawing of "Aged Ignorance," in which an old man with an idiot's face is clipping the wings of a young Cupid struggling towards the rising sun. The proper study of mankind is the natural man, which in practice means that the most fertile themes of the creative imagination will be gossip, slander and domestic trivia.

Sense experience is not the whole of man's contact with nature: there is reflection on it and the evolution of general and abstract ideas. Therefore for the Augustans the innate hostility of poetry and abstractions must be overcome as far as possible, for one of the most important functions of poetry is the expression of generalized platitudes and proverbial philosophy like "A little learning is a dangerous thing." Further, the immediate source of poetry is not so much an external nature as a stock of sense experiences and reflections which have been accumulated, selected and preserved by the memory. The memory is therefore the source of the forms and themes of poetry: imagination is concerned only with the unfunctional decoration which follows the creative process. The *locus classicus* of this theory, to which Dryden and Pope gave qualified support, is Hobbes, and Hobbes' view of art is perfectly consistent with his views of politics and religion:

Time and Education begets experience; Experience begets memory; Memory begets Judgement and Fancy: Judgment begets the strength and structure, and Fancy begets the ornaments of a Poem. The Ancients therefore fabled not absurdly in making memory the Mother of the Muses.[23]

There is an answer to this in Milton, that poetry is not "to be obtained by the invocation of Dame Memory and her Siren daughters, but by devout prayer to that eternal Spirit who can enrich with all utterance and knowledge." This is another of the passages in which the Holy Spirit is associated with art, and was quoted by Blake in his notes to Reynolds.[24]

Let us pick up Dryden's *Parallel of Poetry and Painting* to see what happens if we follow out the Augustan conception of nature a little. We arrive at a God all right, but what a God! A lone, gloomy divine Selfhood spinning out of his own bowels, like the spider which is an inevitable symbol of the Selfhood, a web of spectral abstract ideas or archetypes. Nature affords a blurred and distorted reflection of these archetypes, for when this God went on from Ulro to Generation and tried to make a physical world, he bungled the job, being a bad artist, though of course we must not say so. Blake would admit that there are archetypes which are visualized by the artist through nature, but they are the images of a higher state of being which is human and divine at once. If the Augustan starts with a solitary prehuman God he is starting with a cipher, and consequently will see in nature only a latent harmony or "mathematic form," reality becoming simpler and more diagrammatic as it becomes clearer until it disappears into non-entity. A technique like that of the stopped couplet, based on the mind's expectation of an inevitable recurrence and on an antithetical rhythm which chimes sweetly in the ears of the devotees of the cloven fiction, is the means by which the Augustan poet permits his readers to hear the underlying harmony of nature, the music of the spheres.

But "harmony" is a static relationship, and the music of the spheres exists in the real eternal world of harp and song, not in a Cabbalistic diagram in which the spheres, or their angels, spend all eternity sounding a single note. Pope, however, believes in a static chain of being stretching from matter to God in which all things fulfill the law of their existence by preserving the *status quo.* Of man he says:

> And all the question (wrangle e'er so long)
> Is only this, if God has plac'd him wrong?

As God did not, mankind is to line up like a docile theater queue which will enter into happiness shortly if no one begins to push. This expands into "Whatever is, is right": that is, natural religion, a worship of the order of nature which admits nothing beyond it and sees nothing fallen in it. The result is a religious and political conformity based on a distrust of the mind, in which Milton's great visions of a regenerate England awakening into Paradise amid the hymns and hallelujahs of saints are regarded as the views of "an acrimonious and surly republican."[25]

The wedge driven by Milton between the "true" Christian and the "false" heathen mythology expands for the Augustans into a cleavage which almost destroyed mythopoeic poetry. The contrapuntal symbolism of the Renaissance fell out of favor, and Blackmore could say of Spenser in his Preface to his own epic on Arthur: "This way of writing mightily offends in this Age; and 'tis a wonder how it came to please in any." Pagan mythology and popular superstitions are by definition untrue: therefore they yield only trumpery and puerile themes. The Christian faith on the other hand is true: therefore it cannot be recreated by the artist, but can at the best be paraphrased. However sympathetic Johnson may be to religious poetry, when sufficiently orthodox, he is both conscious of its difficulty and dubious of its value. For Christianity is revealed religion, and as there is no real place in Augustan thought for revealed religion, it becomes something too cloudy and obscure for poetic expression in any extended form. As Boileau says:

> De la foy d'un Chrestien les mystères terribles
> D'ornemens égayés ne sont point susceptibles.[26]

If Christianity is terribly mysterious it is easy to see why it has no place in art, but difficult to see what becomes of its claim to be revelation.

The cyclic vision therefore decayed in the Augustan age and the epic with it. Dryden and Pope translated epics and even dreamed of writing them, but never did, the problems involved being insoluble on their premises. Dryden attempted allegory in *The Hind and the Panther*, in which a theological discussion is enlivened by being assigned to talking animals, but to follow the discussion we must stop visualizing the animals, and vice versa; and when the panther, or Anglican Church, is compared with the middle spirits living between heaven and hell it is left dangling in midair:

> So pois'd, so gently she descends from high,
> It seems a soft dismission from the sky.

It is only in the playful miniature of *The Rape of the Lock* that mythopoeia is admitted to poetry, and Pope's "heroi-comical" scheme, while it is not a parody of Homer or Virgil, is certainly an indication that the age of epics is over. The only form of mythopoeia allowed by Augustan standards is personification, for that assumes the superiority of the abstract to the concrete and brings out an underlying moral antithesis in life. In the passage quoted above Blackmore goes on to say: "There is indeed a way of writing purely Allegorical, as when *Vices* and *Virtues* are introduc'd as *Persons* . . . which still obtains, and is well enough accommodated to the *present* Age."

To the Augustan, art is an imitation of nature which progressively refines and improves nature. It follows that art shows a progressive refinement and improvement on art itself, as Virgil found nature in Homer rather than in direct observation. Underlying this is an analogy with science: one of the speakers in the *Essay on Dramatic Poesy* says: "If natural causes be more known now than in the time of Aristotle, because more studied, it follows that poesy and other arts may, with the same pains, arrive still nearer to perfection." Poetry, in former times often vague and barbaric, can be made more accurate as civilization progresses, and in fact the arts in England have shown a steady development from Gothic barbarism through Renaissance experiment to their present high rococo finish. At this point Burke's antithesis between the sublime and the beautiful comes in. The more self-conscious and refined artist must always follow the more spontaneous creator: hence tradition shows a gradual increase in refinement and by implication a decrease in creative energy. In all the sublime-beautiful twins of Augustan criticism, Homer-Virgil, Shakespeare-Jonson, Dryden-Pope, Denham-Waller, Michelangelo-Raphael, the man of lesser genius and greater polish has usually more to say to the Augustans. To Johnson it was Dryden who found English brick and left it marble; and if Milton had lived later than Dryden he would, Johnson suggests, have given up his crude blank verse and taken to polishing couplets.[27] With Pope we have reached a perfect dilemma of decorum, and, if Johnson does not actually say that nothing remains to be done in English poetry, he was not friendly to many of the new attempts that were made.

The latent fear of creative power in Johnson is more explicit in Pope's *Epistle to Augustus*, in which a rapid review of English literature shows us that Chaucer is ribald, Skelton beastly, Shakespeare and Jonson commercial, Cowley obsolete, Spenser affected, Milton a quibbler, the Cavaliers dilettantes, the dramatists bawdy, Dryden careless, Pope's contemporaries mainly dunces and the outlook for the future bleak. In critics without any creative ability of their own, Dennis or Rymer for instance, the true form of Augustan criticism, the pedant's abuse of genius for breaking his generalizing laws, appears more clearly. When prudes who think man's power of begetting children unspeakably nasty are so common, it is hardly likely that no one hates his power of creating art. "Believe Christ & his Apostles," said Blake, "that there is a Class of Men whose whole delight is in Destroying."[28] Luther's case was exceptional; the devil usually throws the inkpot first, and the tone Blake adopts toward Locke and Reynolds he regards as self-defensive:

They mock Inspiration & Vision. Inspiration & Vision was then, & now is, & I hope will always Remain, my Element, my Eternal Dwelling place; how can I then hear it Contemned without returning Scorn for Scorn?[29]

Another point in Blake's case against the Augustans remains to be noted. It is admittedly unfair to generalize now about the invariable rationalism of the Age of Reason. But such stereotypes are made in the first place by the generation which is trying to embody its revolt against the preceding one in a concrete form. Queen Victoria was hardly in her grave before poets began explaining why they disliked Victorian poetry, just as Johnson opened his *Lives of the Poets* with an explanation of what he considered wrong with the old-fashioned metaphysical poetry. The former will tell us that Victorian poetry is prissy and saccharine; the latter that metaphysical poetry is a parade of learning intended to produce a kind of literary bric-à-brac. Neither of these things is true, but they are historically interesting. Similarly, the conception of a smug, effete, artificial Age of Reason comes down to us from the second half of the eighteenth century, and from poets who underestimated it because they needed to escape its influence.

For Blake belongs neither to the Augustans nor to the Romantics, either as a representative or a rebel. He belongs to another age altogether; the age, in poetry, of Collins, Percy, Gray, Cowper, Smart, Chatterton, Burns, Ossian and the Wartons. Blake's masters in poetry were Gray, Collins, Chatterton and Ossian, and he believed to the day of his death in the authenticity of both Ossian and Rowley.[30] But the age of Blake is not solely one of poetry; it is a broad cultural movement with ramifications in philosophy, religion, painting and politics, and takes in nearly all of that lusty half of eighteenth century culture which has nothing to do with the Age of Reason. Its chief philosopher is Berkeley and its chief prose writer Sterne. Further, though Blake's greatest prophecies are later than the *Lyrical Ballads*, though he outlived Shelley and Keats and came in contact with Wordsworth, Coleridge and Lamb, he had no roots in the Romantic period. He lived to read Byron and *The Recluse*, but his heart was with *Fingal* and *Aella*.

The age of Blake has been rather unfairly treated by critics, who have tended to see in it nothing but a "transition," with all its poets either reacting against Pope or anticipating Wordsworth. The period is unhappy and tormented enough, however, and it seems doubly unfair to reduce its most positive achievements to potential Romanticism. It is true that the poets of this age were reacting against the Augustans, but in view of the fact that they did not know that the Romantic movement was to succeed them, it seems better to look at them rather as attempting to get English poetry back on Renaissance rails. It is with this shift of perspective that we proceed briefly to refer to some elementary facts about the age of Blake.

· 6 ·

ONE of the most obvious features of the reaction to the Age of Reason was the development of a poetry concerned with what we have called Blake's archetypal myth; that is, with man in the religious perspective, surrounded by the huge conceptions of fall, redemption, judgment and immortality. Young's *Night Thoughts* and Blair's *Grave*, both popular and conspicuous poems, are essentially apocalyptic prophecies, and both were exhaustively illustrated by Blake. Their method is less elaborate than Blake's, and is concerned only with the Bible; but it is significant that they prefer these larger visionary themes to the comparatively minor ones suggested by sense experience. The poets of gloom and graveyards were not mere victims of a passing fad: they knew that the proper study of mankind is *fallen* man, and that the man who does not see himself in this perspective does not see himself at all. As Young says, in a passage which contains several Blakean symbols, and may have been the source of the "Mundane Shell" mentioned so often in the Prophecies:

> Embryos we must be, till we burst the shell,
> Yon ambient, azure shell, and spring to life,
> The life of gods! Oh transport! and of man.
>   Yet man, fool man! here buries all his thoughts;
> Inters celestial hopes without one sigh.
> Prisoner of earth, and pent beneath the moon,
> Here pinions all his wishes; wing'd by Heaven
> To fly at infinite; and reach it there,
> Where seraphs gather immortality,
> On life's fair tree, fast by the throne of God.[31]

This expansion of perspective leads to an emphasis on the "sublime" part of Burke's antithesis, on the side of spontaneous and gigantic vision. The result was a revival of the Elizabethan process of making the Classics more prophetic and the Bible more poetic. The latter was aided by the fact that "Longinus," the popular authority on the sublime, had referred to Moses as providing an example of it. Further, a preference for the sublime implies that sublime poets reach heights that no refiner or imitator can approach. And as the refiner comes later than the rugged genius, art never improves. The development of this line of thought is twofold. In the first place, the primary models of poetry, Homer, Shakespeare and Milton especially, are to be regarded more as divinities than men, hence the notion of the divine inspiration of poetry comes back into criticism. In the second place, the Augustan evolutionary theory of art, according to which the merits of a nation's art are in direct ratio to the refinement of its civilization, is no longer held. In fact, as the sublime usually precedes the beautiful, the ratio may actually be inverse. This reminds us again of the Elizabethan tendency to trace Classical myths back to the dawn of civilization, in the time of Orpheus and Zoroaster.

There was a strong desire all through the eighteenth century to write religious poetry, but little of permanent merit was produced, for the Augustan idea that orthodoxy was a matter of assenting to truth rather than of recreating a vision persisted, and the hymns of Watts, Cowper and the Wesleys are not much nearer to Blake than Pope's *Messiah*. The three visionary Renaissance traditions we have mentioned reappear, but, except fitfully in Smart's *Jubilate Agno*, do not coalesce. Methodists, like the Quakers, were essentially of the Anabaptist tradition, holding to an inner light and an indwelling Spirit, and Methodism is one of the few contemporary forms of Christianity for which Blake shows any sympathy.[32] But though the main current of religious energy ran through Methodism, it contributed little if anything to the revival of the creative imagination in poetry.

The chief reason for this seems to be that poets were once more reaching towards a claim to divine inspiration which all the orthodox churches would have denied. When the new poets spoke of "enthusiasm" they meant literally divine possession, however vague their divinity may have been. Once more, as in Elizabethan times, the prophet is a *vates* or seer, the successor of ancient bards, and the teacher of higher truths than reason knows. It is in Collins' *Ode on the Poetical Character* that the most daring claim is made. There, not only does the poet in his creation imitate the creative power of God, but is himself a son of God and Fancy, a "rich-hair'd youth of morn" associated with the sun-god, like the Greek Apollo, a prophet and visionary of whom the last exemplar was Milton. This youth is the direct ancestor of Blake's Orc.

What then is this God-filled enthusiasm or fancy? Obviously the new rush of poetry about the solitary lover of nature wandering through rural surroundings with his head full of dreams does not represent a "return to nature" in any sense of a surrender to its influence. The fanciful poet is using nature as material, and is creating out of it a higher nature. True, he is not taking this process very seriously, and even for the Wartons fancy still means something more reflective than creative; consequently this higher nature is romantic rather than paradisal, and the product of reverie rather than vision. But still the poet is not interpreting nature but releasing the power of his mind; and when Joseph Warton writes an ode to Fancy in which he sees her

> Waving in thy snowy hand
> An all-commanding magic wand,
> Of pow'r to bid fresh gardens blow,
> 'Mid cheerless Lapland's barren snow . . .

he is approaching Blake's idea of the image-forming imagination which creates a paradisal garden out of the wilderness of nature.

We can now perhaps understand more clearly the real motive of eighteenth century poetic primitivism. The Augustan process of developing a poetic tradition within a civilized environment no longer appealed to a poet who wanted to recapture for himself the primary creative mood in which the more sublime visions of earlier ages had been produced. He turned to solitude and direct contact with nature in order to apply to poetry, so to speak, the imaginative intensity of Robinson Crusoe. But the fact that the source of his inspiration is enthusiasm and fancy means that he does not want to be stimulated by nature into moral reflections: he wants to animate nature, to people her with the fairies and screech-owls and will-o'-the-wisps and jolly swains and shepherds which are not natural or human objects but human creatures, products of human creative power. Hence he finds a kinship with the primeval simplicity of the time when "the ancient Poets animated all sensible objects with Gods or Geniuses."

In other words, the poets of the age of Blake wanted to go back to mythopoeic poetry; yet those with any accuracy of poetic instinct wanted to avoid both worn-out Classical mythology with Philomela's "mechanick woe" (a phrase of Cowper's) on the one hand and mere Biblical paraphrase on the other. The immediate solution was to substitute what Blake called "Fairies of Albion" for "Gods of the Heathen." Thus Spenser, the great creator of English Faerie, began to come back into his own; the *Midsummer Night's Dream* and *The Tempest* took on a new significance in the canon of Shakespeare, and nothing that Milton wrote awoke more eighteenth century echoes than *L'Allegro* or *Il Penseroso*. Here was another way in which the imagery of the Bible could be put to poetic use, for in it the animation of nature, from the singing hills of Isaiah to the dragons of the deep praising God in the Psalms, is at its boldest and most vivid.

The main results of this new mythopoeia need only be mentioned: the folklore devils and witches of Burns; the interest of Collins not only in Highland superstitions but, as the subtitle of his poem on the subject indicates, in their value to the poet; the revival of interest in more romantic and fabulous aspects of Gothic culture. It was a curiously accurate instinct that led the eighteenth century to slight Old English and concentrate on the medieval period, for Old English is hieratic and Byzantine; it contains little of what the eighteenth century poets were looking for, though doubtless they could have made the author of *Beowulf* a primitive as easily as the nineteenth century made him a nostalgic Wagnerian pagan. Middle English, on the other hand, animated nature in a more youthful and exuberant way, as did the ballads, the Celtic and even the Norse literatures which were more thoroughly studied and translated. It is here too that the influence of Ossian comes in, for Ossian constantly describes his heroes in terms of the natural world and vice versa; and the kennings he employs, such as calling the echo the "son of the rock," are in the same tradition.

Yet the imaginative animation of nature, or seeing men afar, was in Classical poetry too, and the poetic technique derived from it can be seen in the more enthusiastic Classical writers.

Gray, for instance, finds it in Pindar. He begins his *Progress of Poesy* with an image which he feels requires a full explanatory note, beginning: "The subject and simile, as usual with Pindar, are united." This drew a sneer from Johnson: "Gray seems in his rapture to confound the images of *spreading sound* and *running water*. . . . If this be said of *Musick*, it is nonsense; if it be said of *Water*, it is nothing to the purpose." Gray's point is to some extent, however unconscious he may have been of it, an assertion of a poetic idealism resembling some aspects of Berkeley's thought: Johnson's criticism is that of a man who never did understand what Berkeley was driving at. In his *Descriptive Catalogue* Blake quotes a very similar image from *The Bard* and calls it "a bold, and daring, and most masterly conception, that the public have embraced and approved with avidity"[33]—this last perhaps with a glance at Johnson's charges of esoteric obscurity against Gray, charges to which Blake was peculiarly sensitive, for obvious personal reasons.

Just as the Augustan attitude was a politically conservative one, so most of the poets more congenial to Blake were Whigs and associated their new conception of fancy or imagination with liberty. They did not exactly follow Milton into revolutionary thought, but, consistently with their interest in the primitive, took a quasi-Rousseauist line, asserting that the creative imagination is most free where society is most simple and the restraints of civilization least evident, just as rough mountaineers are usually in the vanguard of political liberty. Gray has a note in *The Progress of Poesy* which reads: "Extensive influence of poetic Genius over the remotest and most uncivilized nations; its connection with liberty, and the virtues that naturally attend on it." It may conceivably have been from this passage that Blake picked his phrase "Poetic Genius" as a synonym for the imagination. Even more significantly, the view of the fall of the Roman Empire was beginning to take the form of a contrast between the primitive liberty-loving Goths and the enslaved and effeminate Romans.[34]

Thus in various ways an immense expansion of literary interests was bringing to the attention of poets much that had been left outside the direct line of development from Homer to Pope. The Arthurian and Eddic myths, which we have seen to be integral to Blake's symbolism, were discovered or rehabilitated. The whole poetic scene was filled with Welsh and Scandinavian translations and adaptations, not wholly out of fashion even when Blake opened his *Descriptive Catalogue* in 1809 with an imitation of Welsh "triads." Bishop Percy's literary career is a good example of the new variety of taste: besides his famous collection of ballads, he translated Mallet's introduction to his history of Denmark, one of Blake's most important sources, translated Norse poetry, and translated a Chinese novel from the Portuguese. New contributions were pouring in from as far afield as Persia and India, and Blake was among the first of European idealists able to link his own tradition of thought with the *Bhagavadgita*.[35]

Here, however, we have passed through fairyland and romance to mythology, and in myths, as in languages, there are endlessly suggestive analogies hinting that an underlying single pattern in the variety of *mœurs des nations* can be seen if one knows how to look for it. There was Biblical authority for Blake's statement that "all had originally one language, and one religion"[36]: perhaps with sufficient industry and learning a scholar might get some idea of what these originals were. It was in Blake's time that the foundations of a systematic study of comparative religion were laid, and in Blake's time that several English scholars, excavating more for buried treasure than for foundations, boldly plunged into the search for its archetype.

Most conspicuous among these, for our purposes, were Jacob Bryant and Edward Davies. The former's *Ancient Mythology*, in three quarto volumes, was a once famous effort to demonstrate that Classical legends are derived from an earlier "Amonian" culture. This mausoleum of misinformation and bad etymology is referred to by Blake as authority for his "All Religions are One" thesis; but the present writer has read it with sufficient care to hazard the guess that Blake had not. Davies' *Celtic Researches*, on the other hand, may have influenced *Jerusalem*. These men were not only unsuccessful in their enterprises, but to some extent deserve George Eliot's caricature of their type of scholar in the Casaubon of *Middlemarch*. Both were clergymen, which in their day meant that they were badly handicapped by an impossible view of the Bible. Both wasted great pains and immense erudition in trying to construct the roots of a pre-Babel language out of guesswork, without understanding the phonetic principles on which the Lord had confounded it. Yet they were by no means charlatans; they were, in their groping way, the Frazers of their time, and all their hopeless philology and dubious history does not obscure the outlines of an impressive idea. For the conception of a morphology of symbolism is of great literary importance; as we have tried to show, it has haunted English criticism at least since Elizabethan times, and has always been to some extent assumed by mythopoeic poets of all ages.

Blake follows Davies and another antiquary named Stukeley in identifying the original world-culture with Druidism. According to Davies, the Druid culture began with the dispersion at Babel; Stukeley, who was the first important antiquarian to pronounce Stonehenge a Druid temple, thought it began with Abraham. Neither suggests that the Druid culture was pre-Adamic, but the idea that Druid civilization was titanic, or rather gigantic, Blake may have taken over from Davies.[37]

This idea of the antiquity of the Druids was not a freakish or jingoistic one: it could have been worked out from Classical references alone by anyone with a decent education in those tongues. Even Milton casts a few glances in its direction. Diogenes Laertius mentions Druids as among the most ancient philosophers, ranking them with Pythagoras and the Persian Magi. But Pliny suggests that the Druids taught the Magi, and the story of the golden arrow brought to Pythagoras by a certain "Abaris" from the north seems to indicate that Pythagoras owed a good deal, perhaps including his doctrine of reincarnation, to the Druids. There are even suggestions that the cult of Apollo, most typically Greek of all Classical gods, came from the "Hyperboreans."[38] Davies considers that the Greek initiatory rites were Druid, pointing out that the katabasis of the eleventh book of the *Odyssey* took place in the far west, and he comes as close as he dares to suggesting that the sign in which Constantine conquered was the emblem of a Druid sun-god.[39]

These traditions of the west as the cradle of civilization seem to go with others about the western locality of the inhabitants of the Golden Age. The account of Atlantis in Plato is only one of a group of legends of paradisal or "Fortunate" Atlantic islands such as the story of the garden of the Hesperides. This Atlantic mythology retained its prestige in medieval times, and after the discovery of America it merged into the curiously persistent beliefs in an Eldorado and a fountain of youth, which are still serving literary purposes as late as *Candide*. Traditions of sunken land formerly possessed by England, notably Lyonesse, are of different origin but similar shape; and so perhaps are legends of an earlier discovery of America. The Madoc story, the subject of a contemporary epic by Southey, implies an association between America and the fellow-countrymen of Geoffrey of Monmouth, and is the apocryphal version of a fact which would have been equally interesting to Blake, that the real first discoverers of America belonged to the culture which produced the Eddas.[40]

The work of Bryant and Davies influenced few besides Blake, but there was a great deal of poetry written about Albion and its ancient bards, in which "Druid" and "Gothic" are not always clearly separated. To Blake the essential point to which all this led was simple enough. There seemed to be evidence, preserved in Classical writers, that the British Druid culture is the oldest on record. To Blake's contemporaries, with a greater primitivism in their bias, that suggested an idealization of the Druid period in which the word "Druid" would be practically synonymous with "inspired bard." Thus Collins speaks of Thomson as a Druid in his elegy on that poet. In Collins' *Ode to Liberty* the episode corresponding to Blake's fall of Atlantis, the deluge which made Britain an island, is followed by a description of a temple of liberty hidden in Albion's forests and associated with Druids, an association which is impossible in Blake. For as there is equal evidence that Druid civilization was one of murderous human sacrifice, there seemed to Blake little point in idealizing it. Their civilization had evidently declined from a still earlier one, and a hint of what that earlier one was is contained in the Atlantis legend, and thence, by the process we have traced before, to the giant Albion, the Northern myth of Ymir which tells of his fall, and finally, a lost myth of a Golden Age of which even the Bible preserves only a reminiscence. This, then, is the key to all mythologies, or at least to the British and Biblical ones; and, armed with this, one may proceed to write an epic which will re-establish the unity of British and Biblical symbolism, lost since Spenser.

None of Blake's contemporaries went so far, but much of what they did write seems less bizarre when we look at it as fragmentary glimpses of the conception just outlined. Thus the Rowley poems are a cycle of visions of an earlier Britain, or rather of a British land of Faerie, which exists not in the past but in an imaginative eternity: in what Blake might have called a spiritual fourfold Bristol. The Ossianic poems also form a cycle of visions connected with an ancient Britain peopled by huge cosmological figures in whom human and natural worlds can hardly be distinguished, so that they come very near to Blake's "Giant forms." In Southey the same mythopoeic interest stretches beyond England to include the world as a whole. He says: "While a schoolboy at Westminster, I had formed an intention of exhibiting the most remarkable forms of Mythology, which have at any time obtained among mankind, by making each the ground-work of a narrative poem."[41] There is no hint here of an underlying unity to these different myths, yet surely Southey intended his complete scheme to be a unity, an epic-romance of a scope even broader than Spenser's. From Blake's point of view, Southey was rather in the position of the man who could have written *Hamlet* if he had had the mind, and perhaps it was from the above passage that Blake formed the totally erroneous notion that Southey might be interested in his *Jerusalem*.[42]

In Smart's *Song to David* there is no British or mythopoeic interest, but the other half of Blake's outlook is there in his great vision of all nature, under the power of the inspired prophet-poet David, praising God and soaring upward into the apocalyptic state of innocence. In what with sufficient control could have become an equally great poem on a far larger scale, *Jubilate Agno*, there is more of Blake than in any other eighteenth century poem. Here, too, the poet is a seer of the apocalyptic vision and the expounder of the Word of God: he sees in every object of nature an "augury of innocence," and unites it to a name from the Bible which is evidently the human spirit within it: he makes associations of the most far-fetched kind within his own experience in order to suggest an underlying form in nature which is to be clearly revealed at the last day. There are several hints of Blake's Anglo-Biblical symbolism and much the same use of occult sources. *Jubilate Agno* is not, of course, a work of art any more than a shattered stained-glass window is; but its fragments are the most eloquently pathetic symbols we possess of that age of *poètes maudits*.

· 7 ·

BLAKE's first and only printed volume of poetry was called *Poetical Sketches*, and appeared in 1783. It was published through the patronage of Blake's friend Mathew, who contributes an apologetic preface. He explains that the book contains poems written by Blake between the ages of twelve and twenty, which Blake had not bothered to revise because he had determined to abandon poetry for "his chosen profession," *i.e.*, engraving. This may mean that Blake already had some scheme in his mind of a canon of engraved poems. *Poetical Sketches* falls into two parts, a group of lyrics of startling beauty and a less distinguished group of dramatic and rhapsodic experiments which are obviously the first attempts at the prophetic form. Though not in the canon, *Poetical Sketches* is of the highest importance to us, partly because it shows Blake's symbolic language in an emergent and transitional form, and partly because it confirms our point that Blake is organically part of his literary age. Chatterton, Ossian, Goldsmith, Percy, Collins and to a lesser extent Thomson and Gray, Gothic horror, the charnel house and the graveyard, primitivism, northern antiquities, oligarchic mercantilism, the renewed appreciation of Renaissance poetry, all find echoes of one kind or another here. The book, in short, shows a receptivity to a poetic environment which only a young poet of confident and assured originality would dare to assume.

A few of the lyrics, including four on the seasons and the famous "To the Evening Star," are related to the convention of the descriptive landscape poem. But Blake cannot describe anything inanimate: his seasons and evening stars are human figures, though even in his adolescence he is careful to call them angels and not gods. He has taken a step beyond personification, and his morning has become a holy virgin, his winter a

> direful monster, whose skin clings
> To his strong bones,

his summer a charioteer with "ruddy limbs and flourishing hair," his spring the earth's lover. In one lovely little song we can see even more clearly Blake's humanizing vision bursting out of eighteenth century abstract nouns:

> Love and harmony combine,
> And around our souls intwine,
> While thy branches mix with mine,
> And our roots together join.
> Joys upon our branches sit,
> Chirping loud, and singing sweet;
> Like gentle streams beneath our feet
> Innocence and virtue meet.

There is only one relapse into simile: the rest is the identification of subject and simile which Gray found in Pindar. Again, we have spoken of the bold and exuberant nature of Biblical imagery, and the Psalmist who wrote of the sun as a bridegroom and an athlete finds a responsive disciple in Blake:

> O radiant morning, salute the sun,
> Rouz'd like a huntsman to the chace, and, with
> Thy buskin'd feet, appear upon our hills.[43]

There are several attempts to work out an antithesis of innocence and experience, and in the song we have quoted from, "Love and harmony combine," there is quite an advanced symbol of innocence: the two lovers are trees, the male in fruit and the female in flower, which recalls the Classical *ver perpetuum*.

Poetical Sketches also shows some startling illustrations of the consistency of Blake's mind. One of the finest of the lyrics, the one beginning "How sweet I roam'd," which tells how a bird was caught in a "silken net" and shut in a "golden cage" by a "prince of love" who is also a sun-god, is said to have been written by Blake at the age of fourteen.[44] In one of the most complicated myths of that very complicated poem *The Four Zoas*, written when Blake was about forty, we discover a "key" to this little lyric which is necessary, not to understand it, but to understand something about Blake. The early lyric looks like a conventional Petrarchan love-song, and has the ambiguous tone of one. In the second Night of *The Four Zoas* we find a version of the Phaethon myth which tells us that one of the main events of the Fall was the seizure of the sun, which belonged to the Prince of Light, or Urizen, by the Prince of Love, or Luvah. The fact that the Eros of "How sweet I roam'd" is a sun-god accounts for the silk net and gold cage, which are also doing duty in lyrics written thirty years later in an exactly similar, though more elaborate, context.

Again, in reading "To the Muses" it is not necessary to read into it Blake's later contrast between the "Daughters of Beulah" or inspiration, who come from the human mind, and the "Daughters of Memory," the Classical Muses, who are assembled from the elements of nature. But it is clear that the lyric is the germ of the myth. The great "Mad Song" is also the germ of Blake's whole conception of "Spectres." A maddened world of storm and tempest is the objective counterpart of madness in the human mind; and the madman is mad because he is locked up in his own Selfhood or inside, and cannot bear to see anything. In order to have his world a consistently dark one he is compelled to rush frantically around the spinning earth forever, keeping one jump ahead of the rising sun, unable even to sleep in his everlasting night. He is a prisoner of space as well as time, for he thinks of heaven as a solid vault. The poem, like many of Blake's, has more humor than it is usually given credit for.

"King Edward the Third" is an exercise in the idiom of Elizabethan drama, just as the songs are, if more successfully, exercises in the corresponding lyrical idiom. It is a very curious piece. Apparently, if one believes that England has always been the home of democracy and constitutional government, and France— at least until the Revolution—a hotbed of tyranny and superstition, one can also believe that the Hundred Years' War was a blow struck solely in the interests of progress. The English are famous for transforming their economic and political ambitions into moral principles, and to the naïve mercantile jingoism of the eighteenth century, which assumed that freedom of action was the same thing as material expansion, there seemed nothing absurd in thinking that the unchecked growth of England's power involved the emancipation of the world. At any rate, Akenside, in his *Ode to the Country Gentlemen of England*, seems to have had a vague idea that war with France is somehow connected with the principles of Freedom, Truth and Reason as well as Glory, and refers to the Hundred Years' War as a crusade in favor of these principles. Akenside was a Whig; Thomson and Young, who wrote a good deal to the same effect, were also Whigs, the liberals of their time, and it is not really surprising if the young Blake, looking for a historical example of the fight of freedom against tyranny, should have selected the exploits of Edward III. A good deal of the poem is simply "Rule Britannia" in blank verse:

> . . . if so, we are not sovereigns
> Of the sea; our right, that Heaven gave
> To England, when at the birth of nature
> She was seated in the deep, the Ocean ceas'd
> His mighty roar; and, fawning, play'd around
> Her snowy feet, and own'd his lawful Queen.

The most puzzling feature of "King Edward the Third" is the frankness with which Blake admits that economic ambitions are the cause of the war. Industry, commerce, agriculture, manufacture and trade are the gods directing the conflict, but the conflict is glorious and the gods worthy of worship. There seems to be no use looking for irony here, though of course there is an innate shrewdness which greater experience could easily make ironic. Such commercial expansion is caused by liberty: it is liberty, "the charter'd right of Englishmen" (another "Rule Britannia" echo), fighting against slavery in its "invisible chains" which Edward III's campaign represents. Those who die fighting for England are immediately transported to Paradise, and peace can only be a *pax Britannica*.

If we have seemed to emphasize the faults of "King Edward the Third" rather than its virtues, it is only to insist that Blake's ideas developed logically from his environment, and the sterility of much of that environment is no argument against the fact that his genius grew up in it. Besides, Blake's palinodes are prompt and frequent. The first is a "Prologue" intended for a play on Edward IV. Now if Blake chose Edward IV as a subject with the same care that he chose Edward III, here is the sign of a swing from mercantilist Whiggery to the radicalism that made him a sympathizer with the French and American revolutions. For the War of the Roses was very obviously the result of the purposeless folly of the ruling classes. The "Prologue," which is in King Cambyses' vein, gives no hint, as "King Edward the Third" does, of the incisiveness with which the poet places the origin of war in profiteering, but it is the first real statement of Blake's revolutionary attitude.

Blake's imagination being what it is, his revolutionary poetry is obviously going to require two central characters, a protagonist fighting for liberty and an antagonist defending tyranny. There is another "Prologue" intended for a play on King John, in which patriotic duty this time is connected, not with assaulting a foreign country in order to steal its trade, but with destroying tyranny in one's own. Here the two central characters are given in an elementary personified form, and Albion is a woman, as England or Britannia is in *Jerusalem*:

Then Patriot rose; full oft did Patriot rise, when Tyranny hath stain'd fair Albion's breast with her own children's gore.

In a much more interesting poem, the ballad called "Gwin, King of Norway," which shows the influence not only of ballads but of Chatterton, the battle is on. Gwin is a king supported by nobles who exploit the poor: Gordred the giant leads a workers' revolution, and a spirited description of a battle follows in which Gordred cuts the tyrant in two, but whether the revolt was a permanent success or not Blake does not say—an equivocation which meets us again in *Europe*. The conflict is fought on a heroic plane, the two champions being giants, with the result that it is sufficiently dramatic to be melodramatic, but not dramatic enough to gain the advantage of a human situation. The revolutionary sentiment is partly Puritan and partly Whiggish. The rebellion seems to be largely a middle-class one, recalling "King Edward the Third," in which the stronghold of political liberty is the independent yeoman, and the phraseology, like the use of giants, recalls the Old Testament:

> The Nobles of the land did feed
>   Upon the hungry Poor;
> They tear the poor man's lamb, and drive
>   The needy from their door!

But obviously this is hardly Blake's line. It is not natural to him to think of liberty as "the charter'd right of Englishmen": in the later poem of "London," in the *Songs of Experience*, the word "charter'd" is used with the whole power of his irony behind it. Nor, for him, would the Biblical precedents for freedom consist, as in Milton's regicide pamphlets, in the rebellions of the chosen people against their no less chosen conquerors, but in the far more radical upheaval envisaged by the prophets. Blake's two characters,

then, must derive from his conception of tyranny as the defense
of the fallen world and of liberty as the effort of the imagination
to recover the state of innocence. It is therefore out of his symbols
of innocence and experience, of Summer with his "ruddy limbs
and flourishing hair" and "the direful monster" Winter, that the
two great figures of Orc and Urizen emerge.

It seems clear that the main outlines of Blake's archetypal
myth were in his mind from a very early age. In "King Edward
the Third" there is an early sketch of the parallel between
English and Hebrew history which is the ground plan of *Jerusalem*, though in terms of a symbolism he later repudiated. In
the closing chorus, the legend of the Trojan origin of Britain
obviously recalls the Biblical story of an exodus from enemies,
a wandering to a land of destiny, a rapid conquest of giants, and
a prophecy of everlasting peace and prosperity. Another poem
called "The Couch of Death" is dated back to "former times,"
"when the cold clay breathed with life," and the theme is in
rough outline one of the episodes in the later fall of Albion. More
extensive and more remarkable is a long theogony written at the
same time as *Poetical Sketches*, in which we find in embryo the
three major themes, the cycle of history, the role of the artist
in society, and the Fall, of Blake's later poetry.[45]

· 8 ·

IN his versification Blake is also following contemporary models
while experimenting in all directions for himself. We have seen
that for Blake the meter of a poem should be an inference from
it rather than a condition of it. The rhythm of major poetry is a
supple and fluent thing, and it is much harder to give variety to
rhythm than to give regularity to it. In Shakespeare, though we
have no reason to suppose that Blake knew this, there is a development from regular end-stopped verse with frequent rhyme to an irregular unrhymed verse which goes at such a speed that an entire
speech or paragraph becomes the rhythmic unit rather than the
pentameter line. In Milton, too, the blank-verse paragraph is the
unit of the epics and expands into an even greater freedom from
pentameter in *Samson Agonistes*. These paragraphs are thus a
kind of combination of blank verse and the stanza, though it is not
necessary that they should be unrhymed. The metrical revolts

against the couplet in the eighteenth century, therefore, included not only the revivals of blank verse and the stanza which the imitation of Milton and Spenser made inevitable, but experiments in the half-cadences and intertwining rhythms of paragraphic verse. This is the basis of the ode form, and Collins' *Ode to Evening* has got away from the rhymed *canzone* pattern of the usual ode into a shimmering texture of evenly diffused sound.

In Blake's *Poetical Sketches* there is an "Imitation of Spenser" in which each stanza is a different variation of the Spenserian model; and the first six poems are experiments in the unrhymed lyric. The pentameter is the basis, and Blake attacks it with a great variety of modulation, trying to avoid end-stopped lines and weld a whole quatrain or sixain into a single rhythmic unit. Enjambement is an essential part of this; weak endings are almost an affectation, and a curious kind of syntactic enjambement takes care of the strong ones:

> O deck her forth with thy fair fingers; pour
> Thy soft kisses on her bosom; and put
> Thy golden crown upon her languish'd head
> Whose modest tresses were bound up for thee![46]

We are concerned here with derivation and experiment, not with the triumphant successes of Blake's lyrical genius. The next step for Blake, having mastered the short lyric, is to develop a more continuous rhythm to carry a longer poem. In a raucous but interesting piece of Gothic horror, "Fair Elenor," complete with charnel houses and echoes from *Hamlet*, Blake falls into the slow beats appropriate for making one's flesh creep and begins to show something of his power in handling accents in a long line:

> and now fancies she hears
> Deep sighs, and sees pale sickly ghosts gliding.

In "King Edward the Third" the effort to produce a decorous imitation of Elizabethan style clashes with a much stronger desire to talk in his own idiom, and the pentameter stretches out uneasily into a less confining rhythm:

> Say, Lords, should not our thoughts be first to commerce?
> My Lord Bishop, you would recommend us agriculture?

Sometimes these stretches are more successful, and Blake can insert an Alexandrine into blank verse with considerable skill. The significance of such passages is that Blake is dissatisfied with the obtrusiveness of recurrent accents in the pentameter line as he handles it, and that his tendency is to lengthen the line rather than build up paragraphs, as a more direct way of increasing the speed.

Most of the "prophetic" sketches are printed in the form of that unreadable anomaly, the prose poem. Blank verse, as one edition has somewhat grimly shown, is still the underlying meter; but whereas in the lyrics Blake had the whole weight of a great tradition behind him, in these he has only Ossian and his own originality. They show that Ossian played an important part in liberating Blake's meter, but Ossian helped him very little with his two chief technical problems of diction and rhythm. The imitation of Ossian involves the reproduction of his very conventionalized poetic diction, and Blake did not want a poetic diction of any kind. A glance at the thundering anapests of *The French Revolution* will show, too, that its author had more ideas about a powerful and cumulative rhythm than he could ever have got from the exclamatory gasps of Ossian.

Let us take the problem of diction first. Blake's vision is based on a theory of knowledge and demands full understanding rather than mere sensibility; hence there is in his poetry a good deal of doctrinal exposition. To invent, like Spenser and Milton, a hieratic form of poetic speech would cause Blake to sound most pompous and artificial when he was being most earnestly explicit. So whatever difficulties there may be in Blake's poetry, difficulties of style are not among them. "The Mental Traveller" is not an easy poem to understand, but its vocabulary and syntax are limpidly pure. Blake, even more than Wordsworth, sticks to the *koiné* of normal English speech, with all its colloquial clatter, the pounding accents of its monosyllables, the rumbling mutter of the longer Latin words, the machine-gun fire of auxiliaries and prepositions. There is very little in Blake of the archaic idiom of Romantic poetry, and no trace of the professional beggar's whine of "dying falls" and self-consciously evocative phrases. Blake distinguishes in *Jerusalem* "terrific," "mild and gentle" and "prosaic" passages; and it is in the last that his assimilation of the rhythm of poetry to that of informal speech is most clearly marked.

But however complex the thought, the speech is consistently simple. Not since Donne had so direct a style been able to express such a variety of moods from apocalypse to ribaldry.

If Blake had worked within the limits of the pentameter, he would no doubt have gone on evolving blank verse paragraphs. But he could not be satisfied with this: he wanted an English dactylic hexameter, a line spacious enough to carry the roll and thunder of apocalyptic visions. This he found in the old medieval septenarius, the meter which Chapman had used to reproduce the rhythm of the *Iliad*, the meter of the ballads and of historical and didactic epics down to Warner's *Albions England*. For some of his shorter prophecies Blake developed a kind of "free verse" recitativo in which the septenarius is mixed with lyrical meters. His greatest achievement in this form is *Europe*. He also wrote three poems, *The Book of Urizen*, *The Book of Los* and *The Book of Ahania*, in which he used a short line of three or four beats, and which brought him back very close to Ossian again, as may readily be seen if an extract is printed in prose form. Evidently Blake intended at first to make this the meter for the longer epic scheme he then had in mind; but when he began *The Four Zoas*, the first of his three long prophecies, he abandoned it and fell back with an audible gasp of relief on his long swinging line:

The Song of the Aged Mother which shook the heavens with wrath,
Hearing the march of long resounding, strong heroic Verse
Marshall'd in order for the day of Intellectual Battle.[47]

English being so strongly accented a language, a line of this length gets out of hand very easily, and the more conventional the treatment the harder it is to break it in for serious work. Too settled a metrical pattern will produce infuriating monotony: rhyme or alliteration are constant temptations to let it relapse into jingle. Blake saw that for his purposes such a line would have not only to dispense with all recurrent ornament, but with a recurrent prosodic unit as well: it would have to be treated as a line of seven beats rather than of seven feet. The exception to this rule, *The French Revolution*, has a consistently anapestic roll to its meter, but it is early and Blake did not repeat the experiment, though it was by no means an unsuccessful one. The other poems show a gradual development of fluency from the early

Book of Thel, where there is still an underlying iambic pattern, to *Milton* and *Jerusalem*, which have achieved the kind of rhythm we find in music. That is, in music any number of notes, within limits impossible to define by strict rules, may be contained within a single rhythmic unit, and Blake's prophecies, particularly the later ones, are musical poetry in this sense.

In this connection a musical term employed by Blake takes on some significance. Of all Blake's engraved prophecies, only *The Book of Ahania*, which is a sequel, lacks some kind of introduction, and the three abandoned poems (*Tiriel*, *The French Revolution* and *The Four Zoas* were never engraved) all start *in medias res*. Blake seems to have felt the necessity of beginning with some kind of single vision of his theme which would serve both as the motto of the poetry and the emblem of the engraving. This introduction he calls several times a "Preludium," a statement of the essential harmonies underlying the contrapuntal intricacies of his thought.

For the more fashionable and less liberal tastes Blake's "Chariot of Genius" will always seem a noisy and rattling vehicle. But it has been thought worth-while to mention the affinity of Blake's rhythm to music because his theory of art applies equally to music, poetry and painting. His work presents a "parallel of poetry and painting" which carries the Elizabethan doctrine of *ut pictura poesis* to its logical conclusion, and in his lyrics the Renaissance "emblem" has been transfigured from allegory into vision. On the other hand, the freedom of music from sense experience is the goal to which his theories of painting and poetry lead. Blake's engraved poems, therefore, not only continue the medieval tradition of the illuminated book, but present, ideally, a unified vision of the three major arts to the individual as the musical drama, with its combination of speech, sound and setting, presents it to the audience.

THE THIEF OF FIRE

ONCE we begin to look at Blake's engraved works as a canon, we can discern certain structural principles within it. *The Marriage of Heaven and Hell*, the form of which is fundamentally that of a prose satire, rises out of the midst of the "minor prophecies" in a class by itself. But there are three poems which are evidently intended to form a single group: *America, Europe* and *The Song of Los*, the last of these being divided into two parts called respectively "Africa" and "Asia." *America* is clearly a revolutionary poem; so is "Asia," and so is another poem on the French Revolution, which was never engraved. These four poems and *The Marriage of Heaven and Hell* revolve around the character whom Blake calls Orc, and are concerned, like a good deal of Milton's prose, with the interconnection of three themes: the theme of satire, or the prophet's denunciation of society; the theme of achieving liberty through revolutionary action; and the theme of apocalypse. We begin with the theme of satire.

It has doubtless occurred to the reader already that Bacon, Newton and Locke do not look very convincing in the role of three-headed hellish Cerberus which Blake assigns them. It is not so much that Blake is unfair to them personally: a thinker should be judged by the quality of his influence as well as by his own views. That is, it is an error of fact to call Locke a Deist, but it is not an error of interpretation to see many affinities between Deism and Locke's theory of knowledge. But Blake's unfairness is more extreme than that. After all, Bacon had a profound respect for the imaginative communication of truth in allegory and parable, and if it does not bulk large in *The Advancement of Learning* it was only because he considered that poetry was doing fairly well and needed no advancement. Blake would no doubt have disagreed with Bacon's approach to allegory in his *Wisdom of the Ancients* if he had read it, but the fact that Bacon wrote such a book at all makes it difficult to dismiss him as a mere Philistine whose "first principle is Unbelief." Locke's virile contempt of slavery, his defense of toleration and even the primacy he gives to sense experience in his theory of knowledge are all Blakean qualities. Newton's work in science certainly did not make him a "Deist"; he had an interest in apocalyptic thought which deserved something better, from Blake's point of view, than the ridicule which Blake seems to give it.[1] Not one of these thinkers are as opposed to Blake's mode of thought as, for instance, Hobbes, whom he never mentions, where there are barriers against Blake's apocalyptic humanism far more rigid than anything his three favorite antagonists erect.

Now whether Blake had read Hobbes or not, he is by no means unaware of the force of this objection. But we have already seen how important to Blake is the Baconian principle that truth comes more readily from error than from confusion. What Blake most fears and hates is more easily defended by hypocrisy or self-deception than by frankness. "Truth," he says, "can never be told so as to be understood, and not be believ'd."[2] The inference is that falsehood can never be told so as to be understood, and not be recognized as false. The very honesty of Hobbes lets the tyrant's cat, or rather Leviathan, out of the bag. It is the reasonable and persuasive Locke who is likely to attract a well-meaning audience, and it is far more important to attack him than Hobbes, who could be plausibly denounced by even a stupid or malicious person. Similarly, though predestination was a doctrine Blake loathed, he does not attack it in Augustine or Calvin; he attacks a tendency to it in his master Swedenborg.[3] Again, the Deist belief that an idea of God is innate in man is in a sense closer to Blake than it is to Locke, who denies it, and certainly closer than atheism is. But Blake saw in Deism, not atheism, the really pernicious foe of Christianity.

This idea that truth in a false context is worse than outspoken falsehood leads in Blake's thought to a distinction between a "contrary" and a "negation." In society the contraries are the "Devils" and the "Angels" already mentioned. Blake and Locke are contraries: both feel that imagination, liberty and life are in their systems, and they must clash or we shall never know who is right. Hobbes is a negation: he cares too little for imagination or liberty to clash with any defender of it. In *Milton* Blake calls the negations "the Elect from before the foundation of the world"[4]; an ironic reference to the theory of predestination. They are the Pharisees who turn all religion, Jewish, Christian or Deist, into a routine of ritual and morality. They are the righteous whom

Jesus did *not* call to repentance, and of whom he says with grim ambiguous irony: "They have their reward." The contraries Blake calls the "Reprobate" and the "Redeemed": they correspond to Rintrah and Palamabron. The former are the persecuted and outcast prophets: the latter are the timid well-meaning orthodox whose good qualities emerge only after the prophets have hammered their timidity to pieces. The clash of contraries is thus an essential part of the "redemption" of mankind. In *The Marriage of Heaven and Hell* a "Devil" makes a violent attack on an "Angel," who becomes converted. "This Angel," says Blake, "who is now become a Devil, is my particular friend."[5] Similarly, in the final consummation of the world portrayed in *Jerusalem*, we see "the innumerable Chariots of the Almighty "

And Bacon & Newton & Locke, & Milton & Shakspear & Chaucer,[6]

taking equal place in the vision.

The same distinction between a contrary and a negation occurs in Blake's theory of ideas. All real things have qualities in them, and qualities always have opposites. This is particularly true of moral qualities, as every virtue has its corresponding vice. All "good" men by any standards may be "bad" by other standards, just as an egg that is bad to eat may be good to throw at someone. But the believer in the cloven fiction prefers to identify a real thing with one of its qualities, because things become easier to generalize about when classified into qualities. Now as things are good or bad according to circumstances, the cloven fiction leads to the absolutizing of circumstances. The deader a thing is, the more obedient it is to circumstances, and the more alive it is the less predictable it becomes. Hence the believer in the cloven fiction finds it much easier to understand the behavior of dead things, the objects of exact science under the law of "mathematic form." And in studying human activity he again finds it easiest to understand when it is most automatic. So insensibly he tends to call "the passive that obeys Reason" good, and "the active springing from Energy" bad. The result is that illegitimate pun on the word "law" which associates a description of a predictable process in nature with the definition of an ideal standard of human conduct:

> And this is the manner of the Sons of Albion in their strength:
> They take the Two Contraries which are call'd Qualities, with which
> Every Substance is clothed: they name them Good & Evil
> From them they make an Abstract, which is a Negation
> Not only of the Substance from which it is derived,
> A murderer of its own Body, but also a murderer
> Of every Divine Member: it is the Reasoning Power,
> An Abstract objecting power that Negatives every thing.[7]

In society, the contraries and negation are the reprobate visionary, the elected tyrant and the victim whom the visionary has to redeem. This means that the victim, not the tyrant, is the prophet's contrary, and the object of his attack. The source of all tyranny is the mental passivity induced by abstract reasoning in the victim's mind, and until that is got rid of all rulers will be compelled to be tyrants.[8] "The tygers of wrath are wiser than the horses of instruction"[9]: the glittering intensity of prophetic vision sees its real prey in the stupid, blinkered vision that distorts forms into frightening monsters.

We may push this opposition of visionary and reasoner a little further. Blake assigns to Aristotle the dictum that "Characters are either Good or Bad," and comments, "A Horse is not more a Lion for being a Bad Horse: that is its Character: its Goodness or Badness is another consideration."[10] To the artist a horse's character is its form: he may make a perfectly good use of what would in other respects be a bad horse, as Cervantes did of Rozinante, and he has no further interest in its goodness or badness. The moralist or reasoner, on the other hand (the two words are synonyms in Blake: we shall see why presently), will select certain forms of behavior and reject others; denounce this and commend that. He will not understand what "use" an artist can make of anything except in relation to choosing what he calls "good" and avoiding what he calls "bad"; and if he had his own way with the arts, he would censor and expurgate along these lines. It is necessary then for art to have some line of defense against theoretical invasions. Such a line of defense would naturally be a satire directed against the pretenses of the reasoning moralist.

Hence there is frequently an antiphilosophical bias in satire and the literary precedents for Blake's attack on Bacon, Newton and Locke in English literature are the attacks of Samuel Butler and Swift on Cartesian logic and Royal Society virtuosi. We could see this more clearly if Blake had selected, say, Descartes for his target instead of the three Englishmen. Of course Butler and Swift are equally merciless on an occult tradition for which Blake had more sympathy, but still *The Marriage of Heaven and Hell* (which incidentally gives quite a rough ride to Swedenborg) is closer to them than to the occultists. For the hostility to science and philosophy displayed in the Laputa section of *Gulliver's Travels* and *The Elephant in the Moon* is neither irresponsible nor incidental: it springs from the artist's insistence that the totality of experience is far greater than all attempts to summarize it in formulas. The scientists in *The Elephant in the Moon* who deliberately rule out inconvenient evidence are not simply dishonest men: there would be little point in the satire if they were. They symbolize the scientific preoccupation with the small part of life capable of logical and experimental treatment. Such preoccupation according to Blake is oversimplified and in the long run inhuman, and he charges the "reasoner" with a self-absorbed introspection only one remove from schizophrenia. He is anticipated in Swift's portrayal of the scientific dignitaries of Laputa who need flappers to recall them to the world.

· 2 ·

BLAKE's most important literary production between *Poetical Sketches* and the earliest engraved works was that extraordinary prose satire (with verse interludes) which has been given the name of *An Island in the Moon*, and is a satire on cultural dilettantism. In this work we touch on one of the very few aspects of eighteenth century culture we did not meet in *Poetical Sketches*: caricature. The uncompromising misogyny of "Hail, Matrimony," and the physical awareness of the repulsive in "When old corruption first begun," are in the Swift tradition, and Blake's power of reducing cultured conversation to the chattering of sophisticated monkeys shows a Hogarthian command of the grotesque. The characters, as we should expect, are not so much individuals as representatives of the various types of "reasoning" which are satirized. The three philosophers who begin the discussion are a Cynic, an Epicurean and a Pythagorean; but, as Blake says, "tho' the sects are not ever mention'd there, as being quite out of date;

however, the things still remain, and the vanities are the same." This anticipates his later remark that "Bacon is only Epicurus over again," though these three turn out to be various kinds of primitivists. But though types, the characters are more carefully differentiated than the casual reader may think. There are vivid sketches of an adolescent schoolboy, a sententious lawyer, a spoiled "genius" typical of a circle of dilettantes, a brainless young woman. And the various techniques employed by Blake, the juggling with "Phebus" and "Pharaoh" in Chapters 3 and 4, the farcical conversational deadlock of Chapter 5, the self-absorbed irrelevance reminding one rather of Chekhov in the discussion "if Pindar was not a better Poet than Ghiotto [*sic*][11] was a Painter," all contribute to an impression that Blake was building with large units.

In the final chapter of this Gargantuan nightmare we stumble upon three of the most delicate and fragile of the *Songs of Innocence*, appearing for the first time in surely the most inappropriate context that could have been devised for them. It is an interesting context, however, as it suggests that the idea of associating them with parallel songs of experience was already in Blake's mind, and was in origin an idea connected with satire, a point to which we shall return. For these three lovely songs of the child's unfallen world are followed by two others which proceed to reproduce the accents of a real schoolboy and a real schoolgirl. The first begins:

> I say, you Joe,
> Throw us the ball,
> I've a good mind to go,
> And leave you all.

The poem goes on to tell how this schoolboy's handkerchief has been used to clean the ball after it had fallen into an unsavory location; he had previously produced what was doubtless the same handkerchief and had applied it to the glass of a scientist's microscope. The link with *The Elephant in the Moon* needs no comment. The girl has her turn:

> Leave, O leave me to my sorrows,
> Here I'll sit & fade away;
> Till I'm nothing but a spirit,
> And I lose this form of clay.

which in its satiric tone is midway between "Ah! Sunflower" and some of the more ribald epigrams in the Rossetti MS. After her contribution we go back to drunkenness and equivocal puns, and the world of imagination which for a while had stolen down on the group and reduced them to bemused silence disappears.

There follows a break in the manuscript, with a hint that the missing sheets contained the secret of the engraving process. It is a great pity that there is not more of the *Island in the Moon*, but there remains the torso of a highly amusing satire. If Blake's aphorism is true that "Exuberance is Beauty," the *Island in the Moon* is an extremely beautiful work of art. Had Blake continued to work in this form, he would perhaps have developed a kind of prose fiction in which, as in *Tristram Shandy* and *Ulysses*, the main characters are expanded to individual phases of human existence with encyclopedic ranges of association around them. Slight as it is, the *Island in the Moon* is one of the few connecting links between these two works. The drunken orgy of the ninth chapter, a riotous pandemonium almost entirely in verse, is perhaps the nearest approach in English literature to the technique of the brothel scene of *Ulysses*; and the smashing of the gas jet in the later work recalls the breaking of the test tube in the earlier one.

The glint in the eye of the poet who wrote this never, of course, faded out: it is still there in *The Everlasting Gospel* and the series of sketches called "Visionary Heads," both quite late. One may wonder, in fact, whether Blake's sense of the grotesque, of broad caricature and ribald parody, was really a minor quality, and good only for an occasional *tour de force*. One may wonder whether satire was not his real medium, whether in the long run he was not of the race of Rabelais and Apuleius, a metaphysical satirist inclined to fantasy rather than symbolism.[12] In any case it was to satire, or a modification of it, that Blake returned with far greater success in *The Marriage of Heaven and Hell*, the crowning work of his early period, in which he announces himself as a prophet come of age, declares his independence of his two mentors Milton and Swedenborg, and proclaims the acceptable year of the Lord.

· 3 ·

THE central idea of *The Marriage of Heaven and Hell,* to put it crudely, is that the unrest which has produced the French and American revolutions indicates that the end of the world might come at any time. The end of the world, the apocalypse, is the objective counterpart of the resurrection of man, his return to the titanic bodily form he originally possessed. When we say that man has fallen, we mean that his soul has collapsed into the form of the body in which he now exists. Hence, while no one could be less of an ascetic than Blake, the premise from which the ascetic starts is also his. The body is "vile"[18]: it is the body of a peeled ape, a witch's cauldron of tangled tissues and sodden excrement cooking in blood. This is as true of the nightingale as it is of the vulture, and as true of the tender virgin as it is of the gorilla. The physical nausea so painfully developed in Swift is an example of a soul's disgusted reaction to its degraded state. But where the ascetics go wrong is in forgetting that all mental activity is also a bodily struggle, because based on sense experience. The prophecies resound with bitter complaints of the inadequacy of the body, of the impotence of the eye to see and of the nose to smell, but the moral in Blake is that the body is weak enough already without trying to split it in two. Now we cannot by taking thought add a cubit to our statures; it is a change of worlds that is necessary, the lifting of the whole body to a fully imaginative plane by getting rid of the natural man.

The transformation of the body into a spiritual substance is the Christian doctrine of bodily resurrection. Job puts this doctrine in the form of its essential paradox: "And though after my skin worms destroy this body, yet in my flesh shall I see God."[14] There is no soul imprisoned within the body evaporating at death, but a living man armed with all the powers of his present body, infinitely expanded. The relation of soul to body is that of an oak to an acorn, not of a genie to a bottle. And there are no natural laws which the risen body must obey and no compulsory categories by which it must perceive. It is impossible to picture this except in terms of what we now see, and providing angels with wings is about as far as we can get. As Blake says, "From a perception of only 3 senses or 3 elements none could deduce a fourth or fifth"[15]; and we have no idea how many imaginative powers we do not possess. But Jesus, says Paul:

shall change our vile body, that it may be fashioned like unto his glorious body, according to the working whereby he is able even to subdue all things unto himself.[16]

Esse est percipi, and because we perceive on the level of this body we see an independent nature in a looming and sinister perspective. We are still living in an age of giant stars just as the ants are still living in an age of giant ferns; the natural man is a mole, and all our mountains are his molehills. In the resurrection of the body the physical universe would take the form in which it would be perceived by the risen body, and the risen body would perceive it in the form of Paradise.

The complete conquest of nature implied by the words "resurrection" and "apocalypse" is a mystery bound up with the end of time, but not with death. When the Selfhood is asked what it wants to do, it can only answer, with the Sibyl in Petronius, that it wants to die, and it thinks of death as a resolution. To the imagination physical death isolates the part that lives in the spiritual world; but as that world is the real here and the real now, we do not have to wait to die to live in it. "Whenever any Individual Rejects Error & Embraces Truth, a Last Judgment passes upon that Individual."[17] Similarly, the apocalypse could occur at any time in history if men wanted it badly enough to stop playing their silly game of hide-and-seek with nature. Visionaries, artists, prophets and martyrs all live as though an apocalypse were around the corner, and without this sense of a potentially imminent crisis imagination loses most of its driving power. The expectation of a Last Judgment in the New Testament does not mean that the Christians of that time were victims of a mass delusion, or that they were hypnotizing themselves in order to nerve themselves for martyrdom, but that they saw the physical universe as precariously balanced on the mental cowardice of man. And when Blake and Milton elaborate theories of history suggesting that time is reaching its final crisis during their own lives, they are only doing what Jesus did before them.

The resurrection of the body means the resurrection of all the body, and as the physical body has a sexual origin, the sexual life,

Blake says, becomes a human one, which means that sex is transformed, not eliminated. In eternity, Blake remarks dryly:

> Embraces are Cominglings from the Head even to the Feet,
> And not a pompous High Priest entering by a Secret Place.[18]

That is why in the Bible the apocalypse is often referred to as a
wedding, a union in love in which the relation of man to nature
becomes the relation of the lover to the beloved, the Bridegroom to the Bride. And as the Bride in Blake is Jerusalem, a
city in Eden and a "married land" in Beulah, it is in Beulah that
the sexual aspect of life becomes fulfilled. But Beulah is the
state of existence directly above our own, hence the apocalypse
will begin by "an improvement of sensual enjoyment"[19]—Blake
uses the adjective deliberately.

And as the risen body perceives the new world the old one
perishes in flames. Why flames? Because fire is the greatest possible combination in this world of heat and light, and the risen
body lives in the greatest possible combination of the spiritual
forms of heat and light: energy or desire, and reason or vision.
Fire destroys the solid form of nature, and those who have believed
nature to be solid will find themselves in a lake of fire at the
Dies Irae. But the imagination cannot be consumed by fire, for
it is fire; the burning bush of God which never exhausts its
material. It is this fire that "delights in its form."[20]

The word "consummation," often applied to the apocalypse,
refers both to the burning world and the sacred marriage. Paradise
itself is a place of flaming fire, the fires being the "lustful" passions
which there are fully gratified. They are also "thought-creating
fires"[21] because gratified desire produces reason. Eden is a fiery
city, as is indicated in Ezekiel's speech to the Covering Cherub:
"Thou hast been in Eden the garden of God . . . thou hast walked
up and down in the midst of the stones of fire." Similarly the
three whom Nebuchadnezzar put into a fiery furnace were seen
to be walking unhurt in the fire with the Son of God.

Since the Fall, there has been a flaming sword over Paradise,
and fire is now something to be approached with more circum-
spection. Orthodox theology tells us that in the eternal world
the fires of hell have heat without light, and that heaven is a
blaze of golden light, the question of heat being slurred over.

Remembering that passion and desire are spiritual heat, such doctrines tell us symbolically that desires are hellish and that we shall be tortured forever for having them, whereas those who have emasculated their passions will be admitted to a heaven in which the kind of divine love they enjoy, while its exact nature is unknown, is certain to be something very, very pure. Like forest animals, the orthodox have a fascinated horror of fire and its torments, and when we come down to the skeptical obscurantism of the "new philosophy" "the element of fire is quite put out."[22] What is coming is the union of heat and light, a marriage of heaven and hell. By "hell" Blake means an upsurge of desire and passion within the rising body so great that it will destroy the present starry heaven, and he calls it "hell" because that is what the orthodox call it. Here Blake's meaning has been misunderstood, and deserves more explanation.

Everything that furthers and increases the creative life is really good. The growth of creative energy is the tree of life which enables men to attain an eternal existence. Whatever is pleasing to society, whatever is cautious, prudent and undistinguished, or else vicious and cruel if society happens to be feeling that way, is morally good. The growth of morality is the tree of the knowledge of good and evil which leads to death. The former is the gospel; the latter the "law" under which all non-Christians, and most of the nominal Christians, live. Michael explains to Adam in *Paradise Lost* that it is the business of the law to discover sin rather than remove it.[23] Moral good and moral evil do not represent any genuine opposition. The one wages wars and executes criminals; the other murders. The one exploits labor; the other robs. The one establishes marriage on the destruction of virginity; the other rapes. But they have a common enemy, the power of genius and prophecy. In terms of moral good it is not the murderer or the robber but the prophet who is really evil. Barabbas may be safely released, for it is impossible that his robberies can destroy the social structure of Pilate and Caiaphas; but there is deadly danger in Jesus and John the Baptist, who must be got rid of at all costs.

That is why no one can be saved by moral virtue. But it does not follow that Barabbas is in a higher imaginative state than Caiaphas. This takes us back by another road to our distinction of contrary and negation. The criminal is not the contrary but the negation of the morally good man; he breaks the law, but he has no gospel. And though the prophet is regarded by society as a devil or messenger from hell, he never practises the vice of "hindering another." There is much that is really good in moral good: the prophet is concerned only to disentangle it from the easy virtue of moral cowardice.

The Marriage of Heaven and Hell, therefore, has nothing to do with the simple inversion of moral good and evil which is known as sadism, and which forms an important aspect of Romantic culture. This is a traditional error in the interpretation of Blake,[24] and one which ignores the fact that Blake attaches two meanings to the word "hell," one real and the other ironic. There is a real hell in the human mind, and it achieves the physical form of dungeons, whips, racks and all the miserable panoply of fear. Such a hell consolidates a moral virtue founded on terror with a moral evil founded on cruelty, and it exists because it is believed to be a part of "necessity." The more degenerate the society, the more obvious this alliance of moral good and evil against the power of genius becomes. Those who know better can see that, as evil is a negation, this hell would be, in the spiritual world, nothingness, a monstrous multiple of zero. No one could go on living in it after the Last Judgment, because no one can exist in a state of nonexistence, the postapocalyptic hell of unending torment being, like the fallen sun, "a phantasy of evil Man." Whatever foreshadows the Last Judgment thus foreshadows the annihilation of hell, and of the believers in it who are negations, "the Elect from before the foundation of the world," and can have no existence after those foundations have disappeared. Hence for these "Elect" anything which makes persecution and oppression seem less "necessary," that is, any blow struck for human freedom, is their hell, and the announcement of a new hope, a new courage, a new faith and a new vision is, to them, "the voice of the devil."[25] The darkness does not comprehend the light; evil spirits fade on the crowing of the cock, and from their point of view it is the cock that is the evil spirit, the herald of the light which afflicts them with the "frantic pain" of the spirit in the "Mad Song."

We have more definite evidence for the same point in *The*

Ghost of Abel, which is addressed to Byron and is apparently conceived as an answer to that poet's *Cain*. Cain is provided by Byron with a great deal of imaginative vision. He knows that the tyrant of the sky who demands docility is unworthy of worship, for if Adam had ignorance Jehovah had malice. He knows that his true enemy is death, and suspects that the flaming sword before Paradise has something to do with death. With the aid of Lucifer he journeys into previous worlds far older than Adam of "past leviathans" and a Golden Age of "intelligent, good, great, and glorious things," returning to the earth dizzy with a star-dazzled enlightenment. In the course of the journey Lucifer has dropped the suggestion that "it may be death leads to the highest knowledge," which links itself at once with Cain's own feeling that the understanding of death is his own ultimate victory—in other words, with the converse principle that the highest knowledge leads to death. It is from this that the state of mind develops which prompts him to murder Abel. Blake's conception of Byron's meaning is, apparently, that imaginative vision has something diabolic attached to it, and that the visionary is not only doomed to be an outcast and an exile, but that even crime may well be an inseparable part of a genius above the law, as illustrated in a murder which was the product of an intellectual awakening.

The Ghost of Abel makes the point that murder cannot be part of genius but is always part of morality, and that genius must break with virtue and vice alike. It is "bad" to commit a murder: granted, but it does not thereby become "good" to murder the murderer. That is the monotonous pendulum of revenge which goes on ticking all through history. Abel worshiped a "good" God who wanted sheep murdered; Cain in killing him was sacrificing to a "bad" God who wanted human beings murdered. But both were the same God, and that God Satan, who makes all his virtue out of necessity. Both Cain's murderousness and Abel's desire for revenge encourage this Satan to proclaim, in a parody of the Biblical account, that human blood is more acceptable to him than the blood of animals. The true God descends at once and sets a mark on Cain to prevent the meaningless counteraction of "bad" crime and "good" punishment from going any further.

All philosophies founded on sense experience are founded on a timid fear of expanding the powers of the mind, which uses the senses. All life lived on such principles takes caution and fear to be cardinal virtues. That is why "reason" in the bad sense is the same thing as morality. Here again we see that *The Marriage of Heaven and Hell* belongs in the tradition of great satire. *A Tale of a Tub* shows us how the official theologies of Christianity are all rationalizings directed to one end, the end of getting along with a fallen world, and of achieving as much Selfhood domination in it as possible. In other words, it makes the identification of reasoning and moral virtue complete. The next step is for Swift to add to this portrayal of the intellectual and moral degradation of man, a physical degradation. The body is the form of the soul, and the degraded soul is the filthy and nauseating aspect of the body. The Yahoo, therefore, is man presented wholly in terms of his fall, and represents a conception of that fall not greatly different from the one set forth in Blake.

Satire is an acid that corrodes everything it touches, and Blake saw in the acid bath he gave his engravings a symbol of his approach:

But first the notion that man has a body distinct from his soul is to be expunged; this I shall do by printing in the infernal method, by corrosives, which in Hell are salutary and medicinal, melting apparent surfaces away, and displaying the infinite which was hid.[26]

This implies that condemnation is only part of the satirist's work: his attack on the evil and foolish merely allows what he reveals to stand out in bolder relief. The satirist who does nothing but watch people make fools of themselves is simply pouring acid all over the plate, and achieves only a featureless disintegration. But the great satirist is an apocalyptic visionary like every other great artist, if only by implication, for his caricature leads us irresistibly away from the passive assumption that the unorganized data of sense experience are reliable and consistent, and afford the only means of contact with reality. Satirists often give to life a logical and self-consistent shift of perspective, showing mankind in a telescope as wriggling Lilliputians, in a microscope as stinking Brobdingnagians, or through the eyes of an ass, like Apuleius, or a drunk, like Petronius. In satire like this the reality of sense experience turns out to be merely a series of customary associations. And in Rabelais, where huge creatures rear up and tear themselves out of Paris and Touraine, bellowing for drink and women, combing cannon balls out of their hair, eating six pilgrims in a salad, excreting like dinosaurs and copulating like the ancient sons of God who made free with the daughters of men, we come perhaps closest of all to what Blake meant by the resurrection of the body. Rabelais' characters are what Blake called his, "Giant forms," and they are the horsemen who ride over the earth in the day of the trumpet and alarm, where we, in our sublunary world, see nothing but anguish and death:

The enemies, after that they were awaked, seeing on one side the fire in the camp, and on the other the inundation of the urinal deluge, could not tell what to say, nor what to think. Some said, that it was the end of the world, and the final judgment, which ought to be by fire.[27]

The Marriage of Heaven and Hell, with its blistering ridicule of the wisdom that dwells with prudence, with its rowdy guffaws at the doctrines of a torturing hell and a boring heaven which are taught by cowards to dupes, is perhaps the epilogue to the golden age of English satire. It has been said that in Blake's "To the Muses" the eighteenth century dies to music. The eighteenth century was a little too healthy to expire in any such trifle, and perhaps it would be better to say that in The Marriage of Heaven and Hell the age of Swift and Sterne and Fielding and Hogarth plunges into a vigorous Beethovenish coda which, though organically related to what has gone before, contains much new material and is big with portents of the movements to follow.

· 4 ·

MAN derives the knowledge that he is living in a fallen world from the contrast between his desire and his power, between what he would like to do and what he can do. Lockian common sense makes the least of the former and the most of the latter; Blakean genius always suffers from claustrophobia. Between these are ordinary men whose feelings of dissatisfaction are choked down and suppressed whenever they recur, until a reservoir of anguish and fury is stored up which periodically floods the world in revolution. Revolution is the sign of apocalyptic yearnings, of an impulse to burst loose from this world altogether and get into a better one, a convulsive lunge forward of the imagination. There is thus a connection far deeper than a resemblance of sound between revolution and revelation. The same instinct that made fourteenth century peasants justify rebellion on the ground that there were no gentlemen in the unfallen state of man made Blake feel that the French and American revolutions were mortal blows struck at the gentlemanly prince of darkness and the tyrant Leviathan who in Job is king over all the children of pride. Such revolutions, while they cannot cause an apocalypse, may be symptoms of one. The real causes of the American revolt, for Blake, are set down not in the Declaration of Independence, but in the Battle Hymn of the Republic.

Satire is not necessarily revolutionary in itself, though its hostility to the world of its time may be pressed into revolutionary service later on, as the satire of Chaucer and Langland was taken by Protestants to herald the Reformation. But a poet cannot depend on satire alone if he wants to show his revolutionary sympathies and point out what such revolutions signify. Thus when the fall of the Bastille aroused a wave of enthusiasm in England, Blake turned at once to write an epic on the French Revolution, in which he treated this event *sub specie aeternitatis* as the beginning of the end of the long nightmare of cruelty and injustice which is human history. The "starry harvest" of six thousand years, Blake's conventional figure for the interval between creation and apocalypse, is about to be reaped: men are about to unite into a single Man, who is God, and who will dwell in a new heaven and a new earth. The fall of the French monarchy, like the fall of empires in the prophecies of the Bible, is significant only as the sign of an approaching Messianic kingdom of liberty.

What in Spenser would be called the political allegory of the poem is simple enough. All that we have of it deals with the summoning of the National Assembly and a debate in which Necker, Sièyes and Orleans speak for the French people and the Archbishop of Paris, the king and a "Duke of Burgundy" for tyranny and reaction, while the gloomy Bastille, not yet fallen, broods over a sick and terrified France. The forces of reaction, with an unconscious irony, point to the Bastille as a symbol of the firmament of their power; and the Bastille is really a symbol, that is, an image or form, of the two larger prisons of man's body and the physical world, both of which are about to be broken down. The physical world, with its "starry harvest," its huge meaningless wastes, its blinding sun and wandering moon, is beginning to waver queasily in the sky along with the abstract God who is "the ghost of the Priest and King"[28]:

> An aged form, white as snow, hov'ring in mist, weeping
> in the uncertain light,
> Dim the form almost faded.

Enormous forces of life are pushing their way through the deadened physical bodies of men, which are symbolized by a cemetery, as the true God, the Word made flesh, tears open their graves. It is not only that the French people are to be freed from oppression and war, but that man is beginning to have dreams, and is no longer content to be bounded in a nutshell and count himself king of infinite space.

Hence Blake gives to the speakers in the National Assembly something of the cosmic significance of the "divine king," a nod of whose head may precipitate an earthquake or a hurricane. The common primitive idea that if kings are not hedged about with taboos the world will blow to pieces would have seemed to Blake imaginatively quite correct. The "Duke of Burgundy" rises to speak for the *status quo* in the form of a ghastly parody of the Sistine Madonna: a "bright cloud of infant souls" weeps in his burning robe. Herod's slaughter of the innocents, the instinctive desire of tyranny to murder human beings when its power is threatened, is only a trifle compared to the number of babies, born and unborn, that tyranny murders in war, to say nothing of the number of imaginations it strangles in those it permits to live a "natural" life. There was no Duke of Burgundy at this time, but Burgundy is a wine-producing country, and the winepress is always a symbol of war in Blake. The Archbishop appears as a huge serpent or leviathan, and when the King sees his army outside the window "his bosom expanded like starry heaven," for the starry heaven is as much a guarantee of his power as the army. The fate of the physical world depends on these deliberations as much as the fortunes of France do, and the rhythms of all three are synchronized:

> He ceas'd, and burn'd silent; red clouds roll round Necker;
>   a weeping is heard o'er the palace.
> Like a dark cloud Necker paus'd, and like thunder on the
>   just man's burial day he paus'd;
> Silent sit the winds, silent the meadows, while the husband-
>   man and woman of weakness
> And bright children look after him into the grave, and water
>   his clay with love,
> Then turn towards pensive fields; so Necker paus'd, and his
>   visage was cover'd with clouds.

Such writing should not be regarded as an extravagant misuse of the "pathetic fallacy." In human affairs moral and natural economies are mutually independent, and a crisis in one does not affect the other, a fact of which an artist can make an ironic use. The pathetic fallacy is pathetic because it is a fallacy. But when we are dealing with themes of resurrection and apocalypse, in which man is seen rising into a spiritual world completely subject to his imaginative power, a ritual symbolism, like that of the *Nativity Ode*, in which halcyon days accompany the birth of Christ, or that of the "weop eall gesceaft" of *The Dream of the Rood*, is appropriate.

An apocalyptic poem which on the political level deals with the conflict of liberty and tyranny is perhaps not easy to fit to a historical situation. The "states" Blake deals with can seldom be identified with the very mixed elements of a political event: to do this either blurs the imaginative pattern or falsifies the history, many of the nobles being really noble and many revolutionaries being mere assassins. This objection might not apply to another poet, but the diagrammatic exactness of Blake's symbolism demands more rigorous conventions. The form of *The French Revolution* is dictated by the sequence of historical events, and as a result the comprehensive view of the states of liberty and tyranny which Blake affords us in other poems, in which their political, educational, economic, religious and psychological aspects are all presented as a unit, is lacking; and the cause of liberty at least has not a definite enough protagonist to represent all its various aspects at once. This is a defect which Blake attempted to remedy in *America* by creating Orc. Here Blake is strongest in polemic, in his powerful if somewhat noisy description of the Bastille towers and prisoners, or of the whimpering terror of Nobodaddy at discovering that the working classes are no longer going to be content with that station in life into which it has pleased him to call them:

> My groaning is heard in the abbeys, and God, so long wor-
> shipp'd, departs as a lamp
> Without oil; for a curse is heard hoarse thro' the land from a
> godless race
> Descending to beasts; they look downward and labour and for-
> get my holy law;
> The sound of prayer fails from lips of flesh, and the holy hymn
> from thicken'd tongues;
> For the bars of Chaos are burst; her millions prepare their
> fiery way
> Thro' the orbed abode of the holy dead, to root up and pull
> down and remove,
> And Nobles and Clergy shall fail from before me, and my
> cloud and vision be no more.

The French Revolution is a fine and durable poem. Swinburne called it "mere wind and splutter," although it is the most Swin-burnian of Blake's poems, but it deserves recognition as the one really spontaneous flash of sympathy for the great revolution that English poetry produced.

· 5 ·

IN *America* the Homeric doggerel of *The French Revolution* has quieted down into the more characteristic septenaries of Blake's prophecies. *America* is not only a better integrated and less experimental poem than its predecessor, but more deeply felt and more important to Blake himself. We have pointed out the unusual organic consistency of Blake's symbolism: we can-not trace it back to a time when its main outlines were not clear to him. It is therefore unlikely that the outbreak of the French Revolution made any essential change in his thought at the age of thirty-two. The American Revolution was already firmly in its place as the significant sign of a dawning Last Judgment, and he regards the French Revolution, although the poem he wrote about it is earlier, as merely the inevitable sequel of a far more crucial event. The Duke of Burgundy certainly feels that a vulgar unrest which will take all grandeur and dignity out of

French life, for people like him at any rate, is American in origin:

> Shall this marble built heaven become a clay cottage, this
>   earth an oak stool, and these mowers
> From the Atlantic mountains mow down all this great starry
>   harvest of six thousand years?

The myth which Blake elaborates about "the Atlantic mountains" has been explained, but may be referred to again here. In the Golden Age before the Fall, humanity or Albion dwelt at peace in its Paradise or Atlantis. The Fall produced a chaotic world and the central symbol of chaos is water. The Platonic story that Atlantis was overwhelmed by a flood gets the meaning of this clearer. The Atlantic Ocean, then, symbolizes the fallen world in Blake; he calls it the "Sea of Time and Space." The rise of a new civilization of English origin in America indicates the reintegrating of Atlantis, the disappearance of the Atlantic Ocean, and the return of the Golden Age. For the revolution does not stop with the political independence of America: it plunges on into the sources of tyranny in the human mind. The poem ends with a vision of the imagination bursting through the senses until the chaos of earth and water that we see begins to dissolve in fire.

The hero of *America* is Orc (giant or devil living in what to the orthodox is Orcus or hell),[29] the first of the "Giant forms" or symbolic characters of the prophecies we have met. Orc is the power of the human desire to achieve a better world which produces revolution and foreshadows the apocalypse; and the "Preludium" to *America* represents him as having arrived at puberty determined to set the world on fire as a promising youngster should do. To the reactionaries, of course, he is a demonic and hellish power, rising up to destroy everything that is sacred and worth conserving. "Albion's Angel," the spirit of English Toryism, addresses him in tones of a righteous indignation which does not at all succeed in concealing an acute nervousness:

> Blasphemous Demon, Antichrist, hater of Dignities,
> Lover of wild rebellion, and transgressor of God's Law,
> Why dost thou come to Angel's eyes in this terrific form?

This continually suppressed but intermittently struggling power of desire is expressed in the myths of the Greek Titans and the

Northern Jötuns: both are groups of earth-bound giants hostile to the sky-gods. That the gods in their turn are hostile to man and that the "Giants who formed this world . . . and now seem to live in it in chains" are our allies comes out in the story of the Titan Prometheus, who was martyred for his friendship to man. The gods maintain their ascendancy over men by keeping their enemies fettered under the earth, according to the myth, whence volcanoes and earthquakes proceed to show that the giants are not dead yet. The real underworld is the physical world as the lazy mind sees it, and the real giants are our own mental powers. And just as the smooth unbroken surface of Pangloss' God was rudely shattered by the earthquake at Lisbon, so the natural tendency of men to sink deeper into automatic acceptance or administration of tyranny is violently interrupted by a gigantic revolution. And some day there will be something more than revolution. The Edda tells us that eventually the fettered Loki will break loose, giants and gods will destroy one another in a final "consummation," and the Golden Age will return.

If we turn from human history to nature, however, we see that revolution, in the sense of a renewal of energy and the power to live, is not haphazard but cyclic. The light dies every day, vegetable life every winter and human life at the end of a finite period; the sun rises again, the year returns and new babies are born. Perhaps the first and most fundamental effort of the imagination in this vegetable world, the primary outline of all religion and art, is to see in the death of a man or in the decline of the day and year an image or reproduction of the original Fall, and in the return of human and natural life an image or prototype of the ultimate resurrection.

· 6 ·

ORC, then, is not only Blake's Prometheus but his Adonis, the dying and reviving god of his mythology. Orc represents the return of the dawn and the spring and all the human analogies of their return: the continuous arrival of new life, the renewed sexual and reproductive power which that brings, and the periodic overthrow of social tyranny. He is both a sun-god, the jocund day on the mountain tops,[30] and a god of renewed "vegetable," or natural human, life. In religious ritual there may be a distinction between a sun-god and a fertility-god, but there can be none in a properly clarified vision, for both sun and fertility have their cycles of disappearance and renewal, and both are temporal images of fall and apocalypse. Orc dies as the buried seed dies, and rises as it grows; winter nights become long and gloomy, but at the depth of winter the light slowly returns.

Now as the emergent Orc represents a return of life, he represents also a victory over death. Death in Blake is the reduction of the physical body to inert matter such as rock and sand, the "limit of opacity." Below this is the chaos that would, if it gained ascendancy, lead us into annihilation or "Non-Entity." As it is obviously impossible for nonexistence to exist, it is evident that chaos is kept within bounds. In the Bible this chaos, symbolized by water, is represented by the sea-serpent Leviathan or Rahab. Leviathan is very like the underground monster of many primitive myths who swallows or fights with the sun at night: Job, in cursing the day of his birth, links himself with the children of darkness who hope that some day the sun will be vanquished:

> Let them curse it that curse the day, who are ready to
> raise up Leviathan.[31]

Hence in every sunrise and winter solstice we may see an image of a victory of creative power over something monstrous and sinister, like a dragon.

The orthodox view of the Titanic myth identifies chaos and reviving energy. Thus the false God of *The French Revolution* sees, in a passage we have quoted, the new life emerging in France as the release of the bars of chaos. But chaos and vital energy are opposed principles, and the return of Orc is the defeat of chaos; hence the real monster is Orc's adversary, and Orc himself the monster's conqueror. The myth of the dragon-slayer is a very widespread one, a fact which indicates, on Blake's principles, that it belongs to the fundamental pattern of ideas which man is trying to formulate. In all such conflicts the hero represents the progress of vigorous life and civilization, and the dragon stands for darkness, waste, sterility and death. When the dragon is slain, darkness is succeeded by light, the wilderness blossoms as the rose, new life is begotten, and death, the last enemy to be destroyed, is swallowed up in victory.

In most stories of dragon-killers the dragon is laying waste and tyrannizing over a *nation* of which the slayer is the deliverer, and sometimes the eventual king. This latent political aspect of the myth comes out in *The Faerie Queene*, where St. George by killing a dragon liberates the Church of England from the Papal power. The Messiah, too, in the political allegory of the Bible, is to destroy a monster of tyranny. This tyranny is identified with Leviathan by Ezekiel,[32] and is frequently associated in the Bible with the various countries, notably Egypt, Babylon and Rome, who tyrannized over Judea. The Great Whore of the Apocalypse is clearly linked with the latter two. Hence in *America* the dragon is the spirit of English tyranny.

The dragon-killing is thus a drama both of the reviving powers of nature and of a freedom from some kind of social oppression. Putting the two things together, we get the principle that such a revolution as is occurring in America is a natural renewal of life in society, and that it therefore does not happen irrationally, but at a definite time, like the dawn and the spring. If this is so, then human history, no less than the natural world, has a cyclic rhythm of decline and revival, and history takes the form of a series of cultures or civilizations, each with its own rise, maturity and fall, initiated by a revolution within it and superseded by one without it.

The dragon is rather tentatively developed in *America*, for Orc's real antagonist is the tendency to chaos within the human mind which the dragon represents. That tendency Blake portrays in Urizen, the Old Man, the cloud-gathering Zeus, Jehovah or Odin who in all pantheons is inevitably the "President of the Immortals," the Ancient of Days who in Blake's great painting, the frontispiece to *Europe*, crouches over the world marking its limits (Gk. ὁρίζειν)[33] with a compass. Urizen is a sky-god, for the remoteness and mystery of heaven is the first principle of his religion. He is old, but his age implies senility rather than wisdom. He is cruel, for he stands for the barring of nature against the desires and hopes of man. Whereas Orc is "ruddy," red being the color of revolution, of blood, of rage and of sexual passion, Urizen is a white terror: his white beard, the freezing snows that cover him and the icicles and hoarfrost that stick on him, suggest the "colorless all-color of atheism,"[34] the nameless chilling fear of the unknown, that Melville depicts in his albino Leviathan. Urizen's associations are with bleached bones, rocks and deserts; but actually Urizen, being the human belief in the objectivity of nature, is an abstraction, a hazy ghost that is always just going to take definite shape and never quite does.

Blake's source for this image of the contest of Orc and Urizen is doubtless the remarkable poem of Ossian's called *Carric-Thura,* in which Loda, or Odin, is confronted by the young hero Fingal. Loda is an old, cruel and gloomy God, whose "nostrils pour the blasts of death" and who boasts of his power to kill. He cannot be killed himself, for he is nothing but clouds and air, but he can be struck at and driven away, and as Fingal does this "the form fell shapeless into the air, like a column of smoke. . . . The spirit of Loda shrieked as, rolled into himself, he rose on the wind." That "rolled into himself" reminds us of Blake's "Spectre" and "Selfhood."

As soon as we begin to think of the relation of Orc to Urizen, it becomes impossible to maintain them as separate principles. If Orc represents the reviving force of a new cycle, whether of dawn or spring or history, he must grow old and die at the end of that cycle. Urizen must eventually gain the mastery over Orc, but such a Urizen cannot be another power but Orc himself, grown old. The same is true of the dragon: the dragon must be the hero's predecessor and the hero in his turn must become a dragon. But if the dragon *is* death, then when the hero dies he is swallowed by or otherwise absorbed into the dragon. The Book of Jonah portrays its hero as swallowed by a leviathan who is death or hell and vomited up again—a humorous image befitting the most humorous book in the Bible. (The medieval paintings showing Jesus walking into the open mouth of a monster when he descends into hell may also be noted, as Blake might have seen one.) But if the dragon is itself the old Orc, then surely is not Orc simply a dragon who has the power to shed his skin from time to time? This is a very abrupt change from our young and heroic dragon-killer, but nevertheless Blake continually associates Orc with the serpent, which is an easy modulation of the dragon symbol. The serpent which appeared on the flags of the revolting Americans would then be an emblem of an infant Orc, and may have been the source of the association.

There are seven major historical cycles in Blake's mythology, the Seven Eyes of God previously listed. Each runs from a youthful Orc to an aged Urizen, which in terms of social and political symbolism means that it gets less energetic in its cultural efforts and nearer the state of nature as it goes on. Blake's later symbolism deals, not with a sequence of cycles in history, but with the cycle itself as a seven-times-recurring phenomenon of human life. He elaborates three main phases of it. In its first phase, symbolized by the birth and binding of Orc, it produces most of its great works of imaginative power. As it gets older, its religion becomes more abstract, and its social life takes on the characteristics of its growing belief in a mechanical universe. It then declines into a sophisticated rationalism founded on "common sense," the insight of mediocrity. In this period cultures produce their Aristotles, their Bacons and Lockes, their empirical science and their metaphysics. This second phase is portrayed under the symbol of Urizen "exploring his dens," the Urizenic intelligence gaining the view of the fallen world which is appropriate to it. Eighteenth century rationalism is the seventh of these explorations. The cycle finally dies in a wild cancerous tissue of huge machinery, a blankly materialist philosophy, an inner death of the soul which causes mass wars, and a passive acceptance of the most reckless tyranny. It is in these late periods that new prophets, in whom the spirit of a reviving Orc is stirring, appear to proclaim a new gospel. This last phase is symbolized by the crucifixion of Orc, in the form of a serpent, on the tree of mystery, the binding of human imagination to the vegetable world and the absorption of human life into the order of nature.

The natural world is based largely on the daily return of the sun and the yearly return of vegetable life, and the sun and the tree are therefore the central symbols of the natural cycle. Looked at from the point of view of sense experience, they suggest nothing but a cycle, persisting indefinitely in time. Looked at from an imaginative point of view, their renewal is an image of resurrection into eternity. Hence each of these symbols has two forms, one the form of its eternal life, which appeals to the imagination, the other the form of its death, which appeals to the Selfhood. There is the tree of life man had before the Fall and will have again after it, and there is the tree of morality or death. The latter is Jesus' barren fig-tree, the world-ash Yggdrasil, the tree of mystery and the knowledge of good and evil. The sun of life is, as the Book of Revelation explains, God himself[35]; the sun of death is the scorching furnace to whom Mexicans and Druids offered human sacrifices. Jesus, the seventh Orc of human history, was the true vine and the sun of righteousness, but his empty skin is left hanging on a dead stripped tree, the arms nailed to it horizontally as an image of the spreading rays of the captive sun. Another image of the dead sun is the clawed or hooked cross which Blake evidently associates with the scythed chariots of the "Druid" Britons.[36] The imaginative status of any nation which has adopted either the rayed sun or the hooked cross for its emblem thus becomes clear.

The crucifixion of Orc as Jesus symbolizes the end of the sixth or Jehovah cycle, and must obviously have happened five times before. The earliest cycles after the fall of Atlantis arose in Africa. Orc, Blake tells us, is bound under "Mount Atlas" in northwest Africa, where he will remain until the end of time.[37] In the "Preludium" to *America* Orc is addressed as "the image of God who dwells in darkness of Africa." This means among other things that the enslaved negro, the fallen child of the sun, is one of the central symbols of the oppression of fallen man, and the chimney-sweep and "little black boy" of the *Songs of Innocence* are modulations of this symbol. Here the black skin represents the confined body of fallen man. There is one curious passage in which Blake even speaks of Africa as a giant of the same kind as Albion, and says that he did not wholly fall,[38] which apparently means that the African civilization was equal to, or more probably part of, the Atlantic one. Besides the legends of paradisal Atlantic islands, there are also many allusions in Classical mythology to another prehistoric Golden Age associated with the "innocent Ethiopians" who are portrayed as dwelling with the gods. Both the *Iliad* and the *Odyssey* open with a reference to a paradisal Ethiopia.[39] The decline of this African culture in Egypt is where recorded history begins. This is presumably why in Plato it is the Egyptians who alone preserve the traditions of Atlantis, and why, in the Old Testament, captivity in Egypt is the first great symbol of the tyranny of the fallen world.

It may be interesting to observe that Blake is not the only poet to associate Ethiopia with the unfallen world from which the fallen world, the "spiritual Egypt"[40] of the Book of Revelation, has descended. It is in Abyssinia that Coleridge sees himself with the flashing eyes and floating hair of an Orc who has drunk the milk of Paradise. From Abyssinia Rasselas descends to Egypt and finds there a madman who believes that he controls the universe—an excellent image of a bound Orc. If anyone had explained to Johnson what his imagination had produced, his Spectre would have instantly answered, "Sir, I wrote *Rasselas* to defray the expenses of my mother's funeral"; but Johnson's Spectre did not write *Rasselas*, and knows nothing about it. Swedenborg also gives the Africans a very high place in the spiritual world; on the other hand, Gérard de Nerval, in *Le Rêve et la Vie*, makes them a race of necromancers.[41]

The African civilization comes to a close with the collapse of the third or Elohim cycle, recorded in the story of Adam and Eve, in which the two great symbols of the dying Orc, the cursed serpent and the tree of death, make their appearance. This is described at the end of *The Book of Urizen*. *The Book of Ahania* follows without a break, and describes the growth of new cycles in Asia, the migration to which is reflected in the Biblical account of the Exodus. Then, after a great struggle of Orc and Urizen principles within the Israelites, the former being the pillar of fire that guided them through the night, and the latter the pillar of cloud that befogged them in the day, Urizen, with his moral law and his ten commandments, won out. Orc says in *America*:

> The fiery joy, that Urizen perverted to ten commands,
> What night he led the starry hosts thro' the wide wilderness,
> That stony law I stamp to dust.

The death of this culture was represented by the brazen serpent hung by Moses on a pole, which was accepted by Jesus as a prototype of his own death.[42] In the serpent, the yellow brass and the pole, the symbols of the dead Orc, the dead sun and the dead tree respectively appear.

The hanged serpent is not otherwise directly associated with the crucified Christ, but there is an important connection between them. The serpent of the wilderness was, the Bible tells us, worshiped by the Israelites for centuries.[43] This means that they were worshiping their own death-principle, which in the next cycle would be Antichrist. The dead body of Christ left behind on the cross, his excreted husk, to use Blake's terminology, is the body of Antichrist, "the mystery of iniquity," as Paul calls him, because the dead Christ (not the dying Christ, which is Orc) on the tree of mystery is the achieved form of hell's revenge on humanity.

Implicit in the myth of Orc and Urizen is the allegory of the young striking down the old, the most obvious symbol of which is a son's revolt against a father. This form of the myth meets us in the story of Dionysus. But Urizen *is* sterility: he can only destroy children, not beget them, and can no more be the father of the succeeding Orc than Herod could be the father of Jesus. However, in *The Book of Ahania* Blake changes his mind and makes the rebel of the Exodus a son of Urizen, Fuzon, the element of fire (*focus, feu*) in nature (φύσις) which is never quite put out. The use of a son of Urizen in place of Orc in a poem engraved in 1795 indicates that Blake is becoming increasingly aware that by "Orc" he means something inseparably attached to Urizen.

When the Israelites got from the wilderness into the garden of God which had been promised them, the revolutionary vigor of their revolt against Egypt had collapsed, and all they got was another Egypt from which imagination and desire were excluded as dangerous intruders. This is set forth in the story of the rivalry of Esau and Jacob, in which the red and hairy Esau, the rightful heir, was sent wandering into the desert. The kingdom of Edom remained outside Jacob's priestly theocracy execrated and accursed, and when Isaiah sees the Messiah coming from Edom he is prophesying the destruction of tyranny by the exiled giant of desire.[44] Esau, therefore, is another Biblical Orc. So perhaps is Absalom, the son who rebelled against his father David, David being one of the "Churches" or subordinate phases of the Jehovah cycle. Absalom's body was pierced with a spear while he was hanging on a tree by his golden hair. Blake often alludes to Orc's flaming hair as an image of the sun, and in *The Book of Ahania* there seems to be a link between Absalom and Fuzon:

> His beautiful visage, his tresses
> That gave light to the mornings of heaven,
> Were smitten with darkness, deform'd
> And outstretch'd on the edge of the forest.

The Classical legend of the Golden Fleece doubtless belongs to the same pattern of symbolism. The giant Samson, whose hair was shorn and who went down into the west into the great cities of the Philistines to work at the mill with slaves, is another vision of an Orc cycle, of much larger scope than the others. The mill is Blake's symbol for the late or big-city stage of an historical cycle: we shall see why later. Then there is the Northern story of Balder, slain by the mistletoe which was sacred to the Druids because it was an emblem of both solar and vegetable cycles at once.[45] And there is Odin's account of himself in the *Hávamál* as hanging on a gallows-tree, "whose roots no man knoweth"—a tree of mystery—wounded with a spear, and offered as a sacrifice to himself. (The nine nights for which he is there may be compared with the nine nights of *The Four Zoas*.) The fact that Odin is both a hanged god and a hoary tyrant who appears in Ossian as Loda shows again the identity of the dead Orc with the Urizen who kills him.

The spear and arrow in Blake are quasi-phallic symbols of the release of imaginative power; the bow is the tense energy of the human body. The shield, on the other hand, is an image both of the impervious heaven (compare Homer's description of the shield of Achilles) and the carapace of the brooding Selfhood. In *The Book of Ahania* Fuzon's "pillar of fire" is hurled like a spear and tears open the sterile loins of Urizen; Urizen opposes to this his "pillar of cloud" in the form of a "broad Disk" or shield.[46] The fact that Jesus, Odin and Absalom are all pierced with spears is thus linked with the fact that they are sacrifices to themselves, as Odin says, or dead forms of what they were.

If we look at the sequence of cycles as a whole, we see that the center of historical gravity, so to speak, has moved in a counter-clockwise circle from Atlantis to Africa, from Africa to Asia, from Asia to Europe, and from Europe, with the American Revolution, back to Atlantis again. In legend some memory of the first three of these shifts is preserved respectively in the story of Perseus (who journeyed eastward across the African desert with the serpentine head of a female monster or Rahab which turned Ethiopian warriors to stone, and is the prototype of Blake's Tiriel), the Exodus and the Trojan war. The decline of these three civilizations has produced, up to Blake's time, a threefold tyranny symbolized in the Bible by the names of Egypt, Babylon and Rome.

The first part of *The Song of Los*, called "Africa," sums this up as follows:

> Clouds roll heavy upon the Alps round Rousseau & Voltaire,
> And on the mountains of Lebanon round the deceased Gods
> Of Asia, & on the desarts of Africa round the Fallen Angels
> The Guardian Prince of Albion burns in his nightly tent.

The last line is identical with the first line of *America*.

The seventh Orc cycle, from Jesus to our own time, is described in the very lovely and subtle poem of *Europe*, which outlines its progress from Orc's appearance as Jesus to its decline into a political tyranny based on an inner exhaustion of vitality, eighteen hundred years after Jesus' time, and just as an eighth cycle is opening up in America. But this time something else happens that has never happened before. Orc is not content simply to arise in America and go through the "same dull round" all over again there: he also explodes in the "vineyards of red France," and this is the signal for a world-wide "strife of blood." The brilliant revolutionary polemic in *The Song of Los* called "Asia" postdates *America*, and describes the spreading of the final apocalypse to that continent while the baffled kings of Asia look on in "bitterness of soul." The "Song of Liberty," a pendant to *The Marriage of Heaven and Hell*, also foresees that the power which has torn down the Bastille will go on to tear down Olympus and rebuild the Atlantic kingdom of the Golden Age.

America was engraved in 1793 and *Europe* in 1794. Within the next few years Blake watched the American and French revolutions gradually subside again into the fallen world. The Americans kept on owning slaves, and the statue of the wrong kind of Reason was set up in Paris. Of the "improvement of sensual enjoyment" Blake had prophesied there was no sign, and a poet who proclaimed that the loins were the place of the Last Judgment would find little to cheer him in the approach of the nineteenth century, which obviously had no intention of making the loins a part of revealed religion. Voltaire and Rousseau declined in Blake's estimation from fighters in the vanguard of freedom to enemies of light[47]; and in 1804, the year that Napoleon made himself Emperor and Beethoven tore the dedication to him out of the Eroica symphony, Blake was writing:

I suppose an American would tell me that Washington did all that was done before he was born, as the French now adore Buonaparte and the English our poor George; so the Americans will consider Washington as their god. . . . In the meantime I have the happiness of seeing the Divine countenance in such men as Cowper and Milton more distinctly than in any prince or hero.[48]

The reference to Washington is a little ungracious, considering that Blake had set the Americans the example; it is the last part of the quotation that indicates the direction his thought was taking.

As Blake never abandoned his belief in the potential imminence of an apocalypse, he did not, like Wordsworth or Coleridge, alter the essentially revolutionary pattern of his thinking. But neither could he feel, with Byron or Shelley, any enthusiasm for a political restoration of the Greece and Rome he so much distrusted. The only real change that the decline of revolutionary fortunes made in his thought was in causing him to reject the Orc man as an apocalyptic agent. The only God that exists exists in man, and all religion consists in following the right men. Men of action of the type Blake calls "heroic villains"[49] are not the right men, and the visionary is on a disastrously wrong course if his vision of the divinity of man leads him to hero-worship of this kind, as Carlyle's did. But the Orc man, the revolutionary leader who is fighting for liberty (Washington is not a very dramatic example of Blake's Orc symbolism; the red-shirted Garibaldi would be much better) does make a real appeal to the imagination. Revolution attracts sympathy more because it is revolution than because of what it proposes to substitute; this is connected with the fact that we indulge the young more than old because they are young and not because they are right. But as Orc stiffens into Urizen, it becomes manifest that the world is so constituted that no cause can triumph within it and still preserve its imaginative integrity. The imagination is mental, and it never has a preponderance of physical force on its side:

The Whole Creation Groans to be deliver'd; there will always be as many Hypocrites born as Honest Men, & they will always have superior Power in Mortal Things. You cannot have Liberty in this World without what you call Moral Virtue, & you cannot have Moral Virtue without the Slavery of that half of the Human Race who hate what you call Moral Virtue.[50]

We must look elsewhere for the divine in man, for the pure imagination or creative power which does not depend on nature for the source of its energy. Jesus could not have become the Messiah without renouncing heroism, and his role as a young dying god was forced on him by his persecutors.

Orc is a process of birth, death and rebirth in another individual of the same species or form, though sometimes he may take the form of a power of rejuvenation. (There is no doctrine of "reincarnation" in Blake: that implies a more casual relation between soul and body than he would admit.) In either case Orc is completely bound to the cyclic wheel of life. He cannot represent an entry into a new world, but only the power of renewing an exhausted form in the old one. The sun always gets back safely: its journey is mechanical rather than adventurous, for it is still imprisoned in night, a far greater spiritual night which is the sleep of the human soul, and in which the natural sun that flashes on and off every day is a mechanical device to light up the wall of an underground cave. In the sequence of historical cycles there is, perhaps, as a new dawn begins, a brief flash of an infinitely greater Day, but it is soon lost in the maturing brilliance of the sunrise. No revolution which falls short of a complete apocalypse and transfiguration of the world into Paradise can give us the eternal youth it symbolizes. Wordsworth puts this in terms of its appropriate image:

> Not favoured spots alone, but the whole earth,
> The beauty wore of promise, that which sets
> (As at some moment might not be unfelt
> Among the bowers of paradise itself)
> The budding rose above the rose full blown.[51]

All the achievements, beliefs and hopes of man are parts of gigantic historical movements as closely bound to the natural world, as inevitable in their progress from birth to decay, as the vegetable life which the very word "culture" is linked with. Men have so far never got what they want, for "the desire of Man being Infinite, the possession is Infinite & himself Infinite."[52] The word "revolution" itself contains a tragic irony: it is itself a part of the revolving of life and death in a circle of pain.

· 7 ·

FOLLOWING out the conception of Orc, therefore, we go around the cycle which that conception itself traces, from a revolutionary millennial optimism to a cyclic Spenglerian pessimism. *America* and *The French Revolution* will remind the reader of Shelley: they describe the triumph of man's freedom, symbolized by a Promethean Titan, over the tyranny of convention, symbolized by a sky-god, in revolutionary and apocalyptic language. The rational "Deism" latent in Shelley, the belief in the future of humanity rather than the eternity of a divine Man, would no doubt have drawn sharp protests from Blake had he read *Prometheus Unbound*, but the sympathy of mood is clear enough. As we find out more about Orc, he seems to take on an increasing resemblance to Milton's Satan, who also begins as a Promethean rebel and ends as a banished and execrated serpent. This is the key to the famous attack on *Paradise Lost* in *The Marriage of Heaven and Hell*. Milton's God, Blake says, is the real Satan, the prince of the power of the air, the creator of a physical universe which is the subterranean cave or hell of eternity. The real God dwells in the real Eden, a city of flaming fire. Milton's Satan is Orc, the power of human desire which gradually and inevitably declines into passive acceptance of impersonal law and external reason. Thus Blake's point is not that Satan is the hero of *Paradise Lost*, but that there is no hero of *Paradise Lost*. The poem simply traces the Orc cycle to the point at which all the characters, from God the Father to Eve, are caught in the same quicksand of fatalistic morality. The implication is that if Blake is to do better than Milton he will need a hero, whom we have not found in Orc.

We may now consider in more detail the three phases which recur in each of the seven Orc cycles, already mentioned as symbolized by the birth and binding of Orc, Urizen exploring his dens, and the crucifixion of Orc. These phases are outlined in *The Book of Urizen* and occupy a whole section (Nights V-VIII) of *The Four Zoas*. We are by no means ready to approach *The Four Zoas* as a whole, but we may lift the part dealing with the Orc cycle out of it for our present commentary. In *The Book of Urizen* the three stages of the cycle are tied to one or two more or less recognizable historical pegs; in *The Four Zoas* the reader is undistracted by such assistance.

The birth (and binding, to be explained later) of Orc is a myth which Blake presents in terms of natural symbols, and there is no point in reading historical allusions into it at all, except that Orc is born when Jesus is born, in the dark frozen terror of the winter solstice, when all things seem to be gathering together for a plunge into an abyss of annihilation, the sun reduced to a cold and weak light unable to bring any more life from the earth. The scene gives Blake an opportunity to write some of the finest unread poetry in the language:

> Still the faint harps & silver voices calm the weary couch,
> But from the caves of deepest night, ascending in clouds of mist,
> The winter spread his wide black wings across from pole to pole:
> Grim frost beneath & terrible snow, link'd in a marriage chain,
> Began a dismal dance. The winds around on pointed rocks
> Settled like bats innumerable, ready to fly abroad.[53]

Of the next two stages, that of Urizen exploring his dens represents the point in the cycle at which the seventh has arrived with Deism. For Urizen to explore his dens means that the Urizenic intelligence, the mental attitude of a Bacon or a Locke, is attempting to account for all the phenomena in the fallen world on the basis of that attitude. It is described, with a wealth of imagination and humor, in Night VI of *The Four Zoas*. Here Urizen starts on a journey to find the bound and concealed Orc, whose "deep pulsation"[54] is shaking the whole earth. Urizen, we are not surprised to learn, finds that the relation of the fallen intelligence to the world must always be that of Atlas: wherever we look, an indefinite stretch of stars is always over our heads, with its constant suggestion of our own insignificance. If we go around to the Antipodes, we shall find only more stars, and no mountain leading up to heaven such as Dante imagined. In *Paradise Lost* Satan, that is, Orc, first begins to show his transformation into Urizen when he makes his journey through chaos to the Adamic world. This is the correct vision, for the object of the journey is to bring chaos into cosmos, and make the order of nature chaotic. But as the Creation was the product of the Fall, the real chaos which Urizen stumbles and flounders through is what he considers the cosmos, the yawning abyss of the sun and the other stars.

As Urizen frantically scribbles one system of philosophy after another in an effort to keep up with all the new facts his observation of nature brings in, space eventually takes the form of a "world of Cumbrous wheels"⁵⁵ over his head, a labyrinth of spinning globes. His next effort is to discover the nature of time. His journey goes from the west to the east and thence to the north, reproducing the progression of historical cycles referred to above, and the first half of this suggests the west-to-east underground journey of the sun, the image of a cycle passing through death and the power of darkness to rebirth. But when Urizen struggles into the region of new life and light he finds himself in the grip of a dying and reviving rhythm which is exactly the same thing as the world of cumbrous wheels, only experienced as time rather than perceived as space. That brings him to the Spectre of Urthona, all of whom we need just now is his primary meaning, which is clock time. The fallen knowledge of time leads to the fallen knowledge of life, and this brings the historical wheel full circle, as Urizen comes to the end of his journey, and face to face with Orc. The "pulsation" Urizen is trying to find is really the throbbing heart and lungs of the fallen Albion, but all that he can understand of that is the recurrent cycle of nature. We may draw a moral here: Urizen's view of space, time and life as cyclic is identical with the conception of Orc we have been tracing, which is why he meets Orc at the end of it. Hence the Orc cycle is the vision of life appropriate, not to the visionary, but to the Deist. Blake, therefore, can afford to be disillusioned about the Orc cycle because it is a long way from being the furthest reach of his thought.

After Urizen has comprehended what he can of the "mystery" of life, his next step is to achieve in human society the kind of social organization consistent with his view of it. The central principle of this organization is uniformity. Urizen can understand recurrence well enough, but the presence within time and space of life, of a power which grows and alters its form, inspires in him a feeling of insecurity, a "horrible fear of the future," as Orc calls it. Urizen, like all enemies of Orc, cannot distinguish the release of energy from the release of chaos, and therefore feels that all life should be made predictable, so as to avoid the accidents of change. The way to do this is to establish a moral law in society in the hope that if it is made stringent enough it will bring life down to the automatism of physical law. If so, then the whirling dervish up in the sky will be worshiped in a way befitting his majesty, men having reduced themselves to robots of perfect obedience to a god who is also nature. And if it turns out that none but dead men can achieve "perfect" obedience, men will simply have to kill themselves off. Nature will not tolerate any revolutionary intrusion of unpredictable life into its order; and, in any case, the same tendency that makes an apple fall to the ground makes it "natural" for the human being to surrender his imagination to impersonal laws. As Urizen elaborates his plans for a Utopia based on Deism, he begins to sound remarkably like the more unpleasant pillars of Victorian society in Dickens, and even Dickens never put the motivation for the preaching of "temperance" into more concise language:

> Compell the poor to live upon a Crust of bread, by soft
>   mild arts.
> Smile when they frown, frown when they smile; & when a
>   man looks pale
> With labour & abstinence, say he looks healthy & happy;
> And when his children sicken, let them die; there are enough
> Born, even too many, & our Earth will be overrun
> Without these arts. If you would make the poor live with
>   temperance,
> With pomp give every crust of bread you give; with gracious
>   cunning
> Magnify small gifts; reduce the man to want a gift, & then give
>   with pomp.
> Say he smiles if you hear him sigh. If pale, say he is ruddy.
> Preach temperance: say he is overgorg'd & drowns his wit
> In strong drink, tho' you know that bread & water are all
> He can afford. Flatter his wife, pity his children, till we can
> Reduce all to our will, as spaniels are taught with art.[56]

We should not fail to notice here the association of uniformity with a frigid paternalism. What Urizen wants is *mental* uniformity, common sense, and the social product of this is the rule of tyrants over victims. Two friends of equal status are not necessarily uniform in their minds; a master and a slave are, because the master is as much a product of a slave state as the slave, and is equally enslaved by it.

The next stage in the cycle is the collapse symbolized by the crucifixion of Orc. It is a stage which, failing an apocalypse, Blake expected that Europe would reach very shortly, if it had not already reached it. It is graphically described in Night VIII of *The Four Zoas* in terms of warfare. When Urizen finds Orc, there is a sharp passage-at-arms of superb dramatic irony between them (Night VII), and then Orc is crucified and reduced to "serpent form," whereupon Orc and Urizen combine into Satan as the culture dies, and all the energy of Orc goes into a warfare which is motivated by a destructive nihilism of spirit. War is the expression of the final victory of moral virtue which crucifies Orc, and any renewal or reversal of the cycle is likely to be accompanied by a great outburst of war. As a culture ages, its wars become an increasingly explicit symbol of its growing death-impulse and reversion to nature. It therefore becomes more mechanically elaborate, reflecting the growing prestige of the mechanically revolving heavens. The episode in *Paradise Lost* about the use of cannon by Satan in heaven may therefore have been introduced because Milton saw the machinery of warfare in his time as in more than one sense diabolically ingenious. At any rate Blake says:

> And Urizen gave life & sense by his immortal Power
> To all his Engines of deceit: that linked chains might run
> Thro' ranks of war spontaneous; & that hooks & boring screws
> Might act according to their forms by innate cruelty.
> He formed also harsh instruments of sound
> To grate the soul into destruction, or to inflame with fury
> The spirits of life, to pervert all the faculties of sense
> Into their own destruction, if perhaps he might avert
> His own despair even at the cost of every thing that breathes.[57]

It is interesting to note that Urizen seems to be responsible for the bagpipe. Blake's symbolism here is probably derived from Ovid. He would read the story of the dragon-guarded Golden Fleece as a reminiscence of a hanged Orc, and before Jason could attain the fleece he had to sow serpent's teeth, which sprang up as armed warriors who destroyed one another.

· 8 ·

Now let us sum up what we have learned of the Orc cycle in terms of another symbol. "Where man is not, nature is barren," says Blake, and the wilderness, desert, forest and sea are the symbols of this unorganized chaos. The garden represents man's victory over nature, and the city his creation from it. The word "culture" may indicate in its etymology a garden or Beulah ideal of mankind, as the word "civilization" indicates the city ideal. We saw that the sun and tree have two symbolic forms, one the form of their eternal life, the other the form of their death. So has the city. The cities man builds in this world express his desire to live an eternal civilized life in a New Jerusalem of which the Messiah is the cornerstone. But as they are produced in the Orc cycle, they eventually die and become monuments of man's failure. As the chill of old age comes over the historical cycle, its life dries up in huge tumorous cities, Nineveh, Babylon, Rome, Tyre, which thereupon become the symbols of the tyranny denounced by the prophet. Eventually the cities themselves are abandoned to nature, which creeps back over their stony skeletons as men move elsewhere to build more cities.

Of the six earlier cycles, the sixth has left the ruins of Rome, the Egyptian its pyramids, the Druid one Stonehenge; the story of the Tower of Babel is a reminiscence of another. The seventh one being built by England Blake calls the "Temple of Verulam,"[58] Verulam being the titular name of the Francis Bacon who wrote that all knowledge is pyramidal in shape, with memory at its base and a mystery at its apex. All these relics except the pyramids are ruins, and a ruin is a pile of stones. Now stones are as near as we can get to existence without life; they are at the limit of opacity, the reduction to the inorganic which in Blake's symbolism is both death and Satan. The stone as a symbol of the death-impulse meets us frequently both in the Bible and elsewhere. Samson, one of the many Biblical Orcs, destroyed himself in the ruin of a building. The sleeping Jacob, or Israel, the Biblical counterpart of Albion, saw a ladder stretching to heaven when his head was resting on a stone, and when he awoke only the stone was left: a stone still used, according to the legend, to crown the kings of England. This appears as the "Stone of Night" in *Europe*. In Ossian, too, the stone always has a sinister meaning and is associated with Loda and the Druids, the latter being called "dwellers of the rock." Just as the individual life can be seen from one point of view as a progression from dust to dust, so the historical cycle can be seen from the same point of view as a progression from stone to stone, Orc being a Sisyphus as well as a Prometheus.

Life in this world apparently springs from the lifeless; that is, life seems, in some way we cannot fathom, to form itself out of dead matter. As the rock is the image of dead matter, all new life struggles out of a rock, and relapses back into it at death. This links more closely the two aspects of Orc as an Adonis, a god of dying and reviving life, and a Prometheus, a giant of energy bound to a rock (and also, at the end of Aeschylus' play, under the earth). The struggle of life out of rock is also Orc's victory over the dragon. For as the dragon *is* death, it is not really a living thing but a dead thing, not something to kill but something to push out of the way. When Jesus rose from the dead he pushed away a stone that was rolled against his tomb to prevent his escape. And what Jesus did in the springtime all life repeats, even cycles of history which begin and end in a heap of stones. Thus Orc can be at the same time a St. George, a Prometheus, a Moses (in Egypt, not in the wilderness) and an Adonis; a dragon-slayer, a bound Titan, an initiator of a new human culture and a reviving god.

The vision of life as an Orc cycle is the pessimistic view of life, which in Blake's symbolism means that Orc is the equivalent of Albion in his fallen aspect. It is the fallen Albion, Blake says, who is the Titan Atlas, with his ruined Atlantis over his head. That ruined Atlantis is the physical world in which a recurring human and vegetable life is imprisoned in a rock, and from the imaginative point of view the physical world *is* a rock, within which all life is "vegetable" in the sense of being anchored to it. Blake does not visualize this Orc-Albion either as enclosed within the universal rock or as standing under it: he portrays him as sleeping, like his counterpart Israel, with his head on the "Stone of Night." This stone in reality is not outside Albion's head, but inside it: it is in other words his own skull[59]; but the image, though somewhat misleading, brings out the protective aspect of the "Rock of Ages," the fact that the limit of death is interposed between life and annihilation; that the physical world is solid and permanent, and orderly enough for the imagination to get a grip on it: that, in short, the Creation, though part of the Fall, was the solid bottom of the Fall, and thus "an act of Mercy." Left to itself, matter would disappear into nonexistence, for nature does not abhor a vacuum but longs for it with all her being; but it is held where it is until Man rises in the full power of his Godhead and rolls it away from his tomb.

THERE are still some aspects of the Orc cycle to be understood. In the first place, while within the individual form of life Orc always insensibly merges into Urizen, yet as states of existence Orc and Urizen, youth and age, are eternally different things. They represent, roughly speaking, the "two contrary states of the soul" which Blake calls innocence and experience. This aspect of their relationship brings our commentary to another group of minor prophecies. This group includes the two engraved sets of lyrics, *Songs of Innocence* and *Songs of Experience*, the subtitle to which is quoted above; also *The Book of Thel* and *Visions of the Daughters of Albion*, which deal with the themes of innocence and experience respectively in the form of the prophecy; and another poem called *Tiriel* which did not reach the canon. Here belong too a third group of lyrics, which Blake wrote out but never engraved, preserved in what is known as the Pickering MS.[1] These lyrics, which include two of Blake's most important poems, "Auguries of Innocence" and "The Mental Traveller," were apparently intended to explore the relationship between innocence and experience instead of merely presenting their contrast, as the two engraved sets do. The central conception in this group of poems is the middle stage between the spiritual and the temporal world which Blake calls Beulah, the married land.

New life does not begin at birth: it begins as an embryo within the womb of a mother. But all mothers are a part of Mother Nature, and though the infant life may break from its individual parent, it never escapes the shrouding protection of a natural environment. In relation to the whole of nature, therefore, Orc is an eternal embryo. But only a small part of nature forms the actual environment of any given form of life, and the latter may gain a good deal of control of that small part, depending on its imaginative vigor. Such vigor is greater in human life than in anything else, and greatest of all in a historical cycle, where extensive and dramatic transformations of nature are made. Whatever the form of Orc, he is born in helpless dependence on Mother Nature: as he grows older he gets more control of her, and she thereupon, if the symbolism is to be consistent, must grow younger, that is, cease to be his mother and become his wife. And as in infancy there is no imaginative contact with nature, the mother, as long as she is so, is a virgin. The account of Jesus' birth from a Virgin Mother is connected, though somewhat vaguely, with this: it is clearer in the Classical legends of Adonis and Attis, where the virgin-mothers who loved these dying and reviving gods were also their mistresses. In the "Preludium" to *America* Orc has arrived at puberty and copulates with his virgin mother, "the shadowy daughter of Urthona," whose name, or rather lack of one, indicates her unformed character. After this she becomes Orc's "emanation," Vala. This means that the American cultural cycle has become mature enough to shake off its dependence both on England and on its own pioneer state of nature: it is emerging both from a mother country and a virgin forest. Orc's age, fourteen, signifies not only puberty but the waxing half of the moon, and indicates that another "sublunary" cycle has come to its strength. As the cycle ages, Orc dies on the cross, and the women whom Ezekiel saw in the deserted Jerusalem wailing for the dying god Tammuz represent the nature who has once more been cheated, once more left unawakened by her lover and abandoned.[2] Thus Ahania mourns over her crucified son Fuzon in the book bearing her name. The "Preludium" to *Europe* is spoken by the same "nameless shadowy female" (not quite nameless actually: she is, or as near as makes no difference, Tirzah) who appears in the corresponding "Preludium" to *America*, seeing, at the time of Jesus, that she is about to go through the same painful process of achieving partial form. The dead Orc, now Satan or matter, is reabsorbed in nature, out of which in time another Orc grows.

To visualize the Orc cycle completely we have to take account of a reservoir of life or place of seed, which every form of life dwells in before birth and after death. In Blake this is one of the functions of Beulah, the garden of Paradise. Orc is Adonis, and this place of seed is the "Gardens of Adonis" which we meet in Spenser's *Faerie Queene*. In Spenser the Gardens of Adonis are a place of fertile love, and from thence all seeds of life fall into our world. Spenser does not explicitly link this garden with the Biblical Eden, though he does call it Paradise, but to find the garden of Eden visualized as a place of seed for this world we have only to turn to Dante's *Purgatorio*.[3] Spenser's contemporary Henry Reynolds suggests that the Hebrew "Eden" and the Classical *hortus Adoni* are etymologically connected.[4] Thus the Adonis river, the red earth of which was supposed to be dyed with the blood of the god, is the same as the fourfold river of Eden, the water of life. Blake calls it "the river of Adona," apparently linking it with "Adam," which means red earth.[5] Red clay is one of Blake's symbols of creative power, used in describing the descent of Milton to the physical world, perhaps with reference to a Greek word μίλτον (acc. case), which means ruddle or red ochre.[6]

If we understand this new aspect of Beulah, we are ready to look at "The Mental Traveller." This poem, as its last stanza suggests, describes a cycle, and while this cycle is not exclusively the cycle of history, the latter is the central form of it. Here the infant Orc begins as a rock-bound Prometheus in subjection to an old woman. At puberty he tears loose from the rock and copulates with the old woman, who grows younger as he grows older and becomes his wife or emanation. As Orc declines, his imaginative achievements are completed into a single form or "Female Babe," which is then to be used by other imaginations, just as an appletree sheds its fruit for others to eat. But a plant in its old age begins to scatter seeds, which fall into the fertile ground of another virgin mother and enter the place of seed again.[7] Here the male principle tends to become younger and the female more aggressive and maternal. Orc, now Urizen, dies a seed's death as the world becomes "a dark desart all around," and eventually re-enters the world of Generation as a reborn Orc. Later phases of "The Mental Traveller" cycle may become clearer to us as we proceed.

Such ideas as the tree of life and the water of life relate, as far as our world is concerned, to this reservoir in nature. The tree of life is not a single tree, but the total power of nature to grow trees; the water of life is the whole machinery of rivers, seas, clouds and rain. Beulah is to us, then, nature in its aspect of a nourishing mother, the garden of the world in which the "spring" of living water and of young life is to be found. It is the bed in which we bury the seed before it rises again, and the bed of sleeping love in which new human life is created. Any imaginative life, too, which draws its sustenance from nature is in the same phase of existence. In Beulah the perceiving consciousness of our world becomes a lover or child and the nature of our world beautiful and beloved, a mistress or mother. Beulah is the world of those transient intuitions of eternity which are not hammered into definite form, the fancies that break through language and escape. It is the world of contemplative thought, of the adoration of some vague mystery enveloping us. It is the world of the consolations of religion, of implicit faith and confident hope. It is the world of wonder and romance, of fairy tales and dreams. It is the protected world of the child and the world of the lover's "gratified desire." It is the world which the imaginative soul enters when it is still an infant untried in the ways of eternity, the world of the benevolent Father, Providence or Madonna which the gentler visionaries inhabit. In the Bible Beulah is the abode of pleasant pastures and still waters, and is most fully described in the Song of Songs, the wedding song of a king and a bride who is more definitely Isaiah's married land, the parts of her body being frequently compared to parts of a country.

All life or imagination in the world, from the heartbeat to the creations of genius, shows an alternating rhythm of effort and rest. There is the energy which creates, and the incubation in which further stores of energy are laid up. There is the struggle to create, and the loving contemplation of what has been created. These are not antithetical qualities, but different phases of the same imaginative rhythm. This rhythm occurs more regularly in nature: there is the bursting energy of life in spring and the buried repose of life in winter; the heat of the day and the coolness of the evening. The fact that all imagination or life shows this alternation of rhythm indicates its existence in Paradise. The two forms of eternal existence, Eden and Beulah, are respectively a sunlit city and a moonlit garden, a golden summer of energy and a silver winter of repose. (Our world is sublunary, and Beulah, being immediately above it, is associated with the moon. Blake even suggests that the moon is a broken-off fragment of Atlantis. The "Hyperborean" kingdom of which we hear such odd hints in Diodorus Siculus has lunar overtones, and when we come to *Jerusalem* we shall see how Blake associates the spiritual England with the lunar number twenty-eight.[8])

We have just spoken of the difference between the struggle to create and the appreciation of the created thing. God in the Bible not only creates but sees that his work is good, and establishes in

human life the same rhythm of energy and repose, in a ratio of six
to one. But the relaxation from creative effort is something much
broader than the artist's admiration of his own work after he has
done it: it is the whole difference between the performer and the
audience, creation and response. As the story of Pygmalion indicates, the joy of making something is not the same thing as the
love of what has been made. But in the eternal world, where all
creations are completely real, the story of Pygmalion would have
no meaning, for the statue would be alive in the first place. Hence
the two pleasures would be rather what is suggested in the fallen
world by the father's pride in his children and the lover's adoration
of his mistress.

In the account of "Eden" in Genesis, the unfallen state of man
is presented solely in terms of Beulah: nothing is left of the flaming
city of the sun which Eden must have been. But as long as we think
of the state of Edenic innocence as uncivilized and pastoral we
shall think of it as a protected child's world, and we shall never
really see the fall from it as anything but an outgrowing of it.
Hence the insoluble paradox of the *felix culpa*, or fortunate fall,
which Milton had to struggle with, as all Christians hampered by
a theology founded on moral virtue must do. Further, the great
vision of the heavenly city with which the Bible concludes has
nothing to polarize it. Gibbon describes quite accurately, if not
very sympathetically, the gradual evolution of this vision in early
Christian apocalyptic:

So pleasing was this hope to the mind of believers, that the New Jerusalem, the seat of this blissful kingdom, was quickly adorned with all
the gayest colours of the imagination. A felicity consisting only of pure
and spiritual pleasure would have appeared too refined for its inhabitants, who were still supposed to possess their human nature and
senses. A garden of Eden, with the amusements of the pastoral life,
was no longer suited to the advanced state of society which prevailed
under the Roman empire. A city was therefore erected of gold and
precious stones, and a supernatural plenty of corn and wine was bestowed on the adjacent territory. . . .[9]

But if we do not see a city behind the garden of Eden, we are bound
in consistency to regard civilization as a decline from an ideal state
of nature which was uncivilized, a line of thought leading directly
to the natural religion of Rousseau.

Yet there is a real reason why the Bible confines its vision to Beulah in its account of the Fall. Beulah is a stage intermediate between spiritual and physical existence, and while it is the dawn and spring for us, the source of inspiration insofar as the arts make use of natural imagery (Blake's Muses are Daughters of Beulah) and the place of seed, from the eternal point of view it is a state of repose and of dormant life. For us, the begetting of new life in a state of love represents a higher phase of existence than we ordinarily enter. According to both Classical and Biblical mythology, gods and sons of gods also have to go to bed with a mortal woman to create new human life. But a god, according to Blake, would be a fully emancipated creator, and it represents for him a descent from that state to make use of a separate female body to bring forth his creature. In the state of love the divine imagination is passive, contemplating and adoring, and in such passivity there is deadly danger if it is persisted in too long. If it reposes so long in sleep as to forget on waking up again that its mistress is its own creature, an independent external world begins to separate from that imagination and it is done for. This, Blake says, is what happened to Albion: he adored the nature he had created too long, began to regard it as independent of him, and was then unable to recover his imaginative power when his creature became a separate "female will."[10]

There are, then, two entrances to Beulah. Blake's symbolism here is based on Homer's description of the Cave of the Nereids in the *Odyssey*, a passage which was the subject of an elaborate commentary by the philosopher Porphyry, *De Antro Nympharum*.[11] While Ulysses is sleeping, he is placed in a grotto inhabited by nymphs which has two entrances, a southern one for the gods and a northern one for mortals. The north, as we shall see presently, is the nadir in Blake and the south the zenith: hence mortals approach it from beneath and gods from above.

All life is born in Beulah, and the energy of that life impels the infant Orc to push his way out of it into our world of Generation. When plants grow out of the place of seed, we see the growth as an ascent, but imaginatively it is a descent to a lower world. But as, according to Blake, nothing achieves reality without going through physical existence, the descent must be made. The failure to make it is the theme of *The Book of Thel*. Thel is an imaginative seed:

she could be any form of embryonic life, from a human baby to an artist's inspiration, and her tragedy could be anything from a miscarriage to a lost vision. To insist on an exclusive interpretation would vulgarize the poem into the wrong kind of allegory. Being an embryo in the world of the unborn, Thel longs to be of "use," that is, to develop her potential life into an actual one and hence come into our world of Generation. Like all seeds, she has to be buried in her "grave-plot" in order to spring to life, to pass through a σῆμα to a σῶμα, to use Plato's pun. But, hearing the groans of a fallen world tormented in its prison, she becomes terrified and escapes back to the unborn world. The "shriek" she gives is therefore that of the disappearing ghost or the uprooted mandrake, not the wail with which a baby announces its birth. Thel's abode is the garden "of him that walketh in the garden in the evening time," the Eden of Genesis, by "the river of Adona"; and to enter Generation she goes out by the "northern" bar used by mortals in Homer.

The only reason that comment on so exquisite a poem is justified at all is that we can see not only what Blake has done, but what he has avoided doing. Few poets could have pushed fragility so close to the line of the namby-pamby without crossing it, and we can seldom forget what perilous depths of bathos await the slightest false step. In this *The Book of Thel* is unique in Blake, for there is much more of the rococo china shepherdess about Thel than there is about the hilarious youngsters we find in the *Songs of Innocence*. And this has so important a bearing on the meaning of the poem that it may almost be said to be its meaning. Thel's world is not the real and eternal city of God: it is a world of dissolving and arbitrary fantasy, a looking-glass world of talking flowers. In describing an unborn world Blake had a more difficult technical problem to solve than even Milton's chaos presents, for the analogies suggested in nature are more tenuous.

But from our point of view also Beulah is a place of perilous equipoise, being as it is the region of the imagination which falls short of the disciplined unity of art. Eden is "human"; Beulah is "sexual,"[12] the region of passive pleasure, a Freudian land of dreams in which all images are erotic. Like its prototype in Spenser, it is a world where forms dissolve and substance does not, in contrast to Eden, where the reverse is true. As such, Beulah provides only a temporary escape from the world, not a permanent creation out of it. Wonder that does not stimulate art becomes vacuity: gratifications of appetite that do not build up a creative life become destructive. Everything that enters Beulah must quickly emerge either by the south or the north door; up to Paradise, or back again to this world. Bunyan includes Beulah in his vision, but there is also in Bunyan an "Enchanted Ground," a place of great spiritual danger. Spenser, too, has both a Garden of Adonis and a dangerous Bower of Bliss. In these latter we can see the perils in the state of imaginative passivity that led to the original Fall.

If dwelt in too long, Beulah will soon turn into Ulro. For Ulro is to our world what Beulah is to Eden, and as in Beulah we have not yet got clear of our world, there is an affinity between Beulah and Ulro which in the crisis of vision becomes identity. This highly technical but crucial point in Blake's argument will meet us again. It is illustrated in "The Crystal Cabinet," in the Pickering MS, where the poet enters, perhaps in sexual intercourse, a "crystal" world of a "little lovely Moony Night," is kissed by a "threefold" maiden, tries out of this complicated embrace to achieve something that is not transient but infinite, and collapses at once back into Generation to begin all over again. The triple mirror is Beulah, but the maiden is Rahab,[18] the apocalyptic Whore who at this point is the whole order of nature, including the Enitharmon of the sky and the Vala of this earth. Similarly in Classical mythology Diana is at once the goddess of the moon, an elusive and viciously chaste virgin of the forest, and Hecate or the queen of hell.

The Orc cycle has now expanded into the entire process of life and death which goes on in our world, taking in the whole physical world of Generation, and Beulah insofar as Beulah is related to Generation. The process begins in a form of potential life which is neither Orc nor Urizen, and in later poems is to be called Tharmas. It is then born as Orc, ages as Urizen, dies as Satan, sinks into the potential form of Tharmas again, and is reborn in another Orc. The entire cycle in the later poems is reduced to the single character "Luvah," the eternal name of Orc. From *The Four Zoas* on, Blake tends increasingly to speak of Orc as Luvah, and in *Jerusalem* the name "Orc" hardly occurs at all, except in passages explaining his identity with Luvah. The female principle of this

Luvah, who gets younger as he gets older and vice versa, is Vala,
and Luvah and Vala between them represent the sexual aspect of
existence, sex being the driving power of all natural life, hence
the word "Generation." Thus to all of Orc's other associations we
must add that of Eros, and this aspect of Orc (along with that of
Adonis, who is sexual or natural death as Eros is sexual life) increases in proportion to the frequency with which Blake calls
him Luvah.

· 2 ·

LIFE growing up in this world forces nature to become younger,
but any life or imagination which lingers in Beulah tends to become more helpless and infantile, and its imaginative environment
grows in proportion more broodingly maternal. This is the world
presented in the *Songs of Innocence*. There the divine imagination
is an infant, symbolized in Christianity by the infant Jesus, the
gentle and innocent Lamb of God. God from this perspective is
a loving Father who sees the sparrow fall. Nature is a kindly old
nurse, and a vigilant Providence appoints guardian angels to take
care of the children. As is appropriate to the state of Beulah, it
is especially in sleep and repose that these guardians are invoked.
Here we find the harmonious society which the single organism
represents in this world. All the forces of nature help to find lost
children; glowworms are beacons to bewildered ants; and as in
Isaiah, the lion lies down with the lamb and all animals are
childrens' pets. The world of imagination in its pitying, tender,
sympathetic and feminine aspect is in *The Book of Thel* as well
as the *Songs of Innocence*; but the world of Mary and Susan and
Emily is a world not of the unborn but of real children. Now real
children are not symbols of innocence: the *Songs of Innocence*
would be intolerably sentimental if they were. One finds a great
deal more than innocence in any child: there is the childish as
well as the childlike; the jealousy and vanity that all human beings
naturally have:

> O, the cunning wiles that creep
> In thy little heart asleep.
> When thy little heart does wake,
> Then the dreadful lightnings break.[14]

Childhood to Blake is a state or phase of imaginative existence, the phase in which the world of imagination is still a brave new world and yet reassuring and intelligible. In the protection which the child feels from his parents and his evening prayer against darkness there is the image of a cosmos far more intelligently controlled than ours. The spontaneity of life which such protection makes possible is the liberty of the expanding imagination which has nothing to do but complete its own growth. No one can watch babies, kittens, puppies or even the first green shoots of plants for very long without beginning to smile; and the smile is a partial vision of the state of existence which this infant life is in. It was to the same vision that Jesus was appealing when he put a child in the midst of his disciples.

However, the course of life in this world indicates that there is a higher world to attain to, and that is the world of the Providence and Father itself, which is looked up to in the infantile state. The dawn of imaginative puberty will make one at once impatient with it: one is then no longer a creature but a creator. At twelve Jesus ran away from home, and though his parents sought him as the searching parents in "A Little Girl Lost" do, he was now about his Father's business, ready to become one with his Father.[15] But outgrowing the child's world does not imply abandoning what it stands for. In every attempt of an adult to console a crying child there is a reminder of the fact that as long as a single form of life remains in misery and pain the imagination finds the world not good enough.

The reader needs no commentary to help him understand the terrible indictment of this latter world in the *Songs of Experience*. Contempt and horror have never spoken more clearly in English poetry. But Blake never forgets to see behind all the cruelty of man the fact of his fall. Just as no one can watch a baby without smiling, so no one can see a child tortured for its own "good" or neglected for someone else's: no one can see its parents, blackened and twisted by the St. Anthony's fire of moral virtue, stumbling out of a darkened church and blinking like bats in the sun: no one can see prostitution or war or race hatred or poverty, without groping for some cause of what seems to be utterly pointless evil. The reason can supply irrefutable proofs that in such things the world is behaving illogically and contrary to its own best interests.

The reason will not take us far. Only vision helps us here, and vision shows us the tree of mystery and morality growing inside the human skull; it shows us the prophet calling to the earth to redeem herself and earth answering with a groan to be delivered; it shows us our accusing enemy who frightens us out of Paradise behind the menacing blaze of a tiger's eyes.

This is the only world the child can grow into, and yet the child must grow. The *Songs of Experience* are satires, but one of the things that they satirize is the state of innocence. They show us the butcher's knife which is waiting for the unconscious lamb. Conversely, the *Songs of Innocence* satirize the state of experience, as the contrast which they present to it makes its hypocrisies more obviously shameful. Hence the two sets of lyrics show two *contrary* states of the soul, and in their opposition there is a double-edged irony, cutting into both the tragedy and the reality of fallen existence.

The same imaginative deadlock occurs whenever what may loosely be called the ideal and the actual are brought into conflict. The actual makes the ideal look helpless and the ideal makes the actual look absurd. Historically, the *Songs of Innocence* descend from the pastoral convention, the vision of life as a simplified rural existence. And the pastoral is congenial to satire, though it does not at once appear to be, because the life which it idealizes points up the artificiality of the court or city which it leaves behind. The forest of Arden, where one may find tongues in trees, has its satirist ready to cleanse the foul body of the infected world. The pastoral convention itself is as artificial as anything it satirizes; but that very fact heightens the satire. It is too brittle to last, and we must return to the ordinary world, but what have we gained by returning? To present the pastoral life as a child's world which is soon outgrown is thus quite faithful to the genius of the pastoral form, and for making the pastoral life an image of the unfallen world there is ample precedent: the "July" of Spenser's *Shepheards Calender* is an example.

Once again we see that unless we visualize the unfallen state as a city it will always seem to be impotent and transient compared to the fallen world. As an ideal the Utopia is much more human than the Arcadia. When Swift shows us horses living a pastoral life of nature and reason, surely the real meaning of his irony is that such a life, if possible at all, would be possible only for an unusually gifted animal: man cannot abandon civilization and live in a state of nature. Such a state is not really natural to man; therefore in it he would not be natural but monstrous, not a shepherd but a Yahoo. If this is Swift's meaning, Blake agrees with him against Rousseau and Bolingbroke.[16] Even the Utopia, however, means nothing unless it is conceived in the apocalyptic terms of a New Jerusalem and a destroyed order of nature.

Plato, for instance, in his unfinished trilogy of *Republic, Timaeus* and *Critias*, works out a vision of an ideal state, to be a new Athens as the Hebrew one was a new Jerusalem, and then goes on to link it with a legend of the creation which follows an account of an overthrow of a great Atlantic commonwealth. The Golden Age, according to the *Critias*, was the period of the high civilization of Atlantis, before its decline. The myth that Atlas now bears the whole weight of the world on his shoulders is the missing link between Plato's account of the fall of Atlantis and his account of the creation in the *Timaeus*. With this link, we can see that the creation in the *Timaeus* was a fall, not the evolution of concrete reality out of abstract perfection. Further, we can see that the Demiourgos of the *Timaeus* is the fallen, or falling, giant form of Atlas, the larger human body of the Atlantic society of the Golden Age. The true Republic is the true Atlantis, and in the true Atlantis there is no more Atlantic Ocean.

The irony suggested by the contrast of the two states of innocence and experience is deepened by the tragedy of Thel, the failure to overcome that contrast which is symbolized by all unborn forces of life, all sterile seeds, all the virginity that results from fear. *The Book of Thel* thus represents the failure to take the state of innocence into the state of experience, a failure which establishes one of the poles of the fallen world. *Visions of the Daughters of Albion* is complementary to this, and illustrates the failure to unite the state of experience with that of innocence.

Visions of the Daughters of Albion concerns three characters, bearing the sonorous and Ossianic names of Theotormon, Bromion and Oothoon. The setting recalls Ossian's *Oithona*, but there is little in that very conventional story of a romantic heroine's preference of death to dishonor to remind us of Blake, except insofar as Blake may have been protesting against it. Theotormon and

Oothoon represent, more or less, the precarious type of wedded love that so easily turns into a jealous possessiveness rationalized by a priggish morality. This morality is personified by Bromion (Gk. βρόμιος, "roaring"), a kind of Mr. Grundy. Oothoon has engaged in an extramarital amour, apparently with Bromion, and has inherited the jealousy of her husband and the thunderous denunciations of her lover. In order to horrify Bromion into calling her a harlot it is not necessary, of course, for Oothoon to do more than find pleasure in sexual experience. The stupidity of Bromion, however, is not a cause of his actions but an effect of them: their real cause is a fear based on common sense, a bad theory of knowledge. He lacks neither intelligence nor sensitivity, but he believes that there is an unthinkably mysterious and remote world beyond his reach. Hence, he reasons, only mechanical laws like the law of gravitation can hold it together. These laws are based on the principle of uniformity, therefore acting in accordance with uniform law is acting in accordance with what must be the will of God. These laws must be tyrannically imposed and implicitly obeyed: the alternative is chaos. We have already met the Urizenic principle that the social product of this conception of uniform law is tyranny, and Bromion applies the principle to love. Love is mutual possession, and may exist on the higher legal level of a marriage contract or the lower one of commercial purchase. Theotormon's relation to all this is simply that of the victim to the tyrant, the host to the parasite, the cuckold to the cuckoo. He knows, in a vague and lugubrious way, that Bromion may not be wholly right, but his spirit has been broken by Bromion's arguments, and he has neither the courage nor the energy to settle his cloudy doubts one way or the other.

But Oothoon has "plucked the flower" of imaginative experience and has entered the state of innocence. She cannot argue or rationalize, but she has passed through sense to imagination and can no longer be persuaded against her own direct knowledge that the world is one of uniform law. She knows that every living thing has a unity and integrity of character, and because it has that there is an infinite variety of life which no law can approximate. The ox and the lion have nothing in common; each obeys the law of its own character, and there is no general law which applies equally to both of them. The profiteer who encloses common land can no more understand the laws that govern the happiness of the children on the "Echoing Green" than a bedbug can understand the nature of a bed. But the laws of any society which believes in uniformity are certain to be in the interest of the profiteer rather than the children. Oothoon has learned that we do not have to wait for death in order to obtain the more abundant life which Jesus spoke of. She has learned that this life is a transfiguration of the sexual life of the natural world, and has nothing to do with the refined fantasies of spiritual eunuchs. But once this more abundant life gets loose in the natural world, it will destroy the present form of that world if it is not smothered, and another thing that Oothoon has learned is that there are plenty of people waiting to smother it.

The poem presents a conflict between the tyranny of convention and an emancipated female's demand for free love, hence it may suggest an opposition of morality and nature. But to Blake it is not in any sense natural to behave like Oothoon: it is natural to rely on sense experience and infer uniform generalizations from it as Bromion does. The pattern of Blake's symbolism is rather different. In the crisis of the "ancient history of Britain," the death of King Arthur, the same three figures, more or less, of a weak jealous husband, a rebellious and passionate wife and an avenging moralist, are involved. Blake is applying a similar pattern to America: the reader may be reminded of the tragedy of Hester Prynne and the two sinister men who wrecked her life, which another great visionary made into a parable of such deep significance for American history. Oothoon is the "soft soul of America"; she is one of the Hesperides, a daughter of Atlas or Albion in the West, who has plucked a golden apple from the dragon-guarded tree of life. (In Blake it is a marigold, but the difference between a flower and a fruit in the state of innocence is not significant.) The other daughters of Albion, separated from her across the ocean, form a silent chorus to her tragedy. In the same sense Oothoon is the bound and struggling imagination of America as Prometheus in Aeschylus is that of Asia:

> Oothoon weeps not; she cannot weep! her tears are locked up;
> But she can howl incessant writhing her soft snowy limbs
> And calling Theotormon's Eagles to prey upon her flesh.[17]

Bromion is thus the moral law which continues in America in spite of the revolution, and he is also the possessive economy founded on slavery. He is associated with a cave, the inevitable symbol of the Selfhood from Plato onwards, as the wavering and doubtful Theotormon is with the ocean which still keeps the two halves of Atlantis separate.

Bromion, it should be noted, is not a Puritan but a Deist. Puritanism at its best is the resistance of an integrated mind to the passivity of sense experience: the sort of resistance set forth in the defense of the Castle of Alma against Maleger in Spenser and in Bunyan's *Holy War*. But the contrast between the human and the divine nature which Puritanism insists on tends to make it a withdrawal from sense experience instead, as God can only be an abstract Spectre where such a contrast exists. Hence natural religion, kept out at the door, comes in by the window, and the moral rectitude of Puritanism soon takes the form of the pseudo-"enlightenment" which finds any other world than the physical one an impenetrable darkness. This conception of Deism as the product of the breakdown of Puritanism is an important link in the argument of *Milton*.

In contrast to the unborn Thel, Oothoon is a fully developed imagination, and whereas in Thel's infertile world everything is exquisite and harmless, everything is a whirlwind of energy in the eyes of Oothoon. Thel's canvas is decorated with lambs and lilies; Oothoon's with eagles, whales, glowing tigers and sea fowls. Purity, or negative perfection, is not what Oothoon wants: to her the so-called "impurities" of life are life:

> Sweetest the fruit that the worm feeds on, & the soul prey'd
> on by woe,
> The new wash'd lamb ting'd with the village smoke, & the
> bright swan
> By the red earth of our immortal river.

The river is the same "river of Adona" beside which Thel walked, but Oothoon is not at its spring but at its delta.

It is something of a digression to have to turn aside from our argument and examine the poem of *Tiriel*, which actually deals with a phase of the Orc cycle discussed in the previous chapter. But *Tiriel* is so obviously the complement to *The Book of Thel* which Blake wrote before he wrote *Visions of the Daughters of*

Albion that some consideration of it belongs here. Thel lives in the "vales of Har," located in the east, probably in Ethiopia; Tiriel, the "king of the west," goes eastwards in search of it. Thel fails to achieve physical existence at infancy and Tiriel fails to achieve spiritual existence at senility. The diction and imagery of the two poems also seem to be a deliberate contrast. There are good things in *Tiriel*, in spite of its tentative narrative and its clutter of undeveloped symbols, and though it seems to belong to a period when Blake was thinking of illustrated rather than illuminated poems, it is possible that Blake intended to engrave it and make it one of a group of three, a tragedy of reason as *The Book of Thel* is a tragedy of a will (θέλος) to live, and *Visions of the Daughters of Albion* a tragedy of feeling. The "motto" of *The Book of Thel* is repeated in both the other poems.

The presiding spirits of the place of seed in which Thel lives are called Har and Heva. Heva is a mere reduplicate of Eve, but Har is distinguished from Adam. Adam is ordinary man in his mixed twofold nature of imagination and Selfhood: Har is the human Selfhood which, though men spend most of their time trying to express it, never achieves reality and is identified only as death. Har, unlike Adam, never outgrows his garden but remains there shut up from the world in a permanent state of near-existence. This garden is a prison-Paradise like the Ethiopia of *Rasselas*, and the poem was apparently intended at one time to describe the collapse of the African culture.

Tiriel, as an individual, is a man who has spent his entire life try-ing to domineer over others and establish a reign of terror founded on moral virtue. The result is the self-absorption, symbolized by blindness, which in the advanced age of people with such a charac-ter becomes difficult to distinguish from insanity. He expects and loudly demands gratitude and reverence from his children because he wants to be worshiped as a god, and when his demands are answered by contempt he responds with a steady outpouring of curses. The kind of god which the existence of such tyrannical papas suggests is the jealous Jehovah of the Old Testament who is equally fertile in curses and pretexts for destroying his innumer-able objects of hatred. The use of the name "Ijim" later in the poem indicates a Swedenborgian source for the theme:

With the essence of divine love the essence of diabolic love may now be contrasted. Diabolical love is the love of self. This is called love, but its true nature is hatred; for it loves none outside of itself, nor to do good to any one but itself; in its inmost nature it desires to rule over all, and to possess the property of all, and at last to be worshipped as a god. . . . In hell this love causes its lusts to appear at a distance like various wild beasts; some like foxes and leopards, some like wolves and tigers, and some like crocodiles and venomous snakes; the deserts where they live are merely heaps of stones or barren gravel, interspersed with bogs full of croaking frogs; while birds of ill omen fly screeching over their miserable hovels. These are the ochim, tziim, and ijim, mentioned by the prophets of the Old Testament, where they speak of the love of dominion from the love of self.[18]

These Hebrew words, which occur in Isaiah xiii, 21, are translated in the 1611 Bible as "doleful creatures," "owls" and "satyrs." Swedenborg means, as Blake read him, that deserts and serpents and vultures are the part of nature's character that corresponds to the part of man's character represented by Tiriel. Blake also points out more clearly what Swedenborg suggests, that if the true nature of self-love is hatred, it will end in self-hatred.

As Tiriel is a tyrant, and as a king is the only man who gets a real chance to be a tyrant, Tiriel is a king, and so symbolizes a society or civilization in its decline. The achievements of his maturity are behind him, and, as his children will have nothing more to do with him, he wanders in his blindness through a desert full of mocking voices, like the King of Babylon in hell who in Isaiah represents the collapse of that empire. He is trying to find some kind of rejuvenation, and makes his way back to Har, his journey being an early form of Urizen's journey in Night VI of *The Four Zoas*. Har represents the unborn theory of negative innocence established by obeying a moral law which Tiriel started out with; Tiriel himself is the dying practice of negative experience which has found that law unworkable. Two negations do not make anything positive in life, whatever may be true of grammar, and Tiriel finds Har's world the exact counterpart of his own mind. And of course one finds no rejuvenation in a second childhood. Har and Heva are a couple of hideous imbeciles, senile children, eternally old like Tithonus, yet eternally young like the Norse gods who are kept alive by Freya's apples. They are in charge of an old nurse whose name, Mnetha, recalls both Athena and μνήμη—wisdom founded on memory.[19] She has a bow and arrow to take care of unwelcome visitors—a faint echo of the Covering Cherub—but is otherwise harmless. In this grim parody of the state of innocence there is a weird chill of horror that even the account of the Struldbrugs in Swift does not excel. There is something about these two creatures, with their ghoulish affection for old age, that suggests a pair of staring corpses imprisoned in ice, with the false bloom of life still on them:

> God bless thy poor bald pate! God bless
>   thy hollow winking eyes!
> God bless thy shrivel'd beard! God bless
>   thy many-wrinkled forehead!
> Thou hast no teeth, old man, & thus I kiss
>   thy sleek bald head.
> Heva, come kiss his bald head, for he will
>   not hurt us, Heva.

Wearily returning home from this defunct Paradise, Tiriel encounters a savage and not quite conscious humanity, haunted by primitive fears of lurking demons, called Ijim. Tiriel himself is the Puritanic iconoclasm and brutalized morality that marks the beginning of cultural decadence of which the lassitude of Deism is the next stage, and Ijim is introduced to show the mental affinity between Deism and savagery. Ijim, like all savages, is terrorized by fiends and ghosts; but one usually finds at the basis of savage religion a Creator who made the world but can no longer be approached and leaves its control to vicious subordinates like devils and witches. This is exactly the same careless *dieu fainéant* that one finds in Deism. That is, belief in devils and witches is founded on natural religion, and the growth in a sick and old civilization of a religion like Deism means that it is only a few centuries removed from the fury of barbarian invasions and other signs of the return to the state of nature which Rousseau in Blake's day was urging. Ijim has tried to catch the elusive demons that haunt him in many forms, and thinks he has finally caught one in the form of Tiriel, only to find that he has the real Tiriel. For Ijim's awakening imagination gives him the forms of things even when he is still calling them phantoms, and his natural religion is a real human Selfhood and not a phantom. It is only through his powerful but undirected energy that Tiriel arrives back home at all, just as barbarian tribes pouring in upon a dying empire will often end by propping up its tyranny again. The internal proletariat, so to speak, of the Tiriel society is represented by the idiot "sons of Zazel," the scapegoats of the law.[20]

Tiriel then kills a hundred of his sons: his sons are his cities, and this means that his empire is being abandoned to the jungle and the "doleful creatures" of Isaiah's prophecy. This is the real meaning of the story of the slaughtered Egyptian sons in the Bible.[21] He also kills four of his five daughters, which probably means that all imaginative activity based on the senses disappears except automatic sexual reproduction. Even this proves too much for his moral virtue: he turns the remaining daughter Hela into something monstrous and obscene, a Medusa with serpentine hair, reaches Har again only to curse him in a final flash of enlightenment, and dies at his feet.

· 3 ·

ALL these visions of the Orc cycle are visions of tragedy and failure. In this world innocence is nearly always accompanied by ignorance and childishness, and we buy experience at the price of a decline in vitality. All our imaginative efforts are bound to a wheel of time, which in its turn is imprisoned in a wheel of space. None of the partial conquests of nature which human civilization has made seems to have been more than another turn in the squirrel-cage of nature, and certainly none has touched the real burden of Atlas, the nature over our heads. In *Europe* Jesus descends to the world from an "eternal day," but Enitharmon, the queen of the sky, sits serenely up in her "crystal house" (compare the "crystal cabinet" mentioned above) quite undisturbed, placidly revolving her untouchable stars in an indefinite night of time. The more we learn about the physical world on a Lockian basis the more impressed we are by the independence of that cyclic movement from the will and desire of man.

The whole strength of the Lockian position consists in not thinking it out to its logical conclusion, or rather its real form. It takes the prophet to show that, as we have already suggested in discussing Urizen's exploration of his dens, the vision of life as an indefinitely recurring cycle in time and space is the real form of the view of life suggested by the philosophy of Locke. We may hail an explosion of revolutions as a promise of deliverance from that weary commonness of sense, but before long we find ourselves back where we started, and the circular progress of our experience has only deepened a slipshod theory of knowledge into a tragic vision of life. We still see time and space extending indefinitely in all dimensions away from the present and perceiving center, the latter being reduced to what Blake calls a white dot.[22] And we still see no shape in time or space except cycles, that is, wheels.

It is no wonder, then, that the tragic vision sees life as a wheel of fate or fortune, and certainly some understanding of this wheel is essential to any serious religion or art. The wheel appears in a curious bit of blank verse which introduces the fourth part of *Jerusalem*, described as a "Wheel of Religion" or "Wheel of fire" (notice the echo of *King Lear*), moving from west to east, "against the current of Creation," the direction of Tiriel's journey.[23] But it seems strange that we should use the wheel to represent an external compelling power, when we invented the wheel ourselves to spin our garments and propel our vehicles. A wheel is a tool of human civilization, and unless we can seize this universal wheel and run it ourselves, it is not correctly visualized as a wheel. In his vision of God Ezekiel speaks of "wheels within wheels," which suggests the possibility of reversing our present view of the universe as a huge "mill" of geared machinery:

> . . . wheel without wheel, with cogs tyrannic
> Moving by compulsion each other.[24]

Now Blake says "if any could desire what he is incapable of possessing, despair must be his eternal lot," and goes on to say that the desire of man is infinite.[25] We must, therefore, either accept the hopeless pessimism suggested by the Orc cycle, or find some vision of life that will do what it fails to do, and impose an intelligible human form both on Enitharmon's crystal house and on the time in which it persists.

· 4 ·

IF we want a single word for the view of life as an Orc cycle, we may call it a vision of "Becoming," the totality of change within an immutable framework of time and space. We have so far discovered only that "all things flow," and have been led into pessimism, as Heraclitus, the coiner of the maxim, is said to have become the weeping philosopher. Now if there were no end or total form to space there would be no meaning in the word "universe," and if there is a universe, there is presumably an end and a total form to time, though we have no separate word for it. We do not need one, as it would be the same thing, a combination of time and space in the form of a universal "Being," a word which implies both continuous existence and permanent form. The words "Becoming" and "Being" are not Blake's, but may be used to approximate the meaning of the words he does use, which are Orc and Los.

It would perhaps be difficult to prove completely the axiom that objects do not cease to exist when we have stopped looking at them. Yet it is hard to see how we could maintain a consistent sense of reality without assuming it, and everyone does so assume it in practice and would even assert it as the first article of common sense. For some reason it is more difficult to understand that events do not necessarily cease to exist when we have stopped experiencing them, and those who would assert, as an equally obvious fact, that all things do not dissolve in time any more than they do in space, are very rare. Common sense prefers to see time as a not quite existing present concealed between a no longer existing past and a not yet existing future. But, again, the permanence of time is usually assumed in practice. At every stage of our "Becoming" cycle from childhood to old age we are conscious, not only of a continuum of identity, but of a certain permanent form or character which makes us equally ourselves in all stages. Thus in a crisis an honest man does the honest thing because he knows his life is building up a pattern of honesty which he does not want to spoil. One may call this duty or self-respect or instinct or impulse or intuition or conscience or whatever name comes handy, but whatever we call it he is assuming that he is a "Real Man,"[26] a permanent form as well as a continuous existence. The more imagination he has, the more attention he gives to perfecting this form, and the more aware he is that at all stages of his life some acts belong to it and others do not.

The real man, therefore, is the total form of the creative acts and visions which he evolves in the course of his "Becoming" life. The latter exists in time and space, but his "Being" or real existence is a work of art, and exists, like the work of art, in that unity of time and space which is infinite or eternal. The imagination or Being, then, is immortal, a form constructed out of time but existing in what Paul calls the "fullness of time." We arrive at the conception of immortality as soon as we grasp the idea of a reality which is not merely part of an indefinite persistence of an indefinitely extensive physical world. But for that very reason immortality cannot mean the indefinite survival of a "Becoming" life arrested at some point in its development (that is, not growing older forever, like Tithonus), as in most conceptions of an immortal personality. What is immortal about the man is the total form of his creative acts, and these total forms are the characters, or "identities," as Blake calls them, of the men who made them, the isolating of what is eternally humane in them from the accidents of Becoming. Everyman in the morality play slinks into eternity with his "good deeds," a few pitiful bits of jetsam he has salvaged from the flood of time; but those good deeds are the eternal reality of Everyman's existence, the spiritual form of Everyman.

What exists in eternity persists in time, and an oak tree which dies and reproduces other oaks exists eternally as the total form or genus of the oak. Imagination is life, but we distinguish different levels of consciousness in life, and generally restrict the term "imagination" to the conscious life of the human being—or of some human beings. Similarly Blake appears to imply a distinction between the Being of the oak tree and the Being of man. The former is something much closer to the Platonic idea, in the sense that its total form is an archetype created in the unfallen world, and existing now in a form appropriate to a fallen one. The latter consists of all human "Beings" united in a larger human Being who in Blake's symbolism is one Man at a distance and multitudes of nations on a nearer view. This conception is founded on the Biblical and Christian idea of a Church or City of God, and might be difficult to find in Plato.

The construction of a character or identity out of life is part of the attempt of Albion to emerge from time into eternity as one Man who is also a City of God. Thus the imagination exists immortally not only as a person but as part of a growing and consolidating city, the Golgonooza which when complete will be the emanation or total created achievement of Albion, Jerusalem. In this world we can draw no real distinction between the individual and the social aspects of any creative act, and in eternity even the appearance of a distinction vanishes. The term "identity" expresses at once an individual and a social integration. Thus Golgonooza comprises:

> . . . All that has existed in the space of six thousand years,
> Permanent & not lost, not lost nor vanish'd, & every little act,
> Word, work & wish that has existed, all remaining still. . . .
> Shadowy to those who dwell not in them, meer possibilities,
> But to those who enter into them they seem the only substances;
> For every thing exists & not one sigh nor smile nor tear,
> One hair nor particle of dust, not one can pass away.[27]

The honest action of the honest man is the right one because it is a manifestation of the divine, or truly humane, character of Albion, and is therefore a part of Albion's eternal life. A dishonest action would be part of the debris Albion is trying to free himself from, and when he is free, the debris, the hindrances and restraints on his freedom which constitute evil, will cease to exist, as it is purely negative. Similarly, the disappearance of the Becoming life at physical death will isolate a man's Being only if by that time there is a real man or permanent form to be isolated. The orthodox imagination tries to work this out in terms of good and evil, and postulates a moral conscience in man instead of a divine vision. But a "conscience" adapts a man only to a social criterion of goodness which is, like the criterion of common sense in Locke, placed at the lowest possible limit of normality. One who follows his conscience only may do many really creative acts, but will get them mixed up with the trumpery taboos and fetishes which are always part of moral good. Hence the prophet says:

> I care not whether a Man is Good or Evil; all that I care
> Is whether he is a Wise Man or a Fool. Go, put off Holiness
> And put on Intellect.[28]

On the other hand, we may be so convinced of the insufficiency of humane standards in comparison with divine ones as to assert that only faith in the latter supplies the means of living rightly. Whether this in itself is right or wrong, we cannot visualize non-human standards of judgment, and if we try we shall only dredge out human atavisms, and think of God as an absolute monarch or a judge more fettered by law than his prisoner. There is no revelation except that which unites the human with the divine through human channels, and our moral acts owe their value, not to faith in what we do not see, but to the form of what we do see, the vision of the world as fallen, redeemed and proceeding to apocalypse. This vision is the framework or larger form of all good acts, and the more consciously the good act is related to this vision the better it is. The honest man without such a vision is a spiritual coral insect, helping to build the world above the ocean without knowing how or why, and dying in his own catacomb.

This brings us back to Blake's doctrine set forth by a Devil in *The Marriage of Heaven and Hell*:

The worship of God is: Honouring his gifts in other men, each according to his genius, and loving the greatest men best: those who envy or calumniate great men hate God; for there is no other God.

We are now in a better position to see what constitutes the greatness of the great man. The "heroic villain" and the tyrant are part of the negative evil of the world, and have no real existence in the sense defined above, therefore we can follow them only into annihilation. The revolutionary leader is part of the Orc cycle, and leads us around it. The honest man owes his honesty to a vision of life which honesty by itself is not sufficiently conscious to attain. The great man of will and action, the ruler who is not a tyrant, may do much real as well as moral good, but as the assumption underlying all his actions is the permanence of a natural order, he is never inspired: the breath of a divine spirit is not in him. Even sanctity finds its most typical expression in miracles, or spasmodic disturbances of the order of nature, rather than a systematic creation out of them. Only the creator has the divine spirit. But it would be a dreary outlook if we had to construct a new sacerdotal order out of that not especially attractive class of men whom we know as artists, and attach a superstitious reverence to their persons. The real artist is not the man creating, but the total form of his creation, his art regarded as his vision of life, and as an individual part of the archetypal vision which is the Word of God. And among artists we must distinguish a Reynolds from a Milton, and follow only the artist who is also a prophet. Through him we may learn that, just as the artist exists eternally as the total form of his art, and not as the man who created it, so the true and eternal God is not the Creator of man, but the total form of his creation, which is the larger body of man. This larger body is the human form of God, and the greatness of the great man consists in his "identity" with the unification of the divine and the human which is the body of Jesus.

The rising Orc has been visualized as killing a dragon and as pushing a rock from his tomb, but neither of these images is really exact. When a new life is born, a new form emerges from unorganized matter, and the "victory" of the rising Orc is the only kind of victory that is possible: the conquest of a creator over his material, the reduction of a monster to a shape. We must now superimpose another pattern on this one. Just as Satan or the monster of death is overcome by Orc, so Orc himself is a monster of natural life (hence his association with the serpent) who must in turn be overcome, or shaped into a form, by someone else. And as Orc shapes life out of death, so this someone else shapes the conscious vision out of life which is the imagination proper, the character or identity, and so constructs a Being from the Becoming. Orc brings life into time; the shaper of Orc brings life in time into eternity, and as Orc is the driving power of Generation, so his shaper is the power of "Regeneration."[29] This shaper is the hero of all Blake's later poems, Los the blacksmith, the divine artificer, the spiritual form of time, the Holy Spirit which spoke by the prophets. Blake's Los is perhaps what Carlyle means when he speaks of "that blending and identification of Eternity with Time, which . . . constitutes the Prophetic character," and what Shelley is hinting at when he speaks of time as a redeemer and mediator.[30] Blake says of him:

> Los is by mortals nam'd Time, Enitharmon is nam'd Space:
> But they depict him bald & aged who is in eternal youth
> All powerful and his locks flourish like the brows of morning:
> He is the Spirit of Prophecy, the ever apparent Elias. . . .
> All the Gods of the Kingdoms of Earth labour in Los's Halls:
> Every one is a fallen Son of the Spirit of Prophecy.[31]

Orc, the amorphous cub whom Los has to lick into shape, is Los's first-born son, as Los is the Holy Spirit or incubating power from whom all life proceeds. And as no life reaches eternity without first going through the physical world, the young Orc is bound by Los to the latter. In Blake's earlier symbolism Orc is bound by Los and Enitharmon with a "Chain of Jealousy,"[32] the chain being a symbol both of clock time and the exhaustion of energy to which Orc is subject. Later on Blake puts greater emphasis on the providential aspect of time, as well as of the creation, and drops the chain of jealousy for a new character called the Spectre of Urthona, the temporal existence of Los. As Blake says:

> Time is the mercy of Eternity; without Time's swiftness,
> Which is the swiftest of all things, all were eternal torment.[33]

The Bible tells us that God expelled Adam from Paradise to prevent him from plucking the tree of life, which means that man is prevented by time from living eternally in the world his fall created. In the life of Jesus the binding by Los is represented by the swaddling bands of his infancy and by the fact that he was carried off at his birth by his parents to "Egypt" or the fallen world. It has nothing to do with his crucifixion.

Los is the builder of the eternal form of human civilization, and is therefore a smith, a worker in metal and fire, the two great instruments of civilized life. He is given a great deal to do in *Jerusalem*, and his hammer pounds and his furnaces are heated to an almost wearisome degree. He is chiefly associated with iron, and the iron vessels from which Orc is fed in the "Preludium" to *America* are his work. In the Book of Daniel Nebuchadnezzar's dream of a statue of gold, silver, brass, iron and iron mingled with clay is, as we shall see more fully in the next chapter, a vision of the whole of human history from the Golden Age to the apocalypse. The silver age was titanic and the brazen gigantic; the iron age began with Adam, the present human form, and it is in this age, six thousand years in length, that Los's work has been done.

Los is thus one of the divine smiths whom we often meet in mythology. We are reminded of the smith-god Hephaistos, one of the binders of Prometheus in Aeschylus, who escapes Prometheus' fate because his work in fire has been done for immortal gods rather than mortal men. This Hephaistos in Homer is hurled out of heaven by Zeus and crippled. The crippling, which recurs in the legend of Weyland, is dropped by Blake: it could only symbolize the compensatory origin of genius out of a physical handicap, and Blake, an unusually healthy genius, was not greatly interested in this. In Thor, whose hammer carves out valleys and whose strength was almost, though not quite, sufficient to tear the world-serpent loose, we are closer to Los. Certain taboos on iron in the Old Testament and the fact that the Israelites under the tyranny of the Philistines were denied smiths (a passage referred to in *Areopagitica*) fit the same pattern.[34] The vision of regenerating the universe by some process carried on with metal and fire is the central conception of alchemic philosophy, and this is linked with the fact that Blake's engraving process is an art employing metal and fire.

If we combine the fact that Los is a blacksmith with the fact that Orc is his medium, we get the furnace as a symbol of the natural body. On the level of an unconscious will to live, the hammer is the heart-beat, the bellows the lungs and the furnace the whole metabolism of a warm-blooded animal. The same is true of the risen or spiritual body, but that body is part of Golgonooza, which is conceived as a huge machine shop or foundry, a vast crucible into which the whole physical world has to be thrown before the refined gold of the New Jerusalem can emerge from it. There are seven furnaces in Los's smithy, corresponding to the Seven Eyes, and they are associated with wheels in a way that we shall explain more fully later. In them are to be found Ezekiel's "wheels within wheels," imaginative energy as opposed to the interlocking compulsions of nature which we see represented in physical machinery. The allusions to the finger of God touching the seventh furnace refer of course to the coming of Jesus.[35]

The stone is the unit of the earthly city, and the New Jerusalem is built of stones as well as gold, but they are the "stones of fire" referred to in Ezekiel, the spiritual forms of precious stones. The breastplate of Aaron, twelve precious stones symbolizing the Zodiac, is an image of priestly legalism because the color and brilliance of the precious stones represent the color and brilliance of heavenly bodies that are out of our reach. Here we have the cloven-fiction type of symbolism. John's vision of the New Jerusalem also sees it as constructed of twelve precious stones, but they no longer represent the Zodiac because they are the Zodiac. In the Apocalypse the stars are the stones of fire, and the sun is the Messiah who is the cornerstone of the city. One may also compare the "white stone" which is a symbol of spiritual victory in the

Apocalypse.[36] Isaiah thus associates the building of a New Jerusalem with precious stones and the work of a divine smith:

O thou afflicted, tossed with tempest, and not comforted, behold, I will lay thy stones with fair colours, and lay thy foundations with sapphires. And I will make thy windows of agates, and thy gates of carbuncles, and all thy borders of pleasant stones. . . . Behold, I have created the smith that bloweth the coals in the fire, and that bringeth forth an instrument for his work.[37]

· 5 ·

WE now pass to a group of poems, *The Book of Urizen*, *The Book of Los* and *The Book of Ahania*, which are connected with one another partly by a distinctive meter and partly by a unity of theme. *The Book of Ahania* is a sequel to *The Book of Urizen*, and *The Book of Los* intersects *The Book of Urizen* at its fourth chapter, somewhat as the J and E narratives intertwine in Genesis. We have already had occasion to comment on *The Book of Ahania* and the latter half of *The Book of Urizen*.

There is a curious passage in *Europe* in which Isaac Newton blows the trumpet that heralds the apocalypse. This is partly an ironic allusion to the awestruck reverence with which the age of Deism regarded Newton—one is reminded of the famous "God said, 'Let Newton be!' and all was light"—it is partly Blake's doctrine that the mental attitude represented by Newton moves toward a consolidation of error which could provoke an apocalypse; and it is partly an uncharitable reference to Newton's own commentary on the Book of Revelation. But there is more in Blake's meaning still.

All truths exist as part of more complex mental patterns in individual minds. No man can keep so inclusive an idea as the law of gravitation unassimilated to the rest of his view of life, and if he could it would not be true. Every man who knows the law draws a moral from it, and it is this moral that Blake is interested in. Most scientific discoveries relate to the material world and the state of nature, and those who believe that the state of nature is the only possible one draw this inference from all such discoveries. Had Blake been able to use Darwin instead of Newton as his trumpeter we should perhaps see this more clearly. When a new truth appears, the imagination uses it imaginatively; and to the imagination such a new truth as the doctrine of the survival of the fit in the state of nature indicates how far away from the state of nature we ought to get. To the Selfhood the same doctrine defines an inescapable fact of existence, and so becomes a new excuse for bullying and mass murder. This is not Darwin's fault; he is an announcer or herald, not a conspirator. Similarly with Newton. Newton's conception of the material world proves to the Selfhood that the universe is a vast collection of particles held together automatically by an unconscious power, that intelligence and imagination are accidental sports from this, that force and cunning are more in keeping with the state of nature—and so on to bullying and mass murder. To the imagination the dead cohesion and solidity of the Newtonian universe makes it look more than ever like the stone rolled against the tomb of a sleeping Man-God. The imagination will have its work cut out to demonstrate this, but this is what Blake attempts to do in *The Book of Urizen* and *The Book of Los*.

The fallen world, Blake says, began in a completely lifeless state of fire and rock and water. Life and consciousness have since evolved in it: where have they come from? We may see a plant grow out of a rock, but no one would be naïve enough to say that the plant was a part of the rock that had come to life—except, perhaps, at a distance of a sufficiently bewildering number of eons in the past. And if death could produce life, even the dead world had existence, and where did its existence come from? Perhaps from nonexistence, for we are often told that God made the world from nothing, though the product of nothing and anything is still nothing. But surely it is simpler to assume that what happened in the azoic world was what still happens every spring, and that life came out of it because it had been previously buried in it. Now when a germ of life grows it recreates its original form: if there were no original form of an oak tree the acorn would not know what to do. Similarly, the original form of the germ of life that grew out of the world long ago is most clearly indicated by the most mature and full-grown forms of life that now exist in the world, that is, human societies.

The notion, Blake says, that "before the Creation All was Solitude & Chaos" is "the most pernicious idea that can enter the Mind."[38] If we make a stand on chaos as a beginning, ignoring the question of where it came from, and deny the analogy between the growth of life out of it and the growth of a plant from a seed, then we are at a loss to explain why there should be a *direction* of development, and why life should take on more and more highly organized forms. The solitary God of orthodox theology is far greater nonsense than this. One can see why a Deist, unable to conceive of creation except as an arbitrary starting point of linear time, should use such a God as his breech-block, but there is no excuse for those who call themselves believers in Jesus. In Jesus God and Man are one, and if the Son of God existed in eternity God must have been human from the beginning. A prehuman God is the most meaningless idol ever worshiped. And if always human, God must have been plural, for it is not good for either God or man to be alone. Thus if there is a creative principle which the evolution of life and consciousness is now recreating, it must have been a human society, dwelling in what are now the two forms of existence which we are striving to re-establish, a city and a garden.

At this point the Berkeleian "to be is to be perceived (by man)" and the orthodox "to be is to have been created by God" become the same axiom, as even Berkeley did not wholly see. Our present human society, then, has evolved out of a seed of life dropped in a dead world from a preceding eternal human society, and we cannot ask where the eternal society in its turn came from, because that is pushing the idea of time further than it will go. If we study this image more carefully, we can see that the seed of life *was* the dead world, fallen from eternity, and that the seed will have achieved its original form when the dead world, including the sun and stars, becomes again a city and a garden. The achievement of a permanent human civilization and culture is the next stage in development, and if that is not the end, we shall see what the end is more clearly from there.

The Book of Urizen does not mention Albion, and has only a passing reference to the Atlantic Golden Age which preceded the Fall. It also leaves out the whole "female will" aspect of the Fall which is developed in *The Four Zoas*. Blake imitates Milton in beginning with the fall of the Satanic principle, and the Bible in introducing us first to a world of chaos. But the two essential principles of his thought, that the Creation was a fall and that it

was the fall of a God as well as a man, are clearly there. In Milton
God sets a baited trap before man and as soon as man nibbles
at it the Fall springs on him automatically. God, according to
Milton, knew that Adam would do this, but did not compel him
to do so and is therefore not responsible for the Fall. It is an
ingenious quibble, but if God had foreknowledge he must have
known in the instant of creating Adam that he was creating a
being who would fall. In other words, we can understand the
Fall only as a false step in an act of divine creation. This occurred,
Blake tells us, when Albion sought a pure or negative perfection
from his creative power. This objectified that aspect of Albion's
mind which is Urizen, the power of abstraction. Urizen says:

> I have sought for a joy without pain,
> For a solid without fluctuation.[39]

Such abstractions are arrived at only by withdrawing the mind
from reality and making it passive. With us this leads only to
introspective brooding; but for Albion it means the withdrawal
of a divine mind from its creatures. The divine mind being life,
its creatures die when it is withdrawn from them; and death being
a reduction to the inorganic, the result of Albion's attempt is a
blank dead "world of solid obstruction," in which fire, the habitat
of imaginative energy, becomes a destructive principle.

Albion has succeeded in killing himself, but not in annihilating
himself: he has hit the solid bottom of the Fall, which is matter
and not chaos. He is still a "Being," even if he is not alive. Thus
the world of solid obstruction contains a Los as well as a Urizen,
and Los slowly and painfully begins to awaken it to life. In his
first stage Los is only movement, the still unconquered fire that
splits the rocks of Urizen and breaks them apart into discrete
forms. In his second stage his fall from eternity achieves a mechanical regularity of motion. The cycle thus becomes the basis of all
future developments, and the essential form of Los in this world,
creative time, is established. Then Los's fall "chang'd oblique"[40]—
possibly a reference to the *clinamen* or swerve which starts the
creation in Lucretius—and Los begins to organize crude and
primitive forms of life, chiefly marine, founded on the same
cyclic rhythm that we find reproduced in our own heart, lungs,
digestive and genital systems. The reproductive system and the

splitting of living forms into male and female, symbolized by the birth of Enitharmon, accompanies this. After laying a foundation of unconscious life, Los evolves consciousness and human forms take shape. At this point Orc is born, after evolving through various stages of life in a rather remarkable piece of embryology:

> Many sorrows and dismal throes,
> Many forms of fish, bird & beast
> Brought forth an Infant form
> Where was a worm before.[41]

When a fallen human body is created, the physical universe takes the form in which that body must necessarily perceive it. The physical universe thereby becomes the objective counterpart of the fallen human body. We shall be able to explain this more clearly in a later chapter. The objective aspect of the development of life up to man is symbolized by the creation of a human body out of Urizen by Los in seven "ages," the reference being to the seven days of Creation and the seven times that pass over Nebuchadnezzar in Daniel. Blake leaves it open to the reader to extend these ages as far as he likes.

As soon as humanity appears, Los confines his attention to it, and strives to develop a visionary imagination out of the human mind and to reconstruct the arts of civilized life. And just as the embryonic Orc goes through many stages of life before he reaches humanity, so we may see the colossal foundation of Golgonooza that Los has been building since the beginning of time reappearing in the work of the artist. Fire and stones are still the materials of culture. The natural cycle is not only the basis of life but the basis of the imagination. All civilization and agriculture, the city and the garden, depend on it; art begins in rituals which mark its different stages, and is developed within the artist from a cycle of habit and practice. Art does not imitate nature, but the order of nature is the foundation of the order of art. Science, law and "mathematic form" relate to the involuntary aspects of existence, and find their place in culture underneath, and as the foundation of, vision, as in the human body the heart and stomach do their work underneath the brain. Hence the artist who runs away from nature is no more superior to the artist who surrenders to nature than the criminal is superior to the morally good man.

Thus the Orc cycle has been created by a power which manifests itself first as cyclic movement, then as life, then as conscious life, and finally as human imagination. We may now see what the place of the Orc cycle in Blake's thought is. Man stands at the level of conscious life: immediately in front of him is the power to visualize the eternal city and garden he is trying to regain; immediately behind him is an unconscious, involuntary and cyclic energy, much of which still goes on inside his own body. Man is therefore a Luvah or form of life subject to two impulses, one the prophetic impulse leading him forward to vision, the other the natural impulse which drags him back to unconsciousness and finally to death. The philosophy of Locke, which teaches that the mental life should be based on involuntary sense experience, is thus an Epimethean philosophy which turns its back on what is in front of man and faces what is behind him. That is why the vision of life as a cycle is also that of Locke.

The imaginative vision turns us around to the "forgiveness of sins" which according to Blake is the only thing to be found in Jesus' teaching that cannot be found elsewhere.[42] This forgiveness is a challenge to men paralyzed by their conventional fears to take up their beds and walk: it makes them realize that they are barred from Paradise only by their own cowardice, and cannot shift the responsibility for their misfortunes to God, nature, fate or the devil, all of which are within them. But again, no effort on man's part to free himself from his enslaved state will get him anywhere unless it is inspired by the same vision and realized by the same creative power. Rousseau says, on a basis of nature and reason, that man is born free, and is everywhere in chains. The imagination says that man is not chain-bound but muscle-bound; that he is born alive, and is everywhere dying in sleep; and that when the conscious imagination in man perfects the vision of the world of consciousness, at that point man's eyes will necessarily be open. Thus Los, with the hammer of the smith and the sickle of Time, is Blake's Demiourgos, a word which means both the Creator of the universe and a worker for the people.

· 6 ·

THERE is, then, an evolutionary process in time, and at each stage of this evolution the highest form of existence becomes the medium of Los. Now that men have appeared, is there any evolution in history corresponding to the preceding evolution of life? If we look at the sequence of seven "Eyes," we can see that in the last "six thousand years" there has been some concentric expansion in their progress, that civilization has been gradually covering more and more of the world, dispersing more mysteries and making increasing efforts to unite society. Blake also postulates a historical process which may be described as the exact opposite of the Hegelian one. Every advance of truth forces error to consolidate itself in a more obviously erroneous form, and every advance of freedom has the same effect on tyranny. Thus history exhibits a series of crises in which a sudden flash of imaginative vision (as in the French Revolution) bursts out, is counteracted by a more ruthless defense of the *status quo*, and subsides again. The evolution comes in the fact that the opposition grows sharper each time, and will one day present a clear-cut alternative of eternal life or extermination.

Further, just as the human body functions on conscious and unconscious levels, so the structure of civilization has different levels, which Blake decides to call, for reasons more obscure than their meaning, Golgonooza, Allamanda and Bowlahoola.[43] The first is art proper, and is in society what the brain is in the individual man. The other two correspond respectively to the heart and the stomach of the individual, and they appear in the larger human body of Albion, whom Los is trying to recreate, as the commerce, science and law which hold that larger body together in a mechanical and largely involuntary cohesion. Here, perhaps, we can see an evolutionary process at work. A world-wide commercial unity seems to be emerging from national rivalries; and science evolves an increasingly coherent form out of knowledge, as law does out of conflict. Commerce, science and law in Blake's day seem to be proceeding to some kind of historical finality, simultaneously with the decline of the Christian historical cycle into Deism. It is at first difficult to see how art can evolve in a similar way, for the quality of art never improves. But it may increase in conscious awareness of the implications of vision as the work of a growing body of predecessors accumulates and is, however haphazardly, preserved. Milton is not a better poet than Sophocles because he follows him in time, but his ability to use Sophocles may have given him a more explicit understanding of what his own imagination saw. To pursue this point, however, would be to anticipate the theme of Blake's poem on Milton, which is not our immediate concern.

In history Los's first-born son Orc is succeeded by a series of other sons who are the agents of human civilization, related to it as the "angels" are to the churches in the Apocalypse. First among them are Rintrah, the vision of the isolated prophet, especially typical of Semitic and Indian genius, and Palamabron, a gentler spirit found in Hellenic culture.[44] Or we might distinguish them as the *Iliad* tragedian who sings of wrath and the *Odyssey* romancer who tells of men and cities. Next come the two spirits of *Visions of the Daughters of Albion*, Theotormon and Bromion, of social service and science respectively. Perhaps they are associated with the "soft soul of America" because Blake foresaw that they would be more important in American life than the spirits of art and prophecy. Around these four are grouped a number of other sons with fluctuating and uncertain attributes: Sotha, a spirit of music; Antamon, of outline and modeling; Ozoth, of painting or the imaginative use of the eye, and others. There is also a large company of daughters, most of them identified as emanations of the sons. A long and horridly cacophonous list of them is given in *The Four Zoas*.[45]

All of these sons may under the wrong conditions be perverted, and in fact are usually so portrayed. Rintrah may become fanatical bigotry, Palamabron lazy dilettantism, Theotormon moral cowardice, Bromion dogmatic prejudice, Sotha a berserk lust of fighting, Antamon sensuality, and so on. But there is a particular reason why they do become perverted. Los is the spiritual form of time, and his "emanation," the total form of what he is trying to create, is the spiritual form of space, Enitharmon. But until Los completes his task, Enitharmon will remain elusive and remote, and will be the tyranny which the idea of unbounded space exerts on the mind. That is why she is associated with the sky, the part of nature which man has never attempted to transform. And as an emanation is, up to a point, a wife, Los's sons are her sons too. Now from Los's point of view, there are no spirits except human ones, and his sons, the spirits of civilization, work within men, not as ghosts looking over their shoulders, but as the inspiration and craftsmanship which come with genius and are developed by practice.

Blake says a man's good angel is his leading propensity. To the Enitharmon mind a "spirit" is a mysterious external power, that is, a god. And as all worship of external powers is suggested by the remoteness of nature which is most obvious in the sky, all such idolatry is fundamentally star-worship, which is why the stars bear the names of gods, and vice versa. In the Gospels the total form of human or divine spiritual power in the world is symbolized by Jesus and his twelve disciples, the divine man and the circumference of his influence. This total power returns in *America* as the thirteen angels who are the spirits of the revolting colonies. To the Enitharmon mind, the total form of spiritual power in the world would most naturally be symbolized by the Zodiac surrounding a fallen sun (Orc). The conflict between these opposed conceptions is presented in *Europe*, which describes the triumph of Enitharmon in the decline of Christian culture. A slight echo of the *Nativity Ode* underlines the reference to Jesus at the beginning of *Europe*, and in Enitharmon's roll-call of her thirteen children with their strange names there is both imitation and parody of Milton's catalogue of defeated gods. Under Enitharmon's influence (a word with an astrological origin, in contrast to the "inspiration" which means breathing in one's own spirit) the oracles are re-opened, the ghost-world of demons and nature-spirits re-awakens, and the twelve gods of Olympus come back on man's neck. The product of this is the debased astrology heralded by Newton; less fascinated by the stars, Blake says, than by the empty spaces between them.[46]

In human life Enitharmon is one of the presiding spirits of war. Blake calls war enslaved energy,[47] and the energy he means is the organic energy of Orc. Organic energy, which exists in the world of Generation, is primarily sexual energy, hence war is a perversion of the sexual impulse. The sexual impulse should lead to the higher imaginative state in which the object is not only seen but loved. Love in its turn should lead us to the still higher state where there is no external object at all. The sense of an eternally external world frustrates this rise in the sexual impulse, and so perverts it from creation to destruction. In passing from the state of love to the state of creation the beloved object becomes a creature and ceases to become objective: it surrenders its "female" or independent quality and takes its form from the will as well as the desire of its creator. The refusal of the beloved object to surrender this independence, which of course is really man's inability to make it do so, is the "female will," or belief in an ultimate externality, which blocks our final vision. Now when Orc revives in human life and another great cycle of history begins, Vala, or nature on earth, is "bound down for his delight."[48] But Enitharmon is still an inviolate virgin-mother, and before long begins to oppress the religion and art of the new cycle. Not long after Jesus a "coy mistress" began to make her appearance, inspiring a code of love which was inseparably connected with a code of war. Such axioms as "None but the brave deserve the fair" usually mean by "fair" a statuesque, aloof and rather stupid beauty, who has little animation or friendliness or capacity for companionship, but is, like most divinities, an unwearied poseur. The fallen Enitharmon in Blake is typically the mistress of chivalry, spiritually inviolate because wrapped up in herself in a way which makes devotion to her a teasing mockery of love, a frustration of life to be expressed in murder. As a warrior in *Jerusalem* says: "I must rush again to War, for the Virgin has frown'd and refus'd."[49] In the decline of a cycle the growing ascendancy of Vala adds another female will to Enitharmon's, and this accounts for the increase in the ferocity of warfare which accompanies that decline. But Vala frankly howls her delight in slaughter, whereas Enitharmon hangs silently over it like a grin without a cat.

Under the guidance of Los his sons work in the opposite direction, decreasing instead of increasing the chaos and misery of existence. Uncivilized life is oppressed by external fears and dangers, and true civilization attempts to remove that sense of external oppression within the small portion of nature which it controls. The sons of Los and Enitharmon work for both simultaneously in all periods of human life, and if there is no age without war and tyranny, there is no age either without some perception that a genuine culture does not pollute nature but tries to transform it into a garden or park inhabited by friendly animals; that a genuine culture does not murder its neighbors but attempts to unite with them into a larger human body. The twilight of the Deism of Blake's time, in which the shadows of war and tyranny are growing longer and longer, is also the time in which the imagination feels that a world-wide peaceful society, the millennium of the Apocalypse, is almost realizable, that:

> The whole extent of the Globe is explored. Every scatter'd
>   Atom
> Of Human Intellect now is flocking to the sound of the
>   Trumpet.
> All the Wisdom which was hidden in caves & dens from
>   ancient
> Time is now sought out from Animal & Vegetable & Mineral.[50]

Every event in history, therefore, exists in relationship, first, to a cultural cycle which inevitably declines and dies, and, second, to a universal form evolving out of history and proceeding toward a civilized eternal existence. Hence the period of chaos between cycles shows these two aspects in the sharpest possible contrast. In the Old Testament, for instance, the escape of Israel from the moribund cultures of Egypt and Babylon was obviously interpreted by many as a promise that Israel would in its turn build up as big an empire and possess as great an amount of slave labor. The prophets, on the other hand, saw in this deliverance an image of a far more important deliverance from the tyranny of nature into the eternal city of the New Jerusalem. Similarly the Great Whore of the Apocalypse is not only Babylon and Rome but Mystery. For in the Christian period too there is at the same time a passing of an earlier culture and a replacing of it with a Christian one, and a renewed vision of an eternal City of God that survives the collapse of all Romes and Babylons. In St. Augustine's vision of this City, the ambiguous conception of a new "Church" covers both aspects. The attempt to escape from this ambiguity forms the crisis of vision in *Milton*. It is in these crises of history that it is especially important to realize that the great man is not Enitharmon's Orc, the great Selfhood or hero-Messiah whom we obey or watch perform, but Los's Orc, the universal imagination operating within an individual. The former Orc is someone else; the latter identical with the immortal part of ourselves.

The sons of Los, working for Enitharmon, produce in society the mental attitude of common sense. This mental attitude recognizes at the beginning of knowledge a split between a perceiving subject and a perceived object, but has not the nerve to try to leap across the gulf. The "spectres" of such reasoning are inner reflections on an external world. But as the inside of a natural man is a very limited place, and as the outside of the natural world is of indefinite extent, all such reflections carry with them a sense of the helplessness of the subject and the mysteriousness of the object. The mental fear in which abstract thought is born and bred is too pervasive to be felt as fear, but the wars and superstitions produced by it in human life are eloquently illustrative of it.

When Los's sons work for Los they produce art, and when we turn from reasoning to art we are conscious first of all of a greatly increased sense of reassurance. Art protects us against nature: it would be impossible to find pleasure in a tragedy or laugh at many of the predicaments of comedy if we did not feel this protection. In nature there is misery, in art tragedy; in nature there is mysterious evil, in art ghost stories. This does not mean that art enables us to escape from nature: it enables us to undertake its imaginative conquest. The reasoner peers myopically out into an indefinite world, finds that he can see only a little way into it, even with the aid of instruments which "alter the ratio,"[51] reaches blindness and ignorance at the circumference of his vision, and reports that man lives, as far as he can see, in a cave shrouded in darkness. The artist, by putting concrete images into a mental form, makes the familiar intelligible; and art does what all civilization does: it transforms nature into a home. This is what Blake means when he shows us the sons of Los creating the concrete imagery of art as a protection for the cringing, fighting, hysterical spectres of abstract thought which are born of the direct exposure of the mind to nature:

> The little weeping Spectre stands on the threshold of Death
> Eternal, and sometimes two Spectres like lamps quivering,
> And often malignant they combat; heart-breaking sorrowful
> & piteous,
> Antamon takes them into his beautiful flexible hands:
> As the Sower takes the seed or as the Artist his clay
> Or fine wax, to mould artful a model for golden ornaments.
> The soft hands of Antamon draw the indelible line,
> Form immortal with golden pen, such as the Spectre admiring
> Puts on the sweet form; then smiles Antamon bright thro' his
> windows.[52]

This conception of the clothing of the spectre needs another word of explanation. The struggle of Los with Enitharmon for the control of their sons has for its goal the redemption of Enitharmon herself, the recreation of the idea of unbounded space into a mental form. Hence to the extent that a single civilization does evolve out of history, Enitharmon becomes, in spite of a good deal of sulking, increasingly subservient to Los. In her unregenerate form, she presents us with a vision of endlessly revolving stars, and from this men have developed the conception of life as a wheel of fate under the control of a female power. It has already been mentioned as a curious paradox that men should have taken an image of overmastering fate from one of their own tools, and one which they no doubt invented before they started to speculate about cosmology. Thus Enitharmon, when undergoing the process of redemption, is, like Los, associated with the imaginative use of wheels; and as the wheels of Los are associated with furnaces, so Enitharmon's is a spinning wheel, and develops a complementary "loom." The former is Golgonooza; the latter Blake calls Cathedron.[53] The furnace Los works with is the organic energy of Luvah, and similarly Cathedron represents an imaginative reversal of a natural process belonging primarily to Vala.

All embryos are plunged into the womb either of Mother Earth or of a mothering animal, and we may visualize nature as a vast net or trap into which these germs of life fall. The human embryos that develop enough imagination see this net or trap from the other side, as a mysterious veil interposed between them and reality, confining them in the worst of all prisons, the prison of an endless expanse. Blake's poem "The Golden Net" is a vision of this net or veil of nature, seen at first on "branches," evidently of the tree of mystery, then as extending over the whole sky. The rending of the veil of the temple by Jesus symbolizes the escape of the imagination through this net. Another modulation of the same image of a confining prison of barred windows which the imagination can see through but which the body cannot escape from is a cage. We may remember that in "How Sweet I Roam'd" Blake's awareness of the symbolism latent in both the cage and the net was contemporary with his own entry into puberty. In either case the vision of a wheel and loom of female Fates, spinning, weaving and cutting the threads of life according to a monotonous program of tyranny and mystery, comes primarily through a sense of being wrapped up inside nature like a mummy, or a worm in a cocoon, to use the image employed in *Jerusalem*.

But only infants and corpses permit themselves to be swaddled; the artist, at least, weaves his visions out of nature, and natural images clothe his ideas as he wills. In the first stages of this there is an answering response from nature, for, as "it is impossible to think without images of somewhat on earth,"[54] there is a nourishing maternal power in nature for the imagination as well as for the natural life, if the imagination has enough vitality to use it properly. Hence the artist is no longer tied up so that he cannot see, but is, in Blake's language, woven in the looms of Cathedron, and feels a correspondence between his imagination and nature. But of course he has much further to go than this. So far we are at the doctrine that the physical appearance is the clothing of a mental reality, a line of symbolism made familiar to us by *Sartor Resartus*. But Blake's symbolism is more radical than Carlyle's. The fact that our clothes are separable, and that man is in that sense the only naked animal, indicates that he has unique powers of dispensing with an external nature. The artist does not use natural images to clothe his ideas so much as to give body to them. An abstract idea is a spectre, a collapsing skeleton; a concrete image has flesh and blood. Hence the rather violent image of woven bodies which Blake employs in this context: from the skeleton's point of view it is rather difficult to say whether the flesh is body or clothing.

In making the familiar intelligible, in imposing a permanent vision on the flux of time, the artist creates a body out of nature which has a mental form. He thereby teaches us to see, in the small part of mystery which he has made coherent, the image, that is, the form or reality, of a universal coherence; he suggests, in other words, that if his natural body is a mental form, then the entire body of nature, from atoms to stars, may also be the form of a human mind, if the imagination could only get hold of it. Our fallen senses hollow out a tiny grotto in a boundless stretch of mystery, and this grotto is our home. But the center of the real universe is wherever we happen to be, and its circumference the limit of the radius of our experience. In the perspective of the awakened mind, the radius of our experience *is* the universe, and art reveals to the senses of distant contact, eyesight and hearing, a universal home or Paradise which is ready for us to inhabit. The protection in art we have spoken of, therefore, is also a promise of deliverance, of an eventual awakening in a world free from what now awaits us outside the theater:

> When all their Crimes, their Punishments, their Accusations of Sin,
> All their Jealousies, Revenges, Murders, hidings of Cruelty in Deceit
> Appear only in the Outward Spheres of Visionary Space and Time,
> In the shadows of Possibility, by Mutual Forgiveness for evermore,
> And in the Vision & in the Prophecy, that we may Foresee & Avoid
> The terrors of Creation & Redemption & Judgment.[55]

And however vague one's conception of "heaven" may be, or however far off its final storming, by the human Titans now bound beneath it, in the meantime art introduces us to a real world of continuous pleasure and of continuously intelligible form. If we can see this in art, we are seeing the image, and therefore the form or reality, of what it reveals.

BY 1796 Blake had completed nearly all the "minor prophecies" which belonged in his canon, and his next task was to work out what we have called a cyclic vision of life from the Fall to the Last Judgment in one long poem. This would constitute in a single form the totality of what Blake came into the world to say, and would be his poetic testament or Word of God in him. It would be, in short, his "epic" (which etymologically means "word," as does "myth"). It is evident, then, that Blake was not planning a series of epics, but a single crowning masterpiece. The moment in which the epic poet finally chooses his subject is the crisis of his life, as Dante and Milton at least show very clearly; and his choice, once made, almost precludes the idea of ever finding another. "An epic from Bob Southey every spring"[1] is possible, because Southey's poems are not epics at all, but simply narratives: "epic" in that sense is not the name of a form but literary jargon for "long poem." No poet, unless the *Iliad* and the *Odyssey* are by the same man, has ever completed a second real epic on a theme radically different from the first.

Some of the minor prophecies, notably *The Book of Urizen*, look like early drafts of an epic, but Blake's first real attempt was the poem which was first called *Vala* and later *The Four Zoas*, on which he worked for several years. Yet in spite of all this work the poem was never engraved, and was left abandoned in an extraordinary manuscript. We shall try to suggest reasons for this: in the meantime, *The Four Zoas* remains the greatest abortive masterpiece in English literature. It is not Blake's greatest poem, and by Blake's standards it is not a poem at all; but it contains some of his finest writing, and there is much to show that it would have contained some of his best engraving. Anyone who cares about either poetry or painting must see in its unfinished state a major cultural disaster.

The two titles indicate that Blake revised the scheme of the poem at least once. A second revision appears to have been begun, but before it had proceeded far Blake realized that he was thinking in terms of another poem altogether. At first, evidently, he intended to cast his epic into the form of a prophecy uttered by a

Sibyl, as in the *Völuspa* in the Elder Edda from which he got the name "Vala." As he went on, the working-out of the far richer symbolism of the "Zoas" reduced Vala to a minor character, while the Muse or Sibyl addressed at the beginning shrank into a vestigial "Eno,"[2] a daughter of Beulah or inspiration, so chosen to contrast with the Classical Muse who is a daughter of Memory. Through the eyes of this Eno Blake sees the whole of existence projected in the form of a single drama of fall, redemption and apocalypse. The poem comes nearer than *The Book of Urizen* does to Blake's real theme, the fall of Albion and his recovery of Jerusalem in the apocalypse; but even so Albion remains offstage and asleep throughout the poem, which latter is thus projected as his dream. That is partly why the poem is called a "Dream of Nine Nights," and why, in its lack of explanations, its passionate utterance and its rich suggestive imagery, it forms a complete contrast to *Jerusalem*, and surrounds us with the atmosphere of a dream world as *Jerusalem* very seldom does. Albion is conscious of torment and oppression, of ecstasy and spasmodic struggle, but he does not possess the larger perspective which distinguishes the waking man from the sleeper.

The theme of *The Four Zoas* is, first, the loss of the identity of divine and human natures which brought about the Fall and created the physical universe; second, the struggle to regain this identity in the fallen world which was completed by Jesus; and, third, the apocalypse. The thesis is given most concisely in the following passage:

> If Gods combine against Man, setting their dominion above
> The Human form Divine, Thrown down from their high station
> In the Eternal heavens of Human Imagination, buried beneath
> In dark Oblivion, with incessant pangs, ages on ages,
> In enmity & war first weaken'd, then in stern repentance
> They must renew their brightness, & their disorganiz'd functions
> Again reorganize, till they resume the image of the human,
> Co-operating in the bliss of Man, obeying his Will,
> Servants to the infinite & Eternal of the Human form.[3]

From the point of view of this poem, therefore, the essential barrier between man and his divine inheritance is the belief in a nonhuman God founded on the fallen vision of an objective nature. This is what Blake means by "Religion." The last line of *The Four Zoas*, describing the final emancipation of man, reads: "The dark Religions are departed & sweet Science reigns." By "Science" he means what he means elsewhere when he says: "The Primeval State of Man was Wisdom, Art and Science."[4] That is, wisdom consists in the mental war which is art and the mental hunting which is science, and these constitute the eternal life of a Man who is God. Art is human, but it is also divine because God is a Creator. Science is human, but it is also divine because God can hardly be the lazy and inert Omniscience which a lazy and inert mind is apt to envisage.

In order to understand the scheme of *The Four Zoas* we must first turn to the Book of Daniel and read the stories about Nebuchadnezzar as legends of Albion which have become attached to that king:

All this came upon the king Nebuchadnezzar. At the end of twelve months he walked in the palace of the kingdom of Babylon. The king spake, and said, Is not this great Babylon, that I have built for the house of the kingdom by the might of my power, and for the honour of my majesty? While the word was in the king's mouth, there fell a voice from heaven, saying, O king Nebuchadnezzar, to thee it is spoken; The kingdom is departed from thee. And they shall drive thee from men, and thy dwelling shall be with the beasts of the field: they shall make thee to eat grass as oxen, and seven times shall pass over thee, until thou know that the most High ruleth in the kingdom of men, and giveth it to whomsoever he will. The same hour was the thing fulfilled upon Nebuchadnezzar; and he was driven from men, and did eat grass as oxen, and his body was wet with the dew of heaven, till his hairs were grown like eagles' feathers, and his nails like birds' claws.[5]

The reason why myths of Albion do become associated with historical figures is that the collapse of every great empire, whether Babylonian, as here, or Egyptian, as in *Tiriel*, or Tyrian, as in Ezekiel, or Roman, as in the Apocalypse, or early British, as in the *Morte Darthur*, repeats the original fall of Atlantis. The distinctive features of the above account, once the sulky and malicious Nobodaddy it implies is removed from it, are, first, that "seven times" or cycles have to pass over Nebuchadnezzar, and, second, that he falls from a palace into a state of nature. The Icelandic account of the formation of the world from the body of the giant Ymir explains more clearly what actually happened to the "King" Atlas or Albion who was really the kingdom of Atlantis in the form of a larger human body.

Another story in the Book of Daniel tells how Nebuchadnezzar flung three men into a fiery furnace, heated it "seven times more than it was wont to be heated," then looked in and said: "Lo, I see four men loose, walking in the midst of the fire, and they have no hurt; and the form of the fourth is like the Son of God."[6] In Blake's hierarchy of the four states of existence, Ulro or hell is a single or "Hermaphroditic" world of reflected abstractions, Generation a double one of subject and object, Beulah a triple one of lover, beloved and child, and Eden a fourfold one of imagination, love, wisdom and power. The story is thus an allegory of the passing of the human body, for which the furnace is a symbol, from Beulah to the fiery city of Eden. In his Exhibition of 1809 Blake had a picture of three "Ancient Britons," whom he calls the Strong Man, the Beautiful Man and the Ugly Man, and on whom he comments as follows:

The Strong Man represents the human sublime. The Beautiful Man represents the human pathetic, which was in the wars of Eden divided into male and female. The Ugly Man represents the human reason. They were originally one man, who was fourfold; he was self-divided, and his real humanity slain on the stems of generation, and the form of the fourth was like the Son of God.[7]

Three of these four we have already met. The ugly man is Urizen, the beautiful man Orc, whose female principle is Vala, and the divine fourth is Los. The strong man is a new character called Tharmas, the Zoa of Beulah required to complete that aspect of the Orc cycle worked out in the previous chapter. The epic deals with the interaction of these four principles within human society and the souls of men. We have next to enquire why Blake calls them Zoas.

The body which is the form of the soul's energy is called by Blake the "Vehicular Form." The most natural symbol for this vehicular form in its complete divine state would be either a chariot or a throne, depending on whether the god is conceived as moving or sitting still. The chariot is found in the allegorical pictures of the Renaissance depicting the triumphs of gods or virtues: in the *Bhagavadgita* Krishna, the divine imagination of Arjuna, is Arjuna's charioteer, and the same figure occurs in the *Phaedrus*. Now a chariot is drawn by animals, who thereby become symbols of the god: thus in the triumphs just mentioned Venus is always drawn by doves, Juno by peacocks, Bacchus by leopards, and so on. In Ezekiel God is visualized in a chariot surrounded by four "living creatures" full of eyes resembling an eagle, an ox, a lion and a man. In the Book of Revelation Ezekiel's chariot has become a throne, and here the same expression "living creatures" is used, though Ζῶα is translated in the 1611 Bible by "beasts." Similarly in the *Timaeus*, God "intending to make this world like the fairest and most perfect of intelligible beings, framed one visible animal comprehending within all other animals of a kindred nature." Here also the word translated by Jowett as "animal" is Ζῷον. Blake, very sensibly, takes Ζῶα as a singular and forms from it the English plural "Zoas."

The reason why the animals who draw the chariot become symbols of the driver is that otherwise the suggestion is that the driver is dependent on an external power for his energy. The chariot is actually the vehicular form of the driver himself, or his own body. This symbol helps to clear up the association of wheels and furnaces mentioned in connection with Los. The two most obvious examples of a wheel used for imaginative purposes as a tool of human civilization are the spinning wheel, which belongs to Enitharmon, and the wheel of the chariot or vehicle. The wheels of Los's furnace, therefore, are the wheels of a chariot. Perhaps if the internal combustion engine had been invented in Blake's day it would have simplified his symbolism at this point. Yet, if we consolidate the image still further, the distinction between the physical power of the engine and the mental power of the man who drives it also disappears. The real chariot-furnace is the flaming energy of the spiritual or risen body, and it is the automotive power of the heart and lungs and bowels and brain of this body which we try to represent when we depict angels as winged.

In *Paradise Lost* there is a graphic portrayal of Christ seated on a chariot surrounded, but not drawn, by four "cherubic shapes" as he cuts his way through the rebel angels:

> . . . forth rushed with whirlwind sound
> The chariot of paternal deity,
> Flashing thick flames, wheel within wheel undrawn,
> Itself instinct with spirit, but convoyed
> By four cherubic shapes, four faces each. . . .
>   . . . at his right hand victory
> Sat eagle-winged, beside him hung his bow
> And quiver with three-bolted thunder stored,
> And from about him fierce effusion rolled
> Of smoke and bickering flame, and sparkles dire.[8]

In this passage Milton has from Blake's point of view achieved his clearest vision of God as Jesus, the God-Man, surrounded by the four powers of the unfallen world. This passage must have deeply impressed Gray, who refers to Ezekiel's vision in his note to his description of Milton in *The Progress of Poesy*. Thus Milton's vision of God was used by another poet to describe the apotheosis of the divine imagination in Milton himself, a hint Blake was not slow to develop:

> Bring me my Bow of burning gold:
> Bring me my Arrows of desire:
> Bring me my Spear: O clouds unfold!
> Bring me my Chariot of fire.

Los and Orc are called Urthona and Luvah respectively when spoken of in the context of the eternal as opposed to the temporal world. The whole four represent more or less the four aspects of God's imaginative energy, Urthona being his creative fertility, which reappears in the fallen world as Los; Tharmas his power to bring what he creates into complete existence, the first privilege lost to man at the Fall; Luvah his capacity for love and joy; and Urizen his wisdom and sense of form. Urizen is thus the unfallen or eternal name of what in the fallen world eventually becomes Satan, the dead matter which is the "form" of nature insofar as it has any apart from life.

We perceive a fourfold nature with a fourfold body: that is, we perceive that there are four elements in nature, and we perceive this by means of the four senses of our bodies (taste and touch being counted as one, for reasons presently to be examined). According to the Galenic theory, there are four aspects of existence, hot, cold, moist and dry; and the four possible combinations of these give, in the organic world, the four "humors" which determine the character of the organism, and, in the inorganic world, the four elements of nature. Whatever one thinks of this theory, it does at least preserve the central imaginative truth that organism and nature are alike products of a single spirit. In a materialistic theory like Galen's this spirit is only chaos: in Blake's, the four senses are "the Four Faces of Man & the Four Rivers of the Water of Life."[9] The Adonis or "Adona" river of Eden, the "immortal river" with its red earth, was actually the coursing blood of the unfallen Albion, and is said in Genesis to consist of four branches, which Blake identifies with the four unfallen senses. The four elements in Blake make up the "married land" of whom the city which is built upon it is the lover. Each Zoa is therefore to be associated both with a sense and with an element.

We see fallen space as stretching away from us indefinitely to north, south, east and west. The fallen world knows nothing of position or direction: its center is anywhere and its circumference nowhere, as in some definitions of God. "In Equivocal Worlds Up & Down are Equivocal," said Blake, referring to Dante, and elsewhere he speaks of "supposing up and down to be the same thing, as all experimentalists must suppose"—meaning by "all experimentalists" the disciples of Hermes Trismegistus as well as of Bacon and Locke.[10] But every "living creature" has an up and a down, and every "animal" has a front and a back. The imagination sees the east, not as one of thirty-two arbitrary divisions of what Blake calls a "concave" space, but as the quarter of beginnings, as the region of newborn life and light. It sees the north, at least in Britain, as an attractive magnet pulling all things downward to it. The north, then, is a "nadir" and the east a "center" of renewed energy: the south, the region of intensest sunshine, is therefore a "zenith" and the west with its bounding ocean a "circumference."

We may understand this point more clearly if we go back to the Book of Daniel again to Nebuchadnezzar's dream of himself as a statue with a head of gold, breast of silver, loins of brass and legs of iron. This statue is Albion before his fall, when great nations dwelt together in the form of one Man. Now this Man must have been the form of unfallen space, and it is the form which the prophetic imagination strives to visualize here. We may notice that Nebuchadnezzar forgot his dream and had to have it recalled to him by the prophet.

Albion's golden head in the southern zenith was Eden, the city of the sun, and the unfallen Urizen. The silver breast of the circumference was the surrounding garden of Eden, or Beulah, the unfallen Tharmas. The brazen loins and genitals of the center were the region of generation and sexual desire, the unfallen Orc and Vala. (In *Jerusalem* the metallic associations of Luvah and Tharmas are reversed,[11] but I give what seems to me the only consistent pattern for *The Four Zoas*.) The iron legs were a dark but unfallen "Ulro," more or less the region the imagination now enters when it tells ghost stories, the abode of Urthona. The city, the top or head of the erect man, is above ground, and around it is the garden of cultivated nature, the lower part of which is the soil or bed of sleeping love. If the reader finds difficulty, as he no doubt does, in visualizing this, he should try to read the Song of Songs as Blake read it. The Song of Songs is neither a voluptuous Orientale nor a chilly allegory of King Solomon's love for his country: it is both of these things at once, the copulation of a city of men so integrated in spirit that they are all part of a greater Man with a nature so alive and responsive that everything in it appears as part of the body of a beautiful and beloved woman. The Christian interpretation of it as an allegory of Christ's love for his Church is really Blake's, if the frankly sexual aspect of the imagery is not too hurriedly passed over. Below this bed of love we go underground into the world of "dark Urthona." These four levels of existence are the four levels of consciousness also. Urizen is the highest level or zenith of active awareness, or creation; Tharmas is the lower level of relaxed awareness; Luvah is the still lower level of love and copulation; and Urthona is "subconscious" sleep and dream, the nadir of imaginative energy. Further, this world of city and garden is no longer underneath an indefinite sky. The domain of the unfallen Urizen, Albion's golden head, is the real or mental sun; that of Tharmas the real moon; that of Luvah or Orc the real stars; and that of Urthona the real mountains, full of mines which are fairy palaces. The present physical universe, the underground cave of the mind, or mundane shell, is thus the fallen Urthona's "dens."

Anyone with any imagination at all will associate the four seasons of the year or the four periods of the day with the four ages of a man's life. In the fallen world these different aspects of time follow one another in inevitable rotation, this rotation being the cycle on which the Fall is based. In eternity one chooses the kind of time that accords with a creative mood, as Raphael explains to Adam in *Paradise Lost*:

> For we have also our evening and our morn—
> We ours for change delectable, not need.[12]

Milton thinks of himself as young in *L'Allegro* and as growing old and contemplative in *Il Penseroso*, as spending his lively day in the sunshine and his pensive one at night, from the same point of view. The body must go helplessly from youth to age: the imagination, though of course it is influenced by this, may be contemplative at ten or youthful at eighty. The seasons are similarly bound to time, and the half-emancipated religious imagination follows them, fasting at Lent and feasting at Christmas; but the imagination does not have to wait until October to respond to Keats's *To Autumn* or Shelley's *Ode to the West Wind*.

For the sake of convenience we may draw up a table of associations with the Zoas, including their "emanations," most of whom we have already met. These emanations are not very clearly distinguished in *The Four Zoas*, being shadowy creatures who do practically nothing but wail, and seem to have chiefly a symmetrical function. Vala and Enitharmon we know; Ahania is the Sophia or bride of Wisdom, her name being a faint echo of Athene; and Enion is a mother of life or Venus Genetrix. Like Venus, she springs from the sea. A little study of the poem and of the commentary following may make some of these associations seem less arbitrary than they are apt to look in a table. A number of them have been added merely to complete the pattern, and a number are mere guesses.[13]

1. Eternal Name	Luvah	Urizen	Tharmas	Urthona
2. Time Name	Orc	Satan	C. Cherub	Los
3. Emanation	Vala	Ahania	Enion	(Enitharmon)
4. Quality	Love	Wisdom	Power	Fancy
5. Zoa (Bible)	Bull	Lion	Eagle	Man
6. Sense	Nose	Eye	Tongue	Ear
7. Body Part	Loins	Head	Heart	Legs
8. Metal (Bible)	Brass	Gold	Silver	Iron
9. Position	Centre	Zenith	Circumference	Nadir
10. Nature (Sky)	Stars	Sun	Moon	Mountains
11. Element	Fire	Air	Water	Earth
12. E. Spirits	Genii	Fairies	Nymphs	Gnomes

13.	State	"Generation"	Eden	Beulah	"Ulro"
14.	Place	Soil	City	Garden	Underground
15.	Activity	Weaver	Plowman	Shepherd	Blacksmith
16.	Art	Painting	Architecture	Poetry	Music
17.	Planet	Mars	Mercury	Venus	Earth
18.	Point	East	South	West	North
19.	Season	Spring	Summer	Autumn	Winter
20.	Time of Day	Morning	Noon	Evening	Night
21.	Age	Youth	Maturity	Age	"Death" (sleep)
22.	Son of Los	Palamabron	Rintrah	Theotormon	Bromion
23.	Emanation	Elynittria	Ocalythron	Oothoon	(none)
24.	City	London	Verulam	York	Edinburgh
25.	Evangelist	Luke	Mark	John	Matthew
26.	Color (Fallen)	Red	White	Green	Blue
27.	Virtue	Love	Faith	Hope	Vision
28.	Vice	Hatred	Doubt	Despair	Dullness
29.	Eden River	Pison	Hiddekel	Gihon	Euphrates

The plan of *The Four Zoas* is not difficult to follow. Night I deals with the fall of Tharmas and the end of the Golden Age; Night II with the fall of Luvah and the end of the Silver Age; Night III with the fall of Urizen and the end of the Brazen Age; Night IV with the beginning of the Iron Age or humanity in its present form six thousand years ago and the establishing of the cycle of fallen life (Adam) and death (Satan). Then comes the tracing of the Orc cycle, under the symbols of the birth and binding of Orc in Night V, Urizen's exploration of his dens in Night VI, the crucifixion of Orc and the triumph of moral virtue in Night VII. In Night VII, however, a double crisis takes place, one an imaginative advance, symbolized by the mingling of Los and the Spectre of Urthona, the other a consolidation of error symbolized by the birth of Rahab from the Spectre of Urthona and another character called the Shadow of Enitharmon. In Night VIII this antithesis sharpens into its final form, in the Incarnation of Christ and the epiphany of Antichrist respectively. Night IX deals with the apocalypse. The most obvious source for the nine nights is Young's *Night Thoughts*, the last of which is also apocalyptic in theme.[14]

· 2 ·

THE Fall begins in Beulah, and begins also with a great flood that destroyed Atlantis. If we look at our table, we shall see that Beulah and water are associated with Tharmas, and *The Four Zoas* opens with the myth of the fall of Tharmas and his emanation Enion. Tharmas is also the *power* to create life at will, the first privilege lost to Man. As only an automatic "natural" cycle of life and death is left to the fallen world, the collapse of Tharmas produces the world of time or "circle of destiny,"[15] in which life is born out of unconscious power, and which, because it is both unconscious and powerful, suggests the blank idiot God of fate and first causes. This is symbolized in the separation of Tharmas from Enion and the birth from Enion of Los and Enitharmon, time and space. Enion becomes a mother of life who weaves a web of life which begins to take on "a will of its own, perverse & wayward."[16] That is, natural life has appeared in the world, a life uncontrolled by conscious design, and which can sustain itself only by preying on other forms of life, a tangled web of mutual murder. She suggests the Classical Penelope, who sits weaving and unweaving a web all day awaiting her lord's return from the ocean.

She also suggests a Demeter or Earth-Mother wandering over a wintry world "blind and age-bent" seeking her children who are lost in hell, and her pathetic complaints recur at intervals throughout the poem. The fall of Beulah is primarily a loss of innocence, and the burden of Enion's lament is that of the *Songs of Experience* which record the result of that loss. The world of nature is a completely callous world, and Enion, seeing her children suffering in a life of pain, cannot understand what has happened. She knows only that she can never be comforted as long as pain exists, and that she will not cease to be a wandering and mourning spirit until nature has become again the "happy garden-state" it once was, and in which the vision of God seeing the sparrow fall with concern for its suffering is not a mere "augury" of the state of innocence but its realization. She is the "vain shadow of hope" which finds everything short of a complete apocalypse hopeless. She is the part of our minds which dimly realizes that all pleasure is at least partly a dream under an anesthetic. Something is always suffering horribly somewhere, and we can only find pleasure by ignoring that fact. We must ignore it up to a point, or go mad; but in the abyss of consciousness, to which Enion has been banished, there lurks the feeling that joy is based on exclusion, that the Yule log can blaze cheerfully only when the freezing beggars in the streets are, for the moment, left to freeze. It is a terrible song that Enion sings, and disturbing enough to have in the mind a thought which can lead only either to madness or apocalypse; yet we cannot eliminate this thought without sacrificing some of our humanity, and the implication that true humanity can be found only in either madness or apocalypse is the dilemma to which all history proceeds:

> It is an easy thing to laugh at wrathful elements,
> To hear the dog howl at the wintry door, the ox in the
>   slaughter house moan;
> To see a god on every wind & a blessing on every blast;
> To hear sounds of love in the thunder storm that destroys our
>   enemies' house;
> To rejoice in the blight that covers his field, & the sickness
>   that cuts off his children,
> While our olive & vine sing & laugh round our door, & our
>   children bring fruits & flowers.
>
> Then the groan & the dolor are quite forgotten, & the slave
>   grinding at the mill,
> And the captive in chains, & the poor in the prison, & the
>   soldier in the field
> When the shatter'd bone hath laid him groaning among the
>   happier dead.
>
> It is an easy thing to rejoice in the tents of prosperity:
> Thus could I sing & thus rejoice: but it is not so with me.[17]

Historically, the fall of Tharmas is the flood that drowned out Atlantis and produced the Atlantic Ocean or "Sea of Time and Space," which is to dry up in the apocalypse when there shall be no more sea. To the visionary in England the west is the region of water, the abode of the Zoa of power who has fallen into chaos, and therefore the symbol of the inability of anyone in the fallen world, however strenuous his imagination, to live the fully creative life of a god. Even for the visionary who lives in the divine Paradise in which creation and perception are the same thing, the gulf between Pygmalion's human power that conceived a statue and the divine power that brought it to life still exists. In Blake's symbolism this failure of power is represented by a "Western Gate," which remains closed in all earthly vision and opens only in the final awakening of Albion.

In the fallen world the five senses, according to Lockian philosophy, are passive recipients of all experience: in eternity there are four senses, the four rivers of Eden or water of life, which are the instruments of the active mind. Tharmas represents the combina-

tion of taste and touch which reduces the number. In this world
the senses of distance, eyesight and hearing, produce the major
arts. The chief imaginative use of the sense of contact is in sexual
love on the plane of Beulah, which is the region of Tharmas. Now
in sexual experience the contact is only a temporary union of independent principles of life: the woman still represents the "female
will," the separated nature which man is trying to transform.
The two great divisions of human imagination, art and love, are
thus the broken halves in human life of two powers that are one
in God. Pygmalion cannot transform his creature into an object
of love; the lover cannot transform his loved one into a creature
of the imagination. The child is as independent as the woman, and
in any case is born naturally, from the female body. This barrier
between art and love is part of the closed Western Gate: it will
not disappear until the final apocalypse, when the Creator twisting the sinews of the tiger's heart will be producing a work of art,
a beloved object and a child of his imagination all at once. That
will include the absorption of the material world into the body
of man, which in the fallen world goes on chiefly in neither art
nor love, but in eating and drinking, the province of "taste."
Eating the body and drinking the blood of a God-Man is therefore
a very profound image of the final apocalypse, which in the teaching of Jesus is associated with a harvest and vintage and also with
a wedding supper. It is perhaps not an accident that we speak of
our imaginative control in this world as "taste." Just as sight is the
mind looking through and not with the eye, so taste is the mind
transforming food, and thus "taste" in the intellectual sense is the
mental digestion of the material world. Tharmas, then, is the
tongue of unfallen man, his power to absorb the nonhuman; and
when nothing we touch is any longer outside us, touch and taste
will become the same sense.

Any kind of imagination separated from its material or emanation becomes a Spectre or Selfhood, and when Tharmas falls and
becomes separated from Enion he turns into the Spectre of Tharmas. As such, he is the direct perversion of everything he was in
his former state. Whereas formerly he was the water of life in
Beulah, the liquid imagination which is continually changing its
shape, he is now the spirit of chaos of which the chief form in the
fallen world is the sea, and which continually tries to break out of

its confining rock to overwhelm life in ruin. The only link left
between the unfallen and fallen Tharmas is the attraction which
the moon, a primary Beulah symbol, still has on the sea. The
Spectre of Tharmas thus suggests the Biblical Leviathan, the
water-monster who symbolizes the tyranny of the state of nature,
and who is slain whenever new life is reborn. But as Leviathan
and Behemoth are only forms of the great Covering Cherub or
power of the fallen human Selfhood who keeps man out of Paradise, the Covering Cherub is ultimately what the Spectre of
Tharmas is. The tongue which is the civilized taste of unfallen
man has become the false tongue of the accusing devil, which,
from the anonymity of many-tongued Rumor to the perjury of
the accusers of Socrates and Jesus, continually fights against liberty
and discourages hope. In the tongue-shaped flames of fallen fire,
which continually destroy but never achieve definite form, one
sees an image of this, as well as a perversion of the fire of Eden
which "delights in its form," and which consumes the material
world without torturing or annihilating it, the burning bush of
God. The flaming sword which frightens us away from Paradise
is therefore the devil's false tongue. The fact that our own tongues
are moist unites the symbols of destructive fire and watery chaos:

> Tharmas the Vegetated Tongue, even the Devouring Tongue,
> A threefold region, a false brain, a false heart
> And false bowels, altogether composing the False Tongue,
> Beneath Beulah as a wat'ry flame revolving every way,
> And as dark roots and stems, a Forest of affliction, growing
> In seas of sorrow.[18]

This obscure link in Blake's symbolism is made clearer in the
Epistle of James, which speaks of the tongue as setting on fire the
course of nature and deriving its own flame from hell.[19]

The Spectre of Tharmas spends his time in "self admiring
raptures," for egocentric life, or pride, is the primary sin of the
Fall. One is reminded of the Classical legend of Narcissus, who
fell in love with

> A sweet entrancing self delusion, a wat'ry vision of Man
> Soft exulting in existence, all the Man absorbing.[20]

and whose emanation Echo thereby pined away into a mere
answering voice. If we study this image more carefully we can see

that Echo and the watery reflection of Narcissus must be the same thing.

The reader should now have some idea of what is going on in the first night of *The Four Zoas*. In the second and third nights Luvah and Urizen fall in their turn, and the result, in Night IV, is a collapse into chaos, which means, as the fallen Tharmas is chaos, that "all comes into the power of Tharmas"[21] again. The Fall in its entirety, therefore, is a huge cycle from a first to a second flood, a saga of struggling gods which, like Wagner's *Ring*, begins and ends in the ripple of water. A flood is thus the symbol of the end of a cycle, the passage from life through death into chaos, the reign of the water-dragon over the terrorized kingdom before the cycle turns again and the dragon-slaying hero reappears on the scene. There are two universal floods in the Bible, the one associated with Noah and the earlier one which produced the world of chaos "without form and void," and which we meet at the opening of Genesis. The latter in Blake is the flood that destroyed Atlantis; and the drowning of Pharaoh's host in the Red Sea, the symbol of the collapse of the "African" culture, may or may not be identical with the flood of Noah.

The Old Testament tells us that God promised Noah that there would be no more universal floods. This means that after the second flood limits are set to chaos. In Blake these are the limits of contraction and opacity already described, which are established in Night IV. Life henceforth may descend to death or inorganic matter but cannot go downward into annihilation. Water is restrained from flooding the land, the restraint being symbolized by a protecting wall of rocks. Leviathan is therefore fixed in the form of Satan, the "limit of opacity" or solid matter. This means that the symbol of chaos, the Spectre of Tharmas, drops out after Night IV, for there is no more place for him when the establishing of the two limits of life and death restrains the power of the sea.[22] Satan, the limit of opacity or physical death, is now the final form of Orc rather than Tharmas, and "Druidism" or Satan-worship, the adoration of the continuous martyrdom of natural life, is represented by the crucified Orc, the mangled body bound to the stone or dead tree as a sacrifice to the flaming Moloch in the sky. The symbol of the Covering Cherub is accordingly transferred to the crucified Orc, and the Leviathan symbol is similarly transferred to the Urizen who is now the clutching and strangling Old Man of the Sea on Albion's back.

The sign of God's promise to Noah, we are further told, was the rainbow. Tharmas and Enion are probably the Thaumas and Eione of Hesiod's *Theogony*, and there, as later in Ovid, Thaumas is the father of the rainbow or Iris.[23] Since the second flood the return of Tharmas at the end of a cycle has implied a transition from chaos to new life. The water returns from the ocean to us, but instead of drowning us it falls on us as rain. Hence the curious ambiguity which we often find in the character of the slain water-dragon, in many of the legends dealing with it. When the hero kills him there is frequently a "freeing of the waters," and the land is reawakened from death; for the hero, like Moses, has released the water from the rocky prison in which it must be con-fined for life to continue. Water as well as blood pours from the pierced side of Christ, and indicates the same symbolism. Beulah is the garden of Paradise and our place of seed, and from Beulah the Paradisal "water of life" comes to us as rain. The same is true even of the fallen Beulah which is our ocean. Further, the two universal floods occurred because human beings were then so powerful that nature went to smash with them. The promise of no more floods made to Noah is thus another aspect of the fall of humanity into its "Adamic" form, in which it is too weak to do itself irreparable damage.

The fall of Tharmas and Enion is a fall of innocence, with all the feelings of sin, shame, jealousy and desire for concealment which that involves. When the state of innocence is recovered in the apocalypse, Tharmas and Enion, in Night IX, are reborn into Beulah as the children who have so intimate a relationship to that state. The *Songs of Innocence* are pastoral lyrics, and the unfallen Tharmas is especially the pastoral side of eternal existence, the Zoa of Jesus which makes him the Good Shepherd and the Lamb of God—not the Lamb as a sacrificial victim, which is Luvah, but as the symbol of the ideal Beulah existence portrayed in the twenty-third Psalm. In the Gospels Jesus' control of Tharmas is shown by his ability to command the sea and in the episode of walking on the waves and saving Peter from drowning. Some of the attri-butes of Tharmas recall Lycidas, the shepherd follower of Peter who drowns in the western ocean and is to enter the resurrection

"Through the dear might of Him who walk'd the waves."[24] The passage of the sun across the sky is one of the symbols of the Orc cycle, and the end of Milton's song synchronizes with the falling of the sun into the western sea, the victory of the watery darkness which suggests either the final annihilation of all life or the promise of a final dawn, depending on the extent of one's vision.

· 3 ·

The fall of Luvah and of Urizen are so closely connected that we had best take them together. "Luvah" is the eternal name of Orc. And in studying Orc we saw how he expands into a cycle of youth and age, and how the Promethean Titan bound and straining under the world becomes, when thus expanded, equivalent to the fallen Albion or Atlas. Luvah and his emanation Vala inhabit in the eternal world a region which, though unfallen, was a region of "Generation" or sexual love, the lower part of Beulah, the loins and genitals of Albion as Tharmas is the heart, the soil or bed of love as Tharmas is the garden. Albion's fall began with his adoration of a separate female will in Beulah, and was completed in Generation, the world of Luvah and Vala. The female principle that broke away from Albion therefore was Vala, and Albion thereupon became Vala's lover: that is, he tried to identify himself with the one aspect of himself which Luvah represents: that is, Luvah seized control of him and became the Prince of the fallen world of Generation, the Satan who afflicts Job, the angel who lames Jacob.[25] Once under Luvah's power, Albion began trying to create life by means of an illusory "outside," and thus sex, creation by means of an independent female will, appeared for the first time and became the motive power of a world where all forms of life are born from mothers, where all imagination is nourished by nature, and where man is, as Vala claims, "Woman-born And Woman-nourish'd & Woman-educated & Woman-scorn'd."[26]

In eternity Urizen, the "Prince of Light" or the true sun, is the golden head of Man; in the fallen world the sun is part of the dying and reviving rhythm of "Generation." Hence the usurpation of power by Luvah involves the seizure of the sun from Urizen. There are two sources for Blake's account of this seizure of the sun: one is in the story of Lucifer in Isaiah, the other in the story of Phaethon as told by Plato in the *Phaedrus* and by Ovid. In Blake the fall of the sun is the objective counterpart of the fall of the body into an imprisoned "furnace." In Night II Albion, struggling to regain his balance after the fall of Tharmas, calls upon Urizen, who is still his own brain, to reorganize the collapsing universe, and Urizen does his best, but has to work very differently under the new conditions. In relation to an external nature the universe takes on the form of a gigantic temple like Milton's Pandemonium, still the habitation of man and therefore not quite fallen, but held together by ideas of general symmetry and "mathematical form." This is the mental grasp of the world preserved in the *Timaeus*, which Blake almost seems to parody as he describes the heavenly bodies rumbling and creaking together in an ungainly geometrical machine:

> Others triangular, right angled course maintain. Others obtuse,
> Acute, Scalene, in simple paths; but others move
> In intricate ways, biquadrate, Trapeziums, Rhombs, Rhomboids,
> Paralellograms triple & quadruple, polygonic
> In their amazing hard subdu'd course in the vast deep.[27]

This structure lasts only a short time, then falls to pieces with an appalling crash (Night III), and Man finds himself precariously perched on a spinning globe full of water in a vast abyss of nothingness with all the other heavenly bodies hopelessly out of his reach. Chaos or Tharmas, as explained, has come again, and Luvah and Urizen are both smashed beyond repair. Only one Zoa is left, Urthona, who has reappeared in the lower world as Los, and Tharmas assigns him the task of rebuilding Man. It is under Los that the two limits are established (Night IV), and life begins on the present human plane.

It is at this point that *The Book of Urizen* began. It is, in fact, where nearly all the religious and scientific accounts of the creation of the world begin. All orthodox minds of whatever bias tend to start the creation with an evolution of life out of chaos in time: in Blake's symbolism, with the birth of Orc from Los (Night V) under the power of Tharmas. Tharmas now becomes the power of life, the potential energy of the place of seed. As chaos, too, the fallen Tharmas is the indefinite mixture of elements from which both living and dead bodies are formed, and the rhythm of sprouting and dissolving life in nature repeats the aimless tossing of the sea. Death, or solid matter, then becomes the framework of existence, and a chaotic life-force boils within it throwing up the little bubbles of red mud which is what the word "Adam" means. And these "Adams" are the most highly organized forms of a huge pulpy mass of stinking life which Blake calls the "Polypus," and which he equates with Orc or Luvah, the totality of life in the world of Generation.[28] Out of this unpromising material Los has to shape a human imagination once more. In *The Book of Urizen* the body of Urizen was at first a solid rock: here the rock is the container of the chaos without, or the sea, and the container of the chaos within, or the ferment of potential life, both abodes of Tharmas.

The conception of the physical world as the body of a God-Man who has been torn to pieces meets us in the legends of many countries: we have mentioned the Icelandic Ymir and the Hebrew Adam Kadmon, and the same imagery is found in the Vedic hymns, in the myth of Osiris, and in several Greek stories, mostly connected with the Dionysus cult, where the tearing to pieces has the technical name of *sparagmos*. It is this aspect of life as a scattered Man that Luvah and Urizen represent. Luvah is ruddy youth and Urizen pallid age, for Luvah is the red blood and Urizen the white body, which in its "purest" form is a skeleton of bleaching bones. Luvah is the pride of summer and Urizen the torpor of winter, when life is buried in a white sleep with "the paths of men shut up"[29]; the outline of civilized life concealed in an abstract blanket. (The table refers to the unfallen forms of the seasons.) Luvah, the blood, is the pulsating rhythm of life in time; Urizen, the bones, is the permanence of space. Luvah is liquid movement and Urizen solid equilibrium. Luvah is the energy of the vegetation and the sun which go through a cycle of existence; Urizen is the eternally circular form of that cycle. In their fallen forms Luvah and Urizen represent respectively the active and passive forms of "jealousy." Luvah stands for war, tyranny and the state of nature; Urizen for religion, mystery and reason.

Fallen life is imprisoned in death, and Urizen always gains the mastery over Luvah. Luvah, then, is not only the energy of life but its suffering and martyrdom in the state of nature. The god of fertility must be a dying god. The Zoa corresponding to Luvah in the visions of Ezekiel and John is the ox or bull, the sacrificial victim; and Jesus in his Luvah aspect is the slain Lamb of God, the life of innocence sacrificed to experience. It is as a dying god (not a dead body, which is Satan or Antichrist), with his blood pouring through the wounds of the scourging, the crown of thorns, the nails and the spear, that Jesus appears in "Luvah's Robes of Blood."[30]

The clearest symbol of the natural body, life imprisoned in death, is the furnace or kiln we have already met, in which the heat of energy is confined in an abstract husk with its light shut out. This image of the furnace or prison of lightless heat is the core of the orthodox conception of hell, which traditionally has heat without light,[31] and it exactly fits the eternal torment of life in the Selfhood, "the being shut up in the possession of corporeal desires which shortly weary the man," which is Blake's hell. As the natural man is born as this kind of furnace, he is born in hell, and if he has any intelligence he looks for a way of escape. The clearest assertions that there is no escape and that there is no world but hell and no God but the devil are to be found in the more primitive forms of Luvah-worship: roasting men and children alive in a furnace which is supposed to be an image of God. The cult of Moloch, Blake's second Eye of God, is the most familiar example of this. (In Phalaris' brazen bull the Luvah symbol is even clearer.) The Druid burning of victims in wicker cages is another instance, and so are the Mexican sacrifices to the flaming sun which Luvah has usurped. The Hebrew legends of slavery among the brick-kilns of Egypt belong to the same imagery; and Egypt, which means the fallen world, is called in the Bible a "furnace of iron."[32]

The eternal world is one of mutual co-operation in which all forms of life are nourished and supported by all other forms, as in the economy of the individual human body. In this world the reverse is true, and getting food in nature usually involves killing or maiming life. As all living things are part of the mangled body of Albion, all living things are nourished in a mutual cannibalism: out of the eater comes forth meat, as in Samson's riddle. Hence the red wine that we drink and the white bread that we eat not only symbolize but really are part of the blood and body of a universal God-Man, and are forms of Luvah and Urizen respectively. Luvah's connections with the wine-god Dionysus and Jesus in his aspect of the true vine and the giver of new wine to man need only be mentioned. In the vintage and the harvest this vegetable blood and body is gathered in when it is still at its full power of life, before it has died and become useless for food. Vintage and harvest, therefore, suggest the myth of a God-Man who has to be slain at the height of his power in order that his strength may be scattered and divided among men instead of being, from man's point of view, wasted. The vintage and the harvest are thus symbols of the original *sparagmos* of Albion, in which Albion also appears in Luvah's robes of blood. The fall of Luvah and Urizen begins in a banquet of Titans or elemental Demons who, though not yet conscious of evil, are transforming the world from peace and culture into anarchy and warfare, and the banquet is a meal of bread and wine.[33] The same association of Luvah with wine and Urizen with bread supplies Blake with the images of the winepress and the mill. Both of these are really modulations of the furnace symbol.

The worship of Luvah begins with human sacrifice, and war to Blake is an outgrowth of the sacrificial impulse, connected with the feeling that when a man has reached his full strength and beauty it is better for him to die than grow old. In the natural religion which is most men's real creed, natural death is merely the wasting-away of life, but violent death scatters life in nature and may therefore nourish it, as the violent death of the wine and bread nourish man. Our language about blood attributes to it a much greater capacity to flow and spill than it actually possesses: there seems to be a certain self-mutilating joy in pouring out the fountain of vital energy into the dust as an offering to the larger Moloch of nature which gives to war that quality of perverted eroticism, of Onan's wasting of the seed, which we have already noticed in connection with the deified mistress of the chivalric code:

> But in the Wine-presses the Human grapes sing not nor dance:
> They howl & writhe in shoals of torment, in fierce flames consuming,

In chains of iron & in dungeons circled with ceaseless fires,
In pits & dens & shades of death, in shapes of torment & woe:
The plates & screws & wracks & saws & cords & fires & cisterns,
The cruel joys of Luvah's Daughters, lacerating with knives
And whips their Victims, & the deadly sport of Luvah's Sons.
They dance around the dying & they drink the howl & groan,
They catch the shrieks in cups of gold, they hand them to one
        another;
These are the sports of love, & these the sweet delights of
        amorous play,
Tears of the grape, the death sweat of the cluster, the last sigh
Of the mild youth who listens to the lureing songs of Luvah.[34]

The mill also represents the dissolving of "living form," and the "dark Satanic mills" in Blake mean any unimaginative mechanism: the mechanical logical method of Aristotle, the industrial machinery that requires slave-labor, the mathematical co-ordination of the Newtonian universe, the mechanical ability to turn out uninspired art—anything that compels Albion, of whom Samson is a reminiscence, to remain "Eyeless in Gaza at the mill with slaves."[35] We have noticed that Paine finds the mill a symbol of deep significance for the rational Deist, and its generalizing comminution is a perfect image of this type of mind, which strives to reduce a world of form and beauty to a sandstorm of atoms.

But there is no image of an inscrutable fate which may not also be an image of creative power, and the winepress and mill may represent not only the disintegration of form, but the reuniting of all nature into the body and blood of a universal Man. Thus the gathering-in of life to prevent its death may be a symbol of the apocalypse. Jesus constantly uses metaphors from harvest and vintage to illustrate his teaching on the Last Judgment, and a dramatic passage in the Book of Revelation deals with the same imagery. In Night IX Blake expands this apocalyptic aspect of his bread and wine symbolism into a superb fantasia in which Luvah gathers the vintage and Urizen the harvest, Tharmas winnows the grain and Urthona grinds it in a mill. Of course the winepress and mill even here, the winepress particularly, are symbols of the gigantic annihilation wars, the massacres of tyrants and the frightful disasters of the four horsemen which herald the day of wrath; but still the process is part of the great communion feast in which human life is reintegrated into its real form.

The same regenerative meaning belongs also to the furnace. Man's body may remain a natural hell of unsatisfied desire, or it may become an imaginative purgatory, a crucible from which the purified mind emerges. In the latter case the furnace, the body of Luvah, is operated by Los, and this is the fiery furnace shown us in the Book of Daniel. A furnace which occurs in a vision of Abraham is the basis of Christopher Smart's apocalyptic prophecy that "the furnace itself shall come up at last."[36]

· 4 ·

THE data which Blake has left for a full account of Urthona, the eternal form of Los, cannot be called an embarrassment of riches. Some of the interpretations which follow are tentative. Urthona is the "nadir," the iron legs and feet of unfallen man; in our world the "attractive north" also associated with iron. His element is the earth. In eternity Urizen is a city, Tharmas a garden, Luvah the soil or bed of love, and below this we sink into an imaginative and unfallen underground of labyrinths and caves and fairy palaces, an underworld of gnomes in mountains and mines, a world of shrouded darkness illuminated by the fantastic glitter of gems and precious metals. In the world of the mind the Urthona imagination is that of the dream, the *penseroso* mood of nocturnal romance and mysterious enchantment which is deliberately created and therefore not feared. Urthona is the sleep of winter and night that in eternity is chosen for "change delectable, not need." His greatest imaginative production is music, the dark invisible world of the "labyrinthine ear."[37]

Offhand, one would think that of all four Zoas this was the least likely to produce a Messiah. But the fallen world is the eternal one turned inside out, and the positions of the Zoas in eternity are reversed in the Fall. When Dante enters the bottom of hell he sees Satan standing upright, but as he crawls past him he passes the center of the earth and then sees him standing on his head. (From Blake's point of view, Dante's vision of Satan is an unclarified vision of fallen Albion, the other half of it, the "Veglio" of Crete who is the four-metaled statue of Daniel, being rather arbitrarily stuck into the symbolism in the fourteenth canto.) Blake implies the same inverted position for Albion. Urizen, the head, fell farthest of all into death; Tharmas, at least since the establishing of the two limits, between death and fallen life; Luvah fell into physical life, and what remains to Urthona is therefore fallen consciousness. The domain of Urthona is the underworld of the unfallen world, and as the present physical universe is also that, it can be only within Urthona's "dens," the catacombs beneath the eternal City, that an imaginative power can operate. Again, Urthona, the world of music and the dancing feet, of the sleeping man's existence in pure duration, with the rhythmic beat of the heart the most striking sign of life, possessed the imaginative equivalent of the rhythmic movement which appears in our world as recurring time, and which is finally emancipated in the arts of rhythm, music and poetry. Hence Los, the imaginative control of time which achieves a permanent form from it, is the reappearance of an eternal Urthona. Urthona, like Los, is a blacksmith, and in both the rhythmic clang of the hammer marks the shaping of form throughout, and out of, the ultimate age of iron. The legs of the statue in Daniel were of iron and the feet of iron and clay, and these have become in our world the life in time which is a furnace of iron and the death in space which is a clod of clay.

But time in our world exists in an abstract as well as an imaginative form, hence from Urthona is born not only Los but the "Spectre" of Urthona, clock time. The crisis of the action of *The Four Zoas* comes with the merging of these two descendants of Urthona in Night VII, and in *Jerusalem* the relation between them largely replaces the more cumbersome scheme of the Zoas as the basis of Blake's psychology. The Spectre of Urthona is the isolated subjective aspect of existence in this world, the energy with which a man or any other living thing copes with nature. It is neither the Selfhood, which is Satan, nor the "vegetable" existence, which is Luvah; it is that aspect of existence in time which is linear rather than organic or imaginative. If one had to pin the conception down to a single word, one might call Blake's Spectre of Urthona the will.

If the Spectre of Urthona is linear time, then the part of him that Los absorbs is his own temporal existence. In a poet the Spectre of Urthona is what is usually called the "man" in him, the identity that grapples directly with nature and gets along in the world, that earns a living and meets other people and supports a family and acquires opinions. It furnishes the pride, self-respect and personal ambition without which no genius could function. The will, in short, is the instrumentality of the mind, the means by which the mind functions in nature, and the power that develops the machinery of life.

A good many of the functions called "bodily" or "animal" are functions of the will, but in a real animal the Spectre is the servant of Luvah; that is, the will is instrumental to an imagination identical with an organic development proceeding toward death. Here the machinery it develops does not go beyond the physical body. But a man, unlike an animal, has his imaginative and natural ends in direct opposition to one another, for there is no "will to live" in nature which does not achieve its end by dying, and man wants a life that does not die. The will, however, is not in man necessarily attached exclusively to either.

This conception of the will puts Blake's antithesis of imagination and Selfhood in a different light. In the third chapter we discussed Blake's theory that evil arises only from passivity, the negative refusal to perform a creative act which results in frustrating either one's own development or that of others. In most orthodox theories of conduct, the evil side of man's nature is associated not with passivity but with "passion," which usually means the energy of a rising Orc celebrated in *The Marriage of Heaven and Hell* as "Eternal Delight." Nevertheless the question of how the word "passion" has come to imply action, and action of a feverishly energetic kind, is a curious one, and the paradox of the activity of passivity, the fanaticism which promotes tyranny and cruelty, needs to be examined, however illusory it may be. It is not simply a matter of observing that "the fool foldeth his hands together, and eateth his own flesh"[38]: he does so, and Dante was right in making a paralyzed gnawing cannibalism his final vision of hell; but even inertia must have some kind of energy to counteract life, just as there is a tremendous effort involved in ceasing to breathe. Now if the will is at once an active and a neutral power, identical with neither the imagination nor the Selfhood, the real conflict between the latter two must be a struggle for the control of the will. The possession of the will by the natural man is the basis for the contrast in Selfhood life between the tyrant and the victim.

In this world Los cannot function without the Spectre of Urthona, and all imagination is inseparably attached to personal interests. It is foolish and impossible to try to eliminate the latter on the ground that some of their manifestations are evil: pride may be evil, but without the artist's pride in his work or a mother's pride in her baby no creative life can exist. But at the same time "There can be no Good Will"[39]; there is a perpetual conflict between the imagination and the will to prevent the latter from deserting to the Selfhood, and there can be no free will either, as the will must be attached to one or the other. When we say that a man is marking time we mean that he is not getting anywhere; and once a man takes his mind off his own eternal Being and begins to concentrate on the world of time he is instantly kidnapped by his natural death-impulses.

For example: the will supplies the machinery of life. In creation, therefore, the Spectre of Urthona is the inventive faculty, and invention is the art of finding things in nature: it does not create so much as supply the instruments for creating. The Spectre of Urthona, properly controlled, is the obedient demon who brings his master Los the fire and metals and other physical needs of culture, and brings the artist his technical skill. Whenever Los has a higher status for man in view the Spectre produces the appropriate tools, an alphabet, a printing press, a wheel or a compass. But once separated from creative and imaginative ends, the instrumental becomes an end in itself, its criteria of use and value are made absolute principles, its media, such as money, become more important than the things they circulate, and vast complications of tools and machines are produced out of a sheer automatic compulsion to produce them. Energy becomes linear and formless, directed along the clock time of fallen life, and as that time is pitifully short, the Spectre crowds Los out, takes charge of civilization and drives it along in a steadily accelerating stampede of hysterical fear. This fear prevents the mechanical energy of busyness and getting along in the world from developing into wisdom, and whether disguised as a fear of security or as a "horrible fear of the future," it is fundamentally the panic inspired by clock time, the Chronos who devours his children.

What has happened is that the Spectre of Urthona, the sorcerer's apprentice who is capable of starting but not of stopping an auto-

matic energy, has gone over to the natural man. The Spectre deals
with the useful, and the question, useful for what? has two answers.
If a thing like a sword, which is of no use to the imagination, is
called useful, what is meant is that it is useful to the Selfhood.
The Spectre does not care; he is merely a demon, as ready to
invent swords as plowshares, as quick in finding out gunpowder
as stained glass, as ingenious in making instruments of torture as
instruments of music. Separated from Los, then, the Spectre
becomes immediately the servant of Luvah, as he is in an animal.
But Luvah must go through his cycle to his death as Satan, and the
Spectre must follow him to a common destruction. In the Bible
this is symbolized in the murder of Abel, the prototype of the
dying god Luvah, by Cain, whose name means "smith" and who is
an inventive Spectre of Urthona beating his plowshare into a
sword. What begins as a pursuit of the instrumental and mechanical for its own sake ends in war and in an overproduction of
luxurious and dangerous toys; and what begins as an intensification of moral virtue or temporal activity ends as a natural beehive
society of unthinking workers, unworking drones and periodic
massacres:

> Then left the Sons of Urizen the plow & harrow, the loom,
> The hammer & the chisel & the rule & compasses; from Lon-
> don fleeing,
> They forg'd the sword on Cheviot, the chariot of war & the
> battle-ax,
> The trumpet fitted to mortal battle, & the flute of summer in
> Annandale;
> And all the Arts of Life they chang'd into the Arts of Death
> in Albion.
> The hour-glass contemn'd because its simple workmanship
> Was like the workmanship of the plowman, & the water wheel
> That raises water into cisterns, broken & burn'd with fire
> Because its workmanship was like the workmanship of the
> shepherd;
> And in their stead, intricate wheels invented, wheel without
> wheel,
> To perplex youth in their outgoings & to bind to labours in
> Albion
> Of day & night the myriads ot eternity: that they may grind
> And polish brass & iron hour after hour, laborious task,
> Kept ignorant of its use; that they might spend the days of
> wisdom

In sorrowful drudgery to obtain a scanty pittance of bread,
In ignorance to view a small portion & think that All,
And call it Demonstration, blind to all the simple rules of
  life.[40]

The imagination recreates nature, and recreation implies a
certain amount of control through the will. But as the will is not
the creative power, when the will is in charge of the natural man its
control is reduced to domination, always a sterile and uncreative
form of control. The result is that curious pollution of nature
which we always see in a society in which the instrumental is an
end in itself. In a primitive imaginative form such as a rain-dance
there are present two motives: one an imaginative attempt to
recreate and humanize a phenomenon of nature in a work of art,
the other an attempt of the natural will to bring about rain. The
expressive and subtle power of the art and the worthlessness of the
magic both gradually appear, and one is developed into drama and
the other discarded as mumbo-jumbo. We say that the magic is a
premature attempt to control nature without understanding its
real laws, which is true but not the real point. If a primitive tribe
could control the weather it would make a foolish use of its power
and soon destroy itself. Similarly a "miracle" in the sense of the
display of an arbitrary power over nature "is an impossibility,
not a miracle," and in any case "Ambitious miracle-mongers,"[41]
with whom Blake refused to classify Christ and his apostles, would
obviously be all the more disastrous to humanity if they could
work miracles. In Blake's symbolism, they are trying to open the
"Western Gate" when there is still behind it a Sea of Time and
Space which will rush in and dissolve everything in the chaos of
another flood. This chaos is the fallen Tharmas, the Zoa of power,
and the Spectre of Urthona is related to Tharmas as Mephistopheles in *Faust* is related to the Erdgeist. Since human bodies sank
to the "Adamic" level of impotence, however, there has been
an inner balance in the world that has so far prevented magical
powers from being developed in advance of vision.

The same is true of the mature development of magic and
miracle which generally usurps the name of science. As an attempt
of the uncreative will to domineer over the natural world or other
men, such "science" is pernicious to the extent that it is successful,
because humanity is just as much inclined to destroy itself in scien-

tific as in primitive times, and has avoided doing so only because it did not know how. Very little of the machinery science makes possible is of any use to the imagination—for though Blake, like Morris, ranks "manufacture" with art rather than commerce, he also uses the word primarily in the sense of handwork—and what is not of use to the imagination must be useful to the natural man, and so destructive. Science conceived as will is a murderous complication of such machines; science conceived as imagination is *scientia*, the clarifying of the form of our knowledge of nature. This latter, when under imaginative control, is of great significance, and the fact that it has had so dramatic a development in the final centuries of the Jesus cycle is another indication that that cycle could be the last, as we shall see when we come to *Jerusalem*.

What is true of nature is equally true of man. The creative imagination perfects the form of its vision, and that vision may have a great influence on others, an influence which should be left to take care of itself. Once the artist thinks in terms of influence rather than of clarity of form, the effort of the imagination becomes an effort of will, and art is perverted into tyranny, the application of the principle of magic or mysterious compulsion to society. Here we come back to the opposition of visionary and hero, of the man who inspires with life as opposed to the man who inspires with death.

Occasionally a prophet will become a warrior, like Mohammed, or his disciples will. The underlying motive for this is often that the prophet becomes impatient (the sin of Moloch the child-roaster, according to Blake) and anxious to get his message proclaimed in a hurry to the greatest possible number of people in the shortest possible time, compulsion being usually regarded as a great saver of time. The prophet who wants to see immediate and dramatic results of his visionary power is being oppressed by the spirit of the Spectre of Urthona, the passing time that will very soon tick his seventy years away. But there are no short cuts to vision through violence or unreflecting energy: "The Will must not be bended," Blake says, "but in the day of Divine Power."[42] A society's index of civilization is not in a high proportion of murderers who get hanged, but in a low proportion of murders; and while it takes less time to hang a murderer than to organize society so as to reduce the motives for murder, there is no imagina-

tive progress in the former. Progress comes only from the "forgiveness of sins" which among other things is the transference of the
will from the Selfhood to the imagination.

It is clearly a matter of considerable importance to human life
whether the Spectre of Urthona is under Los's guidance or not, and
as the Orc cycle declines, the question becomes more and more
critical. After the progress of the Orc cycle has been described in
The Four Zoas, therefore, the Spectre of Urthona simultaneously
(or as nearly so as poetry can suggest the simultaneous) merges
with Los and with a fugitive character called the Shadow of Enitharmon, who, if the Spectre is clock time, is presumably yard-
stick space. The former union produces the tradition of art and
prophecy which reaches its culmination in Jesus; the latter produces the fallen perspective of life, the combining of its two great
categories time and space into a single abstract form, on which is
founded a progression of tyranny leading to Antichrist.

The reader will notice that there are two versions of Night VII,
and that the only one we have spoken of so far is the one beginning
"Then Urizen arose." The other is certainly earlier, and in symbolism is an undifferentiated mixture of the present Nights VII
and VIII. Most of what was valuable in it was transferred to
Jerusalem. The conception of the Spectre of Urthona seems to have
broken on Blake quite suddenly when he was proceeding to a
simpler climax, and occasioned the rewriting of Night VII, if not
of the next two Nights as well.[43] Eventually it burst the whole Zoa
scheme altogether, and was one of the chief reasons for abandoning
the poem.

The Spectre of Urthona does two things for Los: it provides
him with a conscious will which makes his vision consistent and
purposeful, and it gives him a sense of the passing of time which
his imagination creates into a vision of the meaning of history.
The latter is the reason why Blake puts the union of Los and his
Spectre directly after his account of the Orc cycle. The passing
of such a cycle increases the conscious awareness in the imaginative
vision of life, as Hebrew prophecy was inspired by the decline
of Egypt and Babylon. Before he merged with his Spectre, Los
had been a primitive visionary, a kind of glorified medicine man
with the random and haphazard vision of "possession" instead
of the deliberate craftsmanship of art.[44] But with the growth of

a sense of perspective in time, Los settles down to producing art in real earnest, and the arts of civilization begin to weaken and undermine the tyranny of war. This merging of imagination and time is the axis on which all Blake's thought turns. It was suggested at the beginning that we should not call Blake a "mystic" too glibly, and it is here that Blake is to be sharply distinguished, if not from all mystics, at least from that quality in mysticism which may and often does make the mystical merely the subtlest of all attempts to get along without a redeeming power in time.

· 5 ·

THE other union of the Spectre of Urthona, with the Shadow of Enitharmon, the consolidation of tyranny and mystery which appears most clearly in human life in its periods of lowest culture and most ferocious warfare, completes the last phase of the Orc cycle, the phase symbolized by the crucifixion of Orc as a serpent on a tree of mystery. The expulsion of Adam from a fatal tree and a cursed serpent being a symbolic account of one of these periods, this episode in *The Four Zoas* is reminiscent of the fall of Adam and Eve. The fruit, as one might call it, of their union is Rahab, the complete body of Mystery which is also the sign of apocalypse: what the author of *Finnegans Wake* might have called the Last Strumpet or the Great Whorn. With Rahab the symbols of Antichrist make their appearance, and we may proceed to them next, summarizing here for convenience the half-dozen Biblical symbols from which they are derived: (1) the Leviathan of Job and Isaiah, who is related to or identified with a number of other monsters including Behemoth and the swallower of Jonah; (2) the dragon of the Apocalypse, and the two subsidiary dragons sprung from him; (3) the Satan of Job and the Gospels, identified by the author of the Apocalypse with his chief dragon, and elsewhere in the New Testament with the serpent in Paradise; (4) the Great Whore of the Apocalypse, identified by Blake both with the Rahab of the Exodus story and with the water-monster of the Psalms and Isaiah who is also called Rahab and associated with Leviathan; (5) the Antichrist of Paul, the "mystery of iniquity"; and (6) the Covering Cherub of Ezekiel, identified by Blake with the angel guarding the tree of life in Paradise.

The numbers four and three, in Blake's later prophecies, are respectively the numbers of infinite extension and of cyclic recurrence. The world of eternity is fourfold, and any imagination trying to reach that level must incorporate a threefold world within itself. In the world of time and space, time is in three dimensions, past, present and future. The visionary tries to combine all these into an eternal vision in which he may say with Blake: "I see the Past, Present & Future existing all at once Before me."[45] Space is in three dimensions also, and the imagination similarly tries to achieve an eternal vision of that. The fourth dimension of time is space and the fourth dimension of space is time, so that a fourfold perception is one which unites time and space in eternity. The body consists of air, water and earth: the imagination tries to make it live also in the fire of Eden. God is Father, Son and Spirit: the imagination tries to see this Trinity in the fourfold unity of Jesus. This vision is set forth in the story of the fiery furnace, where, as the three men enter the spiritual world, they become four. The world of Beulah also is threefold, and we may remember that, according to "The Crystal Cabinet," an unsuccessful attempt to "sieze the inmost Form" in Beulah will turn it into Ulro. Whether the reader at present understands this or not, from now on he should associate all triplicity with Antichrist.

At the beginning of Night VI Urizen, at the outset of exploring his "dens," the untracked wilderness which is the physical world to the fallen mind, meets "three terrific women," spirits of rivers like the Rhine Maidens, who turn out to be his own daughters, though they might more logically have been daughters of Tharmas. Mythology is full of sinister female trinities who suggest the power of a hostile destiny. The stories of Lear and Macbeth are also concerned with a Urizenic tyrant, three women and a deserted heath, and both, especially the former, have left their mark on Blake's symbolism. Blake does not develop these three women, though they reappear in "The Golden Net"[46]; they represent the fallen body living in a fallen world, female because natural. Blake usually expresses this, however, in terms of the Zoas themselves. In the human body the imagination, Los, struggles to control the three fallen Zoas, Urizen, Tharmas and Luvah, whom Blake identifies with the "Head," "Heart" and "Loins" respectively. These words are not very satisfactory: the modern reader familiar with Freud may substitute those of a newer myth of much the same shape, and read "libido" for Luvah, "id" for the stormy Tharmas, and "superego" for the fanatical Urizen.

Antichrist in Blake is a threefold monster, but not exactly three women. The world of Ulro is, like the lowest segment of Plato's divided line, a shadow-world, in which subject and object reflect one another, a monstrous union which Blake symbolizes by the term "Hermaphrodite." The three forms of Antichrist, therefore, are really hermaphroditic. Chief of them is Satan, the Covering Cherub, the dragon form of the objective world with the revolving stars forming the rattles of its tail. Another is the Rahab or Great Whore who sits on this dragon, the ultimate fallen form of Vala, the Lamia who entices men with the evil beauty of an elusive mysterious nature, symbolized by the cloak of shame spread over love, the "foolish woman" of the Book of Proverbs.[47] The third is Tirzah, the shrouding womb of the physical universe out of which we must break to live, the "Necessity" of Plato's *Republic* who turns the spindle of the universe, the physical basis of all nonhuman gods.

The fallen life of warfare is male energy controlled by a hidden religious belief in an external and therefore ultimately female god, as we have seen in discussing Enitharmon. Rahab, "Religion hid in War," therefore is a "Male-Female" hermaphrodite.[48] Conversely, the man who is born in helpless dependence on an outward environment is a male imagination imprisoned within a female will. Tirzah, then, is a "Female-Male" hermaphrodite. But as Rahab and Tirzah are part of the female will, they are usually referred to simply as female. The combining of these three principles is expressed in Blake by multiples of three. The product of Tirzah and Rahab together is the "nine enfolded spheres" which constitute the "ninefold darkness" of Urizen.[49] The product of all three of them is twenty-sevenfold, twenty-seven being the cube of three, the supreme aggravation of three, so to speak; and twenty-seven is the figure Blake always uses for the fallen world or "Mundane Shell":

> The Mundane Shell is a vast Concave Earth, an immense
> Harden'd shadow of all things upon our Vegetated Earth,
> Enlarg'd into dimension & deform'd into indefinite space,

In Twenty-seven Heavens and all their Hells, with Chaos
And Ancient Night & Purgatory. It is a cavernous Earth
Of labyrinthine intricacy, twenty-seven folds of opakeness,
And finishes where the lark mounts.[50]

The threefold historical tyranny of Egypt, Babylon and Rome
is also symbolized by twenty-seven, the number of "Churches" or
historical generations that stretch from Adam to Luther, just
before the twenty-eighth or last age begins. Hence one would
expect all aspects of Antichrist to have Egyptian, Babylonian and
Roman affiliations as well as a few Atlantic overtones. Blake's
Tirzah may be derived from the Calypso whom Homer calls "the
daughter of sinister Atlas,"[51] which in Blake's language means
"the female will of fallen Albion." Her home, Ogygia, though
located in the Western Ocean, is also an old name for Egypt. Rahab
then would be Blake's Circe, whose habitat in the Classical poets
seems to be both Atlantic and Italian; a curious ambiguity, of a
type which recurs in an old name for Italy, Hesperia, used by
Blake in *Jerusalem*, and in the setting of Shakespeare's *Tempest*.
The Great Whore of the Apocalypse is Babylonian and Roman,
and the water-monster she sits on is, or is closely akin to, the
Leviathan whom Ezekiel calls the "dragon in the midst of his
rivers," and identifies with the Pharaoh of Egypt.[52] In *Jerusalem*
there is an ingenious association between the heads and horns of
the apocalyptic dragon and the three-sided tangle of the Nile
delta.[53] There is also an association, though not a very explicit one,
between Rahab and the Sphinx, the Egyptian image of the female
will who destroys everyone who cannot see through her riddle
of fallen man stumbling along a threefold path from infantile to
senile impotence; and who seems, with her human face, dragon
wings, leonine body and bovine feet to be the four Zoas frozen
together in a diabolical parody of Ezekiel's vision of God. One
would expect Blake to have made more of the two "stony forms"
of Egypt, the world's oldest tyranny and the only nation that remembered Atlantis. He seems to be more interested in Shakespeare's great vision of an Egyptian whore who, like her predecessor
the Pharaoh in Ezekiel, is a "serpent of old Nile," and in the
moment of her triumph in death holds another serpent to her
breast like a sucking child.

The two central images of the fallen world are the crucifixion

of Jesus and of Prometheus, the binding of imagination to Generation and Ulro respectively, together constituting the total form of
"Druidism": the sacrificed Luvah, the rock or holy stone, the dead
tree and the cruel sky-god. In Night VIII these two events take
place at the same time, Rahab presiding over the crucifixion while
Tirzah and her four sisters bind down Prometheus and "catch his
shrieks in cups of gold."[54] The golden cup or bowl, whatever its
meaning in the Bible, is in Blake a symbol of female virginity, and
as such it stands for the elusive female will of the virgin-mother.
In the "motto" of *The Book of Thel* the silver rod and the golden
bowl are phallic symbols of the world of "Generation," in which
not only has all life a sexual origin, but in which there is a kind
of residual virginity in all sexual contact owing to the opacity of
fallen bodies. Rahab also appears in the Apocalypse with a golden
cup full of the blood of the saints.[55] The Arthurian story of the
Grail, the golden cup of Christ's blood, the achievement of which is
the final reward of revelation, would then be an alternative version
of the exposure and annihilation of the Whore who is Mystery, and
one more closely linked with Albion, of whom Arthur is a later
alias.

We may now summarize *The Four Zoas* as far as we have gone:
the first four Nights describe the Fall down to Adam's time, and
the next four are concerned with human history and the sharpen-
ing of the opposition between the evolution of Los and the cycle
of Orc. In Night VII the passing of an Orc cycle brings this opposition into focus, and the Spectre of Urthona becomes the basis
both of imaginative art and of tyranny and mystery. In Night VIII
the opposition is complete. The coming of Jesus achieves the
unity of God and Man which marks the redemption of the latter;
but the coming of Jesus began another Orc cycle, and in the course
of it the form of Antichrist emerges, achieving his perfect clarity
with the Deism of Blake's own time, natural religion recognized
as such, admitted to be such, defended as such. The gospel of an
objective nature is a gospel of mystery, and when it becomes plain
that it is mystery, it is forced into that paradoxical dilemma of a
revelation of mystery which is what Deism is. For Deism holds
that everything outside the world of nature and reason is impenetrable darkness, and that the fact that this is so must appear most
natural and reasonable to every man:

> The Synagogue of Satan therefore, uniting against Mystery,
> Satan divided against Satan, resolv'd in open Sanhedrim
> To burn Mystery with fire & form another from her ashes,
> For God put it into their heart to fulfill all his will.
>
> The Ashes of Mystery began to animate; they call'd it Deism
> And Natural Religion; as of old, so now anew began
> Babylon again in Infancy, call'd Natural Religion.

These are the closing lines of Night VIII. Just before the apocalypse begins in the next Night, we are given the gloomiest possible view of human life as an indefinite series of cycles in which everything happens just as it has happened before and will happen again, and in which our highest hope is that "in time" the old disorder will change and yield place to a new one. One is reminded of the point in the Choral Symphony at the end of the first three movements, where there is a pause as the themes of all three hesitantly recur one after another, before the great vision of the "Tochter aus Elisium" who is also the brotherhood of man begins. In fact it would have been quite possible to have stopped at the triumph of Antichrist in the poet's own time. Langland, who is perhaps spiritually closer to Blake than any other English poet, ended the *Vision of Piers the Plowman* here, though not without making much more of the resurrection of Christ, which Blake so far has deliberately ignored. But such a conclusion is appropriate to satire, or at most tragedy, and Blake's complete vision is a divine comedy. Whether a tragedy is concerned with the dying king in the theater or the dying god in the church,[56] the more profound it is, the more readily it leads to a resurrection of the imagination in the spectators, or, as in Aristotle, a purging of the spirit. Without the feeling of an implicit *commedia* or triumph of life out of death, tragedy is a mere adoration of fate, a death-worship of the sort Blake attacks in *Jerusalem*:

> . . . pitying & weeping as at a trajic scene
> The soul drinks murder & revenge & applauds its own holiness.[57]

Similarly if great satire such as we find in *The Dunciad* does not appeal to something beyond itself, we should have to take the parody of the apocalypse with which that poem ends at its face value. Tragedy and satire are artistically justifiable only when their finality is paradoxical, and where a subsequent resolution of that paradox is implied. In an explicitly cyclic vision there can be no truncation: the tragic trilogy must go on to a dance of giants.

· 6 ·

THERE is nothing like the colossal explosion of creative power in the ninth Night of *The Four Zoas* anywhere else in English poetry. There are great visions of hell, of the Creation, of the Fall, of the unfallen state, even of the resurrection; but English poets have been inclined to fight shy of the *Dies Irae*. The City of God has often enough appeared in the distance to the earth-bound visionary: it has often been described, and even reached at the end of a personal pilgrimage; but as an eternal form remote from the world of time, not as a phoenix arising in the human mind from the ashes of the burned mysterious universe. It has been suggested, and with reason, that Milton was ready for such a vision during the decade after the outbreak of the Civil War, and that *Paradise Lost* is the song of experience following an unwritten song of triumph. In any case Milton follows the rule to which Blake is perhaps the only major exception. *Prometheus Unbound* comes a little way along Blake's path, but Shelley's imagination plunges upward to burst into a shower of lyrical sparks, hiding the stars an instant with a strange illumination of its own, then fading quickly and leaving us with what Blake calls "the black incessant sky"[58] once more.

In reading some of the great eighteenth century writers one is struck not only by their acuteness and clarity, but by the way in which this clarity seems to be founded on a curious simplicity. This is no doubt partly the simplicity of honesty, but there is something about their confidence in the adequacy of their type of intelligence that makes the Age of Reason almost an age of mental innocence. Blake's vision has a wider range, but it has none of the sophistication which as a rule is part of the awareness of what lies beyond the senses and the judging mind. There is nothing naïve in Blake, of course, but there is a unique quality of candor, and it is this quality that not only leads him to envisage an apocalypse, but enables him to control what he so well calls the fury of his course among the stars.[59] In this ninth Night Blake seems to have found his way back to the very headwaters of

Western imagination, to the crystalline purity of vision of the *Völuspa* or the *Muspilli*, where the end of time is perceived, not as a vague hope, an allegory or an indigestible dogma, but as a physical fact as literal as a battle and as imminent as death.

The poet works with physical images, and hence every successful vision of a state of existence beyond the physical must be an immense triumph of technical skill. In *Paradise Lost* three such visions are attempted: of hell and chaos, of heaven and the Godhead, and of the unfallen state of man, not all of which stand on the same level of success. A vision of apocalypse presents at least equal problems, but they are not as insoluble as may be thought. For the whole point about an apocalypse is that the darkening sun and the falling stars and the rest of the fireworks represent a kind of vision that is disappearing because it is unreal, whereas what takes its place is permanent because it is real, and if real, familiar. With a deafening clangor of trumpets and a blinding flash of light, Man comes awake with the sun in his eyes and his alarm clock ringing beside him, and finds himself in what he now sees to have been all the time his own home.

The ninth Night begins in the shrouding winter darkness of misery and stupidity that the poet sees in his own time. People dazed by a passive mind and the tyranny of man and nature that such passivity invites, are stumbling into war to die or into slavery to live in hell, until quite suddenly revolution breaks loose. When one is falling over an abyss in a nightmare, the body gives a self-protective jerk and the abyss vanishes as the mind wakes up. And when a revolution begins, whatever may happen to it eventually there is one breathless moment, just as the old tyranny comes crashing down, in which we become aware that we have bound ourselves to observe the rules of a foolish and evil game that we are not obliged to play. Started in self-preservation, the revolution spreads like a fire in withered stubble, until "Mystery's tyrants are cut off & not one left on Earth,"[60] and the entire human race is united once more in brotherhood. The winter of death has become a winter of potential life.

Unity and peace suggest the feeling that humanity is not an aggregate of men but a single Man, whereupon Albion begins to stir uneasily in his sleep. With the end of war comes the end of the torment of fear. A state of insecurity in which anything may happen is what causes Urizen's "horrible fear of the future" and makes him invent the moral law to make activity predictable. As security grows and this fear of the future relaxes, a new audacity comes into the imagination. With its aid men get a sudden vision of the real truth (symbolized in Blake by the revival and death of Ahania) and the apocalypse enters a new phase. This is the end of the preparatory apocalypse which the Bible calls the millennium, the temporary reign of peace and prosperity in the natural world. The millennium is where the vision of *Prometheus Unbound* stops, for Shelley accepts the orthodox confusion of the eternal and indefinite sufficiently to regard eternity with some suspicion. But in Blake the real apocalypse has only begun.

Urizen so far has taken the lead, for the apocalypse is the clearing of the human brain, which is Urizen's rightful place. The imagination sees the physical universe as the underground or Platonic cave of the real world, the den of Urthona. Men have just beaten their swords into plowshares, and by an ingenious modulation of the "harrowing of hell" symbol Blake has Urizen plow up the surface of this cemetery of buried seeds. An imaginative spring is approaching, and the seeds begin to push upward into eternal daylight. Man must now recover, in order, the world of Luvah or unfallen Generation, the eternal soil, and the world of Tharmas or Beulah, the eternal garden. As this represents the recovery of innocence, a long and very beautiful interlude in pastoral symbolism deals with it. The last spring has now gone through the last summer and is waiting for the harvest of the last autumn, a season which can no longer be called a "fall."

As Urizen reaches into the stars for the sickle all creation begins to pour out human life. The sea, the home of the daughters of Oceanus who fell with Prometheus, gives up its dead; slaves and all kinds of crushed and denied life grow into maturity; and animals and plants take on human character. The "metamorphoses" in Ovid, in which nymphs collapse into vegetable and watery existences, are images of the Fall; and in the resurrection they change back to human forms. Luvah gathers the vintage, Tharmas threshes the crop and Los, now Urthona, grinds the corn. The entire imagination of Man is made into bread and wine, and as the poem dies away a second winter approaches, a winter not of death but of repose and the storing of food, an untroubled sleep before Man awakens for his eternal feast with the other Gods in the hall of the reconquered stars.

> The Sun has left his blackness & has found a fresher morning,
> And the mild moon rejoices in the clear & cloudless night,
> And Man walks forth from midst of the fires: the evil is all consum'd.
> His eyes behold the Angelic spheres arising night & day;
> The stars consum'd like a lamp blown out, & in their stead, behold
> The Expanding Eyes of Man behold the depth of wondrous worlds!
> One Earth, one sea beneath; nor Erring Globes wander, but Stars
> Of fire rise up nightly from the Ocean; & one Sun
> Each morning, like a New born Man, issues with songs & joy
> Calling the Plowman to his Labour & the Shepherd to his rest.
> He walks upon the Eternal Mountains, raising his heavenly voice,
> Conversing with the Animal forms of Wisdom night & day,
> That, risen from the Sea of fire, renew'd walk o'er the Earth;
> For Tharmas brought his flocks upon the hills, & in the vales
> Around the Eternal Man's bright tent, the little Children play
> Among the wooly flocks. The hammer of Urthona sounds
> In the deep caves beneath; his limbs renew'd, his Lions roar
> Around the Furnaces & in Evening sport upon the plains.
> They raise their faces from the Earth, conversing with the Man:
> "How is it we have walk'd thro' fires & yet are not consum'd?
> How is it that all things are chang'd, even as in ancient times?"

Gorgeous as it unquestionably is, one eventually comes to wonder, in studying it, how far this ninth Night is the real climax of the vision, and how far it has been added as an effort of will, perhaps almost of conscience. Has Blake's Ode to Joy any inner logic connecting it with the rest of the work beyond a purely emotional requirement of an allegro finale? Certainly there is little connection between its opening and the close of the preceding Night. The Last Judgment simply starts off with a bang, as an instinctive shudder of self-preservation against a tyranny of intolerable menace. If so, then it is not really the work of Los, though the opening action is ascribed to him: it is the old revolutionary doctrine of a spontaneous reappearance of Orc, this time, for some unexplained reason, to be the last one. What Los has actually been doing while Antichrist has been growing in power is not clearly explained to us. There are attempts to explain it, vague hints of a contest of Palamabron and Satan and so on; but they do not really fit, and seem to belong to another poem. *The Four Zoas* has given us an imaginatively coherent account of how we got from an original Golden Age to the world we are now in. It has not given us an imaginatively coherent account of how we can get from eighteenth century Deism to a Last Judgment through the power of Los, not Orc. Even its author could hardly have torn up *The Four Zoas*, but still he had not achieved a definitive vision, and, leaving his great work in manuscript, started again where he had really left off, with the triumph of nature and reason.

PART THREE
THE FINAL SYNTHESIS

And the angel that was sent unto me, whose name
was Uriel, gave me an answer, and said to me,
Thy heart hath utterly failed thee in regarding this
world, and thinkest thou to comprehend the way of
the Most High?
Then said I, Yea, my Lord.

II ESDRAS, iv, 1-3.

In 1800, after Blake had been working for some time on *The Four Zoas*, he was offered a retreat at the village of Felpham in Sussex, by his patron and friend Hayley, himself a poet of sorts, who had also patronized Cowper. Blake was, like most major English writers, a born Cockney who quickly became miserable long outside London, but he naturally did not know that then, and went off very happily to live under Hayley's protection. It was almost the first "event" in a busy but very quiet life, and Blake planned that his stay in Felpham would be a "slumber" in a Beulah of dormant life during which he would gather together all his powers and concentrate them on clarifying the scheme of his epic and the technique of his engraving. He never ceased to speak of it as a slumber, but a quickly developing antagonism between his temperament and Hayley's soon made it a slumber full of nightmares: not an idyllic pastoral interlude or a sheltered hibernation, but an ordeal by fire, a temptation in a wilderness of fashionable smugness. The net result of the Felpham interval, for Blake's canon, was that *The Four Zoas* was abandoned and *Milton* and *Jerusalem* engraved instead.

In an early prose pamphlet which we know that Blake read, for he quotes from it in his notes to Reynolds, Milton distinguishes the "brief" and the "diffuse" epic.[1] The latter is the full-dress affair in twelve books, or some multiple of twelve, for which Homer and Virgil are the models. Milton's example of the former, to which his own *Paradise Regained* is evidently a contribution, is the Book of Job. Blake's three epics, *The Four Zoas*, *Milton* and *Jerusalem*, are all "brief," but they seem to be, as we should perhaps expect, fragments of an original plan for a single "diffuse" one.

With the Felpham period we get for the first time a series of letters of some continuity to aid us—and very treacherous allies they are. It is quite impossible to relate them exactly to the existing body of Blake's work. The first explicit statement of what Blake is doing comes in a letter to his friend Butts dated April 1803:

But none can know the Spiritual Acts of my three years' Slumber on the banks of the Ocean, unless he has seen them in the Spirit, or unless he should read My long Poem descriptive of those Acts; for I have in these three years composed an immense number of verses on One Grand Theme, Similar to Homer's Iliad or Milton's Paradise Lost, the Persons & Machinery intirely new to the Inhabitants of Earth (some of the Persons Excepted). . . .

This passage could conceivably refer to *The Four Zoas*, or to *Milton*, or to both together. But, unless we adopt the very unlikely hypothesis of a lost poem, Blake's language is rather curious. It is easy to understand why some of Blake's readers should think of the Prophecies as much longer poems than they really are, but why Blake himself should speak of a poem of only a little over four thousand lines as "immense," and compare it to the *Iliad* and *Paradise Lost* in a way that suggests an equality of length, is puzzling. *Milton* is only half as long as *The Four Zoas*, and *Jerusalem* can hardly have been written by then in anything like its present form. In July Blake speaks of "a Sublime Allegory, which is now perfectly completed into a Grand Poem."[2] This does not literally apply to *The Four Zoas*, which was never perfectly completed into anything, cannot apply to the still unwritten *Jerusalem*, and yet seems to refer to a bigger poem than our present *Milton*. Apparently the latter, now in two books, was originally planned as a "diffuse" epic in twelve: the *Milton* that we possess, however, is complete in itself.

Possibly *The French Revolution* as we have it, the first of many promised books, represents Blake's first epic plan: if so, the theme would have been simply a revolutionary struggle of Orc and Urizen with Orc ultimately victorious. When the conception of Los grew clear in Blake's mind, he began on the deeper and subtler theme of the Books of Urizen, Los and Ahania. That too seemed to leave out the real beginning of the Fall, the subjection of man to the female will, so Blake moved on to a "Song of the Aged Mother," an epic to be named *Vala*. Vala in her turn suggested the fourfold Zoa scheme, and *The Four Zoas* was begun as a revision of *Vala*. At the end of *The Four Zoas*, the same process repeated itself in Blake's mind. The symbols in which his vision had finally consolidated, Rahab, Tirzah, Satan, Albion, Jesus, Jerusalem, Los and the Spectre of Urthona, formed now a solid structural framework in his mind, in which the rather vaporous Zoas and their emanations, clouds in the brain of the Albion who was his real hero, and veils concealing the Jerusalem who was his real heroine, began to play a minor role. Meanwhile, his change of opinion about the nature of his sojourn at Felpham had brought an entirely new theme into his mind which demanded his full attention. This was the theme of the contest of Palamabron and Satan, a symbolic transformation of his clash with Hayley, first introduced in Night VIII of *The Four Zoas*, where it is somewhat out of place, and with which *Milton* begins. The idea of writing a poem on Milton, which Blake had probably pondered for some time, then combined with this, for reasons we shall presently explain. The poem he had written on the Zoas, the poem he was to write on Palamabron, Satan and Milton, and the further plan, not then clearly visualized, of a *Four Zoas* rewritten in terms of a more fundamental symbolism, may at one time have coalesced in Blake's mind as a single gigantic epic scheme which certainly "existed," though doubtless not in any written-out form.

From this nebulous epic the *Milton* and *Jerusalem* we now have were precipitated. Once they were finished, there was no longer any real place for *The Four Zoas* in Blake's canon, which in any case he had already used as a quarry for the later poems. Considering the great beauty and variety of the poem, the vitality of the sketches in its manuscript, and the fact that without it we do not possess enough of Blake's symbolic apparatus to understand the later books at all, it is unlikely that Blake intended to drop it altogether. We have to remember that much of Blake's obscurity is due to the fact that he never in his whole life received the smallest public encouragement to complete and perfect his canon: the public, of course, never knew that there was a canon. If a revised and shortened version of *The Four Zoas* could ever have been used as the prelude to a trilogy, the three poems taken together might then have made up a single "diffuse" epic of the requisite number of lines and books. But as it is *The Four Zoas* remains forlornly outside the engraved works, though as late as 1809, in the catalogue to his ill-fated Exhibition, Blake is still speaking of a poem he has written about the fall of a fourfold Man into a Strong, a Beautiful and an Ugly Man, which "if God please," he would like to "publish"—whatever that word may signify.[3]

A bald summary of what happens in *Milton* is unpromising enough. It begins with material taken over from *The Book of Urizen* and *The Four Zoas* about the creation, and goes on to a myth of a dispute between Palamabron and Satan which obviously suggests the relations between Blake and Hayley at Felpham. Then Milton, in eternity, determines to "go to Eternal Death," which means physical life, and after a long struggle he enters this world and reincarnates himself in Blake. The first book ends with a moment of illumination in which the whole of reality is absorbed within the perceiving mind of the poet. Then, we are told, Milton's purpose in reincarnating himself was to redeem his emanation, Ololon, who is called "Sixfold," recalling the three wives and three daughters who kept Milton reminded of the "female will" during his life. The descent of Ololon, the final redemption of Milton-Blake, now united also with Los, and the casting-off of Satan-Hayley in the shape of Antichrist form the subject of the second book. To the corporeal understanding this is a sufficiently absurd farrago, which implies that if we put our intellectual powers to work on it it will emerge a great imaginative masterpiece.

· 2 ·

WHILE no literary critic of any experience will make much effort to define his terms, we have suggested that the word "epic" has a more technical meaning than simply "long poem," as Milton implies when he speaks of brief epics. The function of the epic, in its origin, seems to be primarily to teach the nation, or whatever we call the social unit which the poet is addressing, its own traditions. These traditions are chiefly concerned with the national religion and the national history, and both are presented in terms of the activities of "Giant forms," or beings at once human and divine, who are called "gods" in the religious context and "heroes" in the historical one. The religion is not theological nor the history documentary: both are mythopoeic. As the epic mode of thought, both in its visual form and in its universality of range, is most typical of a culture in the first flush of its vigor, the major epic tends to come rather early in the nation's history and hence may form, if it is great enough, a sort of matrix for the whole cultural development that follows it. Thus the entire attitude to life that we think of as "Hellenic" seems to grow organically out of Homer, and the reverence in which the Homeric poems were held indicates that this is something more than a retrospective illusion. The Indian epics have gone a step further, and have actually absorbed much of this later development, the *Bhagavadgita* itself being an episode from one of them.

The Bible has gone further still in consolidating a national culture. The basis of the Bible is, like that of the epic, religious and historical saga concerned with anthropomorphic gods and theomorphic men, part of it legendary history and part prophetic vision. But the Bible is neither a single work of art like the *Iliad,* nor an expanded one like the *Mahabharata:* it is the historical product of a visionary tradition. It records a continuous reshaping of the earlier and more primitive visions, and as it goes on it becomes more explicitly prophetic, until the confused legends of an obscure people take the form of the full cyclic vision of fall, redemption and apocalypse. The Old Testament begins with an account of an escape from Egypt into Canaan led by Joshua, and ends with the prophetic allegorical recreation of this event: the escape of the imagination from a "furnace of iron" into a City of God through the power of a divine humanity or Messiah. The Gospels consolidate this vision of the Messiah into the vision of Jesus, who has the same name as Joshua, and the proof of the events in Jesus' life, as recorded in the Gospels, is referred not to contemporary evidence but to what the Old Testament prophets had said would be true of the Messiah. The imaginative recreation of Old Testament visions in the New Testament, reaching its climax in the dense mosaic of allusions and quotations in the Apocalypse, merely completes a process which goes on to a considerable extent within the Old Testament itself.

Hellenic literature, from Blake's point of view, shows a gradual decline from the visionary clarity of Homer and the dramatists through the abstract reflective thinking of Plato and Aristotle to a final exhaustion in mystical or skeptical contemplations of the cosmic abyss which is Ulro. We can see something similar in the Bible, if we compare Genesis with Ecclesiastes, for instance; but the unique appeal of the Bible to the religious imagination is connected very intimately with its resistance to abstract thought. And this resistance is largely due to the integrity of the tradition it records, to the fact that the Hebrew prophets and poets continually recreated the historical and religious visions they inherited, refusing to follow the Orc cycle into a Urizenic sophisticated decadence. Hellenic culture, then, illustrates Blake's theory of the Orc cycle; Hebraic culture illustrates his other doctrine of the incorporation of history and tradition into eternal vision, the building of the ruins of time into the mansions of eternity[4] which in his symbolism is the subduing of the Spectre of Urthona by Los.

Let us now look at the English epic to see whether its traditions are Hellenic or Hebraic in shape. A peculiarity of English literature is that its national and religious mythologies do not have the same origin, its religion being imported. It may be partly because of this that in its early "Gothic" period it did not produce a poet corresponding to Homer or Virgil. When Chaucer constructs his pantheon of the essential "Giant forms" in the English nation, he simply projects the life around him, giving us a vision of English Christianity more or less as it appeared to him in experience. In spite of Blake's masterly analysis, the *Canterbury Tales* is in too chaotic a state for anyone to say definitely what its complete form would have been, though in the so-called "Marriage Group" at least we can see a faint trace of a larger outline. Langland, whose spiritual affinity with Blake we have mentioned, makes a prodigious effort to combine his English and his Christian perspectives; but it did not occur to him that historical legends had any place in such an effort, and whether he was right or not, the unity of his epic is perhaps more doctrinal than visionary.

It is not until after the religious capital of England had been moved from Rome to London that Spenser gives us a full epic synthesis of English Christianity in a "darke conceit" which is partly a vision of the purified English Christian Church and partly a vision of English history in terms of Arthurian symbolism. These are known to critics as the moral and historical allegories respectively. Spenser has a clear grasp of the unity of British and Christian mythology, but perhaps Blake would have said that an orthodox censor in his mind causes him to make more use of disguise and camouflage in working out his theme than a prophet should do. For example, he proposes to present in Prince Arthur a Renaissance "complete man," and as to a Christian the only complete man is also complete God, the association of Arthur with Jesus would take him straight into the symbolism of Blake's great hymn, "And did those feet in ancient time," which opens *Milton*. But it is not clear that he has the nerve for this. However, he does, in the fourth book of his unfinished epic, speak of Chaucer as reborn in him, in a passage very important for the proper understanding of Blake's attitude to Milton.[5]

Milton, who told Dryden that his "original"—quite a strong word—was Spenser, eliminated the ancient British myth from his epic, but still makes his view of Christianity an illustration of the contemporary history of England; and in *Paradise Lost* the four states of existence, heaven, Eden (which is Blake's Beulah), the fallen world and hell, are much more sharply outlined than they are in Spenser's ambiguous fairyland. If Milton had not been checkmated by the failure of the British nation to purify itself, national and Christian symbolism would probably have been at least as closely unified in his epic as they are in *Comus* and *Lycidas*, and unified around the theme of apocalypse rather than that of creation and fall. Here Spenser had an advantage, for the movement to purify English Christianity in his day had not, from his point of view, failed. But the very fact that Milton has to record a failure causes him to illustrate all the more clearly what we have just implied: that the later a poet comes in his tradition, the more explicitly he has to deal with the question of his personal relation to the society of his time. Milton thinks of himself continually as an inspired prophet sent by God to present his vision to the English people; and if we examine the argument of *Paradise Lost* we can see how far this goes. Adam's fall lost man the paradise of liberty, therefore an interaction of tyrant and victim, of moral good and moral evil, a reign of law and compulsion, will be the essential feature of fallen human life until the apocalypse. In such a society the visionary or messenger of God will inevitably be a neglected or even persecuted prophet. Thus in Milton's attempt to justify the ways of God to man the question of the role of the visionary in human life is of cardinal importance, in fact almost the moral of the poem.

Now any major English poet following Milton will be ambitious to produce a fourth English epic, the unified vision of English Christianity which is appropriate to his age. But he will find that between Milton's time and his own English Christianity has declined from a sectarian sunset into the gaslight of Deism. In Blake's symbolism, he will be in the position indicated at the end of Night VIII of *The Four Zoas*, at the close of the twenty-seventh Church, or age of Luther, which is the last phase of the seventh cycle of history, the "Eye" of Jesus. Ahead of him is the program suggested by the growth of Deism and the ascendancy of Urizen, a skeptical exhaustion of spirit leading to warfare on a vast scale, the expansion and collapse of huge empires, and a new Dark Age pending a rebirth of Orc in America. He has three courses open to him, two of which are wrong. He may follow the Augustan tradition, join the Deists and write Urizenic poetry like the *Essay on Man*. If he feels unable to do this, the theme of the nature of genius and of the poet's role in society then becomes central in his vision, for if he cannot interpret Deism he should know the reasons for his opposition to it. His second course is to visualize his mission as a rebirth of a new Orc. The "rich-hair'd youth of morn" in Collins' *Ode on the Poetical Character*, the youth with flashing eyes and floating hair in *Kubla Khan*, Shelley's Prometheus, and, in a more carefully considered context, Keats's Endymion, are all, in terms of Blake's symbolism, visions of the poet as Orc, like Blake's own painting of the "Glad Day." But Orc is a circular conception, and whether the poet attempts to celebrate the triumph either of him or of Urizen, what he is really celebrating in both cases is the collapse of all progress toward a conclusion of history; in Blake's symbolism, the return of man from "Luther" to where he started six thousand years ago, or "Adam." In Deism the nation has reached the point at which "common sense," or the fallen vision of the world, becomes its dogmatic confession of faith. But this faith assumes the finality of the two primary categories of common sense, time and space. Hence the third course open to the poet in an age of Deism is, first, to visualize the reversibility of time and space, to see the linear sequence of history as a single form; and, second, to see the tradition behind him as a single imaginative unity. These are, more or less, the themes of *Jerusalem* and *Milton* respectively.

Blake told Butts that he was not the author but the secretary of his epic; yet he objects violently to a clear inference from this which he meets in Plato. "Plato has made Socrates say that Poets & Prophets do not know or Understand what they write or Utter,"

he says: "this is a most Pernicious Falshood. If they do not, pray
is an inferior kind to be call'd Knowing?"[6] That is, is the term
"knowledge" to be restricted to the passive awareness of an outward
object, and refused to the conscious state of controlled inspiration
in which poetry is created? Yet Blake's retort does not really meet
the point of the *Ion*, where Socrates puts his finger on one of the
central paradoxes of art: that the most vivid and obviously inspired
art as a matter of fact does often come from artists who are quite
unaware of the larger implications of what they are doing, or have
deliberately ignored them in order to concentrate their powers
on the immediate task in hand. We have even suggested that
Blake's awareness of these implications makes his own characters
more ideographic than they should be in a work of art. We now
have part of the answer to this objection, if it is one, an answer
indicated by the opening of *Milton*, where a number of Classical
writers, including Plato, are attacked and contrasted with the
"more consciously and professedly Inspired Men" of the Bible.

The extent to which a poet may be conscious, in the narrower
sense, of the implications of his own work, depends partly on how
late he comes in his cultural tradition. It is clear that the question
of the poet's relation to society bulks much larger in Milton than
in Spenser, and in Spenser than in Chaucer. But a poet born with
Deists for contemporaries will find his very right to exist questioned
from the start, for dogmatic common sense assigns him at best
only a decorative function in society. Again, his imaginative self-
consciousness will depend partly on the nature of his tradition.
The imagination in Blake *is* the personality, the Selfhood routine
that we usually think of as the personal life of the artist being
to him purely generic. The Hebrew prophets were far less impersonal than the Classical poets, because their vision was more
intense and the social opposition to it more clear-cut; and Christian
poetry, founded as it is on the Bible, inherits this personal tone.
We can see this if we compare Dante and Milton with Homer and
Virgil; though we should note that, for many reasons too complicated to explain here, the main line of Classical vision for Blake
runs through Hesiod and Ovid rather than Homer and Virgil, and
Hesiod and Ovid both gave their personal situations a place in
their visions.

A poet who looks directly at his greatest predecessors and visualizes his own work as a concretion of a literary tradition is following the Hebraic rather than the Classical tradition, Los rather than Orc or Urizen, and is thereby doing what he can to lead culture back to the Golden Age. Pope may have meant something similar when he spoke of Virgil finding nature in Homer, though of course a poet should not be looking for nature. Dante found in Virgil not nature but a human imagination. As a new birth of imaginative power born at the winter solstice, dying on the dead tree and rising in the spring, Jesus was a rebirth of Orc: as the seventh "Eye" or vision of God, extracting a new visionary form out of the earlier "Jehovah" perception; as the Messiah who reformed the earlier prophecies into the new "Word" of a gospel, he was an incarnation of Los. When Blake imagines himself to be a reincarnation of Milton, then, the imaginative power that is reborn is not a different form, as in ordinary life, but the *same* form which in the process of transforming itself has purged and clarified its vision. The relation of Milton to Blake is not the ordinary relation of father to son, for the father never finds that his son is his own perfected self. Jesus, however, owes his divinity to the fact that he was the Son of the same nature as his Father, and the Word or clarified expression of that Father. For Blake, therefore, to imitate Milton is to imitate Jesus, just as, for Virgil, to imitate Homer was to imitate "nature." And for Blake imitation is recreation.

There is no such thing as "reincarnation," in the sense that a "soul" may leave a "body" and then enter another. "In Eternity," says Blake, "one Thing never Changes into another Thing."[7] But there are two possible forms of rebirth. One is the rebirth of Orc, the reappearance of life in a new form, which is the ordinary process of life. The other is the rebirth of Los, the recreation of one vision by another. Milton's imagination was the real Milton, and a deliberate and conscious attempt to recreate his vision, as *Paradise Lost* was a deliberate and conscious attempt to recreate the vision of the Book of Genesis, is the rebirth of the real Milton into the imagination of the poet who makes this attempt. Every great vision is subject to the errors of its age and the Selfhood passions of its creator, but as a culture matures and the Selfhood vision of life consolidates, the imaginative vision also may, if the refining smith is at work within it, become increasingly more accurate and complete. Art does not improve its quality in the course of time, but it may lead to a visionary crisis in time as more and more of its palace becomes visible to poets. But much more is implied here than the commonplace doctrine of temporal immortality, that a poet survives in his work and in the adulation of posterity. If Jesus had been nothing more than a reborn Orc, he would have been merely one more cycle of energy in an unchanged nature, as Orc-Jesus is in *Europe*: the fact that human imagination reaches finality in Jesus is expressed in the doctrine that the end of time is his second coming. Similarly, when Blake visualizes himself as a reborn Milton, he expresses the corollary of this. If, in the Jesus cycle of history, one man's vision returns to another and is recreated with final clarity, a permanent eternal form will appear in time and the fallen perspective of time as a vanishing current will be arrested.

Complete awareness on the part of the poet that the tradition of poetry behind him is not a purely linear sequence but an evolution of a single archetypal form is thus the same thing as a vision of Golgonooza, the whole of human life seen in the framework of fall and redemption outlined by the poets. Once this becomes clear, the missing link in *The Four Zoas* between the vision of contemporary Deism at the end of Night VIII and the beginning of the apocalypse in Night IX is supplied, whereupon the other epic theme, the historical and religious traditions of the nation, clears up as well. If any one visionary attains a final recreation of another's vision, the Man Albion is fully awake in one brain, so that the possessor of that brain is a herald, who not only sees what is coming but is followed by it.

Milton and *Jerusalem*, then, are inseparable, and constitute a double epic, a prelude and fugue on the same subject, for *Milton* is Blake's longest, greatest and most elaborate "Preludium." The lyric "And did those feet in ancient time," which opens *Milton*, is connected even more closely with the theme of *Jerusalem*, and our hymnbooks have rechristened it accordingly. *Milton* is an individual prologue to the omen of something universal coming on. The Last Judgment lies on the distant horizon, and is prophesied in the final line of the poem; and the "Western Gate," the power to realize what the visionary sees to be real, symbolized by the Atlantic Ocean which still blots out Atlantis west of England,

remains closed all through it. *Jerusalem* deals with the complementary awakening in man and the full apocalypse. One is resurrection and the other Last Judgment, corresponding to the first
and second coming of Jesus.

If this sounds like a rather labored attempt to rationalize Blake's
choice of subject, it may not be without interest to examine his
contemporary Wordsworth from the same point of view. While
Blake was pondering his epic, Wordsworth had written part of his,
and had begun with the theme of the poet's mind. *The Prelude* is
a "diffuse" epic because Wordsworth was dealing with a process
of slow growth, and *Milton* is a "brief" one because Blake was
dealing with an instant of illumination, but the identity of subject
is clear enough. It is true that Wordsworth's wish that Milton
could be reincarnated in his own time never went further than
a wish, but that in itself is not a fatal defect. Wordsworth then
announced his next theme, the vision of a fallen world as Paradise
or Atlantis:

> . . . Paradise, and groves
> Elysian, Fortunate Fields—like those of old
> Sought in the Atlantic Main—why should they be
> A history only of departed things,
> Or a mere fiction of what never was?
> For the discerning intellect of Man,
> When wedded to this goodly universe
> In love and holy passion, shall find these
> A simple produce of the common day.[8]

Blake, who read this passage with keen interest, was dismayed to
find that Wordsworth proposed to treat the relation of man and
nature as one of correspondence, each being "exquisitely fitted" to
the other. In other words, Wordsworth was a Deist or natural-
religion worshiper, or at least had enough of that in him to injure
his poetry. Hence he was unable to clarify his vision of the apocalypse, and his *Excursion* is merely a continuation of *The Prelude*,
still concerned with the poetic mind and the inquiring subject.
Worse, this mind is treated, not as imaginative, but as a solitary
and withdrawn Selfhood, a "Recluse." Further, Wordsworth does
not develop a mythopoeic faculty—the discussion of mythology
in the fourth book of *The Excursion* is a singularly barren one—
for he does not really wish to see nature in human form.

The rather different case of Keats may also be mentioned, though Blake has left no evidence of having read Keats. *Endymion* is, in Blake's terms, a brief epic concerned with the poet's mind as a youthful Orc in the state of Beulah. Keats then went on from Beulah to Eden, from the garden of the moon to the city of the sun; and in *Hyperion* he began a vision of the fall of the sun along lines similar to Blake's treatment of the fall of Luvah. But two problems remained unsolved. One was the exact nature of the influence which Milton should exert on the poem, though it was obvious to Keats that it had a peculiar relation to Milton. The other was how to give the theme of the poetic mind the same significance in *Hyperion* that it had had in *Endymion*, the opening of *The Fall of Hyperion* being presumably an attempt to deal with this. Whether this illustration from Keats is considered relevant or not, it is clear that the composition of the fourth English epic is a matter of some difficulty, and even that a fine poem of over four thousand lines should have been treated as a mere *brouillon* by a poet who would never have claimed any superiority to Wordsworth or Keats is hardly surprising.

· 3 ·

MILTON opens with a "Bard's Song" in eternity which inspires Milton to reincarnate himself, and the subject of that song, the contest of Palamabron and Satan, is an expansion of an episode in Blake's own life, his sojourn at Felpham with Hayley. From here on the misunderstandings come thick and fast, and we must walk warily. If we know anything of Blake's biography, we can see that the Bard's Song can be partly interpreted from it: Palamabron is Blake, Satan Hayley, Blake's wife Elynittria, the emanation of Palamabron, and probably one or two of Hayley's relatives or associates are included in the symbolism. It is not necessary to know much of this in order to understand the poem, and by the time we reach the end we are forced to conclude that the Satan of the twenty-seven Heavens and the forty-eight deformed Human Wonders of the Almighty has got rather beyond the eighteenth century author of *The Triumphs of Temper*. It is interesting and valuable to know about Hayley, just as it is interesting and valuable to know in reading *Samson Agonistes* that Milton, like his hero, was blind and a prisoner of Philistines. But the link between

Samson and Milton does not mean that *Samson Agonistes* is an autobiographical poem: it simply means that Milton was the only man who could have written it. Similarly in interpreting Blake's poem a critic should concern himself, not with what a biographer would make out of Blake's relations with Hayley, but with what Blake's imagination made out of them. The latter will be something with which the "real" Hayley has very little, and nothing relevant, to do.

The readiness of even sympathetic readers to confuse a poet's life and his imagination seems to be based on the assumption that the life is real and the poetry a by-product, so that to search for biography in poetry is, from this point of view, searching for the reality under a disguise. The result, in the criticism of English literature, is that the process of interpreting an unchangeable and deliberately created body of poetry has come to be regarded as fanciful, and the process of reconstructing a vanished life out of a chaos of documents, legends, allusions, gossip and guesswork a matter of exact research. But this is an inversion of the poet's own attitude to his life. The linear sequence of events is imaginative material, just as the data of sense experience are, and are there to be cast into the forming crucible of the mind. In the resulting novel or drama we may, if we know the poet personally, recognize things that remind us of past events in his life, but to read the work of art as something to be interpreted by past events is the most arrant Philistinism. To dissolve art back into the artist's experience is like scraping the paint off a canvas in order to see what the "real" canvas looked like before it assumed its painted disguise. A satirist, let us say, goes to visit a friend, and out of some possibly quite irrelevant incident his mind, which is looking for subjects of satire all the time it is awake, evolves a vision of a miser or a parvenu. In his next satire the miser or parvenu will recall his former host to his friends, including the host himself. They will be outraged that he has violated his friend's hospitality; he will be outraged by their ignorance of how an artist's mind works. He will maintain, in short, that "Imagination has nothing to do with Memory,"[9] just as it has nothing to do with sense experience, even when memory and sense experience provide suggestions for the material.

Of course there are writers who use experience not only as

material but as form, who pay off scores and draw systematically from the flayed model. There are also border-line cases where it is impossible wholly to separate art and biography, and Blake's *Milton* is one of them. But we should hardly expect to find that in writing *Milton* Blake turned his back on his whole theory of inspiration, which refuses all importance to any part of a writer's personality except his creative imagination. We shall not get far with *Milton*, in other words, by reading it as a grotesquely over-written account of a squabble between a sulky megalomaniac and a conceited dilettante. It is true that some years later Blake says: "The manner in which I have routed out the nest of villains will be seen in a Poem concerning my Three years' Herculean Labours at Felpham, which I will soon Publish."[10] But he says this after darker shadows had passed across his life, when he was beginning to see his connection with Hayley as part of an organized conspiracy to swindle him, spread the story that he was mad, and exclude his pictures from the Academy. Whatever this passage may refer to, it does not accurately refer to the *Milton* we have, the whole point of which is that Hayley is not a villain and that imaginative enmity and personal friendship can coexist between two men. As a personal revenge on Hayley, *Milton* would have been the most futile revenge ever taken. Besides, Blake had a gift for invective, and could have used much plainer language than the elaborate symbolism he adopts in *Milton* if he had wanted the public to join him in attacking Hayley. We have not yet touched on the real reason for the appearance of Hayley in *Milton*: our present purpose is to insist that the two great illuminations portrayed in that poem do not describe events in Blake's life, but form a visionary drama. Those who have crucial illuminations in their lives and record them in autobiography are mostly converts who up to their conversion have been largely unaware of the mental processes going on within them. Blake being an artist who dealt professionally in illumination, we must see in his poem the vision of the eternal present which he gives us, and avoid confusing it with a remembrance of things past. The importance of this will become clearer as we go on.

The significance of Hayley in his own time has become some-what blurred by his lack of it in ours; yet if one were looking for a representative of Augustan culture who would bring out the whole antagonism between Blake and that culture, one could hardly do better. Even Blake would not have denied that the really great Augustans, Pope and Johnson for instance, had the heat of imaginative energy in them, and fools are of no importance in any age. But Hayley was neither fool nor genius: he was a man of fashionable taste and social intelligence, a patron of the arts and as such a medium between real genius and society. That Blake had genius was clear, and it was the patron's task, as Hayley conceived it, to direct genius into socially acceptable channels. Now as "society" is apt to be conservative and its members something less than brilliant, the artist must, if he is to succeed, hold his genius down to the point at which mediocrities can understand it and conservatives approve of it. The trouble with Blake, thought Hayley, is that he is rather overburdened with genius, and takes himself too seriously; but geniuses, like children, must be tactfully led to understand the world they have to live in. The problem of the poet's relation to society, therefore, should be left to the Hayleys and not to the Blakes to solve.

In a few months Hayley had turned from Providence into a grinning spectre of polite but persistent discouragement which it was impossible to banish. Behind Hayley was the solid body of organized taste he stood for, including many patrons who would, on Hayley's recommendation, give Blake the occasional order for a handscreen. Blake was alone, his wife was ill, he was dependent on Hayley, and all the moral virtue in his character: self-respect, his duty as a husband and provider, his gratitude to his patron, and even, one may say, and Hayley doubtless did say, his duty to his own genius to make it known to the public, all conspired to aid Hayley and postpone his epic. So he tried to fulfill his commissions and learn to be a miniature painter. There were some things harder to learn than that: for instance, the fact that his position toward Hayley's society was that of a flunkey: that he was accepted as a gentleman only because none of them wanted to put him in a livery and pay him a regular salary. As Blake could never have grasped this delicate point, it is not incredible if one of the patrons had to bribe Hayley to keep Blake out of her sight.[11]

Caught in this "silken net" of gratitude, money, friendship and reasonable arguments, Blake had his "Palamabron" mood in which he saw that Hayley was his friend and patron, and a very forbearing and decent one at that, that he was genuinely anxious for Blake's welfare, that he could not help his lack of sympathy for Blake, and that he could not be told to mind his own business because in a sense Blake was his business. At times, too, he was stung into a "Rintrah" mood of fury in which he saw Hayley as a pompous bore and a conceited ass whose only interest in him was to make him over in his own likeness. A muddled man would have finally decided that one of these and not the other was the "real" or "essential" Hayley, but Blake's conception of reality was more complex than that. And if he was thinking of a poem on Milton, he would learn from Hayley that the apostolic succession had gone elsewhere. For it appeared that one Klopstock, a German poet who greatly admired Milton, had written a long apocalyptic poem called *The Messiah*, and that Hayley was returning the compliment to English literature by translating Klopstock into English. However, this only confirmed Blake in his resolve to write on Milton, or suggested it if he had not already made it. Blake decided that Klopstock had defied England to produce the successor to Milton, and that it was up to him to meet the challenge. His brilliant fantasy on Klopstock leaves no doubt that he considered him a kind of poetical Chadband; unfairly, but in the circumstances not inexcusably.[12]

Finally, even Hayley lost his usually triumphant temper, and, no doubt, said the things that an ordinary man does say when exasperated by a great man who is his social inferior. This broke down the deadlock at once. Even if there were mutual apologies and an agreement to forget everything afterwards, Blake had seen, for a few moments, something looking at him out of Hayley's eyes that was not anxiety for his welfare. It was hatred; a half-spiteful, half-horrified mixture of resentment and fear; the response of society to the prophet. After that, Blake knew that neither friendship nor gratitude could ever again tempt him to abandon his genius.

In August 1803 Blake threw a drunken soldier named Schofield (the spelling varies) out of his garden at Felpham, and Schofield went off to take advantage of a wartime hysteria and try to pin a charge of high treason on Blake. Blake was by no means a timid man, but even so the worry hung over him for months, and made all concentrated work impossible. No doubt he did not seriously expect moral virtue to order him hanged, but after all he was on trial with that a possible result of conviction, and Schofield was ready to perjure himself to bring it about. But there was something very curious about the whole business. Why had Schofield come into his garden and made himself offensive? Blake saw evidence that Schofield had "come into the Garden with some bad intention, or at least with a prejudiced Mind."[13] If so, who had sent him? Could Hayley really have been so desperate at his failure to influence Blake in his own direction that he finally, as Blake wrote, "Hired a villain to bereave my life"?[14] It sounds far fetched enough; but Hayley had patronized Cowper, and Cowper had gone mad.[15] He had patronized Blake, and a good many people were saying that Blake was mad. Was it possible, then, that Hayley, having failed either to convert Blake or break his mind, was offering him up as a sacrifice to moral virtue, the sacrifice mimicked by the peasants who carry a figure called "Death" out of their cornfields to free them of bad luck? Blake remembered how:

> Felpham Billy rode out every morn
> Horseback with Death over the fields of corn,
> Who with iron hand cuff'd in the afternoon
> The Ears of Billy's Lawyer & Dragoon.[16]

Here "Death" and "Billy's Dragoon" are clearly Blake and Schofield respectively. This does not mean that Hayley would actually have seen Blake hanged, but he may have felt that a great enough pressure of temporal worries would bring Blake's genius down to a more "normal" outlook. It might also, of course, destroy it altogether, but if Hayley had been responsible for anything in the tragedy of Cowper he was evidently a persistent experimenter. All this, once more, is Blake's creative instinct evolving a dramatic poem out of the situation, and not necessarily Blake's actual state of mind at any given time. When one has a threatening rupture with one and perhaps several more friends, a sick and terrified wife, and a trial for high treason on one's hands; when one is lonely and unable to work through worry; when one has no friends directly acquainted with the situation; and when all this follows close on the heels of the most exultant illumination of mind which produces an intense longing to work, one may not always be sure just what one's state of mind is.

And although Hayley appeared at Blake's trial and gave evidence that helped a great deal, was even perhaps decisive, in acquitting him, Blake still had a poetic theme of some effectiveness. It was rather melodramatic and badly motivated; it was too open to self-pity, and Blake was not fond of martyrdom as a poetic theme. But there is a more important objection to it. Such a theme would make Hayley Blake's enemy, and Blake could make no poetic use of Hayley unless Hayley were his personal friend; unless, as he says, "Corporeal Friends are Spiritual Enemies."[17] The real enemy is the spirit that looked out of Hayley's eyes when Hayley was angry. That is Hayley's Selfhood or Spectre, the Satan in him that hates and tries to destroy all the imagination it finds. It is a weakling's charity to say that we must love our friends in spite of or including their faults: their faults are their diseases, and to love a man's disease is not very friendly to the man. All men are composed of imagination and Selfhood, and all men should cherish the former in themselves and love it in other men, while hating all Selfhoods and trying to annihilate their own. So, while Blake portrayed Hayley's Selfhood as Satan, he wrote friendly letters to its mixture with Hayley's imagination, and did his best to encourage the latter, even to the point of praising Hayley's poems and attempting to illustrate them. But his pencil was shrewder than he, and Blake and Hayley gradually gave each other up. One of Blake's hostile critics, unable to say that the *Songs of Innocence* are bad poems, has wistfully quoted from Hayley's "Little Tom the Sailor" in order to show how bad they would have been if, as he says, Blake had not been supremely gifted as a lyrical poet. Absurd as this is, the equation Blake minus Blake's genius equals Hayley is only a step removed from the real meaning of *Milton*.

When Milton reincarnates himself in Blake and Blake's imagination is purified, Satan is cast out of both of them at once and revealed for what he is. He is a lot of things, but fundamentally moral virtue, the alternative "good" of passive conformity which the world offers the imagination. No one is likely to be tempted by a devil with visible horns and tail, but a decent, respectable friend like Hayley can sing a very siren song to a neglected poet. The "Badman" portrayed by Bunyan as an incarnation of Satan in this world is certainly not an attractive man, but neither is he an untypical product of Restoration society. If bad men could not get along in this world Satan would not be the prince of it. Blake, clarifying this point still further, sees that evil is dangerous in proportion as it is protected and concealed by society. Hypocrisy is more dangerous than crime; self-deception is more dangerous than hypocrisy. The reason why society pays so little attention to its wise men is not that society consists of criminals or hypocrites, but that it consists of "normal" people who sincerely believe in the superiority of common to uncommon sense.

The comparatively trivial nature of the quarrel between Blake and Hayley makes it all the more crucial. Faced with open persecution, one may obediently strike the heroic pose that persecution may inspire even in the indifferent. But it is not in the grandiose but in the petty events of life, where the issues involved seem of too trifling importance to be worth making principles of, that tyranny and the repression of genius achieve their really significant triumphs. The fear of being thought a prig will do far more to weaken the prophet than the fear of social hatred. Again, to the ordinary man, developing the imagination means bringing out the divinity in himself which all men have. To the artist it also means bringing out the genius in himself which most men have not. An ordinary event in an artist's life in which these two aspects of the imagination coincide puts the artist in alignment with his public, providing a common ground of sympathy between the imagination with genius and the imagination without it.

· 4 ·

THE chief difficulty in understanding the "Bard's Song" is that it does not relate a sequence of events, but tells the story of the dispute of Palamabron and Satan and then brings out its larger significance by a series of lifting backdrops. The Biblical symbolism implied rather than expressed in it is worth spending a moment on, as it is of great importance in *Jerusalem*. We all know, the Bard assumes, that Albion was a fourfold Man who in his fall became a strong man, a beautiful man and an ugly man. By a principle which is also important in *Jerusalem*, the events of the Fall are reproduced in civilized life, and the leaders of men may therefore be divided into the strong, the beautiful and the ugly. We shall have to give these three classes the names, not of the Zoas, but of the sons of Los, Los being the genius of civilized life. Let us call them, therefore, Rintrah, Palamabron and Satan, Satan being the youngest born son of Los, that is, the consolidation of error which Los develops out of Urizen.[18]

Rintrah is, as we know, the hermit-prophet in the desert who calls upon an evil world to repent. He is Blake's Elijah who, as Blake says, "comprehends all the Prophetic Characters,"[19] and who in the Gospels is identified with John the Baptist. Blake speaks in the name of Rintrah when he inscribes on the "There is No Natural Religion" plates the prophetic motto, "The Voice of one crying in the Wilderness," and again in the prelude to *The Marriage of Heaven and Hell.* The voice of Rintrah is heard again in any outcast or rebel prophet, an example in Blake's day being Byron, whom Blake addresses as Elijah in the exordium to *The Ghost of Abel.* The Rintrah or strong class of men is thus a "Reprobate" class: its members are always looked upon as dangerous nuisances. They accept none of the conventional values of society and are revolutionaries, iconoclasts and blasphemers of Nobodaddy. Satan, on the other hand, is the prince of this world: he is the spirit of inertia which incarnates itself in compromise. The worshipers of Satan accept established religions, philosophies and social conditions because they are established; they observe all the commandments of the law from their youth upwards, and their days are long and peaceful in the lands they possess. They, therefore, are "The Elect from before the foundation of the World," and their worldly prosperity is a sign of their inward grace.

Between these two stand most honest men, including Blake himself, who are represented by Palamabron. Few artists can become hermits and denounce society from the outside: most of them must work within it, come to terms with it, and improve its culture without any desire either to accept or to quarrel with its anomalies. Such an artist thus spends his life between two opposed duties, both of which may be called "good." There is his duty to his imagination, the necessity within him to say what he must say. There is also his duty not to destroy the effectiveness of his work by prematurely exasperating society; there is his love for his wife, family and friends; there is a need for serenity and quiet. Of course society is always trying to turn everything under its control, especially the artist's family, into traps to cripple his genius; but nevertheless it remains true that, as we said earlier, there is much that is really good in moral good, when attached to the imagination and not made an end in itself. The moral law is the subconscious foundation of the imaginative life, as physical law is the subconscious foundation of the conscious vision. The artist who lives and dies in society without surrendering his imaginative honesty is of the class Blake calls "Redeemed."

As Rintrah is Elijah or the spirit of prophecy, so Palamabron is Moses or the spirit, as opposed to the letter, of the law. Associated with Aaron, Moses is an evil being, a spokesman of the morally virtuous Satan who wrote the ten commandments. But there is much that is good in moral good, and when Jesus came he enabled his followers to release real from moral virtue and attach the former to their imaginations. That is why Jesus appears on the Mount of Transfiguration accompanied by Moses as well as Elijah, and why he said in what seems a paradox that nothing would pass away from a law which he came to supersede. The redemption of Moses, the emancipation of morality from routine obedience to the inward discipline of wisdom, is the Biblical archetype of the saving of the artist from the bondage of the law.

In the eleventh chapter of Revelation we are told of the martyrdom of two "witnesses," who are evidently Moses and Elijah again,[20] by Satan. Their dead bodies "lie in the street of the great city, which spiritually is called Sodom and Egypt, where also our Lord was crucified"[21]—in other words the *civitas terrena* of the historical cycle. In the next chapter we are told of Satan's attack on a "woman clothed with the sun" which is temporarily thwarted by the archangel Michael, in Daniel the champion of the spiritual Israel. The woman is a part of Jerusalem, the city of the sun and the Bride of Man, and the fact that the Satan who attacks her is a dragon whose tail "drew the third part of the stars of heaven" refers to the Satanic origin of the present "Mundane Shell." Now just as Jerusalem is visualized both as a city and as a bride, depending on whether the vision is of Eden or Beulah, so the *civitas terrena*, Sodom, Egypt, the fallen Jerusalem, may also be visualized as a harlot who is Satan's mistress. This harlot of course is Rahab, who appears in the seventeenth chapter with the further associations of Babylon and Rome.

The Bard's Song tells how Satan, who is ugly only when recognized for what he is, and who before that is a gentle, persuasive and attractive spirit, asked Los if he could do Palamabron's work for Palamabron's own good. The work is represented by the curious symbol of plowing the mundane shell, which helps the embryos within it to sprout upwards into eternity: we have met it before in the ninth Night of *The Four Zoas*. The plowman is traditional in the English epic as a symbol of the visionary: there is Langland's Piers who is identified with Christ, the idealized plowman of Chaucer, and Spenser's St. George, whose name indicates his agricultural origin.[22] Los agreed, and disaster resulted, a disaster corresponding in the archetypal vision to Luvah's seizure of the sun. Even so, it was difficult to see what was wrong because Satan was convinced that he was right and that any disaster had been the result of Palamabron's resentment at being displaced. There was a deadlock here which lasted until Satan went over to Palamabron's ally Rintrah; in other words, lost his temper. That cleared the air, in the way we have explained, and Palamabron was thus "redeemed" by the anger of the "reprobate" Rintrah, even though it was found on the other side. The account in Revelation speaks of a conflict between Satan and Michael, which implies an association between Michael and Rintrah, though the characters are distinguished by Blake (and perhaps a corresponding one, not mentioned, between Palamabron and the "affable archangel" Raphael). The connecting link is the reference in the Epistle of Jude to Michael's dispute with Satan over the body of Moses (Palamabron).[23] We shall meet this dispute again in *Jerusalem*.

Once the Satanic nature of Satan has been thoroughly understood, a backdrop rolls up and we see the original Satan who is the prince of the starry universe, whereupon a second backdrop is raised and we see a woman, Satan's harlot mistress, who this time is neither Rahab nor Tirzah but a still more inclusive character called Leutha, a kind of Lilith who is said to have begotten the whole race of demons who make up Antichrist. She is thus a combination of Tirzah, Vala and Rahab, and represents the unified symbol of objective nature corresponding to the Luvah of *Jerusalem* who represents the whole process of fallen life. Like Luvah, she is a fertility spirit in the minor poems. Blake leaves her undeveloped, and goes back to Vala for *Jerusalem*, but here she is the original "female will" of the Fall, and after she appears, history begins and proceeds onward to its climax, the coming of the Saviour of Man whom all society agreed to be a reprobate, blasphemer and transgressor.

The Bard's Song shocks many of those who hear it because it associates a great deal of the kindly and decent behavior of moral people with guilt. Milton, who also hears it, is not shocked, but he is deeply impressed. There was much in his own masterpiece that had grown out of political disillusionment—after the English revolution had gone its complete circuit from Charles the First to Charles the Second he was forced to see that there was no poetic justice in experience. Like the author of Job, he was then forced to consider the problem of why the innocent suffer. The only possible answer is that there is no such thing as innocence; we are all equally caught in the trap of a fallen world. Milton gave this answer as Job had given it before him, and he had given it in terms of the Orc cycle which the degeneration of his Satan illustrates. *Paradise Lost* tells us that the whole world since the Fall is in the remorseless grip of this cycle and can be redeemed from it only by Jesus; that it is the business of the visionary to proclaim the Word of God to a society under the domination of Satan; and that the visionary's social position is typically that of an isolated voice crying in the wilderness against the injustice and hypocrisy of the society from which he has sprung.

All this Milton had seen: what he had not seen was the Behemoth and Leviathan that stood at the end of his vision as they stood at the end of Job's. The fallen Adam lives in a fallen world. In *Paradise Lost* that world is substantially the same world as the one Jesus creates in Book VII; but if Satan is now the prince of it he must have produced a radical change in its nature. It is wrong, therefore, to associate Satan solely with chaos and moral evil: what we call creation is a part of chaos; moral good is part of moral evil, and creation and moral good both belong to Satan. Blake had already asserted that "in the Book of Job, Milton's Messiah is call'd Satan."[24] Milton, therefore, wants to re-enter the world and gain a new vision. This vision will do two things for him: it will enable him to see the physical world as Satanic rather than divine, and it will enable him as a result to see his "emanation," or totality of the things he loves, as part of himself and not as a remote and objective "female will." The former is the climax of the first book of *Milton*; the latter is the climax of the second. (Milton's emanation, Ololon, is "sixfold," there being six women in Milton's family, and so can be viewed from her seamy side as Rahab and the five daughters who are the five fallen senses, and of whom Tirzah is the chief.) The two books also give us the obverse and reverse of the same instant of illumination. The first book is an apocalyptic restatement of the vision which Michael shows Adam at the end of *Paradise Lost*, and in it the entire time and space of the fallen world is seen, not as emerging from the loins and senses of fallen Man, but as reintegrated with him. The second part shows us the counterpart of this, the rejection of the mirage which is implied by the acceptance of reality. It is essentially the vision of *Paradise Regained*, in which Satan offers Christ so many of the "good" things of a fallen world that it eventually dawns on us that the world and the devil are the same thing, and that thing an illusion.

· 5 ·

MILTON's journey to the fallen world, or part of it, repeats the journey of Moses through the wilderness to the boundaries of the Promised Land, and, like Moses, he fails to cross the Jordan and enter Canaan, though all the forces of evil coax him to do so. We shall explain what this means later. Moses, Palamabron, Milton and Blake (and as far as possible Hayley) all belong to the "Redeemed" class which has to be separated from the Satanic element within it. As such, Milton is what may loosely be called a Puritan: he is a mixture of Christian vision with the sterility of moral virtue and rationalism. Those who see him descend, the four Zoas, the "nameless shadowy female," Rahab and Tirzah, even Rintrah and Palamabron, all see in him the Moses of the Exodus, the lawgiver of a hidden thundergod of mystery and cruelty, and look on him with terror or delight, according to their natures. Only Los sees the significance of the return. We said in commenting on *Visions of the Daughters of Albion* that Puritanism was the ancestor of Deism in the sense that everything wrong with Puritanism, its vestigial natural religion, its Pharisaic morality, its scholastic rationalism and its belief in the infallible goodness of the conventionally orthodox, had in the following century been precipitated as Deism. Los sees that Milton must be on his way to reinforce, not the Deists, but the visionaries who have inherited the other half of Puritanism, its belief in the civilizing Word of God; that Deism is a consolidation of error, and that Milton's return is consequently a sign that "the time is at hand," as the New Testament says. So Los allows Milton to pass into the world, Milton enters Blake's "left foot," Blake, in one of those tremendous metaphors which are a main reward of reading him, stoops down and binds the material world as a sandal on that foot, and unites with Los, the spiritual form of time. This union completes the recreation of Milton's vision.

Milton knew from his Cambridge days at least that he was someday to write a great epic of the eternal world, and hence for many years he was under the contradictory impulses of accomplishing his divine mission and of postponing it until he was fully capable of it. Some of his irascibility during that period may be accounted for by the mental strain arising from this paradox of frustration. Certainly his choice of epic themes reflects it. Adam and Christ are both tempted to premature imaginative acts, acts which are not so much wrong in themselves as attempts to force God's hand before the lapse of time which his will has decreed. The sin Adam commits and Christ resists was thus a sin against Los, the Holy Spirit of Time which, as Blake complains, remains a "vacuum" in Milton. In Milton's personal case we must distinguish between the necessity of waiting for his epic to ripen and the temptation to postpone it indefinitely. The latter, which was evil but appeared to him under the guise of patriotic duty, corresponds to the temptation of Blake by Hayley to postpone his epic in favor of more practicable ways of supporting a wife.

This distinction, applied to *Paradise Lost*, affords an interesting criticism of it. Granted for the moment that the punishment of Adam and all his progeny for an act which God knew he would commit is defensible, and redounds in some way to God's credit. Granted even that it is possible to work out a coherent scheme of creation and fall with a prehuman and yet moral God. Even so, the climax of the whole poem, the vista of human life stretching from the creation to the apocalypse which Michael shows Adam, fails to make the very point that justifies it artistically. The descendants of Adam, apparently, suffer for a length of time arbitrarily set by God and terminated by him at his pleasure for inscrutable reasons. But inscrutable reasons will not satisfy an adult inquirer.

The poem would come to a far richer and more suggestive conclusion if some shape in time could be portrayed, a process which goes on in time but can last only a certain length of time, producing first Jesus and then the apocalypse as its simmer and boil, so to speak, so that history itself becomes the gradual recovery of Paradise by God awakening in Man. Jesus himself suggests such a process when he speaks of the Holy Spirit as continuing his work until the last day. If Milton had done this, the Holy Spirit, who is Los or the imaginative form of time, would not have remained a vacuum in his poem. Thus the integration of Milton and Blake with Los results in a complete vision of the shape of time, in which time and history are seen as a single human form, "the world of Los, the labour of six thousand years."[25] The failure of England to rouse itself from sleep in Milton's life may, by weakening his sense of historical crisis, have caused the omission of the form of time from his epic; and the failure in its turn indicated that Los's labor was not yet completed. But a later poet may say:

> if Bacon, Newton, Locke
> Deny a Conscience in Man & the Communion of Saints & Angels,
> Contemning the Divine Vision & Fruition, Worshiping the Deus
> Of the Heathen, The God of This World, & the Goddess Nature,
> Mystery, Babylon the Great, The Druid Dragon & hidden Harlot,
> Is it not that Signal of the Morning which was told us in the
>   Beginning?[26]

When Milton returns to the world, he finds that European civilization is on the point of subsiding into a phase of metropolitan imperialism which will make the pomp of Britain and France one with Nineveh and Tyre. That is the wheel of the Orc cycle. On the other hand, "The whole extent of the Globe is explored," and sharp limits are being set to further centrifugal expansion. What Milton sees first of all is war, and a promise of more and bigger wars. But he also sees that there is, for the first time in history, the possibility that the entire human race will consolidate into a unit, that out of warfare and trade rivalries some kind of international law and commerce will eventually be born. If this happens, it means that Man is subconsciously developing a circulatory and digestive system analogous to that which goes on in ourselves. This constitutes the lower part of the palace of art, Allamanda and Bowlahoola, the heart and stomach of the individual, and the commerce, science and law of Man. Once the heart and stomach of a larger human body appear, a larger human brain will soon follow them, and the Golden Age of Atlantis, when "all had originally one language, and one religion," will be restored. The religion will be the religion of Jesus, the Everlasting Gospel, and the language will be the tongue of Albion. Blake does not mean by one religion the acceptance of a uniform set of doctrines by all men: he means the attainment of civilized liberty and the common vision of the divinity and unity of Man which is life in Jesus. By one language he does not mean English: he means, quoting the Bible and repeating Milton in *Areopagitica*, that all the Lord's people will become prophets: all will speak the language of the imagination, and the perception of the sun as a company of angels will be the rule rather than the exception. Further, he does not say that all were originally of one race or kingdom or empire, and though he symbolizes humanity by the name of his own nation, his "Albion" has nothing to do with the frantic jingoism which a confused idea of the same symbolism might easily develop, and has developed in our day.

A larger human brain will be developed by Man when the whole of human life is seen and understood as a single mental form. This single mental form is a drama of creation, struggle, redemption and restoration in the fallen life of a divine Man. This drama is the archetype of all prophecy and art, the universal form which art reveals in pieces, and it is also the Word of God, the end of the journey of our intellectual powers. And here the antithesis between imagination and memory, the intellectual powers and the corporeal understanding, the vision of life and the vision of death, reaches its crisis. Everything that has ever happened since the beginning of time is part, Blake says, of the literal Word of God.[27] The ordinary historical conception of human existence as a dissolving flux in linear time is therefore the literal approach to life, the corporeal understanding based on memory. History as the total form of all genuine efforts of human culture and civilization is the canon or Scripture of human life. History as linear time is the great apocrypha or mystery which has to be rejected from it.

The primary social function of the epic is to teach the "nation" its own traditions, and in Blakean terms this means recreating dead facts into living truths, the vanished spectres of tradition into the imagination's eternal and infinite present. One of the many reasons why the Bible has a unique claim on our cultural interest is that the Bible shows the evolution of history as past time into history as present vision not only as an accomplished fact but as a process. There is a good deal of what passes for history in the Old Testament, but the more we try to read it as history the more puzzled we get. As history, it is not only often dreary and absurd in itself, but its subject, the annals of an obscure race in a remote land, hardly seems to have the direct connection with our own imaginative needs which the Bible's reputation may lead us to expect. As history, its truth is of little value, and to believe that the accounts of Abraham's dealings with his wives are historically true does not make them less tedious and puerile. And as we read further, we begin to suspect that the motive of all this history is to force the pious Hebrew to accept the crucial importance of the deliverance of his ancestors from Egypt in order that he may unquestioningly follow, in its least details, the ceremonial law which was the final form of that alleged deliverance. Tyranny is hereditary in structure, and is rationalized as the necessary result of a chain of causality in time stretching back to some original contract or covenant which we are powerless to alter and are bound to observe. This is the priestly reason for preserving traditions, and this union of history and law is the "old testament," the clasping of dead hands over a legal contract in a vanished past.

The prophets fought against this moral bondage and Jesus delivered us from it. But the prophets did not turn their backs on their national history: they recreated it, and brought out of it the eternally present archetypes of the fall and redemption of man. Jesus therefore, in completing their work, did not destroy the law, but fulfilled it: he transfigured it by demonstrating its true meaning. The freedom of the Gospel brings with it the freedom to read the Old Testament mentally instead of corporeally, as the allegorical poem of a great civilization, not as the collected legal and historical superstitions of petty barbarians. When Paul reads the stories of Abraham and his wives, they suggest to him the allegory of the two cities which develops out of him into the gigantic Christian vision of St. Augustine's great book and of Blake's Prophecies:

For it is written, that Abraham had two sons, the one by a bondmaid, the other by a freewoman. But he who was of the bondwoman was born after the flesh; but he of the freewoman was by promise. Which things are an allegory: for these are the two covenants; the one from the mount Sinai, which gendereth to bondage, which is Agar. For this Agar is mount Sinai in Arabia, and answereth to Jerusalem which now is, and is in bondage with her children. But Jerusalem which is above is free, which is the mother of us all.[28]

What is true of the history is equally true of the law, which has always been read allegorically by the Christian. The Gospel teaches us not to despise the letter of the law, but to read it as "letters," spiritually, with the full energy of an active and intelligent mind. The law tells us to offer our first fruits to God. The corporeal understanding interprets that as a command to waste our best efforts in an attempt to bribe a ravenously greedy demon of the sky. The least touch of the imagination releases us from the act, and gives us the anthropologist's insight into its meaning. The full imagination transforms the offering of first fruits into one of the archetypes of the human mind: the identification of the created thing with the God who made it. The Bible teaches us to read like this: it is the primer of a cultured and civilized man. It teaches us to see the sun not as a polished guinea but as a company of angels, and it teaches us to see in the records of all past time not a chaos of tyrannies, but the eternal and eventually emerging form of human life, a form which is the larger body of Man and of God. In Blake's symbolism this is the redemption of the moral virtue of Palamabron, or Moses, by the prophetic power of Rintrah, or Elijah, both of whom attend a divine Man in his transfiguration.

But—and here Blake breaks away from most of those who would agree with him thus far—the same contrast of law and gospel reappears in Christianity itself. If the Old Testament is transformed from the puerile to the profound by being read imaginatively, we can hardly plunge back into literalism when we turn to the Gospel. The belief, with its implications, that Jesus existed on earth two thousand years ago, which is the literal or historical core of the New Testament, is, whether in itself true or false, not the basis of the Christian religion. On this level the essence of Christianity is the compulsory acceptance of a vanished event, and if we pull the words "compulsory" and "vanished" out of that clause we may see that tyranny and mystery, the two marks of the Beast, are still involved in such an acceptance of Christianity. It may be objected that, while *Julius Caesar* and *King Lear* are equally products of Shakespeare's imagination, there is a considerable difference between the evidence we have for Caesar's existence and the evidence we have for Lear's, and that the distinction is something we should take into account in reading the New Testament. But it is that very distinction between what must have been true and what may not have been true that is the real trap for the imagination, and the New Testament goes out of its way to prevent us from walking into it. That is why we have four Gospels with different and often quite inconsistent accounts of Jesus' life, and why the historical proofs for that life are hermetically sealed within the Bible itself. No Evangelist has the slightest interest in writing a biography of Jesus. The Jesus about whom a biography can be written is dead and gone, and survives only as Antichrist. The Evangelists tell us not how Christ came, but how he comes: they are concerned not with a vanished past but with the imagination's "Eternal Now." The timid will protest that we are here in danger of dissolving the reality of Christianity into a vaporous allegory: Blake's answer is that the core of reality is mental and present, not physical and past. Past events do not necessarily dissolve in time, but their existence in the eternal present depends on imaginative recreation.

Each of the seven Orc cycles or "Eyes" of history bears a divine name representing the conception of God which it has. The "Eye" of Jehovah is the Hebrew religious imagination. In Blake's *Vision of the Book of Job* Jehovah and Job have the same face because Jehovah is inside Job's mind. But each cycle shows the same antithesis between the imaginative and the legal and historical conceptions of its God. The aggregate of the former is the real Word of God; the aggregate of the latter takes the form of the twenty-seven "Churches" into which these Eyes, or at least the last five of them, are divided. The crisis in Milton's vision comes when he sees Satan as this aggregate of Churches, and, by casting him off, shows that he identifies the conception of the church with history and the law. For the natural man will always try to reach eternity through a historical tradition and a legal contract, whether he associates them with Moses or with Jesus. And the Christian

Church is, as much as the Jewish Church, a historical continuum stretching back to an alleged provision made by Jesus for the observance of a ceremonial and moral code based on the memory of his past appearance in time. Milton's predecessor Luther understood something of this: he understood too that it was spiritually dangerous to be illiterate, and that the essence of Christianity is the direct individual recreation of the Word of God. But as he tried to replace the twenty-sixth church with a twenty-seventh, he is now himself a part of what he condemned.

The temptation of the churches could refer either to joining or reforming an old church, or to founding a new one. The latter aspect of it brings up a curious relationship between Blake and a number of new religions, which may have struck the reader already. (By this time in the poem Blake and Milton are the same person, and Milton's temptation is also Blake's.) If Blake had told us that he had gone to visit the wise men of the East and had learned from them the doctrines which he has set down in his poems, we should know what he meant, or ought to by now. When Madame Blavatsky tells us the same thing we are not sure what she means. If Blake had told us that he had copied a vision of an ancient Atlantic Continent from golden plates given him by an angel we should know what he meant. When Joseph Smith tells us the same thing about the Mormon Bible we are not sure what he means. When Blake tells us that the English are a lost portion of a spiritual Israel or that pain and sin are an illusion, we can accept what he says without question. When Anglo-Israelites and Christian Scientists expound what sound so much like the same doctrines, unquestioning acceptance of what they say would commit us to a great deal more. All these churches start, from Blake's point of view, with a kernel of genuine vision, otherwise they would attract no adherents at all, but sooner or later a ceremonial literalism, or an acid test of compulsory belief in vanished events, appear in them as in every church. All such religions are exclusive, in the sense that however devoted one might be to any one of them, it would take a very impressionable person to believe in them all. But the reader of Blake can see the real or imaginative form of each one of them, and disregard their nonpoetic husks.

If Milton or Blake had joined or founded a church, therefore, they would have lost the real Church, the total vision which is the

city of God, and gained a sect. No visible church will ever identify
itself with civilized art, purge itself of all legal and historical conceptions of truth, and attain the absolute clarity of present vision.
In the long run all churches are more interested in the rational
than the creative aspect of the mind, in excluding from the truth
of what they say the falsehood of what everyone else says instead
of including its truth, in binding together in a ceremonial and
moral unity a chosen people of spiritual Jews. The source of their
revelation has no such interest. Job is a dramatic poem, the Song
of Songs a love-poem, the Apocalypse an allegory, the teachings
of Jesus mainly parables, and all the prophecy and doctrine is
continuously visualized and illustrated. Only the poetic imagination can comprehend the Bible, and the Bible introduces that
imagination to a mental world of inspired wisdom, culture and
beauty in which all religions are one.

This visionary tolerance is the opposite of the rational tolerance
which holds that all religions are equally attempts to solve an
insoluble mystery. This is Deism: the trumpet which gives out
such uncertain sounds can hardly prepare anyone for "Mental
Fight," and will soon dwindle into the sheep-bell tinkle of moral
virtue. The place of honor in art goes to the artist who has passed
through religion and come out on the other side. Such an artist,
in Blake's symbolism, has gone with the church to the upper limit
of Beulah, where it visualizes itself as the Bride of Christ and man
as a creature of God, and has then burst through the ring of fire
into the Eden where man is no longer a creature but a creator and
is one with God. There he is a citizen of the free city which all
human life strives to realize in this world, and which is the Word
of God or body of Jesus; and whenever he speaks to other men in
the language of the creating mind he recreates that Word in time.
Anything short of this will drive him back from the ring of purging
visionary fire into the mundane shell, the world of nature and
reason, where all religions attempt to include the natural religion
which is an "Impossible Absurdity."[29]

The closing words of the above two paragraphs are intended
to suggest that the titles of the sets of aphorisms which introduce
Blake's canon, "There is No Natural Religion" and "All Religions
are One," contain the whole of his thought if they are understood
simultaneously. Any sectarian bigot could assent to the former

alone, and any Deist to the latter alone. But to say "There is No Natural Religion" without being a Thwackum, and at the same time to say "All Religions are One" without being a Square: that is the whole secret of wisdom. The reasoning Thwackum and the naturalistic Square are descended respectively from the theological Jews who thought Christianity a stumbling block and the pagan Greeks who thought it foolishness. To the one Blake says: "If Humility is Christianity, you, O Jews, are the true Christians," and of the other he says: "If Morality was Christianity, Socrates was the Saviour."[30] Humility and morality are the phobias induced by a passive mind, and neither attitude "contributed" anything at all to real Christianity, which was traveling the opposite way.

Similarly, the corporeal understanding of Milton sees him as a hideous twofold monster, half Puritan and half Deist, part of his mind sunk in a superstitious awe of a foolish God, part looking ahead to a society in which everyone will be tolerant about books and have reasonable views of divorce. Blake's poem attempts to recreate the central vision of life, based on the Bible, which made Milton a great Christian poet. In this perspective the tug of war in him between the humble Puritan and the moral Deist becomes an accident of an age which is dead and gone. Blake is, therefore, trying to do for Milton what the prophets and Jesus did for Moses: isolate what is poetic and imaginative, and annihilate what is legal and historical. This is also what he is trying to do for himself, and there will always be a curse on any critic who tries to see the Christianity and the radicalism of Blake as a dichotomy instead of a unity.

· 6 ·

WHAT we now have is a vision of mankind united in peace and brotherhood, their unity sustained not only by law, commerce and an international science, but by a common understanding of that view of life from which all religions and arts derive their meaning. This is a perfectly comprehensible idea, and an attractive one; but as soon as we have grasped it, Blake becomes obnoxious again. There is no reason to suppose that civilization at this level would affect the order of nature much more than it does now: that is, it would impose a good deal of discipline on Vala, or nature on earth, but it would not restore Enion from the depths of the sea or shake Enitharmon out of her crystal house. Yet, Blake says, as long as the sea surrounds us and the stars revolve above us, so long will man be a natural and a fallen man, and so long his natural tendencies will lead him to murder and tyranny. England and America cannot enter a Golden Age until the sea between them gives up its dead, and all men cannot unite except into one Man.

The Apocalypse speaks of a "millennium," a thousand-year period of peace and security, at the end of the six thousand years of history, corresponding to the day of rest which followed the six days of creation. But all through the millennium, apparently, a gigantic power of evil, symbolized by the giants Gog and Magog, consolidates, and the struggle between the divine and Satanic principles, called Armageddon, does not stop short of a final assault on the stars. Those whose vision ends with a millennium or Utopia established in this world are still looking to history and the law, except that they put their Golden Age and their idealized legal contract in the future instead of in the past. Just as the tyranny of the past is the heart of all tyranny, however, so the mystery of the future is the heart of all mystery, and to judge our actions in terms of the perfunctory and generalized gratitude of posterity is merely inverted Pharisaism. But if the past can be recreated into the present, so can the future, and if the creative life begins, as we are told in *The Four Zoas*, with the merging of imagination and history, it must end, as we are told in *Jerusalem*, with their separation, when time no longer exists.[31] This brings us to the other aspect of the illumination of Milton and Blake, the vision of the world as the labor of Los displayed at the end of the first book.

The natural man is, speaking in terms of conscious vision, an imaginative seed. Just as the seed is a dry sealed packet of solid "matter," so the natural mind is a tight skull-bound shell of abstract ideas. And just as the seed is surrounded by a dark world which we see as an underworld, so the physical universe, which surrounds the natural man on all sides, and is dark in the sense that he cannot see its extent, is the underworld of the mind, the den of Urthona, the cave of Plato's *Republic*. The majority of seeds in nature die as seeds, and in human life all natural men, all the timid, all the stupid and all the evil, remain in the starlit cavern of the fallen mind, hibernating in the dormant winter night of time. They are embryos of life only, infertile seeds, and die within the seed-world. The possibility of life within them remains in its embryonic form of abstract ideas, shadows and dreams. Some of the dreams are troubled visions of the real world of awakened consciousness; others are the nightmares of paralyzing horror which all minds in a stupor of inertia are a prey to. Here and there a seed puts out a tentative shoot into the real world, and when it does so it escapes from the darkness of burial into the light of immortality. Such a seed, however, would only have begun its development, for the vegetable life is not the most highly organized form of life, because it is still bound to nature. The animal symbolizes a higher stage of development by breaking its navel-string, and this earth-bound freedom of movement is represented in our present physical level.

The bird is not a higher form of imagination than we are, but its ability to fly symbolizes one, and men usually assign wings to what they visualize as superior forms of human existence. In this symbolism the corresponding image of nature would be neither the seed-bed of the plant nor the suckling mother of the mammal, but the egg, which has been used as a symbol of the physical universe from the most ancient times. We think of cosmic eggs chiefly in connection with Gnostic and Orphic imagery, but the account of creation in Genesis as a watery chaos surrounded by a shell of "firmament," which the Spirit of God, later visualized as a dove, broods upon and brings to life, also has oviparous overtones. In Blake the firmament is the Mundane Shell, the indefinite circumference of the physical world through which the mind crashes on its winged ascent to reality. To the inexperienced eye the egg appears to be a geometrical stone, but the imagination within the egg soon demonstrates that it is something much more fragile. The same is true of the Newtonian universe, the rock rolled against the tomb of divine humanity.

Whether we think of the natural man as a seed in the soil, an embryo in the womb, or an unborn chicken in the egg, however, in any event he is "self-centered," or egocentric. That is, he is a center of perception: everything he regards as real he also regards as outside himself. His senses are all turned outward towards this reality, and everything he takes "in" immediately becomes unreal and "spectral." Socially and morally, he tries to be an armored crustacean alert only for attack or defense: the price of selfishness is eternal vigilance. The closer society comes to the state of nature, the more tightly men huddle together to be on guard against possible dangers from without. This kind of Argus-eyed tenseness proceeds from a sealed prison of consciousness which Blake calls "opaque," opacity being his symbol for the dead matter to which all nature tends, and of which the stone, the infertile egg, the undeveloped seed, the sealed furnace which we met in *The Four Zoas*, and the herd-unity of the tyrannical society, are all images. As soon as a man acquires anything that can be called wisdom, this hostile and suspicious fear relaxes and he begins to be aware of an inner balance. This changes him from a center to a circumference of perception. His imagination begins to surround his experience like an amoeba: he becomes capable of sympathy because he has given other people shelter in his mind, and no longer thinks of them as opaque; and, as he can thereby see through them, he is equally capable of disinterested enmity. This process of mental growth Blake calls "opening a centre."[32]

The man with an opened center is now a "microcosm," a little world in himself. This term generally implies that nature is a corresponding "macrocosm," an objective universal order to which man should adjust himself. But a macrocosm could only be a larger human body: the end of vision is the living form of humanity, not the mathematic form of nature. But how does one get from one to the other? What relation has the physical appearance of nature to the real mental form or body of Man? There is a curious passage in Exodus which tells how Moses went up to Mount Sinai and was permitted to see the "back parts" of God.[33] These back parts are traditionally interpreted as the material world, hence Moses' vision was a vision of the totality of mystery, like Job's of Leviathan and John's of the Great Whore. Here the Bible comes perhaps nearer than at any other point to suggesting what is expressed in the Icelandic myth of Ymir, and in Blake by the description of the binding of Urizen by Los in seven ages, that nature is the scattered and broken body of a human God or Titan.

What we see in nature is our own body turned inside out. From our natural perspective we cannot see this for the same reason that a fly crawling on a fresco cannot see the picture: we are too small, too close, too unintelligent, and have naturally the wrong kind of eye. But the imagination sees that the labyrinthine intricacies of the movements of the heavenly bodies reflect the labyrinth of our brains. It sees that lakes and pools reflect the passive mirror of the eye. It sees that the revolving and warming sun is the beating and flaming heart of the fallen Albion, and is reproduced in the "Globe of Blood" within our own bodies. It sees that the tide flows and ebbs in the rhythm of Albion's fallen lungs. It sees that the ridges of mountains across the world are Albion's fractured spine. It sees that the natural circulation of water is a human circulation of blood. It sees that nature is the fossilized form of a God-Man who has, unlike other fossils, the power to come to life again. It sees that what vibration-frequencies are to color, what a prosodic analysis is to a poem, what an anatomized cadaver is to a body, so the physical world is to the mental one, the seamy side of its reality. And it sees all this because it realizes that when we see ourselves as imprisoned in a huge concave vault of sky we are seeing from the point of view of a head that is imprisoned in a concave vault of bone.

The telescope helps us to escape from this last dilemma, but introduces us directly to a more crucial one. Blake says that everything in eternity has what he calls a "vortex" (perhaps rather a vortex-ring), a spiral or cone of existence. When we focus both eyes on one object, say a book, we create an angle of vision opening into our minds with the apex pointing away from us. The book therefore has a vortex of existence opening into its mental reality within our minds. When Milton descends from eternity to time, he finds that he has to pass through the apex of his cone of eternal vision, which is like trying to see a book from the book's point of view; the Lockian conception of the real book as outside the mind on which the vision of the fallen world is based. This turns him inside out, and from his new perspective the cone rolls back and away from him in the form of a globe. That is why we are surrounded with a universe of remote globes, and are unable to see that the earth is "one infinite plane."[34] But in eternity the perceiving mind or body is omnipresent, and hence these globes in eternity are inside that body.

Before the Fall, Man was absolute wisdom, and was the circumference of everything. Nothing then existed outside Albion: sun, moon, stars, the center of the earth and the depth of the sea, were all within his mind and body, a body fully conscious of being alive, not only in its brain, but in all parts of itself down to the feet. Hence "opening a centre," as described above, is the imagination's way of reversing the fallen perspective of the world, and uniting an individual imagination with the universal one. This union is completed when in our vision the recurrent throb of existence which we know as time becomes the pulsating heart of a sleeping Man, and the revolving globes in the sky, seen as within instead of outside a human mind and body, become the corpuscles in a human bloodstream which is also the fourfold river of Paradise. That is what Blake means when he says that time is a pulsation of the artery, and space a globule of blood.[35] In eternity all the homes of the soul, the body, the palace, the city and the garden, are one; and the eternal community of men is also the real presence of a divine body, whose blood is the new wine created from the water of nature.

· 7 ·

THIS enlightenment destroys the "female will" for Milton and enables him to attain his emanation Ololon. We have spoken before of the ambiguity of the word "consummation" in referring to the two chief aspects of the Last Judgment, the burning world and the sacred marriage. In *Milton*, too, the sacred marriage follows the vision of the absorption of nature into a fiery city. One may compare in Dante the poet's passage through fire at the top of the mountain of purgatory, which completes the emancipation of his vision, and which is followed by his meeting with the young virgin Matilda in the garden of Eden. This in its turn is related to the larger scheme in which Dante's epic predecessor takes him to what in Blake is the upper limit of Beulah, the ring of fire surrounding Eden, at which point the emanation Beatrice takes over. *The Faerie Queene*, too, was designed to end with an epithalamion; this end was never reached, but Spenser did write a poem in this genre for his own wedding, a poem which is part of his total vision. In Donne's Anniversaries, the death of the poet's emanation, who is a child like Ololon, transforms the world into an "anatomy" or skeleton for the hyena of reason to crunch; thus Donne presents the same vision in terms of its corresponding fall.

These parallels have been suggested to show how important

the image of the emanation, the aggregate of all that a poet loves visualized as a bride, is in poetry. It is missing from Milton, and its absence is a radical defect in his vision. There is, of course, much in Milton's portrayal of the "female will" in its sinister aspect which is quite sound. He felt that a wife and family were not so much hostages to fortune as to Satan, that the family was the main breach in the visionary's defenses through which all the powers of compromise come pouring with their threats and their wheedling. The visionary's right to cut himself loose from his family when his genius is in mortal danger was an essential part of Milton's conception of liberty, and was perhaps the real reason for writing the divorce tracts. All this Blake agrees with, having no doubt suffered himself from Hayley's attempts to "act upon my wife,"[36] and he makes it clear in *Jerusalem* that when Satan is the prince of this world,

> A man's worst enemies are those
> Of his own house & family.[37]

Thus, the fall of Adam in *Paradise Lost* is ascribed to his idolatrous adoration of Eve, against which he was particularly warned by Raphael. The Fall began by the separation of Eve from Adam, and once that had taken place Eve became allied with the reasoning serpent. This closely approximates Blake's account of the fall of Albion and his surrender to Vala, while "the vast form of Nature, like a Serpent, roll'd between."[38] The role of Delilah in *Samson Agonistes* is symbolically identical with that of Eve, and the scene in which Samson casts her off shows more clearly what the divorce tracts mean than they do themselves. But one is struck by the fact that Milton never sees beyond this sinister "female will." His vision of women takes in only the hostility and fear which it is quite right to assume toward the temptress who represents moral virtue, like Delilah among the Philistines or Eve before the tree of knowledge, but which is by no means the only way in which women can be visualized. There is no emanation in Milton; no Beatrice or Miranda; no vision of the spiritual nature of love. The love of Adam and Eve before the Fall is shown us only to make clear what dangers are concealed in it, and to contrast with the lust that emerges when those dangers are realized.

This is not simply the result of the nature of Milton's tempta-

tion theme: it is a missing link in his poetic argument. In *Paradise
Regained,* for instance, the proposal to tempt Christ with women
is rejected out of hand by Satan as too obviously useless. Doubtless
it was, but Satan twice assails Christ on the side of his hunger, and
it is not apparent why he should have had so much higher an
opinion of food. But the real crux of the question is *Comus. Comus*
is introduced and concluded by a spirit who tells us that he has
descended from a higher state of being associated with pastoral
life and the gardens of Adonis—in other words, Beulah—to give
instruction to the inhabitants of a fallen world. As he says, in a
passage Blake may well have been thinking of when he put his
little quatrain beginning "I give you the end of a golden string"
into *Jerusalem*:

> Yet some there be that by due steps aspire
> To lay their just hands on that golden key
> That opes the palace of eternity:
> To such my errand is, and but for such,
> I would not soil these pure ambrosial weeds,
> With the rank vapors of this sin-worn mold.[39]

His home is in the Edenic island of the Hesperides, which (in an
obscure passage in the Trinity MS) is associated both with England
and with the "jealous ocean" which surrounds it, the ocean associated in Blake with the jealousy of Tharmas and Theotormon.
The climax of the action is the arrival of the nymph Sabrina, who
belongs to legendary British history and is one of Blake's daughters
of Albion. As Albion is Atlas, in Blake this means that she is also
one of the Hesperides. Comus is a son of Circe, and Circe, whose
home is in a western island, is Blake's Rahab. Like his mother,
Comus is a sorcerer who transforms men into a lower state of
being, and who is a master of hallucination. He is also associated
with night, and it is clear that Blake's description of the rioting
stars of Enitharmon's "crystal house" in *Europe* who represent the
quizzical indifference of the revolving heavens to man owes a good
deal to his interpretation of Milton's masque:

> We that are of purer fire
> Imitate the starry choir,
> Who in their nightly watchful spheres,
> Lead in swift round the months and years.[40]

We should expect *Comus*, then, to tell us something about the fall of Albion, or at any rate something of major visionary importance; but all that follows is an unsuccessful attempt to seduce a virgin. Now in the character of Comus Milton has begun to sketch a Satan far more essentially Satanic than his later prince of throned powers, and to make a seduction a climacteric revelation of evil is a grotesque anticlimax. Similarly, the frozen negative moral virtue of the Lady is praised as something good in itself, whereas in fact it is something much worse than anything Comus proposes to her. The coy mistress who represents an elusive nature is the most evil of all Blake's symbols, and he associates her with the virginal Diana who turned Actaeon into an animal, which was exactly what Circe did to her lovers, and with the Medusa who freezes the living men of Generation into the stony world of Ulro. Blake, therefore, could hardly have read without a wry smile this praise of a virgin who in his own mythology is a whore:

> Hence had the huntress Dian her dread bow
> Fair silver-shafted queen forever chaste,
> Wherewith she tamed the brinded lioness
> And spotted mountain pard, but set at nought
> The frivolous bolt of Cupid, gods and men
> Feared her stern frown, and she was queen of the woods.
> What was the snaky-headed Gorgon shield
> That wise Minerva wore, unconquered virgin,
> Wherewith she freezed her foes to congealed stone?
> But rigid looks of chaste austerity,
> And noble grace that dashed brute violence
> With sudden adoration, and blank awe.
> So dear to heaven is saintly chastity,
> That when a soul is found sincerely so,
> A thousand liveried angels lackey her. . . .[41]

A thousand lackeying angels in livery can belong only to Nobodaddy.

One should not miss the quiet humor in Blake's handling of this point. In the second part of *Milton*, Ololon appears in the world as a twelve-year-old girl, a child with a child's untouchable beauty, not yet a bride of a sacred marriage but a breastless "little sister" like the one in the Song of Songs. She is respectfully referred to as the "Virgin Ololon" for several pages; but as the physical world burns up before Milton's eyes, and all images of a separated female will cease to mean anything, her virginity splits away from her and runs shrieking into chaos, as the bride Ololon, purified of the stain of virginity, stands before the poet in his final consummation.

The Epilogue to the great poem is exquisitely managed. With the four Zoas sounding the trumpets of the Last Judgment in his ears, Blake falls into a swoon, and revives in his garden with his wife bending anxiously over him, and before him a singing lark and a wild thyme, the early-rising bird and the early-flowering plant of the returning spring. One thinks of an earlier William and Catherine awakening on an Easter morning with the church bells ringing as the poet's dream of the triumph of Christ gives place to its audible symbol:

> Tyl the day dawede . these damseles daunsede,
> That men rang to the resurreccioun . and with that ich awakede,
> And kallyd Kytte my wyf . and Kalote my doughter,
> "A-rys, and go reuerence . godes resurreccioun."[42]

Those who find the Prophecies noisy will perhaps not see that it is only the unearthly quiet of Blake's tone that enables him to rise to the two visionary pinnacles of the poem and descend in the conclusion to his own backyard without a sense of anticlimax. Just before his head clears Blake gets a fleeting glimpse of still another vision:

> Rintrah & Palamabron view the Human Harvest beneath.
> Their Wine-presses & Barns stand open, the Ovens are prepar'd,
> The Waggons ready; terrific Lions & Tygers sport & play.
> All Animals upon the Earth are prepar'd in all their strength
>
> To go forth to the Great Harvest & Vintage of the Nations

The last line, which has an entire plate to itself and no mark of punctuation after it, brings the whole poem, as it were, to an expectant dominant seventh, and reminds us that *Milton* is the prelude to a longer poem on the theme it announces, the building of a continuing city in the England of the Satanic mills.

THE "more consolidated & extended Work" of *Jerusalem* bears the date 1804 on its title page, and we are perhaps to take that as the year in which the conception of the poem took its final shape, though the text we have can hardly be so early. Its main arguments were no doubt fairly clear in Blake's mind long before his visit to Felpham was over, requiring only the experience of the Schofield trial to achieve their final form. In a letter dated January 30, 1803, Blake speaks of learning the Hebrew alphabet,[1] and he must obviously have got much further in the language before beginning *Jerusalem*, as that poem, for better or worse, shows, in its treatment of the Bible, the sudden access of significance in detail which always takes place when one turns from a translation to its original. But as *Milton* and *Jerusalem* constitute a single epic, it is unlikely that any long interval of time separates the end of *Milton* from the beginning of *Jerusalem*. The same symbolism runs through both poems, and the same method, employed in all sections except the second part of *Milton*, of starting with a challenging prose manifesto and following it with a lyric which summarizes the main theme of the section. *Jerusalem* is exactly twice as long as *Milton*, having four parts, one hundred plates and four thousand odd lines to *Milton's* two parts, fifty plates and two thousand odd lines; and *Milton* describes the attainment by the poet of the vision that *Jerusalem* expounds in terms of all humanity.

We have explained the importance in Blake's thought of the conception of the recreation of the predecessor which led him to write his poem on Milton. But the real relation to a predecessor is the common relation of both to the archetypal vision. The recreation, for instance, of Leonardo's Mona Lisa by Pater is an attempt to bring out the archetypal significance of that picture as a vision of what Blake calls a female will. Leonardo and Pater are to be connected by their relationship to that vision, not directly with each other. It was Milton's function to recreate the form of Christian vision for an English public, and any attempt to continue his tradition will involve a renewed study of his archetype, the Bible. In reading *Jerusalem* there are only two questions to consider: how Blake interpreted the Bible, and how he placed that interpretation in an English context.

The imaginative vision of human life sees it as a drama in four acts: a fall, the struggle of men in a fallen world which is what we usually think of as history, the world's redemption by a divine man in which eternal life and death achieve a simultaneous triumph, and an apocalypse. These four acts correspond to the four parts of *Jerusalem*. We have dealt with Blake's doctrine that the only defense of error is confusion and mystery, and that every victory of imaginative vision consolidates a body of error into a comprehensible form, and makes it obviously erroneous. Each part of *Jerusalem* presents a phase of imaginative vision simultaneously with the body of error which it clarifies. Part One, addressed to the public, sets the Fall over against Golgonooza, the individual palace or watchtower of art from which the visionary may see nature in its true form as a sleeping giant. This perspective was attained in *Milton*, the theme of which is thus incorporated into the larger design. Part Two, addressed to the Jews, sets the vision of the world under the law over against the evolution of the Bible out of history. Part Three, addressed to the Deists, contrasts the coming of Jesus with the resistance to his teachings which Deism expresses. Part Four, addressed to the Christians, deals at once with the apocalypse and the final epiphany of Antichrist.

Apart from this pattern of contrast, the structure of *Jerusalem* does not greatly differ from that of *The Four Zoas*. Parts One and Two deal with the Fall and the Orc cycle, and Part Three with the crisis of opposition between the imaginative and the natural views of the world precipitated by Jesus. This was the subject of Nights VII and VIII of *The Four Zoas*, and it was undoubtedly from these Nights that Blake derived the antithetical scheme which runs through the later poem. Part Three ends precisely where Night VIII of *The Four Zoas* ended, in the Deism of Blake's day and a vision of an indefinite cyclic recurrence of tyranny expressed in its penultimate line: "where Luther ends Adam begins again in Eternal Circle." Part Four of *Jerusalem* and Night IX of *The Four Zoas* both deal with the apocalypse. But instead of the dazzling pyrotechnics of the earlier poem, we find in *Jerusalem* almost no working-up of climax. Most of the fourth part is given over to defining the Antichrist, and as we continue to read about him, we discover that we are on our way toward an apocalypse, which flashes on us only in the very last plates of the poem. Blake seems to mark his crisis only as it is frequently marked in music, by an intensification of the original theme. We look back to see where the reversal of perspective occurred, but find nothing very tangible, and after so much churning, the mere silent appearance of the expected butter may seem almost an anticlimax. Remembering that it was precisely in the approaches to the apocalypse that *The Four Zoas* foundered, we may see in this suppression of crisis the key to the structure and meaning of the whole poem.

We are not ready to examine this suggestion yet, but it may help to explain why *Jerusalem* makes on the reader the initial impression of a harsh, crabbed and strident poem. Blake first planned his idea of the beautiful book in the age of high rococo, the age of Watteau and Mozart, which in such genius came perhaps as near as any other in history to realizing Blake's ideal of art as the urbanity of the city of light, a clarity of vision beyond all faith from which everything that is not humane has disappeared, a spontaneous yet disciplined speech in language, outline and melody spoken only in a world of fully conscious innocence. He wrote *Jerusalem* in the age of Goya and Beethoven. And this new kind of genius has the analytic quality of a revolutionary age which will not be satisfied with an impressive appearance designed to conceal an ugly reality. Thus Goya refused to take the Spanish nobility as a conventional symbol of greatness, and would paint a queen as an aging syphilitic whore. In doing so Goya was simply taking her literally at her physical or "face" value. *Jerusalem* is analytic in the same sense: its primary effort is to see the Antichrist as the face of things, the literal appearance of a fallen world. That is the fundamental difference in approach between *Jerusalem* and *The Four Zoas*, which latter has much more of the rococo spirit, and much loveliness. *Jerusalem* is harsh: the Lord's Prayer is not very euphonious when said backwards, and *Jerusalem* is continually muttering or howling sinister spells to compel the devil to appear in his true shape. The motive that drives Blake on through his gloomy and tormented visions is the same motive that drove Goya through his recording of the disasters of war. In both cases the charge of ugliness is irrelevant, and intensity, honesty, a grim resolve to portray experience as it is regardless of its horror, and a passionately sincere clairvoyance, are the prophetic qualities involved.

It is also of course obvious that by the time he wrote *Jerusalem* Blake was so accustomed to thinking in terms of his symbols that the latter had become a kind of ideographic alphabet and had thereby lost much of their immediacy, just as the letter "s" no longer conveys a very vivid impression of a hissing serpent. We shall consider this question again. In the third canto of the first book of *The Faerie Queene*, Una, separated from the Red Cross Knight, is threatened by a lion who becomes tame and accompanies her, who then overthrows "blind Devotion's mart," and is eventually killed by Sansloy, by whom Una is carried off. That contains a sequence of hieroglyphics to be translated roughly: "Truth without holiness, as evidenced in Henry's suppression of the monasteries, which though corrupt and not part of the true church, were brutally and wantonly destroyed, acquires a destructive power which results in anarchy." And there is no doubt that such an episode, which fills forty-four Spenserian stanzas, would be given in Blake within even less space than its summary takes up here. The justification for Blake's kind of dehydrated epic is a simple matter of literary honesty. Poems must take their own forms, and these precipitates of meaning are the forms which poetry takes in Blake's crystallizing mind. An epic of such forms cannot be expanded: it can only be padded, and padding is immoral—if Spenser is not padded it is because he thought in different forms. Blake's epics are brief enough to be examined plastically, reread so that their structural unity emerges along with their linear meaning, and as part of it. The beauty of *Jerusalem* is the beauty of intense concentration, the beauty of the Sutra, of the aphorisms which are the form of so much of the greatest vision, of a figured bass indicating the harmonic progression of ideas too tremendous to be expressed by a single melody.

No student of Blake can fail to be deeply impressed by the promptness with which Blake seizes on the machine as the symbol of a new kind of human existence developing in his own time. His poetry is an imaginative mechanism designed to fight the machine age; it has the "wheels within wheels" of Ezekiel's vision which will reverse the direction of the "wheel without wheel, with cogs tyrannic Moving by compulsion each other" which we see in all natural machinery, including the movements of the stars. Hence his vision of the apocalypse is, like that of the Bible itself, presented in a curiously mechanical context, and the word "machinery," in its old-fashioned sense of the articulation of an epic plan, is only too applicable to the symbolism of *Jerusalem*. As a recreation of the Bible, *Jerusalem* fits the parts of that vast and chaotic book together with a more than theological precision. We are expected to make every dry bone in the Bible live, to recognize that its catalogues and genealogies preserve a fossilized memory of otherwise forgotten history, to appreciate the puns and associations of the proper names in their Hebrew significance. *The Spectator* tells us that the Elizabethan occult poet William Alabaster once preached a sermon on the opening verse of Chronicles, "Adam, Seth, Enosh," which by giving the words their Hebrew meanings supplied him with the text, "Man was placed in misery."[2] This is the sort of intensity that *Jerusalem* requires. There is more to be said for this method of reading the Bible than is likely to be said for a long time, but rightly or wrongly Blake insists on it, and there is no help for it but to plunge after him expounding in his wake. The courteous reader who will follow us through our commentary should be rewarded by hearing in the cacophonous noises of Blake's wonderful poem the squeaking axles of "Chariots of fire" lining up for Armageddon.

· 2 ·

LET us start again with Blake's division of history into seven periods identified with the Biblical Eyes of God, and called by Blake Lucifer, Moloch, Elohim, Shaddai, Pachad, Jehovah and Jesus. Each Eye is an Orc cycle, yet each, as an Eye of God can only be the eye with which man sees as God, is a plateau of imaginative development, and there is, thanks to Los, some evolutionary development in their sequence. The sixth of these, the vision of Jehovah or the Hebrew religious imagination, is, like the Palamabron of *Milton*, who is associated with Moses, a mixture of genuine imagination and moral law, and was purified into the former by Jesus. The vision of Jehovah, thus purified, constitutes the essential Bible. But the Jehovah cycle begins where Hebrew history begins, at the Exodus, and the Book of Genesis forms a prelude incorporating fragmentary reminiscences of earlier cycles, so that the Bible as a whole gives a fairly connected account of the six thousand years which stretch from the establishment of the present human body, or Adam, the chief event in the third or Elohim Eye, to the apocalypse accompanying the return of Jesus. But, as each cycle anticipates in its beginning the ultimate resurrection, and repeats in its decline the original Fall, it is neither practicable nor desirable to interpret the Bible too rigorously in terms of the Seven Eyes.

The first two Eyes are the titanic and gigantic "Druid" periods, which produced Stonehenge and were still surviving in Mexico in a very debased form when the discovery of America sounded the first warning bell of the end of time. They are pre-Biblical, though the story of Noah and Ezekiel's reference to the Covering Cherub relate to them. Adam and Eve bring us to the third Eye, and Abraham, under whom the practice of human sacrifice was finally dropped, to the fourth. Pachad, or "fear,"[3] the fifth Eye, is worshiped by Isaac. (It may be noted in passing that while it was doubtless easier to create a pre-Adamic mythology before the time of Darwin, titanic human beings at least would not leave fossils: they would be the changes in nature and "living forms" which we infer from fossils. "Man is the Ark of God,"[4] said Blake, and Noah's ark was Noah's body.)

The Book of Job may go back to the Shaddai period, El Shaddai, "The Almighty," being the name by which it most frequently refers to God. The hero of this drama is not a man but Man, fallen and restored humanity, whose fall is a disaster that turns his house into a ruin and his land into a wilderness, and whose boils and plagues represent the physical misery of the state of nature. The Satan who inflicts these disasters is therefore that nature, the Luvah or world of Generation into which we have fallen. A threefold accuser (this will meet us again), a young self-confident reasoner, and a nonco-operative wife or emanation then make their appearance. The argument is based on the forbidden kind of knowledge: Job's comforters accuse him, or at least the Man he represents, of moral evil, and he defends himself in terms of moral virtue. But at the end God shows him that the question is not a moral one at all: that the source of his misery is simply the nature of the world he is in, symbolized in the irresistible power of Behemoth and Leviathan, with a vision of whom the poem concludes. There is no apocalypse in Job, only restoration, and that rather a perfunctory one, but there is a perception of the restraint of chaos in it which suggests that, whatever its date, it records a phase of the archetypal vision fairly close to the establishment of the two "limits," which interposed a permanent order of nature between men and annihilation.

Besides Job, there are other echoes of what may be pre-Hebraic visions of the fall of Man. The Sisera of Deborah's exultant war-song seems to have some connection with a Man against whom the stars in their courses fought and who was slain while sleeping in a tent by a treacherous female, the act being celebrated by an infuriated prophetess who hounds men on to war like Boadicea.[5] The tent appears in *Milton* as a symbol of the portable universal home which in eternity every man carries about with him, and the nail driven through Sisera's head has obvious crucifixion and Promethean links. Deborah sat under a palm tree, and Blake, in his usual fashion, associates her with another Deborah in Genesis who was buried under an "oak of weeping." Man "between the Oak of Weeping & the Palm of Suffering"[6] is thus fallen under the power of a female and vegetable world, nailed like Jesus between two other trees.

Samson is introduced as an Orc, a gigantic national hero who fights against foreign tyrants. There are many features in his story which make us think of a sun-god and (as in the incident of the foxes) a lord of the power of fire. But as he goes on to his eventual death in the ruined temple of a Philistine city, this vision of Orc expands, as it should, into a vision of fallen Albion, a Titan imprisoned by the power of a female will. In *Paradise Lost* Milton associates Samson with the fallen Adam,[7] and in the peroration of *Areopagitica*, where he speaks of England as "a noble and puissant Nation rousing herself like a strong man after sleep, and shaking her invincible locks," with the awakening Albion. One of the best of Blake's early paintings is the one called "Glad Day," a picture of Orc as the spirit of the rising sun. (It may also be an imaginative self-portrait, in which case it represents the assumption of the character of Orc by the poet, as in *Kubla Khan* and Collins' *Ode on the Poetical Character*.) Twenty years later Blake added a note to this picture beginning with the words: "Albion arose from where he labour'd at the Mill with slaves"[8]: the echo of *Samson Agonistes* indicates the unifying of Orc, Samson and Albion in his mind.

The account of the Fall at the opening of Genesis, not being originally a part of the vision of Jehovah, has to be supplemented by the latter. The garden of Eden described there covers what for the purposes of the Bible is the world, the ancient civilization which stretched from Egypt to Mesopotamia. Of the four rivers of Eden, the Nile of Egypt and the Euphrates and Tigris of Mesopotamia are three: the fourth, Pison, is traditionally connected with India, but according to Blake this river appears in the fallen world as the Arnon, which flows westward into the Dead Sea. The Pison in Genesis surrounds the land of Havilah, which Blake associates with Vala, and the Arnon, also called Storge by Blake, which is Greek for "parental love," is connected with the possessiveness which makes the family so powerful a brake on imaginative development, and repeats in each generation the binding of the infant Orc.[9]

In the unfallen world, which was the body of a Man, these rivers were the circulatory system and the four unfallen senses, channels of the pulsing artery and the globule of blood which are the real time and space. Four rivers in an underworld also make their appearance in Classical mythology. The garden of Eden, therefore, was the unfallen world, and the fallen world, not the vague wilderness outside Eden into which Adam is supposed to have been driven, but the historical tyrannies of Egypt and Babylon which Eden became. Genesis does not explain this, nor that the unfallen Eden must have been a civilized kingdom as well as a garden: we have to infer these things from such hints as Isaiah's reference to "the children of Eden which were in Telassar,"[10] a city of Mesopotamia. But that is why for the rest of the Bible the real Fall is visualized as a subjection to the tyranny of Egypt or Babylon, and redemption as deliverance from it. The historical Egypt and Babylon, however, have little to do with the Biblical legends about them: in the Bible Egypt and Babylon are usually states of prophetic vision, the nature of which is suggested by some of the phenomena in the historical kingdoms.

The hero of Blake's symbolism is Albion, the spiritual form of his own public, and the character in the Bible who corresponds to Albion is therefore the eponymous ancestor of the Israelites, that is, Israel, or Jacob, and most of the stories about Jacob are interpreted by Blake as reminiscences of Albion. Albion when he falls comes under the domination of Orc or Luvah, life in the fallen world, out of which both Satan and Jesus proceed, and of Vala, the female will of an objective nature eventually revealed as Rahab. Luvah thus has a connection with Esau and Edom, already mentioned, and Vala may be dimly descried in the "daughters of fraud,"[11] Leah and Rachel, for whom Jacob had to serve a cheating taskmaster. In the story of Jacob's ladder we catch a glimpse of the unfallen Albion whose connection between heaven and Charing Cross has since dissolved. In the angel who lames Jacob and changes his name to Israel we see Luvah again, the genius of his fall, the Satan of Job.

The incident in Jacob's life which chiefly interests Blake, however, is his descent with his progeny into Egypt. This means that Man has forsaken his emanation Jerusalem, his bride-land (occasionally also called Rachel in the Bible), and has fallen under the domination of tyranny and mystery, the Whore whose name is Egypt as well as Babylon. Jacob has twelve sons, one of whom, Joseph, falls into a deep pit, a pit with much the same significance as the cave of Plato, the physical universe which is the embryo or underworld of the mind. Joseph then finds himself in Egypt and in prison, both symbols of the Fall, the theme of the Great Whore turning up again in Potiphar's wife, and becomes an interpreter of dreams.

The Fall is completed when Jacob and his eleven other sons follow Joseph into Egypt, and the Hebrews sink under all the tyrannies of the Selfhood, the "furnace of iron," as Egypt is later called. This furnace is familiar to us as a symbol of the fallen body. Blake also calls it a brick-kiln, because the making of bricks represents the Egyptian tyranny in the Biblical account. Just why is not clear: perhaps because the brick is a symbol of a mathematic form constructed out of the deadest part of the material world. The pyramids, though not exactly of brick, are a link in the same imagery.[12]

The chaos of nonexistence below death is represented by the sea, and a flood in the Bible means an imaginative collapse. Thus when Noah, who contained all animals within his ark, and is to that extent a reminiscence of unfallen Albion, sent out a raven and dove who did not return, he knew that the flood was over, but that in the new world animals would be permanently separated from human life. In Blake the sea which drowned out Atlantis is the spilt blood of Albion, and the "Red Sea" of the Bible indicates a connection with blood in its name. And although universal floods no longer occur, yet the symbol may still mark the beginning and end of a historical cycle. Hence when we read of Pharaoh's daughter drawing the infant Moses out of the water of the annually flooded land of Egypt, we know that a new cycle has begun and that a distinction between "Hebrews" and "Egyptians," *i.e.*, men who can be redeemed as opposed to men who cannot, is being established.

The Egyptians, being now plunged in the depths of Ulro, fall a prey to various plagues which represent their subjection to the bondage of nature. The plague of darkness is the most obviously symbolic of these, and we have quoted the explanation of it in the Wisdom of Solomon. The turning of the waters of the Nile to blood is a grim parody of what the Nile was in Eden, and the lice and flies and frogs and hail are, like the boils of Job and the apocalyptic locusts, not disasters inflicted by a malicious God, but simply natural events in a world of which Satan is the prince. The plagues end with the slaughter of the Egyptian firstborn, the interpretation of which we must leave for the moment. The crossing of the Red Sea marks the final break between the Egyptian and Hebrew cycles, and confirms the collapse of the one and the birth of the other.

With the Exodus the Jehovah cycle properly speaking begins, for, as God says to Moses, "I appeared unto Abraham, unto Isaac, and unto Jacob, by the name of God Almighty [El Shaddai], but by my name Jehovah was I not known to them."[13] We now have a new appearance of vital energy or Luvah, personified by Moses. Now Luvah is subject to the action of both imaginative and natural forces: he may be transformed by Los or transform himself into Urizen and Satan. These two possibilities are represented in the Bible by the pairings Moses-Elijah and Moses-Aaron, and in the Exodus account by the pillar of fire and the pillar of cloud. Here it is Moses and Aaron who are associated, and so the cycle runs its inevitable course, or rather its undirected and aimlessly wandering course, to the point from which it started in Egypt. The Jehovah of the burning bush becomes the Jehovah of the moral law, hidden in Mount Sinai, and the road to the Promised Land becomes a pathless wilderness. With the erection of the brazen serpent and the golden calf (Luvah, being a dying god, is always associated with sacrificial animals, including the lamb, bull and ox), the new cycle loses its vitality.

We are familiar with this, but in *Jerusalem* the symbolism is expanded to include the sequence of events up to the entry into Canaan. This is preceded by the crossing of the Jordan, which marks the same point in the Hebrew cycle that the Red Sea crossing marks in the Egyptian one. As they near their Promised Land, the Hebrews find themselves opposed to hostile tribes and kingdoms, Moabites, Amorites, Amalekites, Canaanites and so on. These all represent what the Philistines have come to represent since Blake's time, life on its natural plane of conventional stupidity. But though the Hebrews were under a divine command to exterminate all such aspects of the Selfhood, they did nothing of the kind, but merged with them. One tribe, Levi, the priests of the degenerate Jehovah whom Aaron represented, has no land but has instead forty-eight cities within the other tribes. In the second part of *Milton* Satan appears not only as the twenty-seven churches already discussed, but as "Forty-eight deformed Human Wonders of the Almighty," which are these Levite cities, or false religion in the aggregate.[14]

Canaan, therefore, is Egypt all over again, and the crossing of the Jordan represents a re-entry into Egypt or Ulro, the mundane shell or cave of the mind. The Jordan is in the Bible more or less what the Styx and Lethe are in Classical mythology. The fact that Moses never entered Canaan thus has a twofold significance. His death outside the Promised Land means that what he represents, the spirit of the Hebrew law or vision of Jehovah, was not good enough; but his death outside the fallen Canaan means that he was redeemed and not rejected by Jesus, which is why he appears with Elijah on the Mount of Transfiguration.

Of the enemies the Israelites had to fight to get into Canaan, some are giants, Og of Bashan and Sihon of Heshbon being most frequently mentioned. A giant is an obvious symbol of the tyranny of size, and these giants are really "spectrous forms," abstract ideas, creations of terror and mystery which the Hebrews themselves have placed before their own kingdom, like the statues in *Erewhon*. And giants, we are told elsewhere in the Bible, sprang from the union of the sons of God with the daughters of men—that is, from the surrender of the divine imagination to the female will. Now we remember that Milton in his descent passed through the "vortex" of his eternal vision, and after he did so the vortex rolled backward and appeared as a body of remote globes. Similarly after the Israelites have crossed the Jordan, these giants, or forms of nature which the Hebrews are trying to pass through and external-ize, roll away from them into a vast dead heaven over their heads:

> For the Chaotic Voids outside of the Stars are measured by
> The Stars, which are the boundaries of Kingdoms, Provinces
> And Empires of Chaos invisible to the Vegetable Man.
> The Kingdom of Og is in Orion: Sihon is in Ophiucus.
> Og has Twenty-Seven Districts: Sihon's Districts Twenty-one.
> For Star to Star, Mountains & Valleys, terrible dimension
> Stretch'd out, compose the Mundane Shell, a mighty Incrusta-
> tion
> Of Forty-eight deformed Human Wonders of the Almighty....[15]

The Israelites first approached the Promised Land from the south, in Blake's symbolism the zenith or head of unfallen man, but the invasion of Canaan came across Jordan from the east, or center, the loins of another natural cycle. The prophets speak of an apocalyptic entry into Canaan by the Messiah from the south, through Edom, in Blake's symbolism the upper gate of Beulah. A reference to the south turns up in a corresponding place in the Prose Edda.[16]

The crossing of the Jordan, therefore, is the Jehovah version of the Fall, in which the role of Adam is taken over by the eldest son of Jacob, Reuben, who stands by synecdoche for the others. In Part Two there is a graphic account of the establishing of the limit of contraction, with its five imprisoned senses, in terms of this symbolism. The refrain which runs all through the account is "They became what they beheld": the familiar doctrine that we see the world as monstrous because our minds are contorted. And the creation of Reuben fills those who see it with horror or ridicule because the natural man, a life proceeding to death, is to the vision-ary eye the nightmare life-in-death that thicks man's blood with cold. Even for us, who are used to it, there is no more terrifying vision than a ghost, or spectre, a human form at once dead and alive.

Occasionally the meaning of a place-name will show us what kind of allegory we are reading: Heshbon, the capital of Sihon, means "reasoning"[17]; the valley of Rephaim, where the Israelites fought the Amalekites, means the "valley of ghosts"; and the place at which the Israelites crossed the Jordan was called Adam, a fact which connects more closely the Palestinian symbolism of Milton's descent with the diagram of "Milton's track" which Blake draws to represent it.[18] It should be remembered too that, in spite of the great slaughter of enemies recorded in the Book of Joshua, a harlot named Rahab, who helped let the Hebrews in, was carefully spared. The scarlet thread which she hung from the window turns up in *The Four Zoas* as the "line of blood that stretch'd across the windows of the morning."[19]

The image of God carried by the Hebrews was an "ark." The true ark of God is the human body, as Jesus implied when he identified his body with the temple. But as the Israelite culture declined, the term "ark" became attached to a tabooed object, jealously guarded by priests, causing plagues and death to those who touched it, heavily curtained, and used as a palladium in war. What the Hebrews really had, therefore, was an image of the female will or Vala, who later got control of the Jewish temple and the Christian church in the same way. When the Hebrews finally took Jerusalem, made it their capital, and brought the ark into it, Jerusalem thereby became the fallen Jerusalem on the same level with Egypt and Babylon. This fallen Jerusalem is described in the Apocalypse in a verse already quoted as "the great city, which spiritually is called Sodom and Egypt, where also our Lord was crucified." And as the real Jerusalem is the bride of the spiritual Israel, Blake's Albion, so the fallen Jerusalem is called a harlot, especially by Ezekiel. We shall return to this later.

The numbers four and three in *Jerusalem*, as in *The Four Zoas*, are respectively the numbers of infinite extension and of cyclic recurrence. *Jerusalem* has four parts, and the end of the third brings us back to where we started. Numbers built up of fours, such as sixteen and sixty-four, signify imaginative achievements, like the Bible and Golgonooza; numbers built up of threes, notably nine and twenty-seven, are associated with Antichrist. Similarly in the Book of Revelation, where the sacred or imaginative number is seven, the Antichrist is represented as a series of sixes. Twelve, the product of four and three, is the number of humanity as it is born into the fallen world, with its imaginative and natural tendencies fighting one another for its soul. The twelve sons of Jacob thus represent humanity, and, as there is no real place for Adam in this symbolism, his position is occupied, as we have noticed, by the eldest son Reuben. This is not so much because he is called "unstable as water" or spoken of as defiling his father's bed, as because he found "mandrakes" in the field and gave them to his mother.[20] The appropriateness of the mandrake, the human-shaped vegetable which shrieks when uprooted, as a symbol for the natural man, needs no elaboration.

The fall of Joseph into a pit has been mentioned; his brothers threw him in because they resented his dreams, one of which was that the sun, moon and "eleven stars" bowed down to him. The appearance of a Selfhood among the stars is a primary vision of the Fall, and Joseph's misadventure corresponds to Isaiah's account of the hurling of Lucifer from heaven, which is mentioned by Jesus and recurs in the apocalyptic dragon who draws down a third of the stars with his tail. The twelvefold Zodiac thus represents, as it does in *Europe*, idolatry in the aggregate: that is, as the twelve sons of Jacob stand for the whole human race, so the Zodiac stands for all the false gods invented by man and suggested by an external nature, specifically the stars. They are the "Twelve Gods of Asia" who appear at the climax of *Milton*, and who are symbolized in Aaron's breastplate. The old story of the philosopher who fell down a well while gazing at the stars perhaps suggests a certain sympathy with Blake's interpretation of the story of Joseph. So in a way does the story of Icarus, who was stellified as Boötes, a constellation identified by Blake with Arthur and by implication with Albion.[21] This identification implies another between Daedalus and Los which will remind the modern reader of the artist-hero with whom the author of *Ulysses* identifies himself. In *Jerusalem* the building of the mundane shell, which was assigned to Urizen in *The Four Zoas*, is given to Los, so that Los is the architect of the physical world, for which an apt symbol is the labyrinth, the serpentine coiling body of mystery with a monster at its heart, the spiral or vortex, in which all things open into a mental world, as it is seen from our side.

Once settled in Canaan, the wheel began to turn again, each of the seven great cycles having a number of subsidiary "churches" within it. When a "ruddy youth" named David appears mysteriously and begins his career by killing a Philistine giant, we realize that Luvah, the "Babe" of "The Mental Traveller," has been born once more. No doubt David was a historical figure, but the writers of the Bible are primarily interested in the imaginative form of Luvah. Similarly, there are many features in the story of Solomon with which the promiscuous horse-trader of that name can have little to do. Solomon is Urizen, the decadence of state religion and luxury which is always associated with Urizen, and which in the historical cycle regularly succeeds an earlier period of war and conquest. The books in the Bible assigned to David and Solomon are the cultural products appropriate to the Luvah and Urizen stages respectively. This cycle comes to its close with the Babylonian captivity, and in Old Testament prophecies Babylon and Egypt merge into a common symbolism, a symbolism to which the New Testament adds Rome. The Book of Daniel tells a story which is in many respects closely parallel to the story of Joseph: both heroes become chief ministers by interpreting dreams to a prince of the *civitas terrena* who undergoes seven cycles of calamity. The links between Nebuchadnezzar and the fallen Albion have already been traced.

The career of Jesus is visualized in the Gospels as a recreation or epitome of the story of Israel. He comes of the seed of "David," that is, he is a new Orc or Luvah. A "father" who did not beget him, named Joseph, leads him down to "Egypt," Herod's slaughter of the innocents being in counterpoint to the earlier Passover story. Returning from Egypt, he grows up and is baptized in the Jordan, corresponding to the crossing of the Red Sea; then he wanders forty days in the wilderness as the Israelites wandered forty years, resisting all the temptations the Israelites fell a prey to, including at least one not presented as such in the earlier vision, the miraculous provision of bread. He emerges from the wilderness, gathers twelve followers, appears on a mountain with Moses and Elijah, enters and cleanses the Temple, and is finally lifted up like the brazen serpent in the harlot Jerusalem he came to redeem. In the meantime he raised up a new civilization through the power of the unlearned and oppressed people who were most receptive to his teaching. This new historical cycle is symbolized in Blake by Lazarus,[22] who no doubt is both the Lazarus of Bethany and the Lazarus of the parable, and who is, like Samson, a vision of Orc suggesting the larger contours of Albion, whose resurrection may not be far off. Thus the "life" of Jesus presented in the Gospels is really a visionary drama based on the earlier vision of Jehovah, worked out not in terms of historical accuracy or evidence but purely as a clarification of the prophetic visions of the Messiah.

· 3 ·

JESUS came to clear up an ambiguity in the Old Testament conception of "Israel" as a larger human and divine body in whom all Israelites live. On the one hand there is the conception of it as a chosen race, a peculiar people, an exclusive ceremonial code, a secure possession of a little patch of ground in the physical world. This is the legal and historical conception of Israel, the Judaism which rejects the Gospel. On the other hand there is the imaginative or poetic conception of it as a spiritual Israel, the total human form of the awakened imagination of Man. This is what the Apocalypse means when it speaks of the "sealing" of 144,000 "servants of God" who are equally divided among the twelve tribes of Israel. This conception of the whole of "redeemed" humanity as a spiritual Israel is the starting-point of Blake's conception of Albion.

As the spiritual Israel is the new and not the old Jerusalem, a mental state and not a physical place, so the spiritual England is the garden of the Hesperides and the happy island kingdom of Atlantis. England and Canaan are as remote as two countries can well be, but Atlantis and Jerusalem are the same kingdom, and Eden and the Hesperides the same garden. It is only on the spiritual level, therefore, that an English reader can find in Hebrew prophecy something akin to what his own imagination is looking for. The Song of Songs visualizes the final consummation as a sacred marriage between the king, or symbol of the nation united as one Man, and the "married land" who is that nation's bride, "a City, yet a Woman."[23] This vision is correct as long as we realize the universality of its Solomon and Jerusalem, but it may lead to a literal and historical interpretation which would be of interest only to Pharisees. To call the parties of the marriage Albion and London would be correct under the same conditions, but might lead to a perverted misunderstanding which would only pander to the vanity of English jingoes. To make them Albion and Jerusalem would avoid both errors, and preserve both the English and the Christian aspects of the vision, uniting the exotic religion and indigenous history of Britain in a single universal form. Jerusalem, therefore, is the emanation of Albion, and the palace of civilization being built by English imaginative power is a "spiritual fourfold London"[24]: one thinks of the "Cleopolis" of Spenser's *Faerie Queene*. There are many mansions in the eternal world, and the imaginative body into which England evolves through the power of Los is one of them, and the one that Blake is helping to mold.

The symbolism of *Jerusalem* is based on a combination of English and Biblical imagery. There are two aspects to this, one geographical, the other historical. The former is complicated in expression but simple enough in principle. "Canaan" is merely superimposed on England: England's mountains, such as Snowdon and Mam-Tor, correspond to the Palestinian mountains such as the Mount of Olives and Megiddo; the caves in Derbyshire correspond to the caves of Abraham, David and Elijah; the different districts of London such as Paddington (not so full of dark Satanic mills then as now), Highgate, Stepney and so on, correspond to the Zion and Tophet and Vale of Hinnom and other parts of the Biblical Jerusalem. Even more exact is the correspondence of Tyburn to Calvary, and of Lambeth, where Blake wrote most of his minor poems, to Bethlehem, the madhouse of "Bedlam" in the former being an ironic link.[25] Luvah is the Biblical Edom, just outside Israel and its hereditary enemy, the home of Herod, from whence nevertheless Isaiah sees the Messiah returning, and Luvah is also France,[26] from whence a revolution (reborn Luvah) and Napoleon both proceed. Finally, all the counties, first of Wales, then of England, then of Scotland, and at length, when the symbolism permits of it, of Ireland, are systematically and inexorably divided among the twelve tribes of Israel. Whatever sins against literary tact there may be in the way Blake carries out this scheme, the scheme itself is no more unreasonable than an attempt to

domesticate the birth of Christ by associating it with frosty nights
and deep snow. It is even akin to Wordsworth's great idea of the
imaginative rediscovery of the immediate, an idea which Wordsworth failed to apply, as he promised, to the theme of Atlantis;
and Wordsworth could conceive a poor Susan for whom "a river
flows on through the vale of Cheapside" without considering her
mad.

Turning to the historical combination, the material for an
allegorical vision of English history parallel with the Hebrew
history in the Bible is the cycle of traditional legends, or whatever
they are, that comes down from Geoffrey of Monmouth and contains the account of the settlement in Britain by Trojans under
Brutus, a long chronicle of miscellaneous royalty including Lear,
Cymbeline, Sabrina and others, the exploits of Arthur, and the
prophecies of Merlin. For Blake the important sources of this
material seem to be Geoffrey himself and Milton's *History of
Britain*.[27] Geoffrey, like the Old Testament, contains catalogues
of names and other forms of vaguely understood vision, also the
oracular prophecies of Merlin, snatches of folklore, legends of
ferocious female wills like the Gwendolen who flung Sabrina into
the Severn, references to underground labyrinths in which hidden
loves are imprisoned, and other jigsaw pieces with suggestive
contours. Further, he associates the events in legendary English
history with Biblical events which are asserted to be contemporary
with them, and some later histories founded on Geoffrey, such as
Warner's *Albions England*, complete the Anglo-Biblical parallel
by beginning with the Book of Genesis and working down through
the Trojan war to Brutus.

It may be noted for its general interest that this parallelism is
more common in English literature than the casual reader may
think—particularly, of course, during the period when the Geoffrey
legends were accepted as historical. In the two plays of Shakespeare
that deal with the ancient history of Britain, *King Lear* and
Cymbeline, one is struck not only by a curious insistence on certain
coast towns, Dover in one and Milford Haven in the other, which
link Britain with distant lands, but a symbolism consistent with
a pre-Christian world under the law which has many links with
the Old Testament; and at least once Old Testament allusions are
piled up with a Blakean rapidity:

Upon such sacrifices, my Cordelia,
The gods themselves throw incense. Have I caught thee?
He that parts us shall bring a brand from heaven,
And fire us hence like foxes. Wipe thine eyes;
The good years shall devour them, flesh and fell,
Ere they shall make us weep: we'll see 'em starve first.[28]

Here the word "sacrifices," the central idea which the Old Testament deals with, has suggested something in it to Lear, probably the story of Jephthah's daughter. From there he jumps to the destruction of Sodom and the story of Samson and the foxes, thence to Pharaoh's dream of the lean kine who ate up the fat ones or "good years"; and the meaning of the whole chain is: the world shall burn and the golden age come back before our enemies can triumph over us. Of course these are the uncontrolled associations of a vague and wandering mind, but after all *King Lear* is a play, and Shakespeare must have expected from his audience something of the allusive agility that the reading of Blake demands.

Arthur has been the most popular subject for poetic developments of this history from medieval times to our own; but what Blake was interested in was in extracting symbols out of Geoffrey that could be superimposed on the Old Testament as he interpreted it, and for this he found Geoffrey's pre-Arthurian material more useful. The crossing of the Jordan, the fall into Canaan, corresponds to the flooding-out of Atlantis and the insulating of Britain. A parallel image of enclosing the "Female Space" of the fallen world, or Enitharmon, with a wall of fire, which to a modern reader suggests the climax of *Die Walküre*, is also mentioned by Blake, though not developed.[29] The fact that Britain's conquerors are called Trojans corresponds to the fact that the Hebrews by the time they entered Canaan were in the same spiritual state as the Egyptians they had left behind. For the siege of Troy, which began, like the fall of Eden, with the surrender of an apple to a female will, and ended in a struggle over the possession of a whore, is as clear a vision of the triumph of Vala and Rahab as one could find anywhere. Blake regards Troy as a main source of the worship of external gods, whom he speaks of as "gods of Priam,"[30] because the *civitas terrena* of the Jesus cycle which corresponds to the earlier Babylon and Egypt is Rome, and the founder of Rome brought the gods of Troy to it just as the Hebrews brought the ark of Vala into Jerusalem. The Brutus who led the Trojans into Britain corresponds to the Joshua who led the Hebrews into Canaan, and in the exploits of both a conquest of giants figures prominently. Those conquered by Brutus were Druids, and reminiscences of giants who used to smell the blood of Englishmen have found their way into nursery tales.[31]

Albion, like Israel, has twelve sons, and as the sons of Israel represent ordinary humanity, the sons of Albion are for most of the poem the aggregate Selfhood or spectral aspect of human nature. The legend of Arthur's Round Table may contain a reminiscence of them. Unlike the sons of Israel, the sons of Albion are always named in the same order, thus: Hand, Hyle, Coban, Gwantok, Peachey, Brereton, Slade, Hutton, Skofeld, Kox, Kotope and Bowen (spellings are not consistent). The names are of various origins, and some are unknown, but we may recognize Schofield, his companion Cock, and the Peachey, Brereton and Quantock who were judges at Blake's trial. Blake shows no rancor and makes no personal allusions: he simply needed such names in his symbolism. For just as Jesus and the twelve apostles represent the imagination going all over the world and ready to endure any kind of persecution to proclaim its message of hope and life more abundantly, so the judge and his twelve jurors represent the direct parody of this, a human Zodiac bringing the inscrutable and impersonal gaze of moral virtue to bear upon the prophet, estimating his life in terms of the security of mediocrity, and determined to cut it short if it threatens that security. One may compare the related image of the Roman consul and his twelve lictors, whose fasces have been a recurrent and eloquent symbol of Roman tyranny. Long before Blake, Bunyan had used the same image of the jury with powerful effect in *The Pilgrim's Progress*, and it was probably before his own trial that Blake, in *The Four Zoas*, had described the accusation of Christ in a symbolism that unites the jury with the "Druid" sacrificial altar of Stonehenge and the enemies of the children of light:

> Urizen call'd together the synagogue of Satan in dire Sanhedrim
> To judge the Lamb of God to Death as a murderer & robber:
> As it is written, he was number'd among the transgressors.
> Cold, dark, opake, the Assembly met twelvefold in Amalek,

> Twelve rocky unshap'd forms, terrific forms of torture & woe,
> Such seem'd the Synagogue to distant view. . . .[32]

But of course his recent experience had recreated the image in his mind, and the "rapturous delusive trance" of Enitharmon in *Europe,* with her night-imprisoned sun and her Zodiac, was now remote and unreal compared with this new set of "Starry Wheels."

No doubt Blake associated each son of Albion with a corresponding son of Jacob, though he nowhere gives a complete list; but the associations of Hand with Reuben and of Skofeld with Joseph are explicit. Joseph was the son of Jacob who precipitated the fall, and corresponds to Judas among the disciples. Though actually Jacob's eleventh son, he is ninth in Blake's symbolism, the Scorpio or dragon of the Zodiac whose tail draws down a third of the stars. Now we saw that Reuben, Israel's eldest son, sometimes stands for all his brothers, and thereby becomes much the same symbol as Adam, and similarly all the sons of Albion are sometimes represented simply by the eldest one, Hand. Reuben and Hand thus mean the ordinary man and his Selfhood respectively, and Reuben purified of his Selfhood would become a prophetic imagination, which Blake in this case symbolizes by the name of the only ancient British prophet, Merlin:

> Hand stood between Reuben & Merlin, as the Reasoning
>   Spectre
> Stands between the Vegetative Man & his Immortal Imagina-
>   tion. . . .
>
> . . . Reuben is Merlin
> Exploring the Three States of Ulro: Creation, Redemption &
>   Judgment.[33]

Strictly speaking, and Blake speaks very strictly in *Jerusalem,* a symbol of Antichrist should be associated with three, nine or twenty-seven rather than with twelve. The attempt to see the Sons of Albion as ninefold gets the symbolism into some curious gyrations, and Blake soon abandoned it:

> Cambel & Gwendolen wove webs of war & of
> Religion to involve all Albion's sons, and when they had
> Involv'd Eight, their webs roll'd outwards into darkness,
> And Scofield the Ninth remain'd on the outside of the Eight,
> And Kox, Kotope & Bowen, One in him, a Fourfold Wonder,
> Involv'd the Eight.[34]

But when Hand does duty for all the sons of Albion, he is a tri-partite monster like Cerberus or Geryon. Occasionally Hyle is used instead of Hand, with the same associations: the simpler method of using the first three, Hand, Hyle and Coban, is less frequent. We may remember that in Faithful's trial in Bunyan there were three accusers as well as twelve jurors, named Envy, Superstition and Pickthank, and the same image of three accusers turns up in the Book of Job and the trial of Socrates.[35] This for Blake is a much clearer symbol of Antichrist than the jury, because in the Bible Satan is primarily an accuser, and the spirit of Satan in society is the "accusation of sin."

Hand is probably to be connected with the three brothers Hunt, Leigh, Robert and John, who controlled the *Examiner*, a review which made two vicious critical assaults on Blake. The fact that there were three Hunts is a help to the symbolism. Hand thus corresponds to Bunyan's Envy, the hatred of genius by mediocrity which is a death-principle in society, whatever its alleged motive or practical results. *Adonais* is imaginatively correct even if the *Quarterly* reviewer did not actually infect Keats with tuberculosis. Hyle seems to be an echo of Hayley and of the Greek word ἴλη which means both "vegetation" and "matter."[36] Coban is perhaps an anagram of Bacon assimilated to Caliban. For no threefold summary of false doctrine in Blake is complete without being linked with the unholy trinity of Bacon, Newton and Locke. The latter two are to be connected respectively with Hand and Hyle. Finally, as Hand is associated with the wavering and inconstant Reuben, so Hyle and Coban suggest Simeon and Levi, the sons of Israel who stand for the two great institutions of the moral law, war and religion, or, more precisely, murderous vengeance and a tithe-collecting priesthood.[37]

In Blake's day Hand and Hyle have become the two great pillars of Deism, reason and nature, incarnate in Voltaire and Rousseau. Though these two form an illusory contrast, it is merely what Blake calls the war of contraries under Negation's banner,[38] and even the appearance of contrast is rapidly dissolving. That is, it was only in the age of reason that Rousseau could have thought up his conception of nature, and only a Deist age which accepted the goodness of the natural man could have produced the rational-ism of Voltaire. Blake's dislike of Voltaire was at least as great as

Voltaire's admiration for Newton and Deist England, "cette terre plus célèbre que Tyr et que l'île Atlantide."[39] It is difficult to say just what Voltaire Blake had read, beyond the fact that he quotes his *Moeurs des Nations,* but at any rate *Micromégas,* with its insistence on the immense distance and size of the stars, the miserable pettiness of man, and the blatant fatuity of the notion that this universe is anything with a human meaning, is instructively anti-Blakean. Here again rationalism and the mystery of nature become the same thing.

The "sons of Jerusalem" are not mentioned in the Bible, but in Blake they are the ideal of a united humanity that the twelve sons of Jacob are striving to attain, and must therefore be associated with sixteen rather than twelve. They are the twelve sons of Jacob plus four other human principles; our old friends Rintrah, Palamabron, Theotormon and Bromion, "the Four Sons of Jerusalem that never were Generated."[40] They are also sons of Los, but as they were never generated that implies nothing about the relations of Los and Jerusalem. They correspond to the Zoas, Rintrah to Urizen, Palamabron to Luvah, Theotormon to Tharmas, and Bromion to Urthona, but, being sons of Los, they are manifestations of culture within the world of time, and are therefore less inclusive conceptions.

The traditional number of cities in Albion, as recorded by Geoffrey, is twenty-eight, a complete list being duly given in *Jerusalem.*[41] The number twenty-eight reminds us of the twenty-eight "Churches" into which the history of man from Adam to Milton is divided. There is no indication that Blake associated any of the cities with any of the Churches, but numbers with double associations, one referring to time and the other to space, are frequent in Blake: the fifty-two armies of the Spectre of Urthona mean both the counties of England and the weeks of the year,[42] and the description of fallen man as "a Worm seventy inches long" refers both to his height and his years of existence.[43] Now Jerusalem is the emanation of Albion, Albion has twelve sons, and Jerusalem sixteen. Twelve and sixteen make twenty-eight, and in the final apocalypse in which Albion and Jerusalem are united the full complement of twenty-eight will be made up. The Biblical vision of this is again in the Book of Revelation, where God is surrounded by twenty-eight creatures, the four Zoas and twenty-four "elders."[44] The four Zoas are represented by the four sons of Los and the four cities ascribed to them, "Verulam," London, York and Edinburgh. Verulam, the site of a Roman town and the baronial name of Bacon, belongs to Rintrah and Urizen, and in its fallen state is a symbol with at least two obviously sinister associations. London belongs to Palamabron and Luvah, and is therefore the symbol par excellence of the material with which the visionary deals, the redeemable conscious life in the fallen world, a mixture of imagination and nature, like the Biblical Jerusalem a great dream of a heavenly city expanding out of a dirty and iniquitous earthly one. Edinburgh, the murky city of the north, belongs to Bromion and Urthona, and York, with its American descendant, to Theotormon and Tharmas, the spirits of the western ocean. The other twenty-four cities thus correspond to the twenty-four elders, who in the Bible represent the spiritual Israel.[45]

The sons of Albion are Spectres, and must therefore have emanations or female principles which as long as they are Spectres will remain aloof from them and domineer over them by means of that aloofness, encouraging incessant war and a constant belief in mystery. These twelve daughters of Albion are named, in the order corresponding to that of the sons of Albion given above, Cambel, Gwendolen, Ignoge, Cordella, Mehetabel, Ragan, Gonorill, Gwinefred, Gwinevere, Estrild, Sabrina and Conwenna. Most of these names seem to be taken at random from Geoffrey's history: we recognize the three daughters of Lear, Arthur's queen and the Sabrina of Comus. The meaning of these daughters is an aggregate one, and they cannot be individually distinguished, except that the first two are the ringleaders. They form a contrast to the daughters of Beulah who are Blake's Muses and form a sympathetic chorus like the Spirits of the Pities in The Dynasts; and, like the sons, the daughters of Albion are associated in their fallen state with stars. They ride "triumphant in the bloody sky" on the neck of Taurus or Luvah, the sacrificial bull, as the Pleiades and Hyades who are stellified daughters of Atlas (Albion) in Ovid, and whose enticing sweet influences are referred to in Job.[46] The twelve together constitute the fivefold Tirzah, the fallen senses, and Rahab. So did the virginal part of Ololon in Milton, who was sixfold: to make up the full number of twelve Rahab is given an association with the number seven, represented in the Book of

Revelation by the seven hills of Rome she sits on. The reference is to the conventional morality which is a part of Rahab, and which is traditionally connected with seven cardinal virtues and seven deadly sins—the "reflection" part of Locke's philosophy, as distinct from the fivefold "sensation." The five cities of the Philistines and the seven kingdoms of Canaan, the latter recalling the British heptarchy, are also not forgotten when female will is the theme.[47]

In the first part of *Jerusalem* there is a full description of Golgonooza, and outside Golgonooza Blake puts all his symbols of the fallen world. One may note the forest, the fallen garden and in Blake as in Dante a symbol of lost direction, represented in Blake also by the labyrinth, the wilderness and the pathless blanket of winter snow. Blake calls this forest Entuthon Benython. There is also the "lake," the symbol of the mind which passively reflects its sense experience, the Bethesda pool of paralytics with its five porches, which Blake calls Udanadan.[48] Now as England is the fallen remnant of Albion, individual vision, symbolized by the closed Western Gate in *Milton*, is also symbolized in *Jerusalem* by the "Spaces of Erin,"[49] Ireland being the western promontory of the fallen world in Blake's geography. That is why Ireland is left out of the division of the counties of England, Wales and Scotland among the twelve tribes of Israel in the first part, and not introduced until the end of the third, when its thirty-two counties represent the thirty-two nations of the earth which are about to be gathered together from all points of the compass into the body of Albion. The concealment of America during all but the last few centuries of history since Adam's time belongs to the same "Western Gate" symbolism.

If this explanation has sufficiently damaged the tough and prickly shell of *Jerusalem*, we may proceed to extract the kernel.

· 4 ·

In *Jerusalem* the symbol of the wheel has the two sets of associations and the ambiguous meaning which it also has in *The Four Zoas*. One association is with the "vehicular form" or imaginative mechanism, the furnace-chariot belonging to Los and Luvah; the other is with the spinning wheel and loom belonging to Enitharmon and Vala; and the meaning of the symbol may relate either

to the power of civilization which invented the wheel or to the
sense of an inscrutable fate, depending on whether Los and Enitharmon, or Luvah and Vala, are in charge of it. Traces of this
symbolism are scattered through the Bible, and we have dealt with
the Biblical allusions to furnaces and chariots. Most of the references to clothing in the Bible represent the transparent "net"
which the fallen world flings around us, woven by Vala, who also
weaves armor of conflict, shells of stupidity, or coverings of concealment and shame like the fig-leaves of Adam and Eve. The
swaddling clothes of the infant Jesus are a sign of his descent to a
fallen world; and the curtains of the ark, and the veil in the temple
which concealed the nothingness of the Pharisees' God and which
was rent by Jesus, need no further explanation. As the story of
Joseph is an account of the Fall, the coat of many colors is a symbol
corresponding to the coats of skin made for Adam and Eve and
to what those coats represent, their exile from a Paradise of innocence now guarded by the Covering Cherub, the monstrous dragon
who glitters in gold and precious stones. If we understand this
association of ideas we should be able to follow such a passage
as this (the reference to "One Man's Loins" will be explained
later):

> . . . the Eternal Man
> Walketh among us, calling us his Brothers & his Friends,
> Forbidding us that Veil which Satan puts between Eve &
>   Adam,
> By which the Princes of the Dead enslave their Votaries
> Teaching them to form the Serpent of precious stones & gold
> To sieze the Sons of Jerusalem & plant them in One Man's
>   Loins,
> To make One Family of Contraries, that Joseph may be sold
> Into Egypt for Negation, a Veil the Saviour born & dying
>   rends.[50]

On the other hand, the "seamless garment" of the cross and the
linen clothes abandoned by Jesus in his tomb represent the imagination's escape from this through another power, of which Blake
gives us a glimpse in his remarkable picture of the solicitous Fates
in Plate 59. This is the power of seeing the physical appearance
as the covering of the mental reality, yet not concealing its shape
so much as revealing it in a fallen aspect, and so not the clothing

but the body or form of the mental world, though a physical and
therefore a fallen body or form. If we try to visualize this development of the "clothing" symbol, we get something more like a
mirror, a surface which reveals reality in fewer dimensions than
it actually has.

The ambiguity in the meaning of the wheel in Blake's symbolism has often met us before: there is a tree of life and a tree of
mystery, a city of God and a city of destruction, a hell of eternal
delight and a hell of frustrated desire. It seems an easy inference
that all images whatever may be symbols of the world of innocence
when thought of in terms of eternal existence, and symbols of the
world of experience when thought of in terms of death and annihilation. No class of natural images, then, can be identified with
either world: prisons belong solely to experience, but a prison is
a building, and so is Golgonooza. The world in which we live,
therefore, contains a "heaven" or imaginative world in which all
natural objects have a mental significance, and a "hell" or Ulro
in which the same natural objects have an opposite significance.
The latter is thus a parody or mirror-image, "Vegetable Glass"[51]
as Blake calls it, of the world of mental reality.

In *Jerusalem* Blake expresses this relationship by the term
"analogy." He uses the word only twice,[52] but once in a very crucial
place, and as the idea it signifies is about the most important one
in *Jerusalem*, and has no other word attached to it, we shall proceed to make extensive use of it. The occurrence of the word may
raise the question whether Bishop Butler's *Analogy of Religion*
had any influence on *Jerusalem*. Blake, though he was not likely
to read such a book through without some powerful stimulus, may
have read the first twenty pages of practically anything, and there
is no reason why Butler's book should be an exception either way
to that important principle. To what extent this constitutes
"influence" the writer is not prepared to say, but the complete
argument of each would have horrified the other. Butler attempted
to refute Deism by establishing an analogy between a known series
of facts with which natural reason deals, and an unknown series
which is revealed to us by faith. But the attempt to show that reason
is limited by the unknown is, according to Blake, itself a cardinal
doctrine of Deism, and a logical compulsion to accept an ultra-
rational mystery confirms Deism instead of destroying it. It is a

paradox to associate revelation, or vision, with what we do not know rather than with what we can see.

Though the word "analogy" is new, this conception of the world of experience as a parody or inverted form of the imaginative world has often come up before. It is implicit in Blake's doctrine that truth consolidates error into an increasingly obvious negation of itself until it becomes pure negation and disappears. It is implicit in his contrast between the "Identity" and the "Similitude," the image which means itself because it is itself and the image which means something else because it is like something else, the true and the false allegory. Blake's tiger is allegory; the British lion is an allegory of something. But what it is an allegory of, the reality from which it has been abstracted, is ultimately the real lion. It is implicit, again, in the principle discussed in the third chapter, that many aspects of life in the fallen world are inverted or perverted forms of imaginative realities. The heroic leader is the analogy of the visionary prophet; monogamous marriage is an analogy of the emanation; and, to get nearer the symbolism of *Jerusalem*, history and law are the analogy of the Word, Canaan the analogy of the Promised Land, Antichrist the analogy of Christ, and so on. We have also noticed that the four parts of *Jerusalem* are each based on an imaginative contrast of a similar kind.

If we now go back to the wheel with which this discussion began, we have a basis for explaining the central point of the argument of *Jerusalem*. There are two poles in human thought, the conception of life as eternal existence in one divine Man, and the conception of life as an unending series of cycles in nature. Most of us spend our mental lives vacillating somewhere between these two, without being fully conscious of either, certainly without any great impulse to accept either. But the rise of Deism has increased our awareness of the extent to which we are attracted by the latter. Between the beginning of life in our world and ourselves, a long interval of time may have elapsed, and a great development have taken place; but the beginning of our world cannot have been, from a natural point of view, anything more than an incident in the revolving of stars in the sky. As soon as our idea of a beginning of time or creation disappears into the "Starry Wheels," we have attained the complete fallen vision of the world, the Orc cycle, the wheel of death, the conclusion from the premises of Bacon and Locke. (As the rebirth of Orc is the rebirth of a different individual of the same class, unending recurrence does not necessarily mean that the same thing happens over and over, but that the same kind of thing happens over and over.) Such an idea, Blake insists, is a mental cancer: man is not capable of accepting it purely as an objective fact; its moral and emotional implications must accompany it into the mind, and breed there into cynical indifference, short-range vision, selfish pursuit of expediency, and all the other diseases of the Selfhood, ending in horror and despair. But we cannot shut our eyes and deny its reality; we must see its reality as a reflected image of the eternal mental life of God and Man, the wheel of life, the automotive energy of the risen body.

Jerusalem attempts to show that the vision of reality is the other one inside out. The poem shows us two worlds, one infinite, the other indefinite, one our own home and the other the same home receding from us in a mirror. If we recall the image of the vortex or spiral which was used in *Milton*, we may see these two worlds as coming together in the shape of a vast hourglass, the brain of man being their infinitesimal point of contact.

The process of "reflection" in Locke's philosophy, therefore, really does reflect, and the more clearly it does so, the more clearly it reflects Blake's vision. The most myopic form of common sense tries to identify appearance and reality, to deny the existence of any reality except the physical world. Such a fool, if he would persist in his folly, would become wise. For the work of the greatest artists begins in an attempt to make the appearance real, and ends in an attempt to make reality appear. The assumption underlying art, then, is that the natural world is related to the mental world as material is related to form, diversity to unity, the analytic to the synthetic aspect of the same thing.

In the indefinite view of the world, as it is illustrated in Locke, man is a subject contemplating an object, an undividable unit of perception trying to break down a world outside him into a corresponding aggregate of undividable units, which are called atoms when they are too small to be seen and stars when they are too large to be mentally organized. This is called understanding, a word suggesting the pose of Atlas with the physical world on his head, and what the understanding stands under is substance, which sounds like a Latin form of the same word. In this position man's conceptions of both subject and object are oppressed by a mystery. He knows vaguely that there is something "behind" him; that he is not a wholly self-contained unit of perception, and that as an individual he is part of something more than an aggregate; but what the form of this could be he does not know. He knows too that there is something "behind" what he sees, which Locke calls a substratum of substance, for an attempt to define mystery can only be a pleonasm. His mental equipment consists, then, of an objective "destiny" or predictable nature, a subjective "ratio" and a vacuum, all that is left to him of the three persons in an indivisible substance with which the Christian cycle of natural reasoning began; and this is what leads him to the vision of life as indefinite recurrence. But in such a vision subject and object have taken the same form, the starry wheels and the solar and vegetable cycles in nature being a process which includes the natural cycle of his own life. Hence when the Lockian view of reality becomes complete, it becomes exhausted; when man's mind becomes wholly a function of nature, nature becomes a mental category. The attempt to see subject and object in terms of units thus becomes an attempt to see them in terms of unity. But at that point the whole Orc vision turns inside out. In terms of unity, individuals, atoms and stars are no longer simply undividable units; they are all equally corpuscles, little bodies within a larger body. And as this larger body must be common to both subject and object, the mystery of what is behind the subject and the mystery of what is behind the object reveal one another, and become the same thing, the universal form of both, and the body of God who perceives through man. This is a theory of knowledge in which the word "theory" has recovered its original sense of seeing, and is no longer a matter of fumbling in the dark for a "substratum," or for unknown powers of the soul.

Such a reversal of perspective in space will include one in time, as our existence in time is only a small cogwheel within the whole astral machine which we perceive in space. But as the unfallen perspective is the reverse of this, and contains the whole of perception within the eternal existence of man's mind, the focal point of the analogy which the indefinite world reflects back to the infinite one must be sought for in time. And as the Bible presents the imaginative form of time, we have now to apply Blake's doctrine of the analogy to the interpretation of the Bible which he gives us.

The Bible begins with a world of watery chaos and a pair of spiritual infants in a garden who grow up in a wilderness. But by the time we have reached the end we realize that the Bible, like other epics, has started with the action fairly well advanced, and that the Book of Genesis needs a prelude about a fiery city in which a single divine and human body formed the circumference of the whole of nature. Such a prelude, if we could be sufficiently inspired to compose one, would turn out to be very similar to the conclusion of the existing Book of Revelation. All things have proceeded from a divine Man, the body of Jesus, and will be reabsorbed into him; and the total vision of life must have a circular form.

But if the Bible had begun where it now ends, it would have presented its vision in a *closed* circle, and a closed circle would have suggested, as some Indian visions are said to do, the indefinite recurrence, not only of natural cycles, but of the whole progression of life itself from fall to apocalypse. This in Blake's symbolism would be the triumph of the Spectre of Urthona, the sense of unending time, over his master Los, the vision of time as a single form, and would utterly pervert the Biblical meaning of the word "eternity." The final comprehension of the Bible's meaning is in the spark of illumination between its closing anode and its opening cathode, and if that gap were not there the Bible would not stimulate the imagination to the effort of comprehension which recreates instead of passively following the outline of a vision.

Each reader must discover in his own way, therefore, that the true Eden is not a garden but a civilized kingdom, and the larger human body of God, or Jesus. This is where the national tradition to be incorporated with the Bible comes in, and the reader will identify this kingdom with the spiritual form of his own nation, which is Atlantis in the case of England. But the Jesus we attain by this process of pulling the Bible around in a circle is polarized by the Jesus who stands opposite him in the middle of the Biblical narrative. Here again is the contrast between the present Jesus of vision and the past Jesus of history which we met in the preceding chapter, and the thought suggests itself that somehow the Jesus of the Gospels is an analogy or reflected form of the true Jesus.

We have already noticed that Blake identifies the dead body of Jesus with the body of Antichrist, the form which the social hatred of Jesus creates out of Jesus. But on examination there are many other aspects of Jesus' life which it is impossible to separate from this form. We can distinguish a Jesus of action and a Jesus of passion, a healer and teacher who went about increasing the power of the bodies and minds of everyone he touched, and the hero of a tragic drama, whose passion was society's interference with his actions. The Jesus of passion is a foredoomed victim who speaks of a coming "hour," who goes through a sacrificial ritual and who, after a conquest of death and hell, floats elusively off into the sky in a supreme anticlimax after a supreme victory. This Jesus of passion, then, is not so much a divine and human unity as a cloven "nature," a suffering man and an exhaled divinity. His sufferings do not reveal the character of a joyous Creator but the character of Pilate and Caiaphas, and the Jesus of passion, according to Blake, is the "Satanic body of Holiness"[53] which Jesus had to assume in order to consolidate error, and show what the opposite of Christianity is.

The true Jesus is the present vision of Jesus, the uniting of the divine and the human in our own minds, and it is only the active Jesus, the teacher and healer and storyteller, who can be recreated. The passive Jesus can only be recalled, and by means of a cere-monial and historical tradition. In each day, Blake says, there is a moment that Satan cannot find,[54] a moment of eternal life which no death-principle can touch, a moment of absolute imagination. In that moment the mystery of the Incarnation, the uniting of God and man, the attaining of eternity in time, the work of Los, the Word becoming flesh, is recreated, and thereby ceases to be a mystery. The analogy of this is the daily drama of the Eucharist, in which not the mental but the physical body is recreated, not out of time but in time, not as the supersubstantial daily bread of the Lord's Prayer, but as a substance within the order of nature and reason. In his death Jesus represented, as we shall see in a moment, the original fall and *sparagmos* of Albion, and therefore personi-fied Luvah, the fallen form of Albion; and the ritual of the Eucha-rist expresses the fact that the body of Albion is still broken and divided, and will continue to be so indefinitely. Blake's religion is civilized life, the Christianity of imagination, art and recreation as opposed to the Christianity of memory, magic and repetition. Blake says of Baptism and the Eucharist:

All Life consists of these Two, Throwing off Error & Knaves from our company continually & Recieving Truth or Wise Men into our Company continually.[55]

This is a very "humanistic" conception of these rites, but to Blake any sacramental religion which falls short of it is still a mystery-religion, a communion with an unseen world. We said of Butler's treatment of the analogy that from Blake's point of view it gets us nowhere to say that reason is bounded by mystery, and what Butler is trying to do is to establish a sacramental analogy between a physical and a mysterious world, which is Blake's analogy turned inside out.

To the Jesus of passion should be added the infant Jesus, the helpless victim of circumcision and other parts of the Jewish law, overshadowed by a father and mother. Infancy implies virginity, later amplified into a curious frenzy for "purity" and an attempt to erase every "stain" of sexual contact suggested in the Gospels, not only from Jesus, but from his whole ancestry. Blake would agree that in eternity there is no splitting of human beings into half-forms, and no marrying or giving in marriage. But the orthodox idea of a sin inherent in the sex act, which makes a Virgin Birth essential to the divinity of Jesus, is founded on a misunderstanding. Life is born in sin only in the sense that sin is death and all life proceeds to death. The "sin" in the sex act, then, is not that of love but that of parentage, the bringing of life into time. It is the father and the mother, not the lover and the beloved, who disappear from the highest Paradise, and in the vision of Jesus the Holy Family represents the "soft Family-Love" which is the wedge of society's resistance to prophecy and the weakest link in the prophet's own defenses. In the resurrection Jesus is a Melchizedek, without father, mother or descent. As for the theme of virginity, the original fall of Albion from a garden into a waste land was a loss of creative power, and so was an imaginative castration (the paradox that this produced our present world of "Generation" is quite consistent with the pattern of Blake's symbolism). The celibate Christ with his virginal mother is, therefore, a part of the

Jesus of passion, the "Ecce Homo" who illustrates the torment of man.

We reach final understanding of the Bible when our imaginations become possessed by the Jesus of the resurrection, the pure community of a divine Man, the absolute civilization of the city of God. This Jesus stands just outside the Bible, and to reach him we must crawl through the narrow gap between the end of Revelation and the beginning of Genesis, and then see the entire vision of the Bible below us as a vast cycle of existence from the creation of a fallen world to the recreation of an unfallen one. If we remain inside the gap with the Jesus of history, we are still within that cycle, which thereby becomes the circumference of our vision. The gap or place of final break-through, where the cosmic egg of the mundane shell is chipped, the opening in the womb of nature, is the upper limit or south (zenith) door of Beulah, and is apparently the same as the "Gate of Luban." This gate is also the upper limit of Cathedron, the imaginative development possible under the protection of Enitharmon and her "loom." It is situated on a "[lower] limit of Translucence," corresponding to the limits of contraction and opacity which we have met, and this limit is the setting, if that is the word, of the crisis in the argument of *Jerusalem*, when the form of Albion emerges from Los's crucible, a form which can no longer be contained within Cathedron.[36]

To the individual visionary the upper limit of Beulah is the limit of orthodox vision, and as far as a church of any kind will take him. It is a state in which nature is seen as beatified, God as a Father, man as a creature, and the essence of mental life as the subjection of reason to a mystery. It is, or may be, a state of genuine imagination, but, because still involved with nature and reason, with a Father God, and perhaps a Mother Church, it is imaginative infancy, the child's protected world. Many visionaries remain in this state indefinitely, but those who reach imaginative puberty become aware of an opposition of forces, and of the necessity of choosing between them. Ahead of them is the narrow gap into eternity, and to get through it they must run away from their protecting parents, like Jesus at twelve, and become adult creators themselves. They must drop the ideas of a divine sanction attached to nature, of an ultimate mystery in the Godhead, of an ultimate division between a human creature and a divine creator, and of recurrent imaginative habits as forming the structure, instead of the foundation, of the imaginative life. If they fail, the great wheel of existence which still surrounds them then becomes the furthest reach of their vision. They are now drawn toward the other pole of thought, the vision of the unending recurrence of this wheel, and Beulah freezes into Ulro. The historical cycle illustrates a different form of the same movement. Imaginative puberty may occur at any time, or never, in a man's life; in the life of a civilization it inevitably comes when the doctrine of indefinite recurrence becomes unmistakably the goal of natural reason, as it does from Locke's time on.

The conception of a lower Paradise, associated with the moon, moisture and the relaxed aspects of eternal existence, which is yet part of the cyclic movement of the physical world below it, was probably derived by Blake from the *Phaedrus*, and the *Bhagavadgita* expresses a similar idea in a passage concise enough to quote:

Fire, light, day, the waxing half of the month, the six moons of the northern course—in these go hence the knowers of Brahma, and come to Brahma.

Smoke, night, the waning half of the month, the six moons of the southern course—in these the man of the Rule attains to the light of the moon, and returns.[57]

Here Blake's north and south symbolism is inverted, as it is once in Blake himself.[58] In Spenser's *Mutabilitie Cantoes*, too, it is at the sphere of the moon that the vision of the relation of cyclic movement to both the eternal and the temporal worlds is attained.

The man who reaches this crisis in vision is a Luvah, a redeemable man, pulled toward the gap by Los, and pulled toward the opposite pole by Satan, Los being Luvah himself as conscious mental effort, and Satan Luvah himself as a natural life proceeding to death. Thus the struggle of Los and Satan for the body of Luvah is the universal archetype, to be applied to the historical cycle, of the struggle of Rintrah and Satan for the body of Palamabron, which is the theme of *Milton*, and which refers to the individual artist. This is the pattern of the struggle of "contraries" which unites them into one by casting out a "negation," the absorption of the natural into the imaginative man which turns the transcendental into the nonexistent.

The Biblical symbolism in which the crisis of vision is presented centers on the figure of Moses. Moses is the Hebrew historical cycle which began as a reborn Orc in Egypt, attained its vision of Jehovah, and ran its natural course. When Moses comes within sight of the Promised Land he represents Hebrew culture at a crisis corresponding to that of Deism. This is later referred to as a dispute between Michael, the guardian angel of Israel, and Satan over Moses' body. Satan was trying to drag him into the fallen Canaan; Michael was trying to take him to the real Promised Land, the Eden where Elijah, according to the old tradition, also awaits the apocalypse. Both sides won, and separated Hebrew civilization into the literal law of the Pharisees and the letter of the law spiritualized by Jesus.

As Adam is the Luvah of a previous cycle, Adam and Moses, being equal to the same thing, are equal to one another. Thus Moses, standing between Michael and Satan in Edom at the southern gate of the Promised Land, is also Adam standing between Jehovah and the Covering Cherub at the boundary of Eden, and Luvah standing in the garden of Adonis between Los and Satan. (We mentioned Henry Reynolds' association of Eden and Adon, and a similar link between Edom and Adam is very easy in the vowelless Hebrew text.) The mountain of Moses' distant view of the Promised Land is Pisgah, but Mount Sinai, where Moses was alone with the stars and recognized them as the back parts of God, is involved in the symbolism. Jesus' dispute with Satan on the mountain-top, in which Milton saw the central image of the regaining of Paradise, belongs here too.

The redeemable Luvah of *Jerusalem* approaching the crisis of vision is of course not Blake himself, who got past it long ago, but England. The Los, Luvah and Satan of the great struggle, then, are in this case Jesus, Albion and Satan. The England Blake is addressing is Albion in a fallen or sleeping state in the world of Generation which is Luvah's world: that is, Albion at present is Luvah. The function of *Jerusalem* is to recreate the vision of the Jesus of action, the divine man whose impact miraculously increased the bodily and mental powers of those who saw what he was, in order to bring that impact directly to bear on the English public. This occurs at a time when both English civilization and one of its artists have reached the point we have described as imaginative puberty. England has to choose whether to turn its green and pleasant land into Jerusalem or a howling waste of Satanic mills, and Blake is practically the only Englishman who can express the fact that that choice is now before England, and is still a choice. *Jerusalem* is Blake's contribution to the struggle between the prophet and the profiteer for the soul of England which is England's Armageddon: it is a burning-glass focusing the rays of a fiery city on London in the hope of kindling an answering flame.

This fiery city is Jerusalem, the emanation or bride of Albion; as the present Albion is Luvah, and the emanation of Luvah is Vala, Vala is the present London and all the other fallen cities of the world, "that great city, which spiritually is called Sodom and Egypt." And as Jerusalem is the bride of Albion, so Vala may be visualized as a harlot; the bride-city is communal possession in love, and the harlot shows the degradation to which the state of communal possession in love has sunk in the fallen world. (One might also say that the incest of father and daughter, so common in mythology, represents the degradation of the state of Eden in which the beloved is created by the lover. As the emanation of Albion, Jerusalem is really closer to being his daughter than his wife: his wife is an "England" or "Britannia" who disappears at the apocalypse.[59]) We have noticed that the harlot is frequently the symbol of the fallen city in Old Testament prophecy, usually associated, especially by Hosea, with the cities of the ten schismatic tribes. And as the essential gospel of Jesus is forgiveness of sins, the forgiveness of the harlot is one of the profoundest expressions of the activity of Jesus.

The forgiveness of the harlot meets us frequently in the Gospels: there is the scene of the woman taken in adultery described by John, the encounter with the woman of Samaria (notice the name), and the story of the Magdalen, whom Blake identifies with the fallen Jerusalem.[60] The woman taken in adultery has been cut out of many early MSS of John, and whether Blake knew this or not, it confirms what he clearly implies: that this is the aspect of the Gospel story most likely to suffer from editorial prudery. Blake suggests that prudery has also been at work on the story of Jesus' birth, that in the original the reasons why Joseph was not his father were not miraculous, and that Joseph forgave his wife exactly as Hosea did his. Such an episode would symbolize the

fulfilling of the Mosaic code in a subtler law of love, and so mark
the final transition from the old to the new "Eye" of God. The
bride of Israel was Rachel, who was won by a long term of bondage
under a legal contract: the Christian bride is Jerusalem, the
heavenly city to be built in the world by an imaginative power
determined literally to make the best of the fallen city; that is,
determined to redeem a harlot.

The episode of Joseph and Mary in *Jerusalem* (Plate 61) appears
to be a later insertion, but the same idea is repeated in *The Everlasting Gospel.*[61] It seems to be Blake's one attempt at shocking instead of emancipating the orthodox reader, but this is quite out of
character for a deeply serious writer whose wit and sense of paradox, though constant, are never irresponsible. Blake's real attack
is not so much on the Virgin Birth as on the Immaculate Conception, the doctrine of what he calls a "Virgin Eve,"[62] and which
is the attempt to keep the Christian vision associated with an
eternally chaste female principle who is never subject to human
desires. As this principle is the visualized form of an objective
nature, her presence in the archetypal vision inoculates Christianity with the virus of Deism, and seals off the gap at the upper limit
of Beulah. She thus occupies the place of Rahab, the female body
of mystery which interposes itself between man and his divine
apotheosis in the body of Jesus.

The harlot typifies nearly every aspect of the life of fallen man,
and Jesus' forgiven harlot is the real form of whom the triumphant
Whore of the Apocalypse is the analogy. By forgiveness Blake
means a release of imaginative power, the creating of conditions
which make it possible for a harlot to "go and sin no more," as
opposed to the miserable futility of the Pharisaic attempt to destroy
harlotry by killing harlots. In terms of modern life, the forgiveness
of sins which accompanied Jesus' cures of the lame, the blind and
the possessed implies vast improvements in civilization combined
with a corresponding progress in the vision of how to use them.
In the Gospels these cures are presented simply as "miracles."

Now a miracle of the kind described in the Gospels is a work
both of vision and of will, and illustrates the power of the imagination over the world of experience. In Blake this power is Tharmas,
and the closed Western Gate is his symbol for the fact that works
of art do not perform miracles. There is a continuous discrepancy

between the artist's will, which is pressed into the service of clarifying vision, and the social will, which travels in natural circles. Art has brought about with every cycle an increase of society's power to visualize its own ideal existence, the city of God. The individual artist clarifies his own vision, however, independently of its effect on the world of experience, never achieving any miraculous response from that world, but perhaps never quite losing the hope of doing so. Society in the meantime goes its own way, guided at best by the broken and uncertain lights of vision which it obtains from its legal and historical conceptions of the Word of God. Yet the artist belongs in society, and if the illuminations he records in his art referred only to him, they would simply be analogies, passive reflections of vision. The artist is a translucent medium of a vision which shines through him to the public, though as faintly as the light of a star. But if, at the crisis of a historical cycle, when the fiery city and the fallen city come into a line of direct opposition with one another, the pure burning-glass of a work of art is interposed between instead of the usual opaque mystery of nature, there would be not the usual natural eclipse, but the kindling of the world's last fire. Once society can catch the knack of pressing the social will into the service of a vision, as the artist does, it will start building Jerusalem, and this response to art is the final miracle which the miraculous powers of Jesus symbolize. In *Jerusalem* this is expressed by the separation of the Spectre of Urthona from Los, the artist's renunciation of an individual will which takes place at the end of linear time.[63]

· 5 ·

THE difference between the vision and the analogy is closely akin to the difference between the work of art and the dream. The meaning of a work of art is independent of its creator, because a universal imagination is involved in it. The dream is egocentric, and its meaning is to be sought for within the personal life of the dreamer. But even in the dream the process of symbolizing experience is at work, and the symbols of the dream may often be read as analogies, Selfhood parodies of genuine vision. As history, the analogy of the Word, deals chiefly with the Selfhood aspect of life, the visionary sees history, and the life of men in time, as a continuous somnambulism. He therefore interprets much of what he finds in history as analogies, visions expressed in inverted terms. The king, for instance, is the Selfhood's attempt to express the imaginative idea of the unity of society in a single man. The king owes his title to his descent, which shows the legal and historical shape of the idea, and he often descends from an even profounder parody of the one Man, the eponymous ancestor, through whom an entire nation has been drawn into "One Man's Loins,"[64] and thus as it were turned inside out from an imaginative form to a natural one, a kind of historical vortex. The priest is similarly an analogy of the prophet, and both king and priest are symbols of fatherhood, hence parodies of the city of God which is eternal brotherhood and has no fathers. The state or nation, the church, or any exclusive and partial body of men with a defensive shell around it, is an analogy of the community, which is no respecter of persons. When Blake went to Felpham he noted with approval that the people of Sussex were "Genuine Saxons"[65]; but in *Jerusalem* it is the uniquely mongrel assortment of races in England, and the still greater variety assembling in the port of London, that seems to him the real sign of an awakening Albion.[66] The nobility is an analogy of the free and privileged life in an unfallen world, freedom and privilege being interpreted in the Selfhood terms of idleness and domination. And just as the Messiah is the incarnation of the Word, so it is the hero or conquering Messiah whose dream is history. Men of action and will power are dreamers like Pharaoh and Nebuchadnezzar, and they attain the analogy of inspiration in the trance of instinct, the wide-eyed inner balance of the sleepwalker. Their followers are the dreaming herd whose senses are in their leader, like a flock of starlings all raised and lowered at once by the rhythms of a general existence. This is the world of the Joshua who is the analogy of Jesus, of the Arthur who is the analogy of Albion.

Society is at its lowest ebb when these various analogies consolidate into a single form, when the state and church become the same thing, and the ruler is a divine Caesar (the divine Caesar is obviously a part of the complex of Antichrist symbols in Revelation), to disobey whom is at once treason and blasphemy. At this point the two great dreams of time, the Luvah dream of war, tyranny and nature, and the Urizen dream of religion, mystery and reason, focus into one, and war and religion are identified. The typical form of this union is the crusade, the physical fight to gain possession of the old Jerusalem and the empty tomb of Christ, the analogy of the "Mental Fight" to restore the new Jerusalem in (not to) England. In this state-church we have the political expression of the Deist mental attitude, and the clarified analogy of the city of God.

The worse an action is, the more eloquently expressive of tyranny and mystery it is, and so the more clearly it becomes a reflecting death-symbol. That is why public punishments have such strong suggestions of ritual about them, ritual being, as should be clear by now, one of the analogies of the work of art, the death-drama of recurrence in a fallen state opposed to the life-drama of creation out of it. The significance of the judge and jury, as an incarnation of the worship of "Starry Wheels" which breeds accusation of sin in society, has already met us. The persecution of Jews, again, is an analogy of the appeal to them in Part Two of *Jerusalem* to abandon the legal and historical conception of the vision of Jehovah and enter the freedom of the Gospel. Persecution of course springs from just such legal and historical ideas, and those who persecute Jews can only express by doing so the same attitude that Jesus condemned in the Pharisees: belief in a chosen race, a national moral law and a conquering Messiah. Such persecutors are the Pharisees of the Jesus cycle, the Deists to whom Part Three is addressed. It is they who see in the Jews the symbols of their own far deeper hatred of Jesus. We shall see how this point fits into *Jerusalem* as we go along: in the meantime it may explain why in *The Everlasting Gospel* a coarse anti-Semitic remark is inserted into the middle of a violent anti-Christian tirade by, of all people, Caiaphas.[67]

The prophet can see both the real and the reflected vision; the natural man sees neither, but is living in the analogy, and everything he does is part of its symbolism. But as he can do nothing to emancipate or redeem the fallen world, what he does in one way or another repeats some aspect of the original fall of Albion. Hence most victims of moral virtue, including Jesus himself, are incarnations of the dying god Luvah, Albion's fallen form. A man crucified or hung on a tree represents the martyrdom of all men "bound upon the stems of vegetation"; a man broken on a wheel represents the mangling of all men in the "wheel of Religion" which the Fall started turning; a man burned at the stake represents the hell of society's frustrated desires. The Druid captives in wicker cages illustrate the Selfhood's conception of the barred prison of nature which will someday be consumed in fire. Blake says that an individual should not appropriate universal character-istics,[68] and the only ones who completely succeed in doing so are the victims of these hideous dramas. The imagination sees that the mysterious calamities of nature are produced by an evil female will who will someday be stripped and burned. This female will is a universal archetype. When the Selfhood gets the same idea, it looks for an individual woman, seizes one at random, and burns her as a "witch."

Thus the art and culture of a natural society, the single state-church ruled by a divine Caesar or priest-king already referred to, consists essentially in an act of punishment taking the form of a murder symbolizing the continuation of the fallen state of the world. Human sacrifice in all its forms, therefore, is the most eloquently symbolic act which the dreaming Selfhood is capable of performing. It illustrates every aspect of the Fall, and parodies every aspect of eternal life. In its purest form it is a ritual, taking place at regular intervals and connected with the cyclic order of nature. Its victim represents Luvah or the dying Albion, and repeats in his death the original breaking of Albion's body and the spilling of his blood. Hence sacrifice is an analogy of the eventual reintegration of that body, as its bloodless counterpart the Eucharist is an analogy of the last harvest and vintage. (A Luvah slain in full vigor of life, by the way, would pass directly into Satan or death without going through the Urizen stage, and the prominence of the imagery of sacrifice in *Jerusalem* is one reason for the comparative unimportance of Urizen.) Again, sacrifice is the central form of both war and religion, and the expression of the death-impulse which causes them. It is thus an analogy of civilization, which can survive only through conscious acts of friendship, love and courtesy which represent the killing of the Selfhood by the imagination, the "little Death,"[69] as Blake calls it, which we sometimes call self-sacrifice. It makes a public ceremony out of the accusation of sin, the strengthening of society in a tighter bond by removing a marked individual, and so is an analogy of the forgiveness of sins which frees the individual from society in a private illumination. The leading motive of sacrifice is the Selfhood's desire to do what the imagination wants to do, enter into communion with God; but the Selfhood's god is Satan or death, and it can only make that god appear by killing somebody.

Human sacrifice is older than "Adam" and began back in the Druid period, reaching a pitch of frenzy which for a time, Blake says, threatened to depopulate the earth.[70] With the beginning of the Abraham "Church" it began to decline, and such stories as the Passover and the sacrifice of Isaac reveal the attempt of Hebrew culture to escape from the ghastly rite, an attempt carried on in the teachings of the prophets. But it still remains as the symbol of the degeneracy of civilization both in Egypt and in Canaan. Thus the rebirth of the Hebrew cycle in Egypt was signalized first by an Egyptian attempt to murder the Hebrew children and then by the slaughter of the Egyptian firstborn, a sacrifice of tyranny followed by one of mystery, for the only "destroying angel" involved was in the Egyptians' minds. The same symbol recurs at the birth of Christ, with the same meaning. It also had a good deal of prestige in Mexico, where it symbolizes the concealment of America and the closing-up of the Western Gate.[71]

In Part Three there is a long fantasia on the Crucifixion, the point of which is to show that Jesus also was killed as a Luvah in the role of the dying Albion. This is clear in the Passion from the mockery of him by the soldiers, the crown of thorns and the pretense that he was a king. Mockery is closely related to analogy. Remembering that Sisera the Canaanite is a reminiscence of Albion (though he actually had *nine* hundred chariots), we have in the following passage an intricate network of Druid, Mexican, Canaanite and Christian sacrificial symbols, along with a few of Blake's own:

> The Knife of flint passes over the howling Victim: his blood
> Gushes & stains the fair side of the fair Daughters of Albion.
> They put aside his curls, they divide his seven locks upon
> His forehead, they bind his forehead with thorns of iron,
> They put into his hand a reed, they mock, Saying: "Behold
> The King of Canaan whose are seven hundred chariots of
>   iron!"

> They take off his vesture whole with their Knives of flint,
> But they cut asunder his inner garments, searching with
> Their cruel fingers for his heart, & there they enter in pomp,
> In many tears, & there they erect a temple & an altar.[72]

Most of the sacrificial symbolism in *Jerusalem*, however, relates to the Druids. The Bible visualizes a cycle of life from the third Eye of the Elohim to the end of the seventh, six thousand years of history. From the point of view of the imagination, what is outside this is the city of God and the body of Jesus; from the point of view of the memory, what is outside it is the Druid civilization which preceded it, and left Stonehenge in England as its monument. But nature moves in cycles, and if we give ourselves up to nature, what has happened before in England will assuredly happen again. The six thousand years of the Biblical vision is the period of the Adamic body, when men have been too weak to exterminate themselves. But if behind the Bible there is the memory of an age of murderous ogres who perished in a stench of burning flesh, then in front of it there is the apprehension of a returning power of gigantic self-destruction. The former survives in the Bible as the Covering Cherub; the latter is portrayed as the giants Gog and Magog who return with the full power of darkness after the millennium.

The motive for human sacrifice is not superstitious barbarity, but an effort to express the ascendancy of nature and reason in society. We constantly kill enemies and execute criminals, not out of ferocity, but because we think it necessary and morally justifiable. It seems natural and reasonable to us that the interests of society should be preserved by getting rid of those who are dangerous to it. True, we cannot always distinguish a public enemy from a prophet, but when Caiaphas says of Jesus that it was expedient that one man should die for the people,[73] he speaks with a natural and reasonable voice. Besides, capital punishment is a comparatively rare and sporadic form of the accusation of sin. Every attempt to minimize or ridicule the free use of the imagination in the name of common sense is a little murder of human life, and is related to human sacrifice as Hayley in *Milton* is related to Satan. All we need to do is to persist in natural and reasonable tendencies, and in a very short time we shall get the society we want: the society of the Roman Empire which crucified Jesus all over again, only much more so. We shall get a church-state ruled by a divine Caesar; a religion which is a tyranny of custom as pervasive as atmospheric pressure; a government organized for imperial war without any real purpose beyond waging it, and an increasingly obvious desire for the extermination of all human life within reach. When we get to that point, the stage of the crucifixion of Orc will be arrived at, and we shall find ourselves again in front of the icon which represents the full integrity of nature and reason, the body of a flogged, mocked, bleeding, crucified, naked Jewish wretch.

Albion can be "saved" by this masterpiece of Selfhood art, but not because it convicts him of a sense of moral evil: the cure for moral evil is moral virtue, and he has far too much of that now. Nor because it fills him with the fear of his own approaching doom: the natural man fears death, it is true, but he fears life much more, and cannot very well be frightened into annihilating himself. The saving power of the vision of the hanged Orc is negative; it shows man the form of his own bondage. For, Blake says, we become what we behold; forms of ourselves cannot remain at a distance, and if we see life in the form of the hanged Orc, as an inevitable recurrence of natural vitality ending in death, we shall soon find ourselves not before a cross but on one. For the pattern of contraries and negation reappears even here: there is not only a "reprobate" Messiah but a thief redeemed by seeing him as such, and a mocking "elect" thief representing the Barabbas whom the "Fiends of Righteousness"[74] in society invariably prefer to Jesus. The latter thief is in the pure natural state of man, the state in which the highest imaginative pleasure consists of observing pain. The former has realized that nothing short of the exact opposite of this state will release us from being perpetually tied to it; nothing short of the pure vision of the identity of God and Man in an eternal civilized body, stripped of all trappings of nature, reason, authority and mystery.

The crucified Christ is a vision of irresistible fate, and illustrates what man has always done in the world, is doing now, and will always be fated to do as long as he remains in the state of existence in which fate is to be found. The life of Jesus is eternal joy and freedom; the death of Jesus represents the total achievement of that aspect of human life which consists of temporary painful necessities. But if we could escape from the necessity, we should also escape from time and pain.

Now we derive the idea of necessity from the passivity with which we see things. As the crucified Christ is the clarified analogy of pure vision, it is the perfected form of the sleeping Albion's dream of death. A dream is the process of taking a subreality to be real which is induced in us by bodily and mental inertia. But a complete understanding of a dream includes the knowledge that it is one, a knowledge which at once wakes us up. The crucified Christ is the visible form of Man's dream state, and as whatever is completely visible is transparent, that means that the crucified Christ is a prism or lens of reality, that is, an eye, which Man is slowly trying to open. The word "eye" associates itself at once with another part of Blake's symbolism. Seven Eyes of God, seven increasingly clear visions of the unity of God and Man in one body and one city, have completed their work, and we are now searching for the eighth. He is still elusive, still hiding in the forests, as Blake says,[75] and when we do get him we shall have a new perception of God which will be a final confirmation of either the Blakean or the Lockian view of reality, either a newborn God or an Antichrist. Of Antichrist Paul says: "And ye know now what withholdeth that he might be revealed in his time," and Blake adds, "But you cannot behold him until he be revealed in his system."[76] He also tells us to look through and not with our own eyes.

The vision of the city of God, as focused and clarified by the prism of art, is pressing down on Albion's retina, and as long as it remains there as a passive image of something outside, brought in by chance, it will be the inverted form of itself. If we look with our new eye at what we cannot help seeing, we shall see the form of what God is not, a remote world in space, a hopeless future in time, and a continuously martyred imagination. Satan, Blake says, is a "Reactor"[77]; he never acts, he only reacts; he never sees, he always has to be shown; and if our attitude to what we see is "reactionary," we are done for. But there is consciousness behind the retina of Albion, and as soon as it is stirred by the inverted image into the act of vision, the image will right itself and assume its proper form. Again we become what we behold, for the image of God is the form of human life, and the reality of ourselves.

The drift of the involved symbolism which Blake uses to express all this is as follows: As the Jesus cycle of history nears its close in Part IV, all the powers of darkness endeavor to make sure that the next rebirth (here Hyle, or "nature" as it is in Blake's time, replaces the less specific symbol of Orc) will take place in a bondage to the female will so complete that the new imagination will never be able to get the most fleeting glimpse of reality, but will emerge as a perfect Deist, completely confined to nature and reason. In order to do this the female will belonging to Hyle, Gwendolen, now his virgin mother in the place of seed, wraps him up in the cocoon of a "falsehood," or perverted vision of life, preparatory to getting him reborn as a "Winding Worm," an earthbound existence of which the cursed serpent, the caterpillar (which reminds us of our mother's grief because it represents the pain of natural life) and the worms who are the only guests at the natural man's last supper, are all images.[78] Gwendolen hopes that when this worm does develop wings it will become merely a winged worm or dragon, that is, one of the brood of the Covering Cherub, or totality of fallen life stretching between fall and apocalypse and blocking our view of what life was like before it fell. And as before the Fall Man existed as an eternal city, so the Covering Cherub is the whole body of the fallen city, Eden with its Gihon (Nile) and Euphrates perverted into Egypt and Babylon, man in his complete serpentine or natural form, covered like Aaron with the gold and gems gathered by tyranny and exploitation, and so an analogy of the gold and precious stones of which the revealed city is composed. If we were to look at, or with, this basilisk, we should be absorbed into his own stony death; if we look through him, we see him as a mirror-image, as Perseus saw Medusa, as the reflecting analogy of the true Eden and the true Jerusalem. This analogy Blake calls Canaan, the fallen form of the Promised Land, which is to that Promised Land as eighteenth century England is to Atlantis, and therefore *is* eighteenth century England, the Promised Land and Atlantis being the same thing. At that point the true form of Albion emerges, as the true form of Jesus emerges from the pupil of this new Eye, which is Jesus' analogy the hanged Orc, life bound by the Druids or Satan-worshipers to the tree and the stone.

There is one more point necessary to our commentary, though it is not explicitly made in the poem. After Jesus had consolidated the whole body of error in his society into a resolve to destroy him, he was seized in a garden by soldiers, accused of treason and blasphemy, of sin against church and state, and put to death in a bloody ritual of scourging, mockery, bearing a cross and crucifixion in which he assumed the roles of the dying Luvah and the fallen Albion. Then the great wheel of tyranny rolled over him, and proceeded on its course. While meditating *Jerusalem*, one of England's few prophets encountered a soldier in a garden and found himself accused of treason, and what amounted to blasphemy, the remark ascribed to him, reproduced by Blake as "D - - n the K - - g,"[79] being clearly an insult to the Head of the Church. Originally, the complete punishment for this treason was another bloody ritual of hanging, drawing, castrating and quartering, each phase reproducing a different aspect of the fall and *sparagmos* of Albion. The wheel was ready to roll again, but this time something went wrong. Blake was released, of course, because society did not think him dangerous enough. In any case he is allowed to continue his work—in the next chapter we shall see in more detail what he considered that work to be. But perhaps the slight falter and rattle in the machinery suggests, to an acute ear, something seriously out of order, something that may even cause a breakdown. Perhaps some prophet of the age, whether Blake or another matters little, may achieve the final triumph of the prophet, a triumph accorded in the Bible only to Jonah, who did not appreciate it, of finding his prophecy of impending disaster fail because it is being listened to. Perhaps the cloven fiction of the reasonable Hand and the natural Hyle will not freeze into Druidism after all; perhaps they will be shocked by it into a better kind of unity, as their nursery-rhyme prototypes forgot their quarrel in the shadow of an approaching fear. Perhaps the Prometheus in the human mind is getting tired of being nailed down by his five foolish virgins, who have no light of their own and no idea where they can get any. Perhaps he is already gaining the sensuous wisdom that will lead him into the great Marriage, when the Bridegroom comes out of his chamber with the rising sun, when the cock crows and the evil spirits vanish, and the dawn of a fourfold vision breaks on the night of a threefold denial.

WHEN *Jerusalem* was complete the canon of Blake's poetry was complete too, or nearly so. However its final table of contents would have read, he had little organically to add to it. As it contains history, prophecy, creation myths, apocalyptic and wisdom literature, it perhaps would have contained, to round off the Biblical parallel, *The Everlasting Gospel*, which is later than *Jerusalem*. But in its essentials Blake's poetic testament or "Bible of Hell" was ready for the world, apart from engraving, by about the end of 1808, and Blake lived until 1827.

This idea of an individual canon, apart altogether from the choice between good and bad poems which every poet makes, is neither peculiar to Blake nor a mark of egomania. If a man of genius spends all his life perfecting works of art, it is hardly far-fetched to see his life's work as itself a larger work of art with everything he has produced integral to it, as Balzac was not simply a man who wrote novels but a man whose novels constitute a *Comédie Humaine*. Blake is exceptional only in having said all he had to say in middle life, with twenty years of work ahead of him. We have mentioned Milton's distinction between the brief and the diffuse epic: it occurs in a passage in which he speaks of them as two of the three great forms of poetry, the third being the drama. The passage is early, but nevertheless after reading it one realizes that *Paradise Lost, Paradise Regained* and *Samson Agonistes* make up a single poetic testament. Similarly when Spenser imitates Virgil in beginning with pastoral and going on to an epic, one can see that Spenser is also creating a canon out of his poetry.[1]

The development of Spenser implies that, as an epic is necessarily a product of poetic maturity, the young poet will begin with lyrical forms, the pastoral being one of the most congenial of these. We have noticed that the pastoral form contains within itself a suggestion of satire on the imperfect nonpastoral reality of the world. Blake's earlier poems are similarly lyrical both in mood and form, and tend to be either pastoral songs of innocence or satirical songs of experience. But as soon as Los appears, the tone becomes more didactic, and the characteristics of lyrical poetry, notably its profusion of natural images and its reproduction of the immediate impact of poetic vision, become subtilized. This development away from the lyrical mood is paralleled in the greatest poets, as we can see if we compare, say, *Coriolanus* with *A Midsummer Night's Dream*, or *Paradise Regained* with *L'Allegro*. Those who think that Blake's rich vein of poetry becomes increasingly varicose as he goes on, and that *Jerusalem* would be a better poem if it had more of the kind of beauty that *The Book of Thel* has, therefore assume that Blake should not have allowed himself to develop in the same direction. In any case, in *Jerusalem* the didactic tone has finally been absorbed into the form of the epic.

The fact that Blake finished his epic in the prime of life suggests, by elimination, that there was still before him a crowning period of dramatic art.[2] This, though it sounds oversymmetrical, happens to fit Blake's own views. The epic, in Blake's sense, is a "divine vision" of the whole of life, and the drama in Blake's sense is an episode of the divine vision. But here we imply a distinction between *a* divine vision, which is an epic, and *the* divine vision, which is something infinitely greater than any individual imagination can achieve. The drama relates to the latter, and illustrates episodes of an implicit and unformulated vision broader than any epic can suggest. Shakespeare, for instance, draws on a vision of such scope that it is doubtful if the most heroic effort of criticism would go far in formulating it. As Shakespeare was never an epic poet, he presumably never tried to formulate it himself; but he illustrates the fact that whereas the epic poet attains to a single vision of the world, the dramatic poet attains a perspective in which everything he sees takes on the universal significance of a still wider vision. The goal of this is what we have described as the universal perception of the particular, seeing the world in a grain of sand.

Now the drama proper demands a public support of a kind Blake was not very likely to receive. It is wrong to say that Blake could never have made a dramatist: Blake could have done anything. But the stage and he could never have been friends, and in any case the silent unity of vision in painting makes painting at least equally good as a dramatic medium, and a medium that Blake had already mastered. And of all forms of painting, fresco-painting on walls of public buildings is the most obviously dramatic. After writing *Jerusalem*, therefore, Blake began to experiment with different fresco mediums, and laying plans for a public appearance with a public proposal.

The English nation in Blake's day has come to the historical crisis in which it has to choose whether it will follow the Orc cycle to its end or make the imaginative recreation of itself that will achieve a spiritual England as the Hebrew prophets achieved a spiritual Israel. Winter is approaching, and a great harvest of culture and prophecy is waiting: the English may gather it in and await a millennial spring, or allow it to rot in the fields. So far, they are considering the ways of the grasshopper and being foolish. Lockian doctrines of a passive mind and an external nature have spread over all the arts, to their infinite damage. The English still have the Bible and their great poets, but no longer understand how to use their imaginations in reading them, and the visionary tradition is now a broken and straggling line.

Blake will of course be told that England is at war with Napoleon and is too busy for extra things. This is exactly his point. The decline of imaginative power in England is closely connected with the fact that England is an empire at war, and is approaching barbarism not so much because it is at war as because it is an empire. If Napoleon wins (a very possible view in 1809), Blake may help England, under a *pax Gallica*, to lead captive her conqueror, as Greece did Rome[3]; but the centrifugal force of imperial ambitions, which sucks all genius out of the country, will only be stimulated by victory. The probabilities indicate that London will follow the Orc cycle to where Rome has gone, and where Babylon and Egypt went before Rome; that England will become a natural and reasonable state in which religion and philosophy will subside into fatalism and moral virtue, art into a luxury trade, and mass war, mass tyranny and mass slavery crush its great cities into swarming anthills, while genius and prophecy go wherever there are still living men to be found.

A certain exhaustion of vitality, at the end of a cycle of civilization, is inevitable insofar as it is part of an organic process. But a man should grow wiser because he must grow older, and the same is true of a nation. The function of the prophet is not to point out what is inevitable, but to show what can be built up out of an inevitable development. The real lesson of history is contained in the instructive contrast between the evolutionary Hebraic and the cyclic Classical cultures, and the violent hatred of the latter which Blake expresses from *Milton* on, and which incites him to such utterances as "It is the Classics, & not Goths nor Monks, that Desolate Europe with Wars,"[4] is motivated by his intense desire to point this moral. To the rule stated above that empires do not inspire major art the chief exception is Virgil, and Virgil shows the cloven hoof in the sixth book of the *Aeneid*, where the Sibyl's prophecy assigns conquest to Rome and the arts to more effeminate nations, a passage which really means that Rome's greatest poet is acquiescing in the degeneration of his own culture.[5] The Hebrew prophets, by the imaginative recreation of their culture, produced Jesus: the English, if they do the same thing, can produce a second coming of Jesus.

Blake, therefore, must come forward to insist that "Empire follows Art & Not Vice Versa as Englishmen suppose."[6] He will use his canon as a new testament for English culture. He will teach the English how to use their imaginations, how to develop the immense reserves of power that they are leaving untapped. A savage confronted with a modern metropolis is confronted only with a minor example of what the same human imagination that exists in himself can do. Between a commonplace England and a spiritual England there will be the same link but a far greater contrast, and an awakened England would make short work of Napoleon, as of all the rest of its previous dreams. The answer to the popular estimate of the comparative values of a civilized and a practical life is:

I am really sorry to see my Countrymen trouble themselves about Politics. If Men were Wise, the Most arbitrary Princes could not hurt them. If they are not wise, the Freest Government is compell'd to be a Tyranny. Princes appear to me to be Fools. Houses of Commons & Houses of Lords appear to me to be fools; they seem to me to be something Else besides Human Life.[7]

It is perhaps not a wholly satisfactory answer, but it belongs to the type of thinking that Blake feels he must introduce to the English mind. Otherwise he would be what he is called in *Point Counterpoint*: "the last civilized man." Had Blake heard himself so described in his lifetime, it might have been the one thing that could have broken his spirit.

Blake's primary objective is to revive public painting: the revival of other aspects of civilization will then follow more easily. Against him will be the whole trading combination of commercial painters, with their patrons and connoisseurs: with him will be the common sense of English public opinion. It will be necessary for Blake to write manifestoes explaining the facts of the situation. He will have to tell the public something of his own career in order to establish his right to speak and to clear himself of an unusually malicious series of personal slanders. And if he explains that his reputation as a fool and madman has been built up by a clique of unscrupulous competitors, and brings forward his pictures to prove it, the public is bound to listen to him. "Truth," he had said, "can never be told so as to be understood, and not be believ'd."[8] He will also have to explain that there is no mystery about art, and that those who insist on one are humbugs. The sense of mystery comes from a timid lack of confidence in the imagination. The best that has been thought and said, or painted or composed, in the world, is within the reach of everyone, and those who do not possess the highest pleasures and the richest wisdom are being swindled, whether by themselves or by others.

In the periods of highest civilization, the arts which depend on social co-operation are in an especially flourishing state. These are the dramatic or public arts produced by a group for the benefit of a group, as an ensemble performance for an audience. The chief arts of this kind are music, drama, fresco-painting and architecture. It was during the Gothic and high Renaissance periods, the ages of Chaucer and Michelangelo, that these arts were at their highest development. The lack of fresco-painting in England may be explained by the fact that it never did develop in England to the extent that it did in Italy. But music and drama did; and of all the arts in England in Blake's time none are in a more pitiful condition than those two. Blake's immediate program, being concerned with the re-establishment of fresco in public buildings, involves an overthrow of the easel oil-painting monopoly and a return to the pure colors and sharp outlines which only fresco and water-color can give. It also involves a renewed appreciation of the merits of Gothic and Renaissance culture, when art had more of its proper social basis and a generally understood language of symbolism.

By 1809 Blake had found a very simple formula for making fresco-painting commercially practicable. Take, he says, a surface of wood or canvas, spread a plaster coating over it, and paint the fresco on the plaster. Such a fresco is painted, not directly on a wall to remain there as long as the building itself does, but on a temporary or removable wall, and can be changed at pleasure or transferred somewhere else. Blake thereupon held the first private exhibition of his life and wrote for it a full *Descriptive Catalogue*. This catalogue was intended, first of all, to set forth his new idea, and the pictures of the exhibition were to illustrate what the process would do and how durable it was. With the utter guilelessness that one finds only in genius and sanctity, Blake urges the reader to see how some of the pictures have been "laboured to a superabundant blackness" and how others "have been bruized and knocked about without mercy, to try all experiments."[9] Second, the catalogue was to hint at the infinite possibilities of such a scheme: how gigantic public projects rivaling the greatest works of the Italian Renaissance would be possible, and how, if the right people would give commissions, a very dingy country would suddenly find itself in possession of majestic frescoes of startling brilliance and freshness of color, like brand-new Giottos. Third, the catalogue was to point out the disadvantages of oil, show how blurred and smudged its effects are and how unsuitable it is as a medium for heroic painting, which demands a jewel-like clarity in the smallest details. Fourth, it was to indicate how the man of vision looks at his time, and how political events and figures are evolved by the artist into imperishable forms. Blake includes pictures of the "spiritual forms" of Pitt and Nelson, which he explains could be executed in the same medium in a public building on a colossal scale. Fifth, it was to give a rough outline of the British archetypal myth, showing how the legends of Albion, Arthur, Druids, ancient Bards, the island of Atlantis and other fragments fit together into a pattern by means of which the British nation can develop a set of historical conventions for the artist to use, as religious conventions were employed in medieval painting. Blake refers in passing to having written a poem which explains this myth more fully. Sixth, it provides an elaborate criticism of

Chaucer in order to show the British public what immense store-houses of genius they have in their own poets if they will only read them with some effort of the imagination, and in order also to show what the despised Gothic age could produce. Blake was clearly not aware that he was living in the middle of the Romantic movement. Many other points are dealt with in this catalogue, including the bringing of Swedenborg and the *Bhagavadgita* to public attention, but these are the chief ones.

The *Descriptive Catalogue* was to be the opening gun of the campaign: a "Public Address" explaining Blake's own position and attitude to art would follow, and a history of art (which prom-ised to be of phenomenal inaccuracy) putting the fresco-painting of the Gothic and Renaissance ages in its true perspective and re-ducing the stature of the oil-painters to something more like its proper level.[10] The English public would also be taught what to look for in contemporary painting, and how to find more of it in a great mind like Fuseli than in a fashionable eclectic like Reynolds. In this connection it may be noted that the vitriolic marginalia to Reynolds' *Discourses*, written about the same time, are directly addressed to a reader. The scheme of writing a series of poems in doggerel verse, defending the genuine artists and attacking the sham ones, was probably soon abandoned. The few lines we have from a projected *Barry* and a *Book of Moonlight* do not look very promising.[11] It is possible too that Blake had in mind some biographical prophecies which would round out the symbolism of the Hayley quarrel in *Milton* and the Schofield trial in *Jerusalem* by adding to it other features of the conspiracy of mediocrity against genius which he felt to be taking shape in his own life. As he says: "Secret Calumny & open Professions of Friend-ship are common enough all the world over, but have never been so good an occasion of Poetic Imagery."[12]

So Blake hopes that his quiet little Exhibition will be the birth-day of the Renaissance of English art, and perhaps of greater things still, for Blake, like Milton, felt that his talents were not given him to hide and that the right genius at the right time might speak the great Word that would shatter the walls of the human prison. Besides, "if a man is master of his profession," Blake says, "he cannot be ignorant that he is so,"[13] and there can be no reason-able doubt that his is the greatest creative genius working in

England in 1809. It is therefore his duty to step forward and guide England into the road leading to a clean and beautiful civilization. He is not, like his enemies, a clever advertiser; but he has his work and his plan, and if he does his duty he may expect England to do hers. Robert Hunt of the *Examiner*, the only one who reviewed the Exhibition at all, gave England's answer:

. . . an unfortunate lunatic whose personal inoffensiveness secures him from confinement, and consequently of whom no public notice would have been taken, if he was not forced on the animadversion of the *Examiner* in having been held up to public admiration by many esteemed amateurs and professors as a genius in some respects original and legitimate. The praises which these gentlemen bestowed last year on this unfortunate man's illustrations to Blair's *Grave* have, in feeding his vanity, stimulated him to publish his madness more largely, and this again exposed him, if not to the derision, at least to the pity of the public. . . . Thus encouraged, the poor man fancies himself a great master, and has painted a few wretched pictures. . . . These he calls an Exhibition, of which he has published a catalogue, or rather a farrago of nonsense, unintelligibleness and egregious vanity, the wild effusions of a distempered brain. . . .[14]

· 2 ·

It is unpleasant to have to admit that there is anything in the public reception of Blake's offer to be defended, but there is a very real sense in which Blake was on the wrong track. It is clear that Blake had much more to demonstrate than his technical ability to carry out such a scheme. A long line of prophets between Blake's day and our own, including Ruskin and Morris, have not yet achieved even the beginning of what he hoped for. Like most of his successors, Blake insists that communal art, in particular fresco-painting, is essential to a civilized society; like them, he realizes that social reform is really a revival of art; like them, he points to medieval and Renaissance culture as providing in many respects, with all their faults, a healthier milieu for art than capitalist imperialism. Blake's failure indicates that, like many men of genius, he was inclined to overestimate the ease with which a public can transform itself into another kind of public; at least he overestimated its willingness to try. The artist follows Los and the New Testament: for him, anything that we want to do, whether abolish war, settle a country, plan a society or enter the millennium, we can do and do at once, and his motto is always "The time is at hand." Society follows the Spectre of Urthona, and, even when it agrees on the desirability of the goal, it insists that all such changes take a very long time, and that it will take centuries for some vaguely defined historical ghost to work up the courage to improve its status.

It would have been possible, even in Blake's time, for a nation's imaginative energies to become centripetal and national rather than centrifugal and imperial, and in an atmosphere of growing national and racial consciousness his plan might have received more attention. But a cultural leader bent on reviving dramatic art in such a milieu, whether in music, drama or fresco, would have to be a very different kind of man. He would have to give the public what would appeal not only to their sense of community but to their sense of herded solidarity; that is, he would have to appeal to both the best and the worst tendencies of his nation, and would therefore himself have to be both genius and megalomaniac. As a genius he would visualize great things, and as a megalomaniac he would carry them out in the teeth of frantic opposition. As a genius he would give his nation its archetypal vision, but his achievement would be too egocentric to leave an integrated tradition behind. But Blake was not Wagner, nor was England Germany. Blake had had to sacrifice a great many things to purify his art, but the public was now forcing him to reject one thing more, and it was something it was on the whole as well that he should reject.

There is no question of the social value of art or of the social significance of the artist. But Blake's willingness to become a public leader of art shows a confusion in his mind between two things which are carefully distinguished in the Prophecies: the imagination and the will, Los and the Spectre of Urthona, the struggle of art to perfect its vision and the attempt of the will to alter the world of experience. If Blake had listened to the "Rintrah" within him, he would have been told that as a public figure he would have to give the public what it wanted: an ambiguous phrase, resting on an inability to distinguish between what the public imagination wants and what the public Selfhood wants. The only legitimate compulsion on the artist is the compulsion to clarify the form of his work, and in accepting other compulsions he is at once trapped in compromise. His forms are spoiled by the shifting of emphasis necessary for didactic purposes; his tone is made raucous by the self-hypnotism with which a constant and expectant audience may infect any artist. There is simply no such thing as a "Hero as Poet," and when Milton, for instance, was gloating over his duel with Salmasius, a public joust for liberty "with which all Europe rings from side to side," he was talking nonsense and writing imaginative trash. And if the artist cannot be a public hero, neither can he be wholly a public servant. He must compromise as little as possible with the "necessary" social hypocrisies of the kind which force him to idealize whatever at the moment is being idolized, such as Pitt or Nelson, either of whom may be vilified next day *pour encourager les autres*. And although Blake's Pitt and Nelson are not idealized, but are in fact very sinister figures, that will merely develop the cleavage between the select few and the misunderstanding many which will destroy all public art.

There is of course more to be said about the artist's relation to society than this, but Blake's great value as a personal influence in English literature is that he is so outstanding an example of a precious quality of mental independence. Very few writers even in England have been so startlingly free of accepted shibboleths in religion, morality or politics. His attitude of mind is a kind of reverent Philistinism, with a broad humor that delights to spread banana peelings in the paths of heroes, a simple pleasure in seeing the aura of sanctity around traditional arcana as a fog, and a tough honesty that continues to repeat that war is always damnable and tyranny always stupid and persecution always evil, however "necessary" at any given moment. Cockney cheek and the Nonconformist conscience, two of the most resolute and persistent saboteurs of the dark Satanic mills in English life, combine in Blake to establish an incorruptible mental court without appeal to which all apologies for the traditional and conventional are referred. The public's contemptuous neglect of Blake was as wrong and foolish as it could be, but nevertheless Blake owes much of his integrity to his isolation. We have said that Blake's theory of poetry would have been more easily accepted had he lived in the Renaissance, but as he lived when he did, we have a unique example of an artist saying what he pleased without the least tendency, which social recognition often encourages, toward the parasitic in literature, the sycophantic in politics or the malignant in religion.

· 3 ·

PRACTICALLY all the poetry Blake wrote after *Jerusalem* was occasional. One such poem, the dedication of his "Last Judgment" to the Countess of Egremont, written in 1808, speaks of the canon as more or less closed. This occasional poetry shows no sign of a falling-off in technical competence: it shows only that Blake still could write exquisitely or powerfully whenever he wanted to and that he no longer often wanted to. As an artist, however, Blake has one of the busiest lives on record: he had been in his youth an infant prodigy who refused to burn out, and he was to become at seventy a veteran who had wasted no time in search of a style. With his scheme of portable frescoes ignored he would have to turn to something else. And, if our interpretation is correct, he would find something in his own restricted sphere of activity at least as important to art as his portable frescoes would have been, even if Parliament had given him *carte blanche* to fill England with them.

The transition from prophecy to painting is at first only a shift of emphasis. In the first place, Blake stops illustrating poems and starts commenting on pictures. Take, for example, his treatment of the Last Judgment. In *The Four Zoas* we have a long and ecstatic poetic treatment of this theme: in *Milton* and *Jerusalem* the treatment is far more compressed and is set in a pictorial design. Following *Jerusalem* come pictures with commentaries. The Last Judgment design in the illustrations to Blair's *Grave* referred to by Hunt is still an illustration to a poem, but an illustration quite independent of its text. Then we have the great painting for the Countess of Egremont, with the descriptive commentary preserved in a letter, and the short dedicatory lyric mentioned above. As a climax to this series comes the still larger design, perhaps intended to be the first of the great masterpieces of the last period, of which nothing remains except a commentary. In the second place, Blake's chief interest in writing passes from creation to criticism, and from poetry to prose. Even in the prophecies themselves we can see that the poetic utterance becomes for Blake increasingly a means of explanation or comment on the central form of the poem, and after *Jerusalem* all his important literary ambitions were concerned with prose criticism. The prophecies were re-engraved, but with one exception were not rewritten or redesigned.[15]

We have seen how important in Blake's theory of art is his conception of the recreation of the archetype, the process which unites a sequence of visions, first into a tradition, then into a Scripture. The next step for Blake is obviously, therefore, to illustrate other poets' visions so that their readers may more easily understand their archetypal significance. Blake had always done this to some extent, but not so systematically as he began to do it now. Here he found a formula for uniting the work of the creator with that of the teacher, of combining mythopoeic art with instruction in how to read it, not as spectacular as the one he had planned, but possibly no less rewarding.

The most important works that fall under this classification are the Chaucer painting, the Milton and Bunyan series, the Biblical illustrations, the Dante and the Job. Here we have again a steady advance in objectivity. There is only one Chaucer painting, with an elaborate criticism of the poet. The illustrations to Milton's lyrical poems are simply described, with a few suggestive hints,[16] and those to his epics have no explanatory text at all. Blake may have had some idea of presenting the whole Bible, including the pseudepigraphic Book of Enoch which was first made available to him in 1821,[17] in the form of his own vision, and some fragmentary annotations to the Book of Genesis which still remain may be a relic of this.[18] The Dante sketches and engravings, wonderful as they are, are a little out of the line of Blake's development, as Dante was not the fructifying influence on Blake that the Hebrew and English poets were; in any case Blake has left us only a few rather disgruntled comments on the other great Gothic poet.[19] Finally comes the *Vision of the Book of Job*, where comment is made entirely by quotation. There is also a steady increase in independence of the subject, from the Chaucer painting, where Blake boasts of his fidelity to Chaucer's text, to the recreation of the drama of Job in a sequence of plates which, though a profound commentary on that poem, is clearly not a series of illustrations to it, but an independent art-form.

The two units of art, to Blake, are the audible unit, which is the word in poetry, and the visible unit, which is the image or outlined form. Words in their turn may have suggestive associations of sound both with one another and with the images they represent. All languages develop words of great onomatopoeic effectiveness, and while most of this may be called accidental, it is the poet's business to make as systematic a use as possible of such accidents. What we call imitative harmony in poetry is thus a poet's attempt to unite more closely the audible and the visible units of art. The same point is also illustrated by the words which the poet invents, such as names of characters. Lilliputian is a good name for a pygmy because it suggests the sounds of "little" and "puny," and Ebenezer Scrooge a good name for a miser because it suggests the sounds of "squeeze" and "screw." Similarly Blake's Luvah contains the sound of "love," Urizen of "reason," Urthona of "north," "earth" and "throne."[20]

The sounds of words are represented by letters, and letters, though visual signs, are now largely arbitrary ones. The alphabetic system of writing can be traced back to the Semitic people of "Canaan," and perhaps if we knew more about it we should discover that it was not a moral code but an alphabet that the Hebrews learned at Mount Sinai, from a God with enough imagination to understand how much more important a collection of letters was than a collection of prohibitions:

> Who in mysterious Sinai's awful cave
> To Man the wondrous art of writing gave.[21]

The names of the Hebrew letters are also names of things, which suggests that the letters were originally pictographs, units at once of sound and of imagery. It is understandable then that Hebrew traditions should have preserved in Cabbalism a respect for the letter as well as the word of their Scripture, and perhaps one may see in the Cabbalistic frenzy of superstitious pedantry an "analogy" of the vision of a God who is Alpha and Omega. (The intensity of thought is often in proportion to its verbalism, and the most important of all human disputes, the Arian controversy over whether Jesus was the "Similitude" or the "Identity" of the God-head, was fought over literally a single iota of difference.) It was no doubt the influence of what he knew of Cabbalism that caused

Blake to say of *Jerusalem* that not only every word but every letter in it had been "studied." After *Jerusalem* we can see in his work a development toward the pictograph, and in the Job engravings we are getting down to the very bedrock of imaginative communication, a series of images which are at once pictures and hieroglyphs, rather like what the characters of Chinese must originally have been, in which the common basis of writing and drawing, that is, of poetry and painting, has been re-established.

At the end of the sixth chapter we suggested that the combination of musical, pictorial and poetic characteristics in Blake's prophecies made them unified visions of the three major arts, presented to the individual as the musical drama, the Greek play with its chorus, the Elizabethan play with its songs, or the modern opera, oratorio or ballet, present them to an audience. Of all these forms, the ballet unites music and drama on their common basis in the dance, just as the Job engravings unite poetry and painting on their common basis in hieroglyphic, and it can hardly be an accident that Blake's vision of Job makes an excellent ballet. In all periods of his life, Blake moves toward undifferentiated art, art addressed not to a sense but to the mind that opens the senses.

Blake's pictographs are to be interpreted in terms of their sequential relationship to one another, as a progression of signs which, like the alphabet, spell out not a word but the units of all words. According to Bacon the experimenter searches nature for its underlying principles or forms, and Bacon believed it probable that there were comparatively few of these forms, which, when discovered, would be to knowledge what an alphabet is to a language. And, reading imagination for experiment and art for nature, Blake also seems to be striving for an "alphabet of forms," a Tarot pack of pictorial visions which box the entire compass of the imagination in an orderly sequence. The alphabet itself, if we may do some illustrative guessing, may be a fossil of some such work of art, the Zodiacal signs another, and the Tarot pack (with which the Job series has been associated[22]) a third. The *Vision of the Book of Job* has twenty-two plates, the number of letters in the Hebrew alphabet, just as the Homeric epic, according to its Alexandrian editors, has a book for every letter in the Greek alphabet. Here we have gone from a dramatic medium into a new kind of epic. For the equivalent of the epic in the plastic arts is evidently the kind of imaginative alphabet seen in its "brief" form in Blake's Job and in its "diffuse" form in the encyclopedic symbolism of the medieval cathedrals. The former was what Blake actually produced; the latter was what he offered to take the lead in helping to reproduce.

· 4 ·

IT is clear that the argument over whether art is complete in itself or suggests something beyond itself, whether it is pure form or a guide to better living, amoral delight or ornamental instruction, is dealt with by Blake as he deals with all questions that are cracked down the middle by a cloven fiction. According to Blake, no such dilemma exists: if it were possible to delight without instruction, there could be no qualitative difference between painting the Sistine ceiling and cutting out paper dolls; if it were possible to instruct without delighting, art would be merely the kindergarten class of philosophy and science. There is nothing to be said for the shivering virgin theory of art, according to which art is a fragile evocation of pure beauty surrounded by rough disciplines such as theology and morals, and in constant danger of being polluted by them. There is nothing to be said either for the thus-we-see theory which finds the meaning of art in a set of moral generalizations inferred from it. The work of art suggests something beyond itself most obviously when it is most complete in itself: its integrity is an image or form of the universal integration which is the body of a divine Man. All Blake's own art, therefore, is at the same time an attempt to achieve absolute clarity of vision and a beginner's guide to the understanding of an archetypal vision of which it forms part. We cannot understand Blake without understanding how to read the Bible, Milton, Ovid and the Prose Edda at least as he read them, on the assumption that an archetypal vision, which all great art without exception shows forth to us, really does exist. If he is wrong, we have merely distorted the meaning of these other works of prophecy; if he is right, the ability we gain by deciphering him is transferable, and the value of studying him extends far beyond our personal interest in Blake himself.

Any student of Blake may come to feel that he insists too much on revelation, that his lights are too intense and glaring, that he does not sufficiently sympathize with a reader's tendency to feel

let down when a tantalizing mystery is fully explained. Surely the
deliberate illusion of the magician has a place in art as well as
mental enlightenment. This is more or less the feeling already
referred to that the Prophecies are too diagrammatic to have the
poetic impact of great art, or even to be consistent with Blake's
own condemnation of arid and "spectral" rationalism. We tried to
explain this, however, in terms of Blake's historical context. It is
all very well for Socrates to point out that the poet's inspiration
is one thing and his conscious understanding of what he is saying
another. The Greek dramatists contemporary with Socrates could
make mythological figures humanly credible because a great deal
of their work was done for them: they were interpreting religious
and historical traditions to which their audiences were already
prepared to attach an archetypal significance. The same is true of
Milton's Satan: it is even true, though less obviously so, of many
of Shakespeare's characters. It is, for instance, impossible to understand the significance of Shylock, the Jew who represents a humor
of revenge and a confidence in a bond and a law and a just judgment, without a fairly comprehensive grasp of the argument of the
Christian Bible; and however the Puritan preacher around the
corner might thunder against the godless playhouse, he would
sooner or later, if he knew his job of expounding Scripture, educate
his hearers in the understanding of Shylock.

The audience of a Greek or Christian poet would find it difficult to understand barbarian or heathen symbolism unless it were
first translated into the terms familiar to them. That fact does not
affect the poet, or limit his universal significance; it relates solely
to the audience. In Christian times most of Virgil's readers assumed
that his fourth eclogue was a prophecy of the Christian Messiah.
That has the great advantage of seeing an archetypal pattern in
the poem, and is far ahead of the merely incompetent criticism
which sees nothing in it but extravagant flattery. Insofar as such
readers conceived of the truth of Christianity as rational rather
than visionary, it has the disadvantage of distorting Virgil's
meaning. That is a serious but by no means fatal defect; interpreting Virgil's symbolism in Christian terms is translation, and
translation may be legitimate even though it always has to ignore
many aspects of the poet's original achievement. It is better to
read Virgil in the original symbolism as well as the original lan-

guage, but the one, like the other, must have a meaning communicable to us. Every poet, including Blake, must first be studied in connection with his own age, but there comes a point at which the value of this study becomes exhausted and the conception of "anachronism" is rendered meaningless. What makes the poet worth studying at all is his ability to communicate beyond his context in time and space: we therefore are the present custodians of his meaning, and the profundity of his appeal is relative to our own outlook.

It is here that Blake comes in with his doctrine that "all had originally one language, and one religion."[23] If we follow his own method, and interpret this in imaginative instead of historical terms, we have the doctrine that all symbolism in all art and all religion is mutually intelligible among all men, and that there is such a thing as an iconography of the imagination. Blake suggests to the student of English literature that to recognize the existence of a total form of vision would not be a new discovery, but a return to essential critical principles that should never have been lost sight of. If we look back at Elizabethan scholars, with their rhetorical textbooks and mythological handbooks, their commentaries on Plutarch and Ovid and their allegorical interpretations of Homer and Virgil, we may see that when Chapman spoke of "not onely all learning, gouernment, and wisedome being deduc't as from a bottomlesse fountaine from him [Homer], but all wit, elegancie, disposition, and iudgement,"[24] he meant exactly what he said. It is merely an attempt to complete the humanist revolution, then, to point out that the conception of the Classical in art and the conception of the scriptural or canonical in religion have always tended to approximate one another; that the closer the approximation, the healthier it is for both religion and art; that on this approximation the authority of humane letters has always rested, and that the sooner they are identified with each other the better. Such a cultural revolution would absorb not only the Classical but all other cultures into a single visionary synthesis, deepen and broaden the public response to art, deliver the artist from the bondage of a dingy and nervous naturalism called, in a term which is a little masterpiece of question-begging, "realism," and restore to him the catholicity of outlook that Montaigne and Shakespeare possessed. And though the one religion would be, as far as Blake is concerned, Christianity, it would be a Christianity equated with the broadest possible vision of life, so that it would simply be reading Virgil with the maximum instead of the minimum of imaginative power to see once again the form of the Prince of Peace in Pollio's baby, and unite the Roman poet's *"occidet et serpens"* with the tempter of Eve and Midgard.

The great value of Blake is that he insists so urgently on this question of an imaginative iconography, and forces us to learn so much of its grammar in reading him. He differs from other poets only in the degree to which he compels us to do this. The disadvantage of demonstrating a total form of vision from Homer or Shakespeare is that they give so much for so little effort, and it is easy for their commentators to incur the charge of needless oversubtlety. The advantage of demonstrating it from Blake's Prophecies is that without it, except to the rare and lucky possessor of a set of the original engravings, they give almost nothing. Homer and Shakespeare are not superficial, but they do possess a surface, and reward superficial reading more than it deserves. The reason for Blake's uniqueness is that in his day certain conditions which he blamed, perhaps with some reason, on Locke and the Deists, had brought about a great decline both in mythopoeic art and in the public ability to respond to it. With the exaggeration natural to one in his position, he thought of his age as much less mythopoeic than it actually was; but still he was essentially right in his feeling that archetypal symbolism in his day, if not exactly, in his own words, drawn into one man's loins, was still rare enough for a very explicit treatment of it to be poetically justifiable.

Mythopoeic art revived in the Romantic period, but under the influence of a metaphysic that tended to think of the world of appearance as the object of knowledge and the world of reality within it as unknowable, or, at best, revealed only in flashes of intuition. Hence the importance of suggestive evocation in Romantic art, with its implication that the comprehension of symbolic meanings is a haphazard and fitful process. Our art has passed beyond Romanticism, but our criticism is still largely in it. It is still generally felt that the mythopoeic faculty in art is subconscious, and that if one wishes to produce effective symbolism one must, as Johnson said of Ossian, abandon one's mind to it. Poets are still studied in terms of the Romantic psychological myth

of a subliminal real self conflicting with a censorious rational consciousness. Great Christian poems from *Beowulf* to *The Faerie
Queene* and beyond have been explained as glossing an instinctive
paganism by a perfunctory Christianity, and great tragedies have
been interpreted as more or less disguised expressions of philosophical pessimism, of the kind fashionable in the Romantic
period. And though we should not get far in science or mathematics without a feeling of pleasurable excitement in solving
puzzles, the complicated pattern is felt to be somehow vulgar
in poetry. We are encouraged not to rack the arts to search their
profundities, but to respond to them with a sensitive receptivity,
a relaxed awareness of "appreciation" which, whatever may be
said for it, is clearly not what Dante and Spenser expected from
their readers. And now that poets have become, in Shelley's phrase,
unacknowledged legislators, critics, with one great exception, have
largely forgotten their own language, like Kingsley's gorilla.
Ruskin spoke that language in a diffuse splutter with a thick moral
accent, but he did speak it, and illuminated four or five arts with
his knowledge of it. But this part of his work attracted few disciples, and the present response to symbolism in art seems to be
content with a state of amiable confusion.

The allegorical approach to literature is often, therefore, spoken
of as a fantastic freak of pedantry, though it lasted for centuries,
and probably millennia, whereas our modern neglect of it is an
ignorant parvenu of two centuries and a half. Surely if the word
"pedantry" means anything, it means that kind of contact with
culture which consists in belittling the size and scope of the conceptions of genius, the "nothing but" principle of reading everything on the minimum imaginative level. It is of course true that
one may read too much into a poem, but as Blake says, "If the fool
would persist in his folly he would become wise," and oversubtlety
is an example of the sort of folly he had in mind. Imaginative intensity applied to a wrong or inadequate object can be corrected; a
deficiency in intensity never can be. Of course those who are incapable of distinguishing between a recognition of archetypes and
a Procrustean methodology which forces everything into a prefabricated scheme would be well advised to leave the whole question alone. But it is with symbolism as with etymology: the true
course is neither to accept all resemblances as proving common

descent from a single ancestor, nor reject them all as coincidence, but to establish the laws by which the real relationships may be recognized. If such laws exist, it will be quite possible to develop an imaginative accuracy in reading the arts which is not, like the accuracy of pedantry, founded purely on inhibitions.

The Romantic tradition has one thing in it of great value: it encourages the poet to find his symbols in his own way, and does not impose *a priori* patterns on his imagination. Blake could have told Baudelaire that if he pursued his vision of evil far enough, it would eventually take the form of a gigantic, cruel, elusive and shadowy whore, drunk with the blood of poets and part of the indifference of the order of nature, whom Blake himself calls Rahab. And it was perhaps an advantage to Baudelaire not to be told that. But the advantage of having a large public able instantly to recognize his giantess would far outweigh the very remote possibility that he would not have had sense enough to realize, as Blake did, that he should create his own symbolic system and not be enslaved by another man's.[25] It is with criticism as with so many other aspects of contemporary life: for better or worse the reign of *laissez faire* is over, and the problem of achieving order without regimentation is before us.

It is fortunate that art does not have to wait for critical theory to keep pace with it. The age that has produced the hell of Rimbaud and the angels of Rilke, Kafka's castle and James's ivory tower, the spirals of Yeats and the hermaphrodites of Proust, the intricate dying-god symbolism attached to Christ in Eliot and the exhaustive treatment of Old Testament myths in Mann's study of Joseph, is once again a great mythopoeic age. In *Finnegans Wake*, apparently, we are being told once more that the form of reality is either that of a gigantic human body or of an unending series of cycles, and that the artist's function is to achieve an epiphany of the former out of the chaos of nature and history. Here again is a work of art in which every letter as well as every word has been studied and put into its fit place, which is a puzzle to the intellectual powers and utter gibberish to the corporeal understanding. To all the symbols mentioned above there are many suggestive analogues in Blake, and a theory of symbolism broad enough to develop the critical and appreciative side of contemporary culture will almost have to draw heavily on him.

Blake's doctrine of a single original language and religion implies that the similarities in ritual, myth and doctrine among all religions are more significant than their differences. It implies that a study of comparative religion, a morphology of myths, rituals and theologies, will lead us to a single visionary conception which the mind of man is trying to express, a vision of a created and fallen world which has been redeemed by a divine sacrifice and is proceeding to regeneration. In our day psychology and anthropology have worked great changes in our study of literature strongly suggestive of a development in this direction, and many of the symbols studied in the subconscious, the primitive and the hieratic minds are expanding into patterns of great comprehensiveness, the relevance of which to literary symbolism is not open to question. Anthropology tells us that the primitive imaginative gropings which take the forms of ceremonies and of myths invented to explain them show striking similarities all over the world. Psychology tells us that these ritual patterns have their counterpart in dreams elaborated by the subconscious. And whether we accept Blake's conclusion or not, a less far-reaching inference is almost irresistible.

Neither the study of ritual nor of mythopoeic dreams takes us above a subconscious mental level, nor does such study, except in rare cases, attempt to suggest anything more than a subconscious unity among men. But if we can find such impressive archetypal forms emerging from sleeping or savage minds, it is surely possible that they would emerge more clearly from the concentrated visions of genius. These myths and dreams are crude art-forms, blurred and dim visions, rough drafts of the more accurate work of the artist. In time the communal myth precedes the individual one, but the latter focuses and clarifies the former, and when a work of art deals with a primitive myth, the essential meaning of that myth is not disguised, or sublimated, or refined, but revealed. A comparative study of dreams and rituals can lead us only to a vague and intuitive sense of the unity of the human mind; a comparative study of works of art should demonstrate it beyond conjecture. In the meantime, Blake's Orc may help us to understand that a connection between sex and fire does not exist only in the fact that incendiarists are often sexual perverts, and Blake's ghost of a flea may illustrate the fact that an identification of the character of an animal with the character of a human being does not exist only in totemism.

It is conceivable that such a study—the study of anagogy, if a name is wanted—would supply us with the missing piece in contemporary thought which, when supplied, will unite its whole pattern. Twentieth century culture has produced a large number of theories which seem to demand some kind of fitting together, and we have found a good many analogues to them in Blake. There are theories of history as a sequence of cultural organisms passing through certain stages of growth to a declining metropolitan phase which we are in now, as the Roman Empire was in it before us, which may remind us of Blake's Orc cycle. There are at the same time theories of history as a sequence of revolutionary struggles proceeding toward a society completely free of both exploiters and their victims, which may remind us of Blake's Seven Eyes. There are metaphysical theories of time, and of the divine as the concretion of a form in time, which may remind us of Blake's Los. There are psychological theories of contending forces within the soul which may remind us of Blake's Four Zoas. There are anthropological theories of a universal diffusion throughout primitive society of archetypal myths and rituals underlying all religion and art and connected chiefly with the cult of a dying and reviving god, which may remind us of Blake's Druidism. There are scientific theories of the relativity of the physical world to its human perceivers, and of the mystery of the universe as the analytic aspect of its reality, which may remind us of Blake's vision of Golgonooza. There are new formulations of the Christian conceptions of visionary understanding and of the recreation of the Word of God, new occult conceptions of creative imagination, and new cults with new historical and theological traditions, which have a resemblance to something in our poet. Besides all this, we now have certain facts about the social developments of "Deism" over a century which confirms a good deal of Blake's analysis of them.

The combination of ignorance and lack of space has caused all this to be expressed very baldly, but it would not be honest to omit all mention of the obvious contemporary references of Blake's thought, and in any case the professional caution of a lawyer is not for Blake's interpreters. Now of course the critic's task is to stimulate the understanding of his poet, not belief in what he says, and one naturally resents being told that Blake has "a message for our time." That, however, is the precise opposite of the point we are trying to make. Blake once drew a "Visionary Head" of someone he called his "spiritual preceptor," a vaguely Oriental-looking creature with an expression of baffling inscrutability[26]; and any student of Blake may feel that he too is something of a "preceptor," an oracular revealer of mysteries. But if the reader is left with the impression that there is, or that the writer thinks that there is, something uncanny about Blake's insight, the whole purpose of this book, which is to establish Blake as a typical poet and his thinking as typically poetic thinking, will be overthrown. Anyone who accepts Blake as a preceptor will find his first precept to be that any poet whose work is on a big enough scale will yield an equal harvest of thought if we will take the trouble to learn something about the synthetic and concrete processes of the poetic mind.

The modern reader of Blake may amuse himself, as suggested above, by finding in Blake the germs of ideas later developed by so many of the most important thinkers of our day. In each case the propriety of comparing an exhaustive research into a subject with a few suggestive hints about it may be doubted: it is the poetic articulation, the imaginative unity, of Blake's ideas that is important. Now Blake says that "Real Poets" have no competition[27]: the primary impression which the real poet makes on the reader is not that of comparative greatness, but of positive goodness or genuineness. And this sense of genuineness is the unity of the positive impressions we receive. We are back at Blake's doctrine that "Every Poem must necessarily be a perfect Unity,"[28] with which we began. When we try to express the "quality" of a poem we usually refer to one of its attributes. Blake teaches us that a poem's quality is its *whatness*, the unified pattern of its words and images.

A novelist can say "he ran like a rabbit" without involving the rabbit in a larger pattern of symbolism; but if he does indicate a central symbol, a scarlet letter, a white whale or a golden bowl, he forces us to consider his story as an imaginative unity. And at a certain pitch of concentration peripheral and random images begin to disappear: it has been shown by several critics of Shakespeare that there are very few images in the later plays without some thematic significance. And here the framework of archetypal symbolism provided by Blake may be of some value in trying to unify in our minds the symbolism of another poet. The student of Blake, reading Keats's *Endymion*, may see in the pattern of its symbols, the moon, love, silver, water, sleep, night, dew, "eternal spring," triple rhythms, and its drowsy, relaxed and rather feminine charm, a vision of the state of existence which Blake calls Beulah. He will be able to see how the themes of the elusive virgin, the young shepherd poet, the kingdom under the ocean, the "fabric crystalline" presided over by Circe, the escape from a watery world by exploring the "symbol-essences" of all forms and substances, and so on, fit together.[29] He will be able to see the relation of the world of *Endymion* to Spenser's Gardens of Adonis and Bower of Bliss, and so understand how Keats interpreted and made use of Spenser. The meaning of a poem by Keats is not in Blake, it is in Keats: but it *is* in Keats, and a knowledge of Blake may make it easier to see it there. And after we have met an archetypal symbol employed by Blake, Keats and Spenser in a few more poets, a far bigger problem in interpretation begins to take shape, and here again we may find Blake of unique value as a vademecum.

Behind the pattern of images in poetry, however, is a pattern of words. In poetry the word is a complex of ideas and images, ambiguous and associative in meaning, synthetically apprehended. In ordinary speech the word is something much more blurred and commonplace. Even Blake's favorite words "imagination" and "vision" are now rather tarnished, because so long used for the sentimental vagueness associated with them by vague and sentimental people. The point of view which Blake associates with Locke will attach still other meanings to them. But as the poet must use recognized words, his literary tact can go only so far: he cannot overcome a confirmed habit of responding only to words in their commonplace meanings. One can see this very clearly in translation. It is impossible that a Greek tragedian can have meant by *ananke* what the average English reader means by "necessity." But the translator must use some word, and the real difficulty lies in the reader's inability to recreate the word "necessity" into a conception with the associative richness of *ananke*. It has been said of Boehme that his books are like a picnic to which the author brings the words and the reader the meaning. The remark may have been intended as a sneer at Boehme, but it is an exact description of all works of literary art without exception.

Where are we to find the meanings of words? Sophocles is dead, and eke his language, and both at once are buried in dictionaries which give only the translator's equivalent. The meaning of *ananke* must be sought in the meaning of the poetic form in which it is found, in the *raison d'être* of Greek tragedy. Here a knowledge of the historical origin and context of Greek tragedy is necessary, but we have explained why we must eventually move beyond this. Just as we must find the meaning of *ananke* in its relation to its context in Greek tragedy, so we must find the meaning of Greek tragedy in its relation to the context of all tragedy, the great drama of death and redemption of which it forms a crucial episode. Thus in pursuing the meaning of a word in poetry we follow the course of the meaning of the word "word" itself, which signifies the unit of meaning, the Scripture, and the Son of God and Man.

We have seen that in his relation to English literature Blake attaches himself to a certain unity of ideas held in the English Renaissance, most clearly illustrated in the first book of *The Faerie Queene* and *Areopagitica*. We traced this unity of ideas in the sixth chapter, and are now in a position to sum it up more briefly as the unity of the meanings belonging to "word" in the above paragraph. In its Renaissance context it was a combination of certain Protestant and humanist tendencies, of new ideas about the Word of God combined with new ideas about the words of man. If we understand that to Blake there are no puns or ambiguities or accidents in the range of the meaning of "word," but a single and comprehensible form, we have wound up all of his golden string and are standing in front of his gate. But gates are to be opened, and there is still much to be seen by the light of the vision Blake saw—perhaps the same light that broke in on the dying Falstaff when he babbled of green fields and played with flowers, and on his hostess when she told how he had gone into "Arthur's" bosom, and how he had talked of the Whore of Babylon.

NOTES

THE word "mystic" has never brought anything but confusion into the study of Blake, and, in my anxiety to prevent it from cluttering up this book, I have begun by conceding, as a sort of opening gambit, the conventional mystic's attitude to the artist as the imperfect mystic who cannot wholly detach himself from the sensible world. But it does not follow that I am willing to let the conventional mystic remain in possession of the field.

The significance of the term "analogy," as Blake uses it in *Jerusalem*, is that Blake is working out an *analogia visionis* which, unlike the more orthodox analogies of faith and being, excludes natural religion and yet allows of a human response to revelation. This *analogia visionis* is as far as *Jerusalem* takes us. Now as long as the vision is something, the analogy will be something too; and the real apocalypse comes, not with the vision of a city or kingdom, which would still be external, but with the identification of the city and kingdom with one's own body. But when this happens the external aspect of the unfallen world becomes a void, and the analogy of the unfallen world, or body of Jesus, would then be the Creator alone in nothing whom we meet on page one of all orthodox cosmogonies.

When we have taken this short and inevitable step beyond *Jerusalem*, the struggles of the mystics to describe the divine One who is all things, yet no thing, and yet not nothing; to explain how this One is identical with the self yet as different from the self as it can be; to make it clear how the creaturely aspect of man does not exist at all and yet is a usually victorious enemy of the soul, begin to have more relevance to Blake. From this point of view, Blake's "art" becomes a spiritual discipline like the Eastern "yoga," which liberates man by uniting him with God. The true God for such visionaries is not the orthodox Creator, the Jehovah or Isvara or Nobodaddy who must always be involved with either an eternal substance or an eternal nothingness, depending on the taste of the theologian, but an unattached creative Word who is free from both. Unity with this God could be attained only by an effort of vision which not only rejects the duality of subject and object but attacks the far more difficult antithesis of being and non-being as well. This effort of vision, so called, is to be conceived neither as a human attempt to reach God nor a divine attempt to reach man, but as the realization in total experience of the identity of God and Man in which both the human creature and the superhuman Creator disappear. Blake's conception of art as creation designed to destroy *the* Creation is the most readily comprehensible expression of this effort of vision I know; but the effort itself is the basis of, for instance, Zen Buddhism, which with its paradoxical humor and its intimate relationship to the arts is startlingly close to Blake. It seems also to be the basis of the great speculative Western school which forms a curiously well-integrated tradition at least between Eckhart and Boehme, and which is often called mystical.

If mysticism means primarily a contemplative quietism, mysticism is something abhorrent to Blake, a Selfhood-communing in Ulro; if it means primarily a spiritual illumination expressing itself in a practical and (in spite of its psychological subtlety) unspeculative piety, such as we find in the militant monasticism of the Counter-Reformation, the word still does not fit him. But if mysticism means primarily the vision of the prodigious and unthinkable metamorphosis of the human mind just described, then Blake is one of the mystics.

Nos. 4 and 6 are line engravings; the others are prints, some hand-colored in the original and others left uncolored, of relief-etchings made by the process Blake employed to produce his engraved works, the details of which are not yet certainly understood. The statement on p. 6 that the text was engraved backhanded has been declared impossible: some favor the theory of a counterproof, but that offers at least equal difficulties.

1. Frontispiece to *Europe*, generally known as "The Ancient of Days Striking the First Circle of the Earth" (1794). See text, pp. 34, 52, 98 and 209. One of the most famous deathbed stories in literature tells how Blake's last complete work was a version of it. The deity is, more or less, Urizen, and the compasses come from Prov. viii, 27, via *Par. Lost* vii, 225 f, with a hint or two from the *Timaeus*. They are held in, or grow out of, the left or "sinister" hand: for this symbolism in Blake, see J. H. Wicksteed, *Blake's Vision of the Book of Job*, London, 1924 (rev. ed.). It should be realized that they outline the circumference of the subjective fallen world, or the human skull, as well as its objective counterpart.

2. *Songs of Experience*: "Holy Thursday" and "The Sick Rose" (1794). The dead child under the barren and poisonous tree of mystery links the images of the slaughter of the innocents and the winter solstice. In a sense the child has fallen from the tree, which represents the "vegetable" world of ordinary experience. See text, pp. 74, 203 and 237. For the sexual symbolism of the worm in the rose, see below, ch. 9, n. 28 (the worm is part of the serpent and dragon complex).

3. *America*, Plate 14 (1793). The phallic serpent again, this time aiding the female will in teaching the young Orc the mysteries of "Generation," or the world of nature, sex and reason. Below, a rudimentary leviathan forms a counterpoint in similar motion to the serpent: both are aspects of a Covering Cherub which faces westward towards America and is also in itself the ocean covering Atlantis. A typical example of the way in which the designs of Blake's prophecies illustrate the text.

4. *Glad Day* (1780, 1800). The traditional title, derived from *Romeo and Juliet*, III, v, 9-10. See text, pp. 129, 170, 207, 320 and 362. The second state of the famous portrait of Orc, which exists also in a color-print version. An early work, done before Blake's study of Renaissance prints made him conscious of muscles and before he had begun to explore the symbolic possibilities of distortion, this superb nude is his finest vision of the "spiritual body."

5. *Jerusalem*, Plate 28 (engraved 1818-20). See Laurence Binyon, *The Engraved Designs of William Blake*, London, 1926, 130, who correctly identifies it as Jerusalem and Vala assimilating into one in the Lily of Havilah. The ambiguous vision of Beulah, "where no dispute can come" because the mental reality and the physical appearance both

exist, is part of the contrast of form and reflection, vision and analogy (suggested here also by the watery background) that runs all through *Jerusalem* but is particularly important in Part Two, which deals with the ordinary Adamic man who is a focus of both eternal and temporal vision. For Part Three, addressed to the Deists, the solidified threefold Beulah-Ulro referred to in the text, pp. 234 and 389, is similarly the theme, and is represented at Plate 53 (Binyon, *op. cit.*, Plate 75).

6. *Vision of the Book of Job*, Plate 20 (1825). See the commentary *ad loc.* in Wicksteed, *op. cit.*, and S. Foster Damon, *William Blake: His Philosophy and Symbols*, Boston and New York, 1924, 235-36. The "stretto" of the Job series. Job is not restored to his former state of pastoral innocence, but raised to the unfallen world which that state reflected, a world in which his "emanations" are united to him, and in which the tragedies that befell him are portrayed as works of art existing "in the shadows of Possibility." These pictures are on the walls of Job's mind, for the room he is in is identical with his own body. That does not make them subjective, for Job is no longer a subject: he is one with God, not the Creator of the natural leviathan shown in our first illustration, but the creative Word of God who tames it.

The six illustrations have been chosen to show in order the major crises in Blake's cyclic myth: first, the Creation-Fall; second, man's awareness of his fallen state and its misery; third, his awareness of a power within him oppressed by tyranny and mystery; fourth, the triumphant emergence of this power, still an undifferentiated mixture of creative and organic energy; fifth, the effort of Los to separate the former from its natural reflection; and sixth, the recovery of the unfallen state.

NOTES TO THE TEXT

1. All references to Blake's own works are accompanied by the page reference to *The Writings of William Blake*, ed. Geoffrey Keynes, 3 vols., London, 1925. These page references are preceded by the letter "K" and the number of the volume.

2. The Arabic numeral following a reference to an engraved poem is the number of the plate; following a reference to *The French Revolution* or *Tiriel*, it is the number of the line as given in *The Poetical Works of William Blake*, ed. Sampson, Oxford U.P., 1905; following a reference to *A Descriptive Catalogue*, it is the number of the page in the original edition; following a reference to *Public Address* or *A Vision of the Last Judgment*, it is the number of the page of the Rossetti MS; following a reference to marginalia, it is the number of the page in the copy annotated by Blake. References to *The Four Zoas* are accompanied in parentheses by the line number as given in *The Prophetic Writings of William Blake*, ed. Sloss and Wallis, 2 vols., Oxford U.P., 1926. This variety of reference is confusing, but not easily avoidable.

3. The following abbreviations for Blake's works have been employed:

A.R.O.	*All Religions Are One*
B.A.	*The Book of Ahania*
B.L.	*The Book of Los*
B.T.	*The Book of Thel*
B.U.	*The Book of Urizen*
D.C.	*A Descriptive Catalogue*
E.G.	*The Everlasting Gospel*
F.R.	*The French Revolution*
F.Z.	*The Four Zoas*
G.P.	*The Gates of Paradise*
I.M.	*An Island in the Moon*
J.	*Jerusalem*
M.	*Milton*
M.H.H.	*The Marriage of Heaven and Hell*
N.N.R.	*There Is No Natural Religion*
P.A.	*Public Address* (Rossetti MS)
P.S.	*Poetical Sketches*
S.E.	*Songs of Experience*
S.I.	*Songs of Innocence*
S.L.	*The Song of Los*
S.Lib.	*A Song of Liberty*
V.D.A.	*Visions of the Daughters of Albion*
V.L.J.	*A Vision of the Last Judgment* (Rossetti MS)

CHAPTER ONE

1. Poem in Letter to Butts, Aug. 16, 1803: K2, 251; cf. "Mary": K2, 228.
2. D.C., Advertisement: K3, 89.
3. For his view of obscurity cf. Marg. to Reynolds' *Discourses*, 194: K3, 44. See also ch. 10, n. 6.
4. Darrell Figgis, *The Paintings of William Blake*, London, 1925, 30. The vine is from Gilchrist, *Life of William Blake*, ch. xii.
5. "The Caverns of the Grave I've seen": K3, 85.
6. Letter to Trusler, Aug. 23, 1799: K2, 176. This is an important letter: the reader should particularly notice the sentence: "The wisest of the Ancients consider'd what is not too Explicit as the fittest for Instruction, because it rouzes the faculties to act."

7. M.H.H. 10: K1, 186.
8. "I rose up at the dawn of day": K3, 86. The word "mystic" occurs only in J. 53: K3, 245.
9. Letter to Butts, July 6, 1803: K2, 246. The reference seems to be to the *Phaedrus*.
10. *On Homer's Poetry*: K3, 361.
11. Dante, *Convivio*, ii, 1.
12. V.L.J. 68: K3, 145.
13. J. 77: K3, 284.
14. For his knowledge of French see the quotation from Voltaire in Marg. to Reynolds (introduction): K3, 6. In a letter to his brother James, dated Jan. 30, 1803: K2, 242, he speaks of "going on" with Greek and Latin, implying a rather elementary stage of study, and beginning Hebrew. The date is late for the student of his poetry, and when he speaks of reading Greek fluently he means New Testament Greek, where he knew the crib by heart. With Blake, as with other poets, proof that he knew something about a language is not proof that he could read it, and proof that he could read it is not proof that he habitually did so.
15. J. 10: K3, 177.
16. Marg. to Watson's *Apology*, 3: K2, 156.
17. Cf. H. Crabb Robinson, *Reminiscences of Blake*, s. 1825 (in *Blake, Coleridge, Wordsworth, Lamb, Etc., being Selections from the Remains of Henry Crabb Robinson*, ed. Edith J. Morley, Manchester U.P., 1932, 18). Landor made a similar remark about Blake and Wordsworth.
18. Cf. Marg. to Spurzheim: K3, 352, and *The Pencil Drawings of William Blake*, ed. Keynes, London, 1927, 47.
19. M.H.H. 13: K1, 188.
20. Marg. to Watson, 3: K2, 156.
21. Marg. to Reynolds, 244: K3, 49.
22. Letter to Butts, July 6, 1803: K2, 247.
23. V.L.J. 95: K3, 162.
24. *Lives of the Poets*: "Cowley" and "Pope."
25. Marg. to Reynolds, 61: K3, 25; and xcviii: K3, 13.
26. Marg. to Berkeley's *Siris*, 213: K3, 355.
27. Marg. to Lavater's *Aphorisms on Man*, 532: K1, 107.
28. Letter to Cumberland, Apr. 12, 1827: K3, 392.
29. Marg. to Reynolds, 35: K3, 20.
30. See the poem beginning "Mock on, Mock on, Voltaire, Rousseau": K2, 214.
31. Marg. to Reynolds, 61: K3, 25.
32. A.R.O., Argument: K1, 131.
33. G.P. 5: K3, 348.
34. "Auguries of Innocence": K2, 235.
35. M.H.H. 4: K1, 182.
36. A.R.O. 1: K1, 131.
37. M. 4: K2, 309.
38. Marg. to Reynolds, 34: K3, 20; M.H.H. 8: K1, 185; G.P.: K3, 338.
39. Marg. to Lavater (conclusion): K1, 116-17.
40. Marg. to Bacon's *Essays*: K2, 172.
41. M.H.H. 7: K1, 184; D.C. 37: K3, 108.
42. V.L.J. 91-95: K3, 162.
43. N.N.R. II, ii: K1, 130.
44. N.N.R. II, iv: K1, 131.
45. Marg. to Reynolds, 157: K3, 41; and 58: K3, 24-25.
46. M.H.H. 4: K1, 182.
47. M.H.H. 7: K1, 184.
48. A.R.O. 5: K1, 132.

49. D.C. 44: K3, 111. For his view of the trustworthiness of records in history cf. Marg. to Watson, 15-16: K2, 165.

CHAPTER TWO

1. Marg. to Berkeley, 219: K3, 356; Laocoön Aphorisms: K3, 358.
2. M.H.H. 23: K1, 194.
3. M. 35: K2, 356.
4. Marg. to Swedenborg's *Divine Love and Divine Wisdom*, 24: K1, 120-21.
5. Marg. to Swedenborg, 11: K1, 119.
6. Laocoön Aphorisms: K3, 358. The preceding phrase is from Browne, *The Gardens of Cyrus*.
7. *On Virgil*: K3, 362.
8. *Moby Dick*, ch. cxix.
9. Marg. to Lavater, 426: K1, 102.
10. V.L.J. 68-69: K3, 146.
11. Marg. to Lavater (conclusion): K1, 117.
12. M.H.H. 10: K1, 186.
13. "Auguries of Innocence": K2, 235.
14. See below, ch. 5; and cf. H. Crabb Robinson, *Reminiscences of Blake*, s. 1826 (*Selections*, ed. Morley, 23).
15. Letter to Butts, July 6, 1803: K2, 246.
16. Marg. to Lavater (conclusion): K1, 117; cf. J. 3: K3, 167.
17. D.C. 38: K3, 108; cf. I Cor. xiv, 32.
18. Marg. to Wordsworth's *Recluse*: K3, 379.
19. Marg. to Lavater, 342: K1, 98.
20. J. 88: K3, 305.
21. V.L.J. 71-72: K3, 146.
22. M.H.H. 7: K1, 184.
23. A.R.O. 1: K1, 131. For Ovid cf. V.L.J. 79: K3, 148.
24. Poem in Letter to Butts, Oct. 2, 1800: K2, 190.
25. F.Z. v (121-26): K2, 58-59.
26. Milton, *Of Reformation Touching Church Discipline in England*, Book ii, Introduction.
27. V.L.J. 76-77: K3, 149.
28. S.I., "A Little Girl Lost": K1, 150-151.
29. Laocoön Aphorisms: K3, 359.
30. Wordsworth, *The Prelude*, vi, 634-39.
31. "Auguries of Innocence": K2, 232.
32. M. 26: K2, 341.
33. V.L.J. 91-92: K3, 158.
34. M.H.H. 7: K1, 184.
35. Marg. to Lavater, 407: K1, 101.
36. See especially *Divine Love and Divine Wisdom*, i, 40-82. Cf. M. O. Percival, *William Blake's Circle of Destiny*, Columbia U.P., 1938, 83 f.
37. *Lives of the Poets*: "Yalden."
38. Isa. lxii, 4.
39. Ezek. i; Rev. iv.
40. Poem in Letter to Butts, Nov. 22, 1802: K2, 209.
41. Marg. to Berkeley, 241: K3, 356.
42. M.H.H. 6: K1, 183.
43. D.C. 46: K3, 112.
44. N.N.R. II, Application: K1, 131.
45. See Illustration 1, and note, p. 433.
46. Laocoön Aphorisms: K3, 359. Cf. *Faust*, I, 1224-37.
47. Swedenborg, *True Christian Religion*, 115. Cf. M.H.H. 3: K1, 182.

CHAPTER THREE

1. Marg. to Lavater (conclusion): K1, 117.
2. M.H.H. 10: K1, 186.
3. D.C. 26: K3, 103.
4. Marg. to Lavater, 489: K1, 105.
5. Marg. to Watson, 14: K2, 164.
6. Marg. to Bacon: K2, 172.
7. *Ibid.*
8. Eph. vi, 12.
9. Marg. to Watson, 25: K2, 166.
10. Marg. to Bacon: K2, 171.
11. F.Z. i (14): K2, 2.
12. Marg. to Thornton, *A New Translation of the Lord's Prayer*: K3, 387-88.
13. "Let the Brothels of Paris be opened": K1, 249.
14. M.H.H. 24: K1, 195.
15. Marg. to Watson, 25: K2, 166.
16. M.H.H. 7: K1, 184.
17. *Ibid.*; M. 31: K2, 351.
18. E.G. *d*: K3, 329.
19. S.Lib.: K1, 197.
20. V.L.J. 91-92: K3, 158-59.
21. Marg. to Lavater, 479: K1, 105.
22. V.L.J. 86, 90: K3, 159-60.
23. Letter to Cumberland, Apr. 12, 1827: K3, 392. Cf. Mark Schorer: *William Blake: The Politics of Vision*, N.Y., 1946, 170, which appeared when the present book was in proof.
24. V.L.J. 86, 90: K3, 159.
25. E.G. *d*: K3, 328.
26. V.L.J. 84: K3, 156; cf. D.C. 18: K3, 100.
27. M.H.H. 3: K1, 182.
28. F.Z. ix (852): K2, 147.
29. Marg. to Lavater, 36: K1, 87.
30. M.H.H. 12: K1, 187.
31. V.L.J. 92-95: K3, 161. Cf. John xvi, 2.
32. M. 9: K2, 318.
33. Letter to Butts, Jan. 10, 1802: K2, 201.
34. Marg. to Lavater, 409: K1, 101.
35. J. 27: K3, 205.
36. This may be the meaning, or part of the meaning, of the poem beginning "Why was Cupid a Boy?": K3, 77. Cupid or Eros is certainly a boy in Blake's symbolism, being identical with the youthful Orc.
37. K1, 247.
38. S.E., "London": K1, 287.
39. Laocoön Aphorisms: K3, 358.
40. Marg. to Watson, iii: K2, 153.
41. Laocoön Aphorisms: K3, 359.
42. "Auguries of Innocence": K2, 233.
43. V.L.J. 82-84: K3, 155.
44. Marg. to Reynolds, 15: K3, 17.
45. Poem in Letter to Butts, Nov. 22, 1802: K2, 207.
46. M.H.H. 23-24: K1, 194.
47. John ii, 4; cf. S.E., "To Tirzah": K1, 292.
48. Cf. Marg. to Watson, 117: K2, 169, where "Nero" may be a rhetorical substitute for Marcus Aurelius.
49. Marg. to Lavater, 309: K1, 97.

50. Marg. to Watson, 12-13: K2, 163.
51. E.G. *a*: K3, 323.
52. V.L.J. 80-81: K3, 153.
53. Marg. to Swedenborg, 181: K1, 123.
54. V.L.J. 86, 90: K3, 159.
55. V.L.J. 82-84: K3, 156.
56. Laocoön Aphorisms: K3, 357.
57. V.L.J. 87: K3, 160.

CHAPTER FOUR

1. Laocoön Aphorisms: K3, 358.
2. Marg. to Berkeley, 214: K3, 355.
3. N.N.R. II, v: K1, 131.
4. J. 72: K3, 278-79.
5. Cf. Marg. to Lavater, 342: K1, 98.
6. Laocoön Aphorisms: K3, 357.
7. Marg. to Reynolds, i: K3, 7.
8. P.A. 66: K3, 131; Marg. to Reynolds (introduction): K3, 5.
9. Cf. H. Crabb Robinson, *Diary*, s. Dec. 10, 1825 (*Selections*, ed. Morley, 3).
10. Marg. to Reynolds, 244: K3, 49.
11. Marg. to Reynolds, 124: K3, 35.
12. P.A. 60-62: K3, 130.
13. Marg. to Reynolds, 157: K3, 41.
14. V.L.J. 82-84: K3, 154.
15. Marg. to Reynolds, 157: K3, 41.
16. Laocoön Aphorisms: K3, 359.
17. Marg. to Reynolds, 32: K3, 20.
18. Marg. to Reynolds, 33: K3, 20.
19. Marg. to Reynolds, ii: K3, 7.
20. D.C. 64: K3, 119.
21. Letter to Cumberland, Apr. 12, 1827: K3, 392.
22. D.C. 63-64: K3, 119.
23. Marg. to Reynolds, 200: K3, 46.
24. D.C. 55: K3, 115-16.
25. Marg. to Reynolds, 120: K3, 35.
26. Marg. to Lavater, 532: K1, 108.
27. Marg. to Reynolds, 71: K3, 27.
28. Marg. to Reynolds, 154: K3, 41; D.C. 46: K3, 112.
29. Marg. to Reynolds (introduction): K3, 5.
30. P.A. 18-19: K3, 133.
31. P.A. 66: K3, 132.
32. Marg. to Reynolds, 274: K3, 52.
33. Marg. to Reynolds, 131-32: K3, 37.
34. Marg. to Reynolds, 90: K3, 29.
35. Marg. to Reynolds, 99: K3, 31.
36. D.C. 48: K3, 112.
37. Cf. Letter to Cumberland, Aug. 26, 1799: K2, 177.
38. P.A. 51-57: K3, 127.
39. For Romano cf. P.A. 18-19: K3, 134; for Poussin cf. Marg. to Reynolds, 139: K3, 39; for the Carraccis cf. Letter to Butts, Nov. 22, 1802: K2, 204.
40. Marg. to Reynolds, 114: K3, 33.

CHAPTER FIVE

1. V.L.J. 70: K3, 145.
2. V.L.J. 71-72: K3, 146.

3. M.H.H. 24: K1, 195.
4. Marg. to Watson, 22: K2, 166.
5. Laocoön Aphorisms: K3, 359.
6. M. Preface: K2, 305.
7. D.C. 43-44: K3, 111.
8. *On Homer's Poetry*: K3, 361.
9. D.C. 17: K3, 99.
10. D.C. 19-20: K3, 100-1.
11. Marg. to Wordsworth: K3, 377.
12. Eccl. xii, 12; John xxi, 25.
13. J. 3: K3, 167.
14. V.L.J. 68: K3, 145.
15. Marg. to Berkeley, 213: K3, 355; *On Homer's Poetry*: K3, 361. For the contrast of similitude and identity cf. Marg. to Reynolds, 200: K3, 46.
16. Laocoön Aphorisms: K3, 360.
17. J. 3: K3, 166.
18. Marg. to Watson, 4-5: K2, 158.
19. *The Faerie Queene*, III, x, 60.
20. V.L.J. 68: K3, 145.
21. *Convivio*, II, i (Temple Classics tr.).
22. Marg. to Swedenborg, 12: K1, 120.
23. Marg. to Reynolds, 60: K3, 25.
24. F.Z. viii (1): K2, 100.
25. J. 27: K3, 202. Cf. Emerson, *Nature*, viii.
26. *Northern Antiquities*, London, 1770, Percy's translation of Mallet's introduction to his history of Denmark, contained a not very accurate translation of the Prose Edda. References to Percy's book will be made from the Bohn's Library edition, London, 1847.
27. D.C. 42-43: K3, 110. Cf. *The Faerie Queene*, IV, xi, 16. For Ariston cf. *America* 10: K1, 267. The name comes from Herodotus, vi, 61 f, and the same name is associated with Poseidon in Diodorus Siculus, iii, 42. The story of Ariston, the Spartan king who stole another man's "emanation," is a reversed form of the story of Menelaus, and expresses Blake's belief in the derivative nature of Greek culture. For Blake's knowledge of Plato and the Neoplatonists, see F. E. Pierce, "Blake and Thomas Taylor," *PMLA*, 1928, 1121-41.
28. "The Caverns of the Grave I've seen": K3, 85. For Blake and the Atlantis myth see Bramwell, *Lost Atlantis*, London, 1937.
29. From ἐναρίθμιος, "numbered," or ἀνάριθμος, "numberless," probably the former. Cf. Damon, *op. cit.*, 69.
30. Gen. vi, 1-4. The Book of Enoch was published in 1821; see *Pencil Drawings*, 80.
31. Num. xxvii, 1 f; xxxvi, 10 f; Josh. xvii, 3 f; Cant. vi, 4. The five Valkyries in Gray's "The Fatal Sisters" also helped to build up the symbol.
32. F.Z. viii (387-95): K2, 112-13. Cf. M. 14: K2, 322; J. 55: K3, 248; Zech. iv, 10; Rev. iv, 5.
33. Cf. Gray's note on Lok in "The Triumphs of Owen."
34. Cf. *Northern Antiquities*, 14.
35. For Mexico cf. the rubric in F.Z. iii (opp. 90-91): K2, 40; and J. 43: K3, 229.
36. Figgis, *op. cit.*, pl. 13.
37. Geoffrey of Monmouth, *History of the Kings of Britain*, I, ii; IV, xix. Cf. Malory, *Morte Darthur*, III, ii.
38. Marg. to Watson, 6: K2, 159.
39. *Ibid.* Cf. Eph. ii, 2.
40. D.C. 4-5: K3, 94.
41. D.C. 21-22: K3, 101. Blake's Priam may be connected also with the Priamus who appears in *Morte Darthur*, V, x.
42. J. 5: K3, 170.

43. D.C. 41: K3, 110.
44. *True Christian Religion*, 279.
45. *Par. Lost*, xii, 310.
46. *Convivio*, II, i (Temple Classics tr.). Cf. *Purg.* ii, 46.
47. Wisd. Sol. xvii, 3.
48. J. 56: K3, 250.
49. M. 41: K2, 364; J. 75: K3, 283.
50. Rev. x, 7.
51. Marg. to Berkeley, 205: K3, 354; cf. Gen. ii, 10; Rev. xxii, 1.
52. *Par. Lost*, ix, 835-38.
53. *Par. Lost*, x, 215-18.
54. Ezek. xxviii, 13-16.
55. J. 33: K3, 214; *Europe* 5: K1, 297.
56. Job xxxviii, 11; Rev. xxi, 1; cf. Ps. lxxiv, 13.
57. Job xli, 34.
58. Josh. ii. For Rahab as Leviathan cf. Isa. li, 9; Ps. lxxxix, 10; and more especially Ps. lxxxvii, 4; Isa. xxx, 7 (R. V. rdg.)
59. Rev. xii, 9.
60. II Thess., ii
61. *Prose Edda*, 24.
62. Marg. to Swedenborg, 133: K1, 122.
63. Josephus, *Antiquities of the Jews*, III, vii.
64. *Morte Darthur*, II, xi.
65. *Europe* 8: K1, 298-99.
66. Laocoön Aphorisms: K3, 357.
67. D.C. 40: K3, 110.
68. *Morte Darthur*, V, iv.
69. *The Faerie Queene*, I, xii, 26. Cf. I, vii, 43.
70. *The Faerie Queene*, I, i, 5.
71. *The Faerie Queene*, I, xi, introductory quatrain (the phrase comes from Rev. xii, 9). Cf. I, xi, 29 and 46. Duessa is identified with the Great Whore in I, vii, 16.
72. J. 77: K3, 284.

CHAPTER SIX

1. M.H.H. 22: K1, 193-94.
2. *On Virgil*: K3, 362.
3. Laocoön Aphorisms: K3, 357.
4. D.C. 31-32: K3, 106. The next sentence refers to "Joseph of Arimathea," K1, 54 (for which cf. Heb. xi, 37-38).
5. "The Grey Monk": K2, 230; J. 52: K3, 243.
6. D.C. 16: K3, 99.
7. Agrippa, *Vanity of the Arts and Sciences*, anon. tr., London, 1684, 5.
8. Agrippa, *op. cit.*, 345.
9. *The Works of Thomas Vaughan*, ed. A. E. Waite, London, 1919, 135-36.
10. J. 58: K3, 253. For a much fuller account of the relation of alchemical symbolism to Blake than I am qualified to give see Percival, *op. cit.*, ch. x.
11. Jonson, *The Alchemist*, I, iv, 25-29.
12. Butler, *Hudibras*, I, i.
13. Agrippa, *op. cit.*, 343.
14. *Critical Essays of the Seventeenth Century*, ed. J. E. Spingarn, Oxford U.P., 1908, I, 170.
15. Ovid, *Fasti*, vi, 5. Cf. *Elizabethan Critical Essays*, ed. Gregory Smith, Oxford U.P., 1904, I, xxiii, 232.
16. Gregory Smith, *op. cit.*, II, 3.
17. H. Crabb Robinson, *Diary*, s. Dec. 10, 1825 (*Selections*, ed. Morley, 6).

18. Num. xi, 29, quoted in M. Preface: K2, 306.
19. Spenser, *Letter to Raleigh.*
20. *Tatler*, 11.
21. I.M. ch. 9: K1, 72.
22. P.A. 39: K3, 138; Letter to Hayley, May 4, 1804: K2, 270.
23. Spingarn, *op. cit.*, II, 59.
24. Marg. to Reynolds, 50: K3, 22. Cf. Milton, *Reason of Church Government*, ii, Introduction.
25. *Lives of the Poets*: "Milton."
26. Boileau, *L'Art Poétique*, iii, 199-200.
27. *Lives of the Poets*: "J. Philips."
28. M. Preface: K2, 305.
29. Marg. to Reynolds, 244: K3, 49.
30. Marg. to Wordsworth: K3, 377.
31. Young, *Night Thoughts*, i, 132-41. (Illustrated by Blake.)
32. J. 52: K3, 243.
33. D.C. 35: K3, 107.
34. *Northern Antiquities*, 57-58.
35. D.C. 59: K3, 117.
36. D.C. 44: K3, 111.
37. Davies, *Celtic Researches*, London, 1804, 84.
38. Herod. iv, 36; Diod. Sic. ii, 47; cf. Diog. Lat. i, 1; Pliny, *Hist. Nat.*, xxx, 1. See also Saurat, *Blake and Modern Thought*, London, 1929, Part Two; Hungerford, *Shores of Darkness*, Columbia U.P., 1941, Part One.
39. Davies, *op. cit.*, 143.
40. Cf. the reference to the "tribes of Llewellyn" in J. 83: K3, 298.
41. Southey, Preface to *The Curse of Kehama.*
42. H. Crabb Robinson, *Diary*, s. July 24, 1811 (*Selections*, ed. Morley, 1).
43. P.S., "To Morning": K1, 5 Cf. Ps. xix.
44. Malkin, *A Father's Memoirs of His Child*, London, 1806, quoted in most of the secondary sources.
45. K1, 54.
46. P.S., "To Spring": K1, 1.
47. F.Z. i (1-3): K2, 2.

CHAPTER SEVEN

1. *Europe* 11: K1, 301. See below, ch. 8.
2. M.H.H. 10: K1, 186.
3. See Marg. to Swedenborg, *Wisdom of Angels Concerning Divine Providence*: K1, 176.
4. M. 7: K2, 313. The conception of three classes may come from the "Gunas" of the *Bhagavadgita*, xiv.
5. M.H.H. 24: K1, 195.
6. J. 98: K3, 318.
7. J. 10: K3, 177.
8. Cf. P.A. 18-19: K3, 134.
9. M.H.H. 9: K1, 185.
10. *On Homer's Poetry*: K3, 361.
11. Intended not only to represent an incorrect pronunciation of Giotto, but to suggest the ludicrousness of the mistake in Italian (the word *ghiotto* means "glutton"). Some knowledge of Italian on Blake's part may be implied.
12. In W. B. Yeats, *A Vision*, London, 1937, 137, Blake is classified with Rabelais and Aretino.
13. Marg. to Wordsworth: K3, 380. Cf. n. 16.
14. Job xix, 26.

15. N.N.R. I, iii: K1, 130.
16. Phil. iii, 21.
17. V.L.J. 82-84: K3, 156.
18. J. 69: K3, 273.
19. M.H.H. 14: K1, 189.
20. F.R. 189: K1, 209.
21. S.L. 4 ("Asia"): K1, 341.
22. Donne, *An Anatomie of the World*, 206.
23. *Par. Last*, xii, 290.
24. Swinburne, *William Blake*, London, 1868, 158n. Cf. Mario Praz, *The Romantic Agony*, London, 1933, 223, 278.
25. M.H.H. 4: K1, 182.
26. M.H.H. 14: K1, 189.
27. Rabelais, II, xxviii (Urquhart tr.).
28. Marg. to Thornton: K3, 388.
29. Cf. the note to "orcneas" in line 112 of *Beowulf*, ed. Wyatt and Chambers, Cambridge U.P., 1933, 8.
30. See Illustration 4, and note, p. 433.
31. Job iii, 8 (mg. rdg. in AV).
32. Ezek. xxix, 3.
33. F. E. Pierce, "Etymology as Explanation in Blake": *PQ*, 1931, 395-96.
34. *Moby Dick*, ch. xlii.
35. Rev. xxi, 23.
36. Cf. the reference to the sun as a "Scythed Chariot of Britain," J. 56: K3, 250.
37. S.L. 2 ("Africa"): K1, 339.
38. J. 45: K3, 234.
39. ἀμύμονας Αἰθιοπῆας, *Il.* i, 423; cf. *Od.* i, 23. Cf. also Ariosto, *Orlando Furioso*, xxxiii, 109-10.
40. Rev. xi, 8.
41. *True Christian Religion*, 835-40; de Nerval, *Le Rêve et la Vie*, I, viii. Cf. *Finnegans Wake*, N.Y., 1939, 75-76.
42. John iii, 14.
43. II Kings xviii, 4.
44. Isa. lxiii, 1; cf. M.H.H. 3: K1, 182.
45. The mistletoe is referred to in J. 66: K3, 267.
46. B.A. i, 3-6: K1, 323-24. The image is that of the sun hidden, not by clouds, but by the opaque interposed body of the earth at night.
47. Cf. F.R. 282: K1, 215 with S.L. 3 ("Africa"): K1, 340. Note that in the former passage the pillar of fire and the pillar of cloud are not yet contrasted. For the loins as the place of the Last Judgment see J. 30: K3, 211.
48. Letter to Hayley, May 28, 1804: K2, 273.
49. Marg. to Bacon: K2, 171.
50. V.L.J. 92-95: K3, 160-61.
51. *The Prelude*, xi, 117-21.
52. N.N.R. II, vii: K1, 131.
53. F.Z. v (30-35): K2, 56. The reason for the absence of historical symbols here is that their presence would lead to the idealization of the earlier stages of a historical cycle, which would have given Blake's revolutionary sympathies the medieval reference that we find later in William Morris. Blake is concerned to make one point only about the historical cycle: that "Deism" (Urizen exploring his dens) is potential and imminent "Druidism" (crucifixion of Orc).
54. F.Z. v (238): K2, 62.
55. F.Z. vi (193): K2, 69.
56. F.Z. viia (111-29): K2, 77-78. Cf. Sir Joseph Bowley in *The Chimes*.
57. F.Z. viii (124-32): K2, 104. Cf. Ovid, *Metamorphoses*, vii.

58. *Europe* 7: K1, 298. Cf. Bacon, *Advancement of Learning*, ii (Everyman's Library, 95-96); Spenser, *The Ruines of Time*, 41.
59. *Europe* 7: K1, 299. For the symbol of the "south" in this passage see below, ch. 9.

CHAPTER EIGHT

1. The Pickering MS contains the following poems: "The Smile," "The Golden Net," "The Mental Traveller," "The Land of Dreams," "Mary," "The Crystal Cabinet," "The Grey Monk," "Auguries of Innocence," "Long John Brown" and "William Bond." See K2, 221 f.
2. Ezek. viii, 14.
3. Canto xxviii.
4. Spingarn, *op. cit.*, I, 176.
5. B.T. 1: K1, 171.
6. M. 21: K2, 330.
7. The passage beginning "He wanders weeping far away": K2, 225 is to be connected with the quaint story in I Kings, i, as well as with *Tiriel*. I am not happy about my interpretation of the "Female Babe."
8. J. 49: K3, 239; Diod. Sic. ii, 47.
9. *Decline and Fall of the Roman Empire*, ch. xv.
10. F.Z. iii (41-98): K2, 38-40.
11. *Od.* xiii, 109-12. This essential link in Blake's symbolism was established by Damon, *op. cit.*, 312.
12. M. 4: K2, 309. ("The Sexual is Threefold, the Human is Fourfold.")
13. Cf. J. 70: K3, 274.
14. "A Cradle Song": K1, 222.
15. Luke ii, 49; cf. E.G. c: K3, 325.
16. Bolingbroke is referred to in M. 46: K2, 369.
17. V.D.A. 2: K1, 255. Cf. Aeschylus, *P.V.*, 412.
18. *True Christian Religion*, 45. Ochim and Ijim reappear in F.Z. viii (349): K2, 111.
19. Cf. Damon, *op. cit.*, 307.
20. Damon, *op. cit.*, suggests that Zazel is derived from "Azazel," the Hebrew word in Lev. xvi, 10, translated in the AV as "scapegoat."
21. Cf. the thirty sons of Tiriel with B.U. ix, 6: K1, 321.
22. J. 33: K3, 214.
23. J. 77: K3, 285.
24. J. 15: K3, 185.
25. N.N.R. II, vii: K1, 131.
26. Marg. to Berkeley, 241: K3, 356.
27. J. 13-14: K3, 183-84.
28. J. 91: K3, 312.
29. J. 7: K3, 174.
30. Carlyle, *Sartor Resartus*, III, x; Shelley, *Defence of Poetry*.
31. M. 26: K2, 341. As a painter Blake has some difficulty in visualizing a human type as appropriate to Los as the youth of the "Glad Day" is to Orc or the old man of the "Ancient of Days" to Urizen. Cf. V.L.J. 91: K3, 159.
32. B.U. vii, 4: K1, 318. Perhaps derived from the ring of Draupnir, *Prose Edda*, 49.
33. M. 26: K2, 341.
34. I Sam. xiii, 19. Cf. Josh. viii, 31.
35. F.Z. iv (276): K2, 54.
36. Rev. ii, 17. Cf. I Pet. ii, 4-8.
37. Isa. liv, 16.
38. V.L.J. 91-92: K3, 158.
39. B.U. ii, 4: K1, 306.
40. B.L ii, 6: K1, 335. Cf. Lucretius, *De Rerum Natura*, ii, 292.
41. B.U. vi, 6: K1, 316.

42. E.G. exordium: K3, 335.
43. M. 26: K2, 341. Apart from the echo of "Golconda" in Golgonooza, the names have a vaguely Indian look: cf. Saurat, *op. cit.*, 113.
44. Cf. S.L. 2 ("Africa"): K1, 339.
45. F.Z. viii (346-54): K2, 111.
46. J. 91: K3, 311.
47. F.Z. ix (151): K2, 124.
48. "The Mental Traveller": K2, 223.
49. J. 68: K3, 271.
50. M. 27: K2, 342.
51. M. 31: K2, 350.
52. M. 30: K2, 348.
53. F.Z. viii (47): K2, 101.
54. Marg. to Lavater (conclusion): K1, 116-17.
55. J. 92: K3, 313.

CHAPTER NINE

1. Byron, *Don Juan*, III, xcvii.
2. Eno appears in B.L. i, 1: K1, 332, as well as in F.Z. i (133 f): K2, 9, and J. 48: K3, 237. Her name may be an anagram of "eon" (Damon, *op. cit.*, 148); though as a rule anagrammatic derivations of Blake's names (*e.g.* Orc from "cor" and Los from "sol") are wrong.
3. F.Z. ix (364-72): K2, 131.
4. J. 3: K3, 167. For war and hunting see M. 39: K2, 360.
5. Dan. iv, 28-33.
6. Dan. iii, 25.
7. D.C. 41-42: K3, 110. Hence the reference to a third of the stars in Rev. xii, 4.
8. *Par. Lost*, vi, 749-66.
9. Marg. to Berkeley, 205: K3, 354.
10. Cf. Damon, *op. cit.*, 466; Remarks on Dante Drawing 101: K3, 382; Letter to Cumberland, Apr. 12, 1827: K3, 392.
11. J. 97: K3, 318.
12. *Par. Lost*, v, 628-29.
13. Nos. 5 and 25 have been added to complete the pattern; Nos. 17, 26 and 29 are guesses. No. 17 is based on a passage in *America* 5: K1, 264.
14. K2, 375.
15. F.Z. i (68): K2, 5.
16. F.Z. i (79): K2, 5.
17. F.Z. ii (616-26): K2, 35. Notice how effectively this bitter cry follows on the "rapturous delusive trance" of Enitharmon.
18. J. 14: K3, 184.
19. James iii, 6.
20. F.Z. iii (47-48): K2, 38. For the meaning of the Narcissus story cf. Gregory Smith, *op. cit.*, I, 65.
21. F.Z. iv (129): K2, 49. For the two floods (in reverse order) cf. Gregory Smith, *op. cit.*, I, 331.
22. Cf. the suicide pact in F.Z. vi (64 f): K2, 65, proposed to Urizen by Tharmas, which Urizen rejects.
23. Hesiod, *Theogony*, 237, 255, 780; Ovid, *Met.* iv, 480.
24. *Lycidas*, 173.
25. F.Z. iii (74-77): K2, 40.
26. J. 64: K3, 262.
27. F.Z. ii (490-94): K2, 31.
28. M. 31: K2, 350. As Luvah is the spirit of "Generation," or the world of sexual life, and as the fallen Orc is associated with a serpent, the serpent is a phallic

symbol. This extends to the Covering Cherub when that character is absorbed into Orc, and forms the symbolic basis of the poem beginning "I saw a chapel all of gold": K1, 220.

29. F.Z. viia (174): K2, 79.
30. F.Z. viii (54): K2, 105.
31. Cf. B.L. i, 9: K1, 333.
32. I Kings, viii, 51.
33. F.Z. i (ii, 97): K2, 14; cf. F.Z. ix (163): K2, 125.
34. M. 29: K2, 346-47; cf. F.Z. ix (746-52): K2, 144-45.
35. *Samson Agonistes*, 41.
36. Smart, *Jubilate Agno*, x, 72, ed. Stead, London, 1939, 92. Cf. Gen. xv, 12-17.
37. J. 98: K3, 319; cf. F.Z. i (12-13): K2, 2.
38. Eccl. iv, 5.
39. Marg. to Swedenborg: K1, 118.
40. F.Z. viib (viia, 168-84): K2, 95; J. 65: K3, 263.
41. Marg. to Watson, 12-13: K2, 164.
42. J. 44: K3, 232.
43. Cf. Middleton Murry, *William Blake*, London, 1933, ch. xi.
44. Cf. F.Z. v (1-5): K2, 55.
45. J. 15: K3, 185.
46. Cf. also J. 56: K3, 250 ("Three Women around The Cross!").
47. Prov. ix, 13-18. Verse 17 is quoted in the "Introduction" to *Europe*: K1, 294.
48. M. 46: K2, 369.
49. B.U. i, 2: K1, 304; Milton, *Arcades*, 64.
50. M. 19: K2, 327.
51. Ἄτλαντος θυγάτηρ ὀλοόφρονος, *Od.* i, 52. Tirzah is the "Adamah" of Gen. ii, 7, referred to in Laocoön Aphorisms: K3, 358. Cf. Percival, *op. cit.*, 115.
52. Ezek. xxix, 3.
53. J. 89: K3, 306-7.
54. F.Z. ix (766): K2, 144; cf. "The Mental Traveller": K2, 223.
55. Rev. xvii, 4; cf. Jer. li, 7, and Eccl. xii, 6.
56. For this association cf. M. 11: K2, 318. (Lines 12-13 of plate.)
57. J. 41: K3, 226.
58. F.Z. ix (78): K2, 122. See Tillyard, *Milton*, London, 1934, 112.
59. Letter to Butts, Nov. 22, 1802: K2, 205.
60. F.Z. ix (79): K2, 122.

CHAPTER TEN

1. Milton, *Reason of Church Government*, Book ii, Introduction.
2. Letter to Butts, July 6, 1803: K2, 246.
3. D.C. 42: K3, 110.
4. Letter to Hayley, May 6, 1800: K2, 180.
5. *The Faerie Queene*, IV, ii, 34.
6. V.L.J. 68: K3, 145-46.
7. V.L.J. 79: K3, 148.
8. Wordsworth, *The Recluse*, 47-55.
9. Marg. to Wordsworth, 374-75: K3, 378.
10. P.A. 51-57: K3, 126.
11. Lady Hesketh; cf. Wright, *Life of William Blake*, Olney, 1929, I, 127. For the handscreen cf. Figgis, *op. cit.*, 41-42.
12. "When Klopstock England defied": K1, 251. I am assuming that the date of 1793 assigned to this poem by most of its editors is wrong, as it assuredly is. That Blake could have read Klopstock in translation at any time is of course admitted: see F. E. Pierce, "Blake and Klopstock," *SP*, 1928, 11-26.
13. Memorandum in Refutation of Schofield: K2, 254.

14. "On H---'s Friendship": K3, 65.
15. "William Cowper, Esqre": K3, 75.
16. "And his legs carried it like a long fork": K3, 54.
17. M. 4: K2, 310.
18. M. 4: K2, 309.
19. V.L.J. 82-84: K3, 154.
20. Cf. Rev. xi, 6, with I Kings xvii, 1, and Ex vii, 20.
21. Rev. xi, 8.
22. *The Faerie Queene*, I, ix, 66.
23. Jude 9.
24. M.H.H. 5: K1, 183.
25. M. 31: K2, 351.
26. J. 93: K3, 314.
27. M. 49: K2, 371. Identified with the Covering Cherub in J. 96: K3, 316.
28. Gal. iv, 22-26. The phrase "Mount Sinai in Arabia" occurs in B.A. ii, 10: K1, 325.
29. M. 46: K2, 369.
30. J. 27: K3, 205; Laocoön Aphorisms: K3, 357.
31. J. 91: K3, 312.
32. F.Z. i (136): K2, 9.
33. Ex. xxxiii, 23.
34. M. 17: K2, 326.
35. M. 31: K2, 349-50. Note that as man is an erect vertebrate, the tree of life is also one of the symbols of the risen body.
36. "On H---'s Friendship": K3, 65.
37. J. 27: K3, 205. Cf. Micah vii, 6.
38. F.Z. iii (96): K2, 40.
39. *Comus*, 12-17.
40. *Comus*, 111-14; cf. *Europe* 12: K1, 303.
41. *Comus*, 440-54. *Visions of the Daughters of Albion* is also to be connected with *Comus*, by virtue of its Hesperidean symbolism and its protest against the identification of chastity with virginity.
42. *Vision of Piers the Plowman*, C-Text, Passus xxi, 471-74.

CHAPTER ELEVEN

1. Letter to James Blake, Jan. 30, 1803: K2, 242.
2. *Spectator* 221. The information comes from the Life of Alabaster in Fuller's *Worthies*.
3. Gen. xxxi, 53.
4. Marg. to Lavater, 533: K1, 108.
5. Boadicea is identified with Cambel, the first daughter of Albion: J. 71: K3, 275.
6. Gen. xxxv, 8; Judges iv, 5; cf. J. 59: K3, 253, and F.Z. i (ii, 206): K2, 17.
7. *Par. Lost*, ix, 1059-62.
8. K2, 194. See Illustration 4.
9. Pison is identified with Arnon in J. 89: K3, 307 (cf. Percival, *op. cit.*, 232), and is called Storge in M. 38: K2, 359. For Vala and Havilah cf. J. 19: K3, 193.
10. Isa. xxxvii, 12; cf. *Par. Lost*, iv, 213-14.
11. J. 69: K3, 272.
12. J. 31: K3, 211.
13. Ex. vi, 3.
14. Josh. xxi, 41; cf. M. 43: K2, 365.
15. M. 42: K2, 364.
16. Isa. lxiii, 1; Zech. ix, 14; *Prose Edda*, 51. For a Swedenborgian source see H. C. White, *The Mysticism of William Blake*, Wisconsin U.P., 1927, 147.
17. Cf. J. 79: K3, 288.
18. Josh. iii, 16; cf. M. 38: K2, 358.

19. F.Z. ix (159): K2, 125; cf. Josh. ii, 18.
20. J. 93: K3, 314; G.P. 1: K3, 347; cf. Gen. xxx, 14.
21. D.C. 40: K3, 109; Ovid, *Met.* x, 450. Cf. Percival, *op. cit.*, 152.
22. M. 26: K2, 340.
23. F.Z. ix (221): K2, 126.
24. J. 53: K3, 245. Cf. *The Faerie Queene*, I, x, 57-59.
25. J. 31: K3, 212.
26. J. 66: K3, 265.
27. D.C. 43: K3, 110. Note the important phrase: "given the historical fact in its poetical vigour so as it always happens."
28. *King Lear*, V, iii, 20-25.
29. B.U. vii, 9: K1, 318.
30. M. 15: K2, 324.
31. J. 43: K3, 231-32. Cf. the traditional association of Gog and Magog with the "Goemagot" of Geoffrey: cf. K1, 276.
32. F.Z. viii (262-67): K2, 108.
33. J. 36: K3, 219.
34. J. 7: K3, 173.
35. See the illustration at J. 93: K3, 313; cf. V.L.J. 86: K3, 158. Hand, who in the Albion complex corresponds to the Spectre of Urthona as Hyle does to Orc, derives his name from the fact that he is the instrumental aspect of the imagination, the search for power rather than wisdom which was the error of Faust, whose name (Eng. "fist") is similar.
36. Hyle-Hayley corresponds to Bunyan's Pickthank: cf. "On H--- the Pick Thank": K3, 72.
37. Gen. xlix, 5.
38. M. 38: K2, 358.
39. Voltaire, *La Princesse de Babylone*, ch. xv.
40. J. 71: K3, 276.
41. J. 40, 46: K3, 225, 235. See ch. 5, n. 37.
42. F.Z. vi (310): K2, 73. Cf. *America*, add. pl. 12: K1, 273.
43. J. 33: K3, 214.
44. Rev. iv, 4-6. Cf. the reference to the twenty-eight "loves" destroyed by the separation of Spectre and Emanation in "My Spectre around me": K2, 211. Their division into four groups of seven is linked with Blake's interpretation of the numerical system of Revelation, in which a fourfold seven is the number of imagination and a threefold six that of Antichrist. A reference to the Book of Tobit may also be involved.
45. I Chron. xxiv, xxv.
46. Ovid, *Met.* vi, 174. Cf. Job xxxviii, 31.
47. M. 46: K2, 369.
48. The lake is first introduced in B.A. iv, 2: K1, 327. Cf. Percival, *op. cit.*, 68.
49. J. 11: K3, 179.
50. J. 55: K3, 247.
51. V.L.J. 69-70: K3, 147.
52. J. 49, 85: K3, 240, 300.
53. J. 90: K3, 309.
54. J. 38-39: K3, 222.
55. V.L.J. 82-84: K3, 156; cf. "My Spectre around me": K2, 213. Both passages are probably based on Prov. ix, 5.
56. J. 92: K3, 312; cf. F.Z. v (76-78): K2, 57. The statement in J. 42: K3, 228, that there is no limit of translucence means that there is no upper limit. In M. 30: K2, 348, a development of vision takes place from Theotormon and Sotha, who have 7,007,700 sons and are in the Gate of Luban, to Ozoth, who has 8,000,008 and is in the eye. These figures mean only that their progeny is innumerable and that they are to be associated with the numbers seven and eight. What is

referred to is the climax of vision in which we pass from the seventh "Eye" of Jesus (associated with Theotormon in "Africa") to the eighth "Eye" of his second coming. The latter is pure vision, as the former is the hearing of the Word, the lesser revelation to the ear (cf. Job xlii, 5) which also ceases at the upper limit of Beulah.

57. *Bhagavadgita* viii, 24-25. Cf. *Phaedrus*, 248. The translation used is that of *Hindu Scriptures*, Everyman's Library, 254.

58. M. 28: K2, 344; unless the phrase "against the east" can conceivably mean "facing the west."

59. V.L.J. 80-81: K3, 152; J. 95-96: K3, 316.

60. J. 62: K3, 259.

61. E.G. *i*: K3, 333.

62. J. 90: K3, 309. Cf. Murry, *op. cit.*, 274-93.

63. J. 91: K3, 312.

64. J. 55: K3, 247. See above, n. 50.

65. Letter to Butts, Oct. 2, 1800: K2, 192.

66. J. 92: K3, 312. Blake's doctrine of "Druidism" should be borne in mind by the modern reader when he finds that treatments of Atlantis legends, dying god myths and the relation of Jerusalem to Albion are associated with foolish or mischievous political ideas. Cf. Alfred Rosenberg, *Der Mythus des 20. Jahrhunderts*, a work with many English and American analogues.

67. E.G. *i*: K3, 334.

68. J. 90: K3, 309.

69. J. 96: K3, 317.

70. D.C. 41: K3, 110.

71. F.Z. iii (opp. 90-91): K2, 40.

72. J. 66: K3, 266.

73. John xi, 50.

74. J. 91: K3, 311.

75. J. 55: K3, 248.

76. See the next note and II Thess. ii, 6.

77. J. 29: K3, 207.

78. For the worm and caterpillar cf. G.P.: K3, 347 (the text to pl. 16 is quoted from Job xvii, 14). As the Covering Cherub is a winged or plumed serpent, it may be associated with birds as well, notably the peacock, whose "eyeless wings" (J. 89: K3, 307) are an analogy of the four Zoas who are "full of eyes" (Ezek. i, 18), and the dying and reviving phoenix (cf. "The Ashes of Mystery began to animate," F.Z. viii [598]: K2, 119).

79. Memorandum in Refutation of Schofield: K2, 253.

CHAPTER TWELVE

1. Spenser, *Shepheards Calender*, E. K.'s Introduction; *The Faerie Queene*, I, Proem, 1.

2. Cf. Joyce, *Portrait of the Artist as a Young Man*, Modern Library ed., 251.

3. "Now Art has lost its mental Charms": K3, 84.

4. *On Homer's Poetry*: K3, 361.

5. *On Virgil*: K3, 361-62.

6. Marg. to Reynolds (introduction): K3, 5.

7. P.A. 18-19: K3, 134.

8. M.H.H. 10: K1, 186.

9. D.C. 52, 59: K3, 114, 117.

10. D.C., Advertisement: K3, 89.

11. K3, 79, 75.

12. P.A. 51-57: K3, 126.

13. D.C. 66: K3, 120.

14. Quoted from Wright, *op. cit.*, II, 41.
15. The exception is *The Gates of Paradise*: K1, 277; K3, 338.
16. K3, 163.
17. See ch. 5, n. 30.
18. For these see Damon, *op. cit.*, 221.
19. K3, 382-83.
20. Cf. Damon, *op. cit.*, 69, 311.
21. J. 3: K3, 166. For the sources see Damon, *op. cit.*, 434.
22. Damon, *op. cit.*, 237.
23. D.C. 44: K3, 111.
24. Gregory Smith, *op. cit.*, II, 299.
25. The resemblance to Rahab is closest in the sonnet beginning "*Avec ses vêtements ondoyants et nacrés.*"
26. *Pencil Drawings*, 48.
27. Marg. to Wordsworth, 43: K3, 376.
28. *On Homer's Poetry*: K3, 361.
29. The phrases in quotation marks are from *Endymion*, iii, 628, 700.

INDEX

Works cited, except Blake's own, will be found under the author's name.

63, 285, 316, 335, 336-37, 351, 352, 354-
55, 356, 362, 393, 397

Fenri, 140

Ficino, Marsilio, 150, 154

Fielding, Henry, 201; Thwackum and
Square, 346

floods, in Blake's symbolism, 130, 139,
283-84

Florentine painting, 106

"Fly, The," 6

forgiveness of sins, 69, 79, 259, 298, 398

form, 15, 27, 89, 122, 124

Four Zoas, The, 6, 60, 117, 178, 185, 186,
215, 219, 234, 243, 256, 261 313-16,
320, 323, 335, 347, 349, 357-58, 368,
369, 375, 380, 414; commentary, 220-23,
269-309

France, 179, 216, 339, 372

French, Blake's knowledge of, 11, 436

French Revolution, 62, 66-67, 134, 179,
180, 194, 202-5, 216, 260, 372

French Revolution, The, 184, 185, 186,
187, 208, 219, 314; commentary, 202-5

fresco painting, 406, 408-11

Freud, Sigmund, 233, 301

furnaces, 253, 273, 286, 288, 291, 300,
364, 380-81

Fuseli, John, 410

Fuzon, 133, 214, 215, 228

Gainsborough, Thomas, 105, 106, 161

Galenic theory of matter, 274-75

Garibaldi, Guiseppe, 217

Generation, 49, 50, 71, 76, 112, 124, 125,
127, 134, 135, 136, 137, 141, 163, 229,
232, 233, 234, 235, 251, 262, 272, 285,
287, 303, 307, 354, 361, 388, 391, 445

Genesis, 37, 50, 120, 126, 127, 133, 135,
136, 137, 138, 142, 231 233, 254, 275,
283, 317, 322, 348, 360, 363, 386, 389,
415

Geoffrey of Monmouth, 130, 132, 175,
373-75, 378, 379, 448

George, St., 141-43, 209, 225, 335

Gibbon, Edward, 161, 231

Giotto, 192, 409, 442

Gnostics, 38, 41, 111, 137, 348

God, Blake's doctrine of, 30-54; as Father, 37, 52-53, 75, 80, 88, 219, 230,
235-36, 322, 389, 395. See also Jesus,
Holy Spirit

gods, 38, 61, 118-19, 121, 171, 177, 272

Gog and Magog, 347, 399, 448

gold, 152, 154, 252, 276, 402

Golden Age, 108, 125, 126, 127, 128, 142,

143, 174, 175, 199, 206, 207, 212 216,
238, 252, 256, 309, 322, 340, 347

Golden Fleece, in Ovid, 215, 223

"Golden Net, The," 266

Goldsmith, Oliver, 177

Golgonooza, 91, 248-49, 253, 258, 260,
266, 323, 357, 380, 382, 425, 445

good and evil, 40, 55-78, 117-18, 135,
189-90, 200, 211, 222, 240, 249, 331,
333-34, 336, 361

Gospels, 80, 108, 116, 262, 284, 299, 317,
333, 341, 342, 343, 370-71, 386, 388,
392, 393, 396

Gothic art, Blake's view of, 34, 100, 104,
148-49, 171, 175, 177, 318, 408, 410

Goya, Francisco de, 358

Grail, the Holy, 141, 142, 303

Gray, Thomas, 167, 177, 178, 440; *The
Triumphs of Owen*, 142; *The Bard*,
172; *The Progress of Poesy*, 172, 274

Greco, El, 105

Greek culture, *see* Classical culture

Grendel, 138, 141

"Grey Monk, The," 149

Gwendolen, 373, 379, 402

"Gwin, King of Norway," 181

Hand, 375-77, 403, 448

Har, 242-45

Hardy, Thomas, 34; *The Dynasts*, 34,
379

harlot, 74, 79, 363, 392-93

Harvey, Gabriel, 116

Havilah, 363

Hawthorne, Nathaniel, 10; Hester
Prynne, 240

Hayley, William, 313, 315-16, 325-32,
337, 338, 352, 377, 399, 410

heaven, 26, 71, 80, 81, 83, 382. See also
Eden, Beulah, Paradise

Hebrew culture, 90-91, 132, 148, 156,
261, 317-18, 322, 360-80, 391, 407, 416

Hecate, 234

Hela, 245

hell, 26, 81, 83, 196, 198, 288, 382, 397;
ironic use, 197-98, 200, 206, 382. See
also Ulro, Satan

Hephaistos, 252

Heraclitus, 247

hermaphrodite, 135, 272, 301

Hermes Trismegistus, 275

Herod, 203, 214, 370, 372

Heshbon, 366, 368

Hesiod, 128, 284, 321

Hesperia, 302

Hesperides, 138, 174, 240, 353, 371, 447